Meeting the Challenges of Global Terrorism

Meeting the Challenges of Global Terrorism

Prevention, Control, and Recovery

Edited by
Dilip K. Das and Peter C. Kratcoski

LEXINGTON BOOKS
Lanham • *Boulder* • *New York* • *Oxford*

LEXINGTON BOOKS

Published in the United States of America
by Lexington Books
A Member of the Rowman & Littlefield Publishing Group
4720 Boston Way, Lanham, Maryland 20706

PO Box 317
Oxford
OX2 9RU, UK

British Library Cataloguing in Publication Information Available

Library of Congress Cataloging-in-Publication Data

Meeting the challenges of global terrorism : prevention, control, and
recovery / edited by Dilip K. Das and Peter C. Kratcoski.
    p. cm.
Includes bibliographical references and index.
ISBN 0-7391-0499-3
1. Terrorism. 2. Terrorism—Prevention. I. Das, Dilip K., 1941–
II. Kratcoski, Peter C., 1936–
HV6431 .M434 2002
363.3'2—dc21   2002012174

Printed in the United States of America

∞™ The paper used in this publication meets the minimum requirements of
American National Standard for Information Sciences—Permanence of Paper
for Printed Library Materials, ANSI/NISO Z39.48-1992.

This book is dedicated to President Horace A. Judson of State University of New York at Plattsburgh in acknowledgment of our gratitude to him for providing generous financial support for organizing the ancillary meeting on "Terrorist Vicimization: Prevention, Control and Recovery" as part of the Tenth United Nations Congress on the Prevention of Crime and the Treatment of Offenders. It is this ancillary meeting that provided the bulk of the papers that are included in the present volume. Dr. Judson's encouragement for assembling a galaxy of international experts on terrorism in a United Nations–leading forum, even before the unprecedented events of September 11, 2001, speaks volumes on his unfailing vision and penetrating insight.

Contents

Foreword

It is a pleasure for me to introduce this very timely and informative book on terrorism and the possible responses to this menace, as reflected in the observations and suggestions of government and police experts and academic researchers.

After considering what message I could convey that would inform readers of the importance of this book, I decided to focus my remarks on ways that universities, through their administrators, researchers, and instructors, can become active partners in the fight against terrorism.

The inspiration for this work was the ancillary meeting of experts on terrorism held in conjunction with the Tenth United Nations Congress on the Prevention of Crime and the Treatment of Offenders, "Crime and Justice: Meeting the Challenges of the 21st Century." Dr. Horace Judson, president of the State University of New York at Plattsburgh, recognized the importance of this meeting and provided the encouragement and financial support that made it a reality.

Dr. Dilip K. Das, professor of criminal justice at the State University of New York at Plattsburgh, was the moving force behind the organization of the ancillary meeting. He gathered experts from around the world who focused their attention on the lessons learned from scores of terrorist incidents and identified the best practices to assist those confronting the terrible threats and consequences of terrorism, including hostage negotiations and providing immediate and long-range services to direct and indirect victims. Dr. Das was so impressed with the quality and scope of the presentations at this gathering that he saw the possibility of collecting the papers presented there in book form. As he and his coauthor, Dr. Peter C. Kratcoski, professor of justice studies at Kent State University, pursued this objective, they asked other practitioners and scholars who had not attended the original meeting, but were well-known for their experience and expertise in this area, to become involved in the project. After the terrible events of September 11, 2001, they realized that the information they had gathered must be made available to a large audience of readers.

This important book became a reality because of cooperation and support among university administrators, justice professionals, and academic researchers and writers. Working alone, none of these could have produced a work of the scope, vision, and practical importance that we see here. Cooperation among these entities must be expanded and coordinated in our continuing fight against terrorism. World events show us that this battle has just begun, that the stakes are very high, and that we must employ every weapon in our preventive and reactive arsenal if we are to succeed. Close cooperation between university leaders, justice practitioners, and academics is vital to this effort.

Last, but not the least, I would like to express sincere thanks to the United Nations for inviting the State University of New York to organize the meeting, which provided an excellent opportunity for this admirable cooperative global venture to materialize.

ROBERT L. KING, CHANCELLOR
State University of New York

Preface

This book has emerged from an important ancillary meeting on "Terrorist Victimization: Prevention, Control and Recovery" held in 2000 as part of the Tenth United Nations Congress on Crime Prevention and Treatment of Offenders. I organized the meeting in close collaboration with Alex Schmid of the United Nations in Vienna who took the initiative for this excellently well-conceived event. I am indeed most grateful to President Horace Judson of the State University of New York at Plattsburgh for providing generous financial assistance for the ancillary meeting and fully supporting my efforts in connection with the terrorism project. The book has been dedicated to him in recognition of his vision and encouragement

Some of the papers which are included in the book, namely, those from Brazil, Egypt, India, Israel, and the United States, as well as the paper from the United Nations, were presented at the ancillary meeting. The authors were both scholars and practitioners working in the area of terrorism in various parts of the world. Later I contacted many other terrorism scholars and practitioners from all over the world specifically for the book. Although the new papers were still focused on terrorist victimization, their scope has gone beyond the theme of the ancillary meeting.

Professor Peter Kratcoski, who has admirably served as an official reporter of the International Police Executive Symposium (IPES) for almost a decade now, was asked to be coeditor of the book. He played an extremely important role in the revision and resubmission of all the papers through his thorough and careful review. As a result, the papers have been updated until the moment of their being sent for publication. Peter received excellent support from Lucille, his wife, and both of them deserve heartfelt gratitude from all of us.

I thank all of the authors for their splendid cooperation and excellent contributions. Our editor, Martin Hayward of Lexington Books, has been an invaluable source of guidance, support, and encouragement throughout the entire process of the preparation of the manuscript. My wife, Dr. Snezana Mijovic-Das, came to Vienna to help me in the organization of the ancillary meeting and assisted a great deal in the preparation of the manuscript.

Finally, I thank Mintie Das for getting the manuscript ready for the press by her superb editorial skills, efficient handling of the diverse contributions, and ability to adhere to the deadline dates. Last and not the least, Thelma Lyon, secretary to President Judson, has provided most valuable assistance in every stage of the entire endeavor. I offer her heartfelt thanks.

DILIP K. DAS

After the events of September 11, 2001 occurred, I realized how important it was for us to produce this book with selections from the practitioners, researchers, and scholars from across the world who have experienced and reacted to terrorism firsthand, researched its sources, forms, and effects, or provided services to its victims. It was an honor to be part of this important undertaking, and I am grateful to Dilip for allowing me to be involved. I was highly impressed with the expertise and academic credentials of the authors, and the task of structuring and editing the selections proved to be a very exciting, educational, and enjoyable experience. We were fortunate to have such a distinguished group of practitioners, researchers, and scholars as contributors. They have offered widely divergent perspectives on this problem, defined and clarified the issues surrounding terrorism, illustrated the many facets of terrorism, and described its effects. My contribution involved summarizing and analyzing the materials available to us, end editing the authors' contributions. I join with Dilip in expressing our gratitude to the persons he mentioned above who have given such wonderful support and assistance to us in this project.

PETER C. KRATCOSKI

I

INTRODUCTION

1

The Nature, Definition, and Uses of Terrorism, and the Range of Rational Options to Deal with It: A Summary

Gerhard O. W. Mueller

The discussion of terrorism presented here is based on three shocking propositions: (1) terrorism is not a crime; (2) terrorism is normal behavior; and (3) terrorism is official legal policy. These statements require some explanation.

Terrorism is not a crime. The American Law Institute, in preparing the Model Penal Code, did not define terrorism as a crime because acts associated with terrorism, including murder, kidnapping, and other types of violence, were already prohibited by existing laws. The institute decided that threats of terrorism should be defined as illegal. Hence, the state penal codes that followed the Model Penal Code list terrorist threats as crimes. No penal code in the world has a terrorist crime category.

Terrorism is normal behavior. This is evident because terrorism is a normal psychological technique for inducing behavior. Think of your own upbringing: When you did something wrong (really wrong, like playing hooky or stealing a cookie from the cookie jar) you were warned by parents that if you continued that behavior you would grow up to be a criminal, would go to hell, be put on a spit, rotated and burned, and the devils would poke you with pitchforks. This is an example of a terrorist threat. It is a normal psychological technique used to bring about conformity of behavior. Whether in school, church, or home, unhappily we use terrorism. Throughout history, terrorism has been an accepted stratagem of warfare. King Frederick I of Prussia tried to make his seven-foot-tall guard soldiers appear to be eight feet tall by putting tall hats on them. When the Austrians saw these giants, they were terrified. The pirates of the Spanish Main terrorized victims. When their pirate ships approached the enemy, they would make nerve-shattering noises. They were dressed in frightful garb. Thus, they terrorized their victims, and half the battle was won.

Terrorism is an officially sanctioned legal policy. We use the word deterrence. We want to deter potential criminals from engaging in criminal activity. Here is the word "terror." At one time, if you were really bad, you would be quartered and drawn, and you could not be buried in a Christian cemetery; you had to be buried at midnight at the crossroads. That was terrorism. We still have deterrence as a legal concept today. There may be as little a threat of punishment as a fine. However, even that can be terrible. A $750 fine for speeding on the freeway is terrible. Parole and prison are no longer as terrible as they once were, but terror nevertheless is their purpose, because deterrence is official policy.

CRIMINAL DEFINITION OF TERRORISM

So, when we talk about terrorism in the post-9/11 world, what do we mean? The concept of terrorism is a criminological one. In my view, the concept has six ingredients:

1. Who is a *potential perpetrator?* Any person or agency, perhaps other than a government vis-à-vis another government. (When a government engages in terrorism against another government, it is war, or a war crime.) So we are dealing primarily with nongovernment persons, real or legal persons.
2. There must be a *victim*. The intended victim may be any place or any person, including innocent targeted population groups. That is where we distinguish the terrorists from the freedom fighters. Freedom fighters do not target innocent population groups. Terrorists do.
3. Next come the *methods*. They are chosen for maximum impact, including destruction, with minimal effort. The selection of symbolic targets is important. The World Trade Center could not have been a more symbolic target, but it was not the first symbolic target. Remember ten years ago when the terrorists attacked a nightclub in Berlin that was frequented almost exclusively by GIs? What was the name of the nightclub in Berlin? Hollywood. You always look for a symbolic target.
4. There must be a *purpose* for terrorism. The purpose is to instill fear and terror.
5. There is a *goal*. It usually is to force a change of governmental policy toward a goal favored by the terrorists. There are short- and long-range goals. The long-range goals can be as far-reaching as the destruction of a whole country, or the proposition that nonbelievers should give back all holy lands.

6. There is always the overarching motive of terrorists: to portray an aura of invincibility and capacity to strike unimpeded anywhere in the world.

RESPONSES TO TERRORISM

There are five general areas that need to be addressed if we are to develop effective counterterrorism programs. They are: (1) remove the underlying causes of terrorism; (2) increase internal and external security to make it more difficult for terrorist groups to hit their targets; (3) improve international global intelligence; (4) perfect a global justice network, including respect for the newly created International Criminal Court; and (5) respond by military action, unilaterally or multilaterally.

Removal of the underlying controversies, a method favored by the United Nations, has proven a successful response under certain circumstances (e.g., Ireland, Kosovo). Target hardening, while expensive, will remain a universal response. A global intelligence network is in the making, with exchange of agents and of information. The creation of a global justice network is just in the beginning, the main obstacle being the mistrust of the United States. Military action has been the U.S.-favored response, often in collaboration with other nations. The method is not favored by most of the rest of the world.

THE UNITED NATIONS RESPONSE

The United Nations has been concerned with the problem of terrorism virtually since its beginning. The unit that I headed, now called the Centre for International Crime Prevention (CICP), has been concerned with terrorism for decades. It now has a special branch, called the Anti-Terrorism Branch, composed of a four-person staff and a secretary. (This unit is primarily concerned with coordinating government activities.) The United Nations has done a great deal in the area of antiterrorism. During the years the United Nations has existed, eleven conventions on counterterrorism have been drafted. The first one of three dealing with aircraft terrorism, The Convention on Offenses and Certain Other Acts on Board Aircraft, was adopted in 1963, and the last one on this topic was the Montreal Convention of 1971, the Convention for the Suppression of Unlawful Acts against the Safety of Civil Aviation. After 1973 (roughly the time I came into office), we received instruction from the General Assembly to deal with terrorism generally and make it a crime. What does it mean to make terrorism a crime? Well, it reminded me of watching a little kid at a birthday party, eyeing the cake. The kid would have liked nothing more than to grab the whole cake and eat it. But that

Gerhard O. W. Mueller

won't work. You have to get a knife and cut the cake into slices. And that is what we did with terrorism in the United Nations. It was like one big cake. We cut it into slices. Dealing with each individual slice was a lot easier than trying to deal with the whole phenomenon of terrorism. I wanted to have slices that were particularly appealing to my consumers, namely, the international diplomatic and political community, as they came together in the United Nations. So why not make it a terroristic crime to attack internationally protected persons, including diplomatic agencies? In no time flat, the Convention on the Prevention and Punishment of Crimes against Internationally Protected Persons, Including Diplomatic Agents (1973) was passed, and it is now law in practically all countries of the world, including the United States. Again appealing to the consumers, the Convention against the Taking of Hostages was created in 1979. Hostage taking concerned everyone at the United Nations and beyond. Then came the Convention for the Protection of Nuclear Materials, the Vienna Convention of 1980. It was drafted in cooperation with the International Atomic Energy Agency. Next came the Convention of Suppression of Unlawful Acts against the Safety of Maritime Navigation (1988), which the United States adopted. It really is a "protection of life" kind of activity. In the United States, we regard life-threatening terrorism by which death is caused as a capital crime. This makes it legally impossible for many other nations to extradite offenders to the United States. The need to mark explosives for the purpose of catching those involved in illegal international shipments of explosives, often for use by terrorist groups, led to the International Convention for the Suppression of Terrorist Bombings that was passed in 1997. The International Convention for the Suppression of the Financing of Terrorism, the most recent convention, passed in 1999.

During the past three decades the number of terrorist acts, and the devastation created thereby, have increased significantly. Criminologists must regard terrorism as one of the most significant criminological problems. While governments ultimately will have to act, the preparation of rational options is up to us.

NOTE

This summary is based on an address delivered to the Internal Section of the Academy of Criminal Justice Sciences, 2002.

2

Terrorist Victimization: Definition, Focus, and Impact

Peter C. Kratcoski and Dilip K. Das

The topics touched upon in this book were addressed at an Ancillary Meeting of the International Police Executive Symposium on the topic of "Terrorist Victimization: Prevention, Control, and Recovery" held at the United Nations Center in Vienna, Austria, on Wednesday, April 12, 2000, in conjunction with the Tenth United Nations Congress on the Prevention of Crime and the Treatment of Offenders. The congress focused on "Crime and Justice: Meeting the Challenges of the 21st Century."

The formal presentations and the discussions that followed concentrated on assessments of the main contemporary trends in terrorism, the politicization of terrorism, the effects terrorism has on primary and secondary victims, the linkage of terrorism with organized crime, and the measures governments, international organizations, and justice agencies can take to curtail and eradicate terrorism, including international cooperative efforts (Kratcoski 2001, 267).

The information provided here was considered so important and vital to world efforts to prevent terrorism that a decision was made to disseminate it in a book, and *Meeting the Challenges of Global Terrorism* began to take shape. Other experts in the field were asked to provide chapters, and the events of September 11, 2001, provided a catalyst for new assessments of the global situation and the possibilities for prevention, control, and recovery.

THE CONCEPT OF "TERRORISM"

The Federal Bureau of Investigation (FBI) of the United States has defined terrorism as "the unlawful use of force or violence against persons or property to intimidate or coerce a government, the civilian population or any segment thereof, in furtherance of a political or social objective." Louis J. Freeh, former director of the Federal Bureau of Investigation, speaking before a Senate Committee on the "Threat of Terrorism in the United States," defined International Terrorism in the following manner:

> International terrorism involves violent acts, or acts dangerous to human life, that are a violation of the criminal laws of the United States or any state, or that would be a criminal violation if committed within the jurisdiction of the United States or any state, and which are intended to intimidate or coerce a civilian population, influence the police of a government, or affect the conduct of a government. Acts of international terrorism transcend national boundaries in terms of the means by which they are accomplished, the intended persons they appear to intimidate, or the locale in which the perpetrators operate. (Freeh 2001, 2)

Freeh (2001) stated that there are three major categories of international terrorist threat. "Loosely affiliated extremists" are groups that are motivated by political or religious beliefs and may be the most dangerous to the United States because of their extreme beliefs and willingness to take whatever action is needed to act on these beliefs. The second category mentioned by Freeh is "formal terrorist organizations." According to Freeh (2001, 2), "typically, these autonomous, generally transnational organizations have their own infrastructures, personnel, financial arrangements, and training facilities." These groups are capable of organizing and implementing terrorist attacks anywhere in the world. The third category, "domestic terrorism," is composed of various groups that represent viewpoints from the entire political and social spectrum, including right-wing extremist groups, left-wing extremist groups, special interest extremist groups, anarchist groups, and hate groups. While these domestic terrorist groups may have different missions and agendas, they nevertheless have many similarities in that they "conduct acts of politically motivated violence to force segments of society, including the general public, to change attitudes about issues considered important to their causes" (Freeh 2001, 4).

Jenkins (1975) observed that the threat of violence can accomplish the same result as actual violence and terrorist acts, because the threat or actual carrying out of violence is designed primarily to instill fear. Mullins (1997) also contended that the threat of violence or destruction may be all that is necessary for the terrorists to accomplish their goals. The fact that the violence could occur is likely to have an effect on those toward whom the violence might be directed. Mohsen (2000, 4), in his paper titled "Challenges of the Terrorist Phenomenon in the 21st Century," observed that terrorism has two major elements: "the use of violence and the desire to obtain publicity or propaganda in an accepted axiom."

An overview of terrorism by the U.S. Department of State (1999, 30) noted that, while the motives for committing terrorist acts have varied, terrorism in such forms as political assassinations, hostage taking, and property destruction has been a tactic employed throughout history by tyrannical rulers, political revolutionaries, those trying to obtain redress for past grievances, and those bent on repression of others. Another difficulty in defining terrorism is that persons seen as terrorists by some portions of society may be regarded as freedom fighters by others. Ward (1985, v) observed that "Terrorists and freedom fighters are frequently considered polar positions in more critical analyses of this form of violence, with all terrorists being bad and all freedom fighters being good. Unfortunately, the real world is not all that simple."

Some terrorists may be viewed as disturbed persons who behave so irrationally and erratically that their true motivations are difficult to discern. Suicide bombers who sacrifice their lives without making any statement of purpose or offering explanations for their actions leave open the possibility that they may have been deranged persons seeking attention for other reasons rather than true terrorists.

Abdelhameed (2001, 1) defined terrorism as: "the exercise of force in a regular, continuous and illegal manner." He also stated: "This comprises all forms of force in its broad material and moral senses involving the element of threat within them. This abstract sense aims at giving the psychological effect which leads to the achievement of the terrorism objective. A main feature of force is the exercise of violence as one, among other means of much milder impact."

Mullins (1997, 33) delineated four basic types of terrorism. *State* terrorism (used by a government to control its own citizens) involves terrorist tactics, violence, and creation of fear; *transnational* terrorism involves terrorist acts conducted by citizens of more than one country but not supported or sanctioned by the governments of these countries; *international* terrorism is supported by a government, but the terrorism is directed against citizens or agencies of other states (e.g., takeover of the American embassy in Tehran, bombing of the World Trade Center in New York); and *domestic* terrorism consists of acts by individuals or groups acting independently of any government support (Ku Klux Klan, Arian Nation). Examples of all of these types of terrorism are plentiful.

Claridge (1998, 75) saw *state terrorism* as having many elements in common with terrorism against the state. He noted, "[State terrorism] in its psychological functions and basic methods of operation is essentially the same as anti-State terrorism, although the actual tactics might differ. So where the non-state terrorist uses kidnap, the State has an equivalent tactic in enforced disappearance."

In the same vein, Oliverio (1998, 5) defined terrorism as "an extreme form of coercive politics."

Alex Schmid (2000) maintained that there is too much concern about the definition of terrorism. He regarded terrorism as both a substantive concept and a political concept. Schmid (2000, 2) observed that "despite debates since 1972, the United Nations has not managed to define 'international terrorism' conclusively to the satisfaction of all member states. Some insist on a distinction between 'illegitimate terrorism' and 'legitimate national liberation struggles.'" He also observed that for the victims of terrorism, those who are taken hostage, injured, killed, kidnapped, or tortured, these distinction have little meaning.

THE FOCUS OF TERRORISM

According to Schmid (2000), there are two major categories of terrorism— focused and indiscriminate terrorism. In focused terrorism, the victims are deliberately selected and the terrorist activities focus on them. In indiscriminate terrorism, the victim just happens to be present when the act of terrorism is carried out. Damphousse et al. (2002), citing research on terrorist victimization, concluded that it is difficult to ascertain the motives of various terrorist groups in regard to primary or secondary victimization. They regarded the targeting of victims as motivated by one or more of several considerations, including efforts to obtain funding for the terrorist organization (robbing a bank, kidnapping for ransom), revenge against persons who have opposed them publicly (the assassination of judges or prosecutors by drug traffickers), attacks on ideologically symbolic targets (a political opponent of members of groups that oppose the terrorists' stand on political issues), or internal targeting of victims (exemplified by punishment of members of their own group for nonconformity). In the categories and examples given by Damphousse et al., the victims appear to be targets of focused terrorism as described by Schmid.

Another motive of some terrorist groups is to instill fear, and they use indiscriminate terrorism incidents in public places to produce this effect. In the case of the victims of the sarin gas attack in the Tokyo subways, the Aum Shinrikyo Group did not have any specific target in mind, but:

> The guru ordered selected members to spray sarin to make the victims "poa" or "phowa," which means that Aum members (the winners of truth) could eliminate all the "evil karma of people" through death, and they could ascend the killed to a higher realm. So the selected members believed they were releasing sarin to save people with evil karma who did not recognize these truths. (Uchiyama 2002, 3)

Karmon (2000) noted that in the 1970s and 1980s the terrorist acts were directed predominantly against Western countries and were of such a nature as bombing of buildings or hijacking of airplanes whereby hundreds of persons were killed. It was very easy to unite sentiments against the perpetrators and to generate sympathy for the victims. In the 1990s, although the quantity of international terrorist attacks diminished, the incidents became more lethal and amorphous, carried out by new terrorist organizations with less clear nationalist or ideological motivations, but grounded in religious or political movements. It was more difficult for the public to assess whether these acts were related to some type of movement to liberate a country from real or imagined ills, or simply the work of criminals.

Mohsen (2000) agreed that terrorism is more deadly and perilous today than in the past. Major reasons for this include new, more sophisticated weapons used by terrorists and new modes of organization and terrorist leadership in which the leaders believe that any action that will further their cause is justified, regardless of the consequences. He also indicated that today there are more victims of terrorist attacks, latent effects, and indirect targets.

Uchiyama's (2002) research revealed that there were 5,311 victims recorded for the sarin gas attack on the Tokyo subway in 1995. Of these, twelve were fatally injured and the remaining persons had physical and psychological disorders of varying degrees. The psychological effects experienced by the victims, such as flashbacks, nightmares, social withdrawal, alienation, depression, and avoidance of the place in which the incident occurred, had diminished considerably when a second survey was completed three years after the incident. Nevertheless, these problems were still quite evident for a number of the victims.

Damphousse et al. analyzed data from the American Terrorism Study, which began in the 1980s and continues to the present time. This study is based on information collected by the FBI on suspected terrorist activity and indictments of terrorists. Damphousse et al. (2002) found that, between 1980 and 1998, there were 340 actual or intended targets of terrorist groups (incidents is which groups planned or carried out acts that injured persons or destroyed property). Of these, 229 were carried out, while the remainder were planned but never completed. A target was defined as a military base, a public or private building, or a church. The actual number of individuals who may have been affected in each incident was not reported. The researchers found that, during the period from 1980 to 1998, the most common target was the government, followed by the military. When the trends in targeting for the period of 1980 to 1989 were compared with those for the period from 1990 to 1998, the government still remained the most common target, but terrorist attacks on other types of targets increased substantially during the 1990 to 1998 time period. Increases occurred in hate crimes and attacks on military installations, economic establishments, and media opposition groups. There were also more attacks on public utilities and public transportation systems (Damphousse et al. 2002, 14).

Schmid (2000) noted that terrorism tends to produce an exaggerated fear of victimization, even for those who are not directly involved in terrorist attacks. The effects of fear on the physical and mental health of individuals are not easy to assess. Citing various statistical sources of terrorism data, Schmid concluded that the annual risk of death rate from political violence was much lower in Northern Ireland during the era of terrorism than the annual risk of death rate from traffic accidents.

Statistics on the terrorist tactics from 1968 to 1993 (Hoffman 1994) revealed that nearly half of the attacks consisted of bombings, and more than 20 percent involved direct attacks on property or persons, while hijacking, kidnapping, and hostage taking accounted for much lower percentages of terrorist activity. Hoffman and Claridge (1998), using figures provided by the U.S. Department of State, showed that both the number injured and the number killed as a result of international and domestic terrorism increased significantly in the period from 1990 to 1993, compared with the much longer period from 1970 to 1983. In fact, the average number killed annually by terrorism for the 1990 to 1993 time period was more than three times as large as the annual number killed by terrorism in the period from 1970 to 1983.

Statistics on the magnitude of terrorist victimization for 1997 showed that attacks on facilities made up more than half of all of the victimization incidents for that year (Pinkerton Global Intelligence Services, *Annual Risk Assessment*, 1997, and U.S. Department of State, Office of the Coordinator for Counter Terrorism, December 7, 1999). The types and magnitude of terrorist activities differed by continent. For example, more than 75 percent of the kidnappings of persons abducted for ransom occurred in South America, with a large number of these occurring in Colombia and Brazil (Control Risk Group, London, 1999; Auerbach 1998). The countries most affected by acts of hostage taking, defined as "holding of a person or persons against their will in a known location with the purpose of seeking compliance with a demand or purely to publicize a cause" (Control Risk Group 1999, 7) included the United States, Mexico, the United Kingdom, Brazil, and Germany. The magnitude of victimization by hijacking from 1992 through 1999 revealed a high of forty-one hijackings in 1994 and a low of eight hijackings in 1998. There was a drastic decline in the number from 1995 through 1998, but in 1999 the number increased dramatically to thirty-one. The former Soviet Union and China were the two countries most affected by hijackings (Control Risk Group 1999, 9).

Subramanian (2002) reported that India has experienced many varieties of terrorism in the past twenty years, with the terrorist acts carried out by

Sikh militants, the left-wing political extremists from the Communist Party of India-Marxist-Leninist (CP-ML), and Pakistan-sponsored Islamic Fundamentalist movements. From 1990 to 2000, there were more than 6,000 civilians and 2,200 security personnel killed in the states of Jammu and Kashmir. In the southern state of Andhra Pradesh, 1,715 civilians and 344 security personnel were killed during the same time period by terrorists from the "Peoples War Group," a branch of the CP-ML.

TERRORISM'S EFFECTS ON ITS VICTIMS

A highly troubling aspect of terrorism is that its victims are most often persons who have no direct connection with the terrorists and no involvement in the issues or profit-oriented activities that motivate the terrorist incident. In addition to the physical injuries and terror endured during the initial terrorism event, many victims experience long-standing emotional effects, including post-traumatic stress.

In some Latin American countries, peasants faced with pressures from guerillas who have infiltrated and virtually taken over rural areas as part of their activity to protect drug production and trade have fled to large cities to escape these dangers. These refugees from terrorism are separated from family and friends, familiar surroundings, and their regional culture, and have little hope of finding meaningful work in their new environment (Millard 2000).

The lives of many persons not directly touched by terrorist activity can also be affected. Attacks on cities or airports can result in the loss of millions of tourism dollars and persons whose occupations are linked to the tourist industry, including hotel and restaurant employees, shop owners, travel guides, or persons who work in factories that manufacture items used or purchased by tourists, may experience financial problems. Funds that were earmarked for economic development must be diverted to hiring more security personnel and developing programs to control or reduce terrorist activity, resulting in reduced quality of life for the general population. Persons affected in this way are the "indirect" victims of terrorism (Mohsen 2000). When persons are taken hostage or abducted for ransom, their families are victimized by the demands made on them and by the trauma of the experience (Schmid 2000). If victims have mysteriously disappeared and are never located, there is the added trauma of uncertainty and lack of closure for relatives. Other indirect victims of terrorism are the rescue or health care workers who experience the traumas of attending to those killed or mutilated in terrorism (Schmid 2000, 4). It has been reported that the number of firefighters and police in New York City who have reported illnesses and psychological problems after the September 11th attack has increased significantly (*Akron*

Beacon Journal 2002, A4). Schmid (2000) summarized the symptoms that may be displayed by victims of terrorism as:

fear, free-floating anxiety, phobias
grief
shock, apathy, numbness
survivor guilt, self-blame
anger, hostility, rage, resentment, resignation
depression, lack of hope, alienation and loneliness
isolation, interpersonal difficulties
physical symptoms of distress: insomnia, startle reactions, nightmares
inability to concentrate, memory lapses, sexual problems
panic
inability to resume normal activity

Another aspect of victimization is the development of cynicism and lack of faith in the established social order and the judicial system (Subramanian 2000). Citizens may be victimized and intimidated by the terrorists, and government agents attempting to control terrorism may impose restriction on the citizens' abilities to move about freely or compromise their human rights through interrogation efforts to discover the identities or locations of the terrorists. Huggins (1998, 162–63) reported that, in the late 1960s, the Brazilian police, under the guise of fighting terrorism and subversion, created coordinated, centralized national police units that were directly under military control. The interconnected national network of police and military security forces had as its mission "to secure intelligence and neutralize terrorists." Specialized squads were created specifically to arrest suspects, others to collect intelligence and interrogate prisoners, and others to analyze the information gained from the informants. According to Huggins (1998, 165), some operatives observed, others interrogated, some tortured, and a group of them even murdered.

Survivors of a terrorism experience may be physically or mentally handicapped by injuries they suffered in the terrorism event or in counterterrorist rescue operations, or they may suffer post-traumatic stress as a result of these experiences or of the pressures of reliving their suffering as witnesses against the terrorists. Programs must be developed to provide services to the victims of terrorism, if they wish to be involved in treatment.

Although there has been some sound research completed on how terrorist activity physically and psychologically affects those who have been exposed to such activity, much of our knowledge on this matter is based on anecdotal material or on speculation. An interesting summary of the research on the effects of prolonged violence on the citizens of Northern Ireland by

Silke (2002) reveals that in Northern Ireland, even though thousands of people have been killed or maimed by terrorist violence and tens of thousands of civilians have witnessed terrorist violence, including children who had been exposed to violence their entire life, the fears that the terrorism would have a significant and prolonged effect on the lives of those who were direct victims or had witnessed violence has not been substantiated by the research.

TERRORISM AND THE MASS MEDIA

If one of the elements of terrorism is the wish to obtain publicity for a cause and create propaganda, the media has obviously overreacted in responding to this desire. Research has demonstrated a link between media coverage of terrorism events and the creation of traumatic reactions from those who view them. One such reaction is fear of future victimization. According to Crelinsten (1997), such fear was manifested by a great increase in demand for guns among those who viewed media coverage of riots in Los Angeles, California. Studies of the impact on viewers of media coverage of terrorism events (Moyers 1996; Nadir et al. 1993) revealed that such viewing triggered post-traumatic stress reactions and other problems in war veterans and in children. Another reaction to media coverage of violence is a desensitization of the viewers to depictions of violence and reduced concern for its victims (Kaftka et al. 1997).

Kam-Yee (2000, 235) believed that the media's sensational reports of violent crime are highly correlated to the public's crime panic. In her research, she discovered that even though the vast majority of violent crimes are specifically focused or targeted, their presentation in the mass media gives the impression of random violence. She stated, "There is an increasingly clear tendency of the mass media to adopt the policy of 'inform-tainment' in their report activities (inform-tainment means 'information' for the purpose of entertainment)." Thus the members of the public become indirect victims of violent crime as a result of their fear of crime.

Not all victims are of equal importance in the eyes of those individuals working in the mass media. Silke (2002) notes that the depth of the mass media's coverage of terrorist activities increases significantly as the number of victims increases. Also, the nationality of the victims is very important in determining the amount of coverage given by the mass media, with domestic victims being given considerably more attention than foreign victims.

How can the impact of media depictions of terrorism be blunted? It has been suggested that protocols should be established to regulate the amount and the nature of potentially trauma-producing material broadcast and disseminated by the media. Shipler (1988) noted that Britain has passed laws limiting news coverage of terrorism.

Although media attention is sought by many terrorists, some acts of terrorism are not primarily motivated by a desire for such coverage. Simon (1996, 110–11) described the situation in this way: "There are of course terrorist groups that thrive on generating media attention. Their actions have led to the perception that all terrorism is media related. . . . But many terrorists go about their violent business without considering media exposure."

Simon (1996, 111) concluded that "the issue of terrorists manipulating the media is limited to particular terrorist groups and to particular terrorist incidents, such as hijackings and hostage taking."

TERRORISM AND ORGANIZED CRIME

In his analysis of the relationship between organized crime and terrorism, Ward (2000, 1) observed, "One of the most perplexing aspects of the changing crime problem throughout the world is an increasing network of criminal activities which crosses traditional boundaries, and merges heretofore separate offenses in pursuit of common goals." According to White (1998, 199–200), "organized criminals are not terrorist" but "they use terrorist methods and their violence has political ramifications. . . murders [are committed] to influence political outcomes. . . . The Russian Federation [is] experiencing an unprecedented growth of criminal organizations using terrorist tactics."

Terrorism that is orchestrated and carried out by organized crime takes various forms. In Latin America, terrorism related to the production and distribution of drugs has been characterized as "narco-terrorism." In his paper "The Forgotten Victims of Narco-Terrorism in Latin America," Millard (2000, 3) stated:

> Narco-terrorism is conducted to further the aims of drug traffickers. It may include assassinations, extortion, hijackings, bombings and kidnappings directed against judges, prosecutors, elected officials and law enforcement agents, and the general disruption of a legitimate government to divert attention from drug operations. Guerrillas protect the drug cultivation sites and trade routes.

In Latin America, organized crime groups have set up mutually beneficial arrangements with insurgent or terrorist groups. Millard (2000, 4) noted, "While the relationship between drug dealers and these groups has been contentious at times, insurgents are sometimes paid to provide security services for drug traffickers, where they often 'tax' drug operations in areas they control, and, in some instances they are directly involved in narcotics cultivation."

Terrorist groups have access to vast funds from the illegal drug trade and other criminal activities. They have used these proceeds to buy heavy weapons and high-tech communications equipment in Eastern Europe. Seized military equipment includes armaments of exclusively Russian origin, suggesting links between Russian organized crime and Colombian guerrillas. The relationship between the guerrilla terrorist groups and narco-terrorism has become so intense that it has become impossible to separate the two. This has resulted in terrible consequences for the people of the affected Latin American countries. As Millard (2000, 15) observed, "It can be seen [that] there is immense suffering by the people, inestimable loss of life, and widespread social instability. This could also be reaching other levels . . . such as the damage to the ecology and irreparable economic disorder."

OFFICIAL GOVERNMENT REACTIONS TO TERRORISM

Subramanian (2000) noted that terrorists use the fear of death as a weapon in hostage taking, kidnapping, and hijackings, and they threaten to take the lives of the victims if their demands are not met. Some governments have countered such demands by proclaiming a policy of "no negotiations with terrorists" but even here they may be forced to deal with the terrorists in some way to try to save lives. In his book *Human Rights and Police* (1998, 143), Subramanian observed that:

> Since causes of political violence are rooted in politics, the cures are to be found in political processes only. In the world history, seldom have political violent movements based on popular causes been put down through force. More often they have achieved their goals. In the war of attrition, it is these elements who outclass the State.

Cohen and Corrado (2002) reported that the power of the Basque separatist group Euskadi Ta Askatasuna—Basque Homeland and Liberty (ETA)—operating predominately in Spain, declined tremendously as the people of the Basque region were able to satisfy their political agenda through peaceful, nonviolent methods. They contend that the terrorist tactics of ETA consisting of kidnapping and murdering of politicians, police, military officers, and even innocent civilians were once favorably received by a large number of the citizens of Euskadi, the Basque country of Spain, but have now lost the support of the Basque people. Cohen and Corrado (2002, 2) stated:

> In effect, it is not the public's growing desire to seek a peaceful solution to the question of Basque independence, but rather the changing structure of Basque society resulting from industrialization and globalization, the institutionalization of liberal democratic values, the political devolution or federalization of Spain

since the death of General Franco, an increased recognition of the economic, social, political, and cultural costs to the Basque region of ETA terrorism, the substantial gains made by non-violent Basque national political parties to protect and defend the Basque culture and language, and the concessions made by the national government to most of ETA's demands [that have brought about the decline in ETA's influence on the people in the Basque area].

Cohen and Corrado (2002) imply that often the goals of terrorist organizations may be perceived as legitimate and worthy of pursuit even though the tactics these groups use to accomplish the goals are not acceptable to the general population. Nevertheless, if the political regime is perceived as being completely insensitive to the goals and is not willing to offer any concessions, the people may perceive the more drastic violent actions of the political terrorists groups as necessary if the goals are to be accomplished.

Ganor (2000) confirmed that even Israel, which has proclaimed a policy of not negotiating with terrorist groups, has deviated from this stand on certain occasions. In a paper titled "The Main Factors in Israeli Counter-Terrorism Strategy," Ganor (2000, 10) stated:

> Israel has the reputation as a country with a "tough" policy of not negotiating with terrorist organizations. Yet this image has not always stood the test of reality. For example, various Israeli governments have made "deals" with terror organizations. Examples are the exchanges in which five soldiers captured by the Fatah were exchanged for thousands of imprisoned terrorists in Lebanon and Israel in 1983, and the exchange of Israeli soldiers held by PFLP-GC for 1,100 terrorists held captive in Israel in 1985.

Ganor (2000, 4), in analyzing defensive action or antiterrorist measure taken by various countries, including Israel, notes that:

> Typical anti-terrorist measures include defensive tactics, such as military and police patrols, roadblocks and ambushes, as well as the application of perimeter defenses such as physical measures (fences, barriers, metal detectors, "sniffers," video cameras, etc.). Which measures are put into place naturally depend on the conditions specific to the protected target.

Ganor (2000) also stated that these antiterrorist measures will generally require considerable manpower and other resources to be effective. In addition, if the counterterrorist tactics employed are excessive, they may place considerable constraints on the everyday activities and lives of the citizens. This, in turn, may cause resentment toward the government and lead to some support for the terrorists.

Raghavan (1999, 64–80) concludes that the most effective way for police to combat terrorism is through preventive action. In India, the intelligence branches of the state police and the district police headquarters keep track of the effects the government's actions have in reducing terrorist activity and they also conduct surveillance of specific religious groups in various states that are known to be dissatisfied with government policies. Dissatisfaction may occur because of shortages of food, fuel, or water, labor disputes, or what may appear to be disrespect for religious traditions. Any of these could trigger protests, violence, or terrorism. Raghavan also notes that the results of terrorist action have included considerable loss of life and much human suffering. Many of those injured or killed were police officers. Regardless of the causes of mob action, violence, or terrorist activity, the police are blamed if they do not handle the situations with restraint and professionalism. From experience, the Indian police forces have developed a professional approach in their responses to terrorism. The police cannot eliminate or even reduce the extreme dissatisfaction many groups feel toward the government. The best the police can do is respond to situations in such a way that this dissatisfaction, fear, or hostility toward the government does not increase as a result of police action, to hold the situation in check, and to try to convince the citizens not to resort to violence or terrorist tactics during the time when the government is trying to alleviate the problem.

Das (1990, 3) described the major steps taken by the Italian police against terrorism: "Coordinated intelligence onslaughts, police arrests of terrorists, destruction of their hideouts, trials and long sentences, and the repentance in terrorist ranks, as well as exposure and discord created by confession were some of the cornerstones of the police action that would evolve over the years."

After the sarin gas attack in the Tokyo subways, Japan's government was determined to prevent a recurrence or a similar terrorist attach. It took several measures to improve security and enacted the Group Regulation Law that allowed close monitoring of organizations or groups that were suspected of plotting or engaging in terrorist activities (Uchiyama 2002, 16).

CRITICISM OF GOVERNMENT RESPONSES TO TERRORISM

Verma (2002, 15), commenting on the states' response to left-wing victimization in India, in which thousands of officials and citizens were killed, abducted, and kidnapped for ransom, concluded that the government was not able or willing to assist the victims, and that the victims did not receive support or compensation. He stated: "In order to prevent and control victimization from left-wing extremism it is necessary that the government reform its style of functioning and evolve a rule of law based on human rights and fairness."

Das (1990, 95–96), in assessing the Italian response to terrorism, noted that frustration with the prosecution of several terrorists, in which immediate results were not obtained, led to the granting of much wider powers to the judiciary and the police in regard to search, seizure, wiretapping, interrogations, and other methods. This led to increased criticism of the police as being too aggressive and violent, and having too many powers to confiscate property and tap telephones. The judiciary was also criticized. Many citizens felt that their civil rights were being compromised in the name of security.

Hocking (2002, 16) expressed the opinion that the rhetoric used by government spokespersons to characterize terrorist group leaders was at times excessive. The characterization of them as "evildoers" and their activity as "terrorist acts against all freedom-loving people everywhere in the world" may be excessive. The use of propaganda by government officials to create the impression that the threat to the nation is so severe that it is necessary to adopt extraordinary measures to combat terrorism might be compared to efforts by the terrorist themselves to frighten citizens.

Dyson (2001, 321) mentioned that "terrorism investigation is the area in which the temptation is the greatest to violate the law for the greater good." In describing the investigation conducted against the Weather Underground Organization and the New World Liberation Front, Dyson (2001, 322) observed:

> Unfortunately, some departments and investigators went too far. For some of these officers, the objective of solving and preventing terrorist attacks justified their investigation and disrupting all anti-war groups, including religious, cultural, and student organizations. Some engaged in "dirty tricks" to solve the problems.

The efforts of the United States to act against terrorists have been viewed by some in a very negative way. Egendorf (2000, 14) observed that it has been said that "the United States has promoted terrorism in Central America, the Middle East, and elsewhere" as part of such efforts. She added:

> Understandably, the U.S. government, along with some supporters, disputes this point of view. At a U.S. State Department press briefing on April 21, 1998, Under-Secretary of State Thomas Pickering defended the Sudan and Afghanistan bombings, [stating], "Our strikes against terrorist targets in Afghanistan and Sudan . . . represent an intensification in our battle against terror."

BEST PRACTICES IN WORKING WITH SURVIVORS OF TERRORISM

According to the UN Commission on Crime Prevention and Criminal Justice, the elements of a victim service program should include crisis intervention, counseling, advocacy, support during investigation of a crime, support during criminal prosecution and trial, support after case disposition, training for allied professionals on victim issues, violence prevention and other prevention services, and public education, including awareness raising campaigns, on victim issues (United Nations Commission on Crime Prevention and Criminal Justice 1997, 23). This programming should take into account the rights of victims, as stated by the United Nations (1999, 3):

The right to be treated with respect and recognition;
The right to be referred to adequate support services;
The right to receive information about the progress of the case;
The right to be present and to be involved in the decision-making process;
The right to counsel;
The right to protection of physical safety and privacy;
The right of compensation, from both the offender and the state.

A UN Voluntary Fund for Victims of Terrorism has been proposed, but it has not yet been established. Brennan (2000), in her paper titled "Addressing the Needs of Victims," reported on a victims' fund established in the United States, through which 90 percent of the revenue from the fines, assessments, and penalties collected by the government from organizations, agencies, and persons attached to terrorist groups was set aside specifically for victims' needs. She stressed that an immediate, clinically grounded community-based response to victimization is needed. A mental health plan for disaster and terrorism victims should be developed to provide immediate and long-term services. Crisis intervention services should also be readily available when the need for them arises in terrorism situations.

INTERNATIONAL RESPONSES TO TERRORISM

International efforts to combat terrorism occurred as early as 1926, when the First International Conference of Penal Code addressed the need to establish an international convention to combat terrorism, but ensuing conferences were unsuccessful in developing a comprehensive international instrument. Proposals for such an agreement were also made to the League of Nations in 1926 and 1934. Although the League produced a Convention for the Prevention and Punishment of Terrorism in 1937, and twenty-four member states signed it, it never went into force because of the outbreak of World War II and the later breakdown of the League of Nations (Mohsen 2000). It was noted earlier that, since its creation, the United Nations have been unable to agree on an acceptable definition of terrorism and to implement a plan of action to combat it.

Although no international convention has been developed that gives a general definition of terrorism and condemns it, international conventions criminalizing specific types of terrorism have been developed. These include:

> Conventions that criminalize hijacking of airplanes and the destruction of airports,
> conventions relating to attacks on ships and fixed maritime platforms, and a convention to mark plastic explosives to aid in their detection.

In addition to these international conventions, regional antiterrorism conventions have been developed by the Organization of American States, the European Union, the South Asian Union for Regional Cooperation (SAARC), the Arab League, and the Organization of African Unity. The involvement of regional organizations in combating terrorism is a positive development, because the member states can agree on policies to prevent illegal arms trafficking and other terrorist activities that are unique to their situations (Mohsen 2000).

Condemnations of terrorism by the international community or regional organizations have also had some detrimental effects (Mohsen 2000). Much of this is due to irresponsible media coverage and is related to identifying terrorist elements or groups with certain religions or cultures, creating waves of negative public opinion and reactions toward them. Another problem related to international reactions to terrorism is the action of certain countries in offering sanctuary to criminal and terrorist groups by considering them refugees and granting them safe havens and/or political asylum as such.

Subramanian (2000, 5) noted that many democracies are tempted to use martial law to restore order in extreme terrorism situations, but he argued that this defines the terrorists as successful. He stated:

> The primary objective of counter terrorist measures is the protection and maintenance of liberal democracy and the rule of law. . . . To believe that for the sake of "order" individual human rights and freedoms can be sacrificed is to embrace the cult of terrorism. . . . Indiscriminate repression is incompatible with the liberal values of liberty, equality, humanity and justice. . . . The best antidote for terrorism is good, honest and efficient grass roots administration. . . . Security forces . . . should adopt the golden principles of proportionality and operational necessity in the use of force, avoidance of unnecessary suffering to the people and careful selection of the means of operation that would cause the minimum damage to life and property.

There is absolutely no doubt that "the need for cooperation is essential" (Taillon 2001, 132). The need for international cooperation to combat terrorism was emphasized by many of the speakers at the United Nations Conference, and the authors of various chapters in this book also allude to it. Some of the measures to prevent and counteract terrorist crime adopted or proposed by the various Arab Gulf states mentioned by Abdelhameed (2002, 13–17) included:

Pledges to cooperate in the planning, organization, and execution of strategies to combat terrorism,

Governments pledge to refrain from participating in any activity that is in any fashion associated with terrorist activity, as well as not to harbor any individuals who are known to be associated with terrorism,

Governments have developed coordinated systems to detect firearms, explosives, and other destructive or assault weapons thought to be destined for terrorist groups,

Governments have reinforced their own internal security systems, cooperated with other countries in tracking terrorist organizations and crimes committed in their territories, conducted investigations, and extradited suspected terrorists for trial,

Governments have exchanged expertise,

Governments have established new legislation that specifically addresses terrorism and provides appropriate punishments,

Governments have adopted measures that address the needs of victims of terrorism and are considering legislation that will provide protection and compensation for victims.

THE PRESENT AND FUTURE FACES OF TERRORISM

Terrorist groups are developing organizational structures that are transnational and decentralized. They are using high-tech weapons and are also using the most advanced communications, including the Internet, to disseminate their political messages and to communicate with the cells in their organizations. Terrorism on the Internet can occur through attacks on the databases of companies or governments. Links with organized crime and the international drug trade have provided terrorist organizations with high amounts of funds and opportunities for assistance from other terrorists. There is a continuing threat of terrorists acquiring weapons of mass destruction, but even the more conventional weapons (firearms, bombs) used by terrorists are becoming more lethal and effective (Mohsen 2000).

Mullins (1997) contends that the amount of terrorism committed by foreigners in the United States is likely to increase in the future. The number of terrorists entering the country legally or illegally is growing. Once in the country, they establish two types of groups. He characterizes one type as "sleeper cells." This type is composed of individuals who immigrate to the

United States, establish identities, are assimilated into the culture, and then await orders from their superiors in regard to their terrorist mission. A second type, referred to as "transient cells," consists of those who enter the United States legally or illegally, complete their terrorist mission, and quickly depart. At times, they may receive assistance from the "sleeper cells." It is difficult for law enforcement officials to penetrate these terrorist groups, since they are close-knit, highly mobile, self-contained, and very efficient in their work.

The dangers of nonconventional terrorism (chemical, biological, radiological, and nuclear) must also be considered. Although incidents of nuclear terrorism have sharply declined, those of chemical and biological terrorism have been rising. The countries of the developed, industrial world have been the chief targets of nonconventional terrorism, and the facilities that are targeted are usually found in these countries (Karmon 2000). Among the forms of nonconventional terrorism, chemical terrorism presents the greatest threat because the materials are readily available and the techniques for employing them are relatively easy to develop. In contrast, the number of incidents involving the use or attempted use of biological agents for terrorism purposes is extremely small. Nuclear terrorism seems to be on the decline, and terrorism through threats of radiological dispersal has not been a problem, although the possibilities of sabotage of a nuclear site or nuclear material shipments always are present (Karmon 2000). The potential for mass destruction posed by nonconventional terrorism make it one of the most fright provoking types of terrorism. As Schmid (2000, 28–29) observed:

> The Terrorism Prevention Branch [of the United Nations] keeps a close watch on this possibility, maintaining a database on terrorist interest in weapons of mass destruction. We also monitor smuggling incidents of radioactive material and precursor elements which can serve the fabrication of weapons of mass destruction. The potential use of such weapons, while still an unlikely threat, warrants close scrutiny.

The threat posed by terrorism should motivate all countries of the world to denounce terrorism and cooperate to reduce it. Measures must be put in place to help contain the existing forces that promote and profit from terrorism. In addition, efforts to increase the standard of living for persons in the countries most victimized by terrorists could have a positive effect.

It is pointed out by Jenkins (1986, 192) that, "terrorism, like poverty, prejudice, and crime, is becoming another of society's chronic afflictions." He adds, "Individual terrorists can be arrested, terrorist groups can be 'defeated,' but governments find it extremely difficult to identify and destroy the violent web of personal relationships, clandestine contacts, alliances with other groups, suppliers of material, and services that sustain the terrorist underground."

Berman (1986, 326) echoes the same concerns. He says that terrorism is "community based." He explains that it is:

> An outgrowth of the social dynamics of particular communities where individuals feel themselves to be beleaguered and ignored both at home and by the international community. When they feel themselves under siege, community members begin to tolerate more extreme behavior in the name of the community causes. The surest sign of imminent terrorist activity is unwillingness of community leaders to condemn their own extreme elements for fear of losing overall support.

CONCLUSION

The contributors to this book and others who have researched the terrorism problem have emphasized that cooperative efforts at the international, national, and regional levels are very important in containing and reducing the threats posed by terrorists. These cooperative efforts should include exchanges of information on the identity and activities of known terrorists and terrorist organizations and training activities to prepare governments, troops, support personnel, negotiators, medical teams, counselors, and other service providers to respond to terrorism incidents (Kratcoski 2001). Collaborative research is another highly important element. Both basic and applied research are vital to understanding the motivations and characteristics of individual terrorists and/or terrorist groups, and the findings of applied research can be used for strategic analysis and control. Good solid applied research would enable those responsible for combating and eradicating terrorism to develop operational analysis and also implement activities directed toward controlling and eliminating terrorism (Kratcoski 2001).

Nations must follow the lead of those countries that have already enacted legislation that delineates exact penalties for terrorism incidents, and details the process for extradition of terrorists who have fled to other countries. Following the rule of law, codes of conduct must be developed for those who apprehend and question alleged perpetrators of terrorism incidents. The rights of victims to receive treatment and rehabilitation must be assured. The mechanisms for assisting victims of terrorism must already be in place when the need for them arises.

Immediate assistance and support must be available from other nations when terrorist events take place, to minimize loss of life and reduce the possibilities of panic and paralysis of the infrastructure. This help may be in the form of advice from experts, based on their experiences in negotiating with or identifying terrorists, or it may involve rapid deployment of medical teams or immediate provision of food and other supplies for the victims.

BIBLIOGRAPHY

Abdelhameed, Mamdooh. 2002. The Anti-Terrorism Strategy in the Arab Gulf States. Manuscript prepared for *Terrorist Victimization: Prevention, Control, and Discovery.*

Akron Beacon Journal. 2002. New Stresses for Firefighters and Police, 24 March.

Auerbach, Ann Hagedorn. 1998. *The Untold Story of International Kidnapping.* New York: Henry Holt.

Berman, William O. 1986. Stricter Penalties Will Not Eliminate Terrorism. In *Can Terrorism Be Eliminated?* edited by David L. Bender. San Diego, Calif.: Greenhaven Press.

Brennan, Noel. 2000. Addressing the Needs of Victims. Presented at the ancillary meeting on Terrorist Victimization: Prevention, Control, and Recovery held in conjunction with the Tenth United Nations Congress on the Prevention of Crime and the Treatment of Offenders, 12 April, at Vienna, Austria.

Claridge, David. 1998. State Terrorism? Applying a Definitional Model. In *Violence and Terrorism,* edited by Bernard Schechterman and Martin Slann. Guilford, Conn.: Dushkin/McGraw Hill.

Cohen, Irwin M., and Raymond R. Corrado. 2002. A Future for ETA? Manuscript prepared for *Terrorist Victimization: Prevention, Control, and Recovery.*

Control Risk Group. 1999. Annual report, London.

Crelinsten, R. D. 1997. Television and Terrorism: Implications for Crisis Management and Policy Making, *Terrorism and Political Violence* 9: 8–32.

Damphousse, Kelly R., Rent L. Smith, and Amy Sellers. 2002. The Targets and Intended Victims of Terrorist Activities in the United States. Manuscript prepared for *Terrorist Victimization: Prevention, Control, and Recovery.*

Das, Dilip K. 1990. Impact of Antiterrorist Measures on Democratic Law Enforcement; The Italian Experience. *Terrorism* 13: 89–98.

Dyson, William E. 2001. *Terrorism: An Investigator's Handbook.* Cincinnati, Ohio.: Anderson.

Egendort, Laura K., ed. 2000. *Terrorism: Opposing Viewpoints.* San Diego, Calif.: Greenhaven Press.

El Din, Ashraf Shams. 1990. The Need for Cooperation among Arab Countries in the Prevention and Control of Crime. In *International Responses to Terrorism: New Initiatives,* edited by Richard H. Ward and Ahmed Galai Ezeldin. Chicago, Ill.: Office of International Criminal Justice.

Freeh, Louis J. 2001. Statement for the Record on the Threat of Terrorism to the United States. *Congressional Statement,* 10 May.

Ganor, Boaz. 2000. "The Main Factors in Israeli Counter-Terrorism Strategy." Paper prepared for the ancillary meeting on Terrorist Victimization: Prevention, Control, and Recovery held in conjunction with the Tenth United Nations Congress on the Prevention of Crime and the Treatment of Offenders, 12 April, at Vienna, Austria.

Hocking, Jenny. 2002. Developments in Australian Counter-terrorist Strategy: Toward a Surveillance Society. Manuscript prepared for *Terrorist Victimization: Prevention, Control, and Recovery.*

Hoffman, Bruce. 1994. Responding to Terrorism across the Technological Spectrum. *Terrorism and Political Violence* 6, no. 3 (Autumn): 369.

Hoffman, Bruce, and David Claridge. 1998. "The RAND-St. Andrew Chronology of International Terrorism and Noteworthy Domestic Incidents." *Terrorism and Political Violence* 10, no. 2 (Summer): 204–16.

Huggins, Martha K. 1998. *Political Policing: The United States and Latin America.* Durham, N.C.: Duke University Press.

Jenkins, B. M. 1975. International Terrorism: A New Mode of Conflict. Research Paper 48, California Seminar on Arms Control and Foreign Policy. Los Angeles, Calif.: Crescent Publications.

———. 1986. Terrorism Cannot Be Eliminated. In *Can Terrorism Be Eliminated?* Edited by David L. Bender. San Diego: Greenhaven Press.

Kaftka, C., D. Linz, E. Donnerstein, and S. Penrod. 1997. Women's Reactions to Sexually Aggressive Mass Media Depictions. *Violence against Women* 3: 149–77.

Kam-Yee, L. 2000. Macau's Triad Violence. *The Police Journal* 73, no. 3: 231–40.

Karmon, Ely. 2000. Trends and Threats in the Terrorism of the New Millennium. Paper presented at the ancillary meeting on Terrorist Victimization: Prevention, Control, and Recovery, held in conjunction with the Tenth United Nations Congress on the Prevention of Crime and the Treatment of Offenders, 12 April, at Vienna, Austria.

Kratcoski, Peter C. 2001. Research Note: Terrorist Victimization: Prevention, Control and Recovery. *Studies in Conflict and Terrorism* 24, no. 6: 267–473.

Kushner, Harvey W. 2000. The Impact of Terrorist Events in the Media on the Traumatization of Society. Paper presented at the ancillary meeting on Terrorist Victimization: Prevention, Control, and Recovery, held in conjunction with the Tenth United Nations Congress on the Prevention of Crime and the Treatment of Offenders, 12 April, at Vienna, Austria.

Millard, George Henry. 2000. The Forgotten Victims of Narco-Terrorism in Latin America. Paper presented at the ancillary meeting on Terrorist Victimization: Prevention, Control, and Recovery, held in conjunction with the Tenth United Nations Congress on the Prevention of Crime and the Treatment of Offenders, 12 April, at Vienna, Austria.

Mohsen, Ashraf. 2000. Challenges of the Terrorist Phenomenon in the 21st Century. Paper presented at the ancillary meeting on Terrorist Victimization: Prevention, Control, and Recovery, held in conjunction with the Tenth United Nations Congress on the Prevention of Crime and the Treatment of Offenders, 12 April, at Vienna, Austria.

Moyers, F. 1996. Oklahoma City Bombing: Exacerbation of Symptoms in Veterans with PTSD. *Archives of Psychiatric Nursing* 10: 55–59.

Mullins, Wayman C. 1997. Future Trends in Terrorism. *The Justice Professional* 10: 31–46.

Nadir, K. O., R. S. Pynoos, L. A. Fairbanks, M. Al-Ajeel, and A. Al Asfour. 1993. A Preliminary Study of PTSD and Grief among the Children of Kuwait Following the Gulf Crisis. *British Journal of Clinical Psychology* 32: 407–16.

Oliverio, Annamarie. 1998. *The State of Terror.* Albany: State University of New York Press.

Pinkerton Global Intelligence Services (PGIS). 1997. Annual Risk Assessments 1995.

Raghavan, R. K. 1999. *Policing a Democracy: A Comparative Study of India and the U.S.* New Delhi, India: Manohar Press.

Sadler, A. E., and Paul A. Winters, eds. 1996. *Urban Terrorism*. San Diego, Calif.: Greenhaven Press.

Schmid, Alex P. 2000. Magnitudes of Terrorist Victimization: Past, Present, and Future. Paper presented at the ancillary meeting on Terrorist Victimization: Prevention, Control, and Recovery, held in conjunction with the Tenth United Nations Congress on the Prevention of Crime and the Treatment of Offenders, 12 April, at Vienna, Austria.

Shipler, D. K. 1988. Future Domestic and International Terrorism: The Media Perspective. *Terrorism* 11: 543–45.

Silke, Andrew. 2002. The Psychological Impact of Terrorism: Lessons from the UK Experience. Manuscript prepared for *Terrorist Victimization: Prevention, Control, and Recovery*.

Simon, Jeffrey D. 1996. Terrorism Is Not Affected by Media Coverage. In *Urban Terrorism*, edited by Bruno Leone, Scott Barbour, Brenda Stalcup, A. E. Sadler, and Paul A. Winters. San Diego: Greenhaven Press.

Simonsen, Clifford E., and Jeremy Spindlove. 2000. *Terrorism Today: The Past, the Players, the Future*. Upper Saddle River, N.J.: Prentice Hall.

Smith, Brent L. 1994. *Terrorism in America: Pipe Bombs and Pipe Dreams*. Albany: State University of New York Press.

Subramanian, S. 1998. *Human Rights and Police*. Hyderabad, India: Association for Advancement of Police and Security Sciences.

———. 2000. Safeguarding Human Rights of People in Counter Terrorist Operations. Paper prepared for the ancillary meeting on Terrorist Victimization: Prevention, Control, and Recovery, 12 April, at Vienna, Austria.

———. 2002. Human Rights in Counter Terrorist Operations. Manuscript prepared for *Terrorist Victimization: Prevention, Control, and Recovery*.

Taillon, J. Paul de B. 2001. *The Evolution of Special Forces in Counter-Terrorism: The British and American Experiences*. Westport, Conn.: Praeger Publisher.

Uchiyama, Ayako. 2002. Victims of Sarin Gas Attack at Tokyo Subway a New Type of Organized Crime—Crimes of Aum Shinrikyo. Manuscript prepared for *Terrorist Victimization: Prevention, Control and Recovery*.

United Nations Commission on Crime Prevention and Criminal Justice. 1997. 1997 Manual on the Implementation of the United Nations Declaration of Basic Principles of Justice for Victims of Crime and Abuse of Power. Vienna: E/CN/15/1997/CRP.9.

United Nations. 2000. Tenth United Nations Congress on the Prevention of Crime and the Treatment of Offenders, 10–17 April, at Vienna, Austria. A/CONF. 287/8 General Assembly Resolution 42/34, Annex. Vienna, UN, 15 December 3, 1999.

U.S. Department of State. Data provided by the Coordinator for Counter-terrorism, December 7, 1999.

Verma, Arvind. 2002. Terrorist Victimization: Prevention, Control, and Recovery Case Studies from India. Manuscript prepared for *Terrorist Victimization: Prevention, Control, and Recovery*.

Vice-President's Task Force on Combating Terrorism, The. 1986. All Political Violence Is Terrorism. In *What Is Terrorism?* edited by David L. Bender. San Diego, Calif.: Greenhaven Press, 1986.

Ward, Dick. 2000. Gray Phenomena: The Changing Nature of Organized Crime and Terrorism. OICJ Office of International Criminal Justice. Chicago: University of Illinois Press.

Ward, Richard H. 1985. Foreword to *Terrorism and Political Violence: An Egyptian Perspective* by Ahmed Galal Ezeldin. Cairo, Egypt: Journalism, Publishing, and Printing.

White, Jonathan R. 1998. *Terrorism: An Introduction.* Belmont, Calif.: Wadsworth.

———. 2002. *Terrorism: An Introduction.* 2nd ed. Belmont, Calif.: Wadsworth.

II

EXTENT OF TERRORIST VICTIMIZATION AND EFFECTS ON VICTIMS

3

Magnitudes of Terrorist Victimization

Alex P. Schmid

INTRODUCTION

Terrorist crimes take a physical, psychological, social, political, and economic toll on primary and secondary victims and society as a whole. The assessment of the full magnitude of terrorist victimization is a terrain that is still largely uncharted. While terrorist perpetrators are the topic of hundreds of books and thousands of articles, terrorist victimization has seldom been studied empirically.[1]

For a variety of reasons, the perpetrator of a crime generally receives more attention than the victim.[2] The rights of offenders were codified in human rights instruments long before those of the victims. Only one international instrument, the UN Declaration of Basic Principles of Justice for Victims of Crime and Abuse of Power, which was adopted by the General Assembly in December 1985, explicitly cites the rights of victims.[3] Some of these rights have been translated into laws in some UN member states. The Tenth United Nations Congress on the Prevention of Crime and the Treatment of Offenders (April 2000) planned to review the progress that has been made in national action plans to boost victims' rights. In particular, the congress focused on better protection for victims in cases of organized crime.

Our concern here goes to the victims of terrorism. We lack good answers to a number of questions:

1. What types of terrorist victimization exist?
2. What do we know about the suffering of victims of terrorism?
3. What is the rate of terrorist victimization?

4. Who are the victims?
5. What are the rights and needs of victims?

THE NATURE OF TERRORIST VICTIMIZATION

Both terms, "terrorism" and "victimization," require clarification.

Terrorism

Like other "isms" (racism, sexism, etc.), terrorism is both a substantive concept and a political label. Its meaning is constantly stretched to serve new
purposes, as in the term *cyberterrorism*. Despite debates since 1972, the
United Nations has not (at the time of this writing, mid-January 2002) managed to define "international terrorism" conclusively to the satisfaction of all
member states. Some countries insist on a distinction between illegitimate
terrorism and legitimate national liberation struggles.[4] Some are particularly
concerned about "state-terrorism" while others worry more about "state-
sponsored terrorism." Yet others want the term to cover "terrorism in all its
forms and manifestations." For the victims who are taken hostage, kidnapped, injured, or killed, these conceptual distinctions are of secondary importance. Yet if one wants to determine the victim population of terrorism,
some conceptual distinctions have nevertheless to be drawn. While we have
many typologies of terrorism, we do not have similar classifications of terrorist victims.

The terrorists themselves often deny the very process of victimization,
even asserting that "there are no innocent victims."[5] In doing so they are
often implying that they mete out punishment to offenders in acts of "revolutionary justice," thereby shifting guilt away from themselves onto the
victims—a semantic trick maneuver. Sometimes there is an indirect acknowledgment of victimization, as in the case of a South Moluccan terrorist
who said that, "if necessary, we create unnecessary victims."[6] To the terrorist, in contrast to the assassin, the immediate victim of violence matters much
less than the ultimate addressee of his violent communication—his target audience. In a way the direct victim is only the skin on a drum beaten to reach
a wider audience, a pawn used to force the real target into action—or freeze
it into inaction. An ancient Chinese saying has already encapsulated this
idea: "Kill one [to] frighten ten thousand."

The production of atrocities to capture and affect specific target groups
and/or to impress mass audiences sharing victim characteristics or concerns,
is what matters for the terrorist. If the target audience pays attention to the
grievances and demands of terrorists or undergoes terror or panic, terrorists
have reached an important goal. When the terrorist group opposes the state,

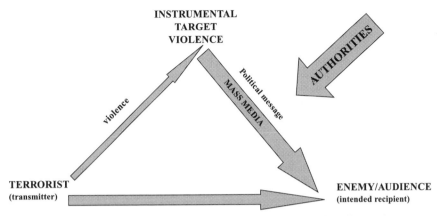

INSTRUMENTAL
TARGET
VIOLENCE

AUTHORITIES

violence

Political message

MASS MEDIA

TERRORIST
(transmitter)

ENEMY/AUDIENCE
(intended recipient)

Figure 1.1   The Triangle of Terrorism. *Source:* **A. P. Schmid.** *Political Terrorism: A Research Guide to Concepts, Theories, Data Bases, and Literature.* **With a bibliography by the author and a world directory of "Terrorist" Organizations by A. J. Jongman. Amsterdam, North-Holland Publishing Company, 1994, 91; as adapted by Jan Oskar Engene. "Patterns of Terrorism in Western Europe, 1950–1995." Bergen, Department of Comparative Politics, 1998 (unpublished Ph.D. thesis), 68.**

it often uses the public, or sections thereof, as victims. Terrorists like to think of themselves as warriors and often call their organization an "army." Yet they are not soldiers. In war, armies attack armies. If unarmed civilians are deliberately targeted, soldiers who do so become war criminals. To produce atrocities in war is bad enough. To produce atrocities without a war is even worse—yet that is exactly what terrorists do. They do not care about the direct victims; they victimize them for its effect on third parties. Successful victimization of sectors of society signals to the public at home and abroad that the state cannot protect them effectively. Depending on the goals of the terrorist—there are usually three: propaganda, coercion, or intimidation—a target of attention, a target of demands or a target of terror is addressed by the terrorist victimization. Human beings killed, injured, kidnapped, or taken hostage serve as message generators to the terrorist. In 1988, after a consultation of academic colleagues, a social science consensus definition was proposed. It runs as follows:

> Terrorism is an anxiety-inspiring method of repeated violent action, employed by (semi-)clandestine individual, group, or state actors, for idiosyncratic, criminal, or political reasons, whereby—in contrast to assassination—the direct targets of violence are not the main targets. The immediate human victims of violence are generally chosen randomly (targets of opportunity) or selectively (representative or symbolic targets) from a target population, and serve as message generators. Threat and violence-based communication processes between terrorist (organization), (imperiled) victims, and main targets are used

to manipulate the main target (audience[s]), turning it into a target of terror, a target of demands, or a target of attention, depending on whether intimidation, coercion, or propaganda is primarily sought.[7]

In a wider sense, the target audience is also victimized, certainly when a campaign of terror raises apprehension to a level where many people worry about the question: "Will I be the next victim?"[8]

Sometimes the execution of the victim is suspended: a human being is kidnapped or taken hostage but its survival is held in suspense, depending on "concessions" being made to the terrorist. In such situations, the families of those abducted or held are certainly also victimized—sometimes they are asked to pay ransom while their worry about the fate of their loved ones, which, in fact, makes them "covictims."

What makes terrorism so different and complex is that the terrorist actor can move and remove the direct target of violence, while also freezing and immobilizing a target of terror, impacting on a target of demands and manipulating a target of attention. Depending on the way the actual victims of terrorist violence are linked to the target of terror, the target of demands or the target of attention, different objectives can be achieved. By activating the interplay between the three target groups, terrorism can create multiple secondary effects which can serve a variety of purposes.[9] The manipulation of government through the victimization of sectors of the public brings about changes in public opinion. It works best in democracies with a free, but uncritical, press.

Victimization

When it comes to crime one usually distinguishes between the perpetrator and the victim.[10] However, there are also crimes in which both sides are willing accomplices, for instance, in some forms of prostitution. Such crimes are termed "victimless crimes." Can there be terrorism without victimization? There is a minority opinion in terrorism research which argues "that 'victims' are not indispensable to a definition of terrorism." Adherents of this school of thought argue that attacks on highly symbolic targets or vital infrastructure can create fear without people being directly victimized.[11] While there is some prima facie plausibility to this, in reality terrorists attack people, symbolic objects, and material facilities and by attacking the latter they endanger the lives of the former. Usually militant groups "progress" from attacks on objects to attacks on people who are either considered as adversaries or as "dispensable cannon fodder" in their campaigns of psychological warfare. Yet political activists are sometimes already termed "terrorists" by the government before they engage in serious political violence and produce human victims in order to "communicate" with their principal target. Victims of terrorism come in two main categories:

Focused terrorism: Discriminately chosen victims, usually part of the target group that is the principal addressee of the terrorist's message, coercion, or intimidation; and

Indiscriminate terrorism: The random victim who happened to be in the wrong place at the wrong time and who was not specifically selected for his or her individual characteristics. In Colombia, for instance, terrorists set up roadblocks and stop cars and busses. They abduct then those who look rich enough for ransom by their families and let the others go. They call this "miracle fishing." Sometimes the nature of a place (e.g., an aircraft or cruiser) or a certain circumstance (e.g., the anniversary of a massacre) determine the terrorists' victim selection. Most innocent victims are targets of opportunity.[12]

The first type of victim is usually involved, though often only passively, in the conflict between the terrorist movement and the adversary. If he is a high-profile political target, the killing might become so focused that it is an assassination. An assassination can cause shock and grief, but, due to its unique nature, rarely terror. The second type of victim—the chance victim—is generally not even remotely connected to the conflict issue.

The Latin word *victima* referred to a sacrificial animal that was chosen as a pure offering to the gods. That meaning can be found in many religions: the true believer—in our case the terrorist—makes an offering, whereby the innocence of the victim in a way enhances its value. The victim of terrorism is usually an involuntary, defenceless victim and the element of unpredictability and randomness in victim selection gives terror part of its power.[13] The sudden transition from normalcy to a situation threatening imminent death, from health to injury, from courtesy to cruelty, from equality to exploitation, makes terrorist victimization especially gruesome. The prototypical form of terrorist victimization is the act of hostage taking. In the context of terrorism, "victim" has been defined by Frank Ochberg and David Soskis as "a person or thing injured or destroyed in pursuit of an object, in gratification of a passion, or as a result of event or circumstance."[14]

The composition of the ingredients in the combination of vulnerability, helplessness, and humiliation, which characterize the state of victimization, is partly dependent on the nature of the victim and the type of victimization. Basically, there are, as Martha Crenshaw has pointed out, two types of victimization:

1. Single phase victimization, as in a shooting attack or a bomb attack, and
2. Dual phase victimization, where there is a time lag between the initiation and the completion of the terrorist crime.

Single phase incidents can be classified in terms of magnitude by looking either at the quantity of human lives lost or by looking at the quality of victimization. Dual phase incidents can be broken into four qualitative magnitudes of victimization.

1. Being taken hostage is bad—but at least the location of the hostage is known—he or she can hope for liberation.
2. Being kidnapped is worse, since the terrorists can kill the victim with impunity at the secret location where they keep the abducted person.
3. Being tortured is even worse. Torture serves several purposes; a major one is to frighten others from opposing the regime that tortures.[15]
4. Worst of all is being "disappeared." The families of the victim do not know the fate of the victim and cannot put the matter to rest, hoping against hope for the reappearance of the one who was first kidnapped, then tortured, and finally murdered and disposed of without a trace.

THE SUFFERING CAUSED BY TERRORISM

Most authors on terrorism deal only with kidnappings and acts of hostage taking and forget about the terror that is created by torture and disappearances. This omission is partly because acts of hostage taking and kidnapping are usually the work of nonstate actors while torture and disappearances are more often the work of secret services and death squads. Yet, we should not forget that a disappearance begins with a kidnapping and ends in murder. Its effects on society are profound and long lasting as the aftershocks from the repression in Chile and Argentina in the 1970s make clear.

When we talk about "Magnitudes of Victimization," there is a qualitative and a quantitative dimension. Yet, we should never forget that it is the individual's psychological and physical pain that matter most. The degree of suffering and the number of those who suffer can both vary. Victims, relatives, target groups all suffer, but in varying ways. The immediate victim experiencing terror—an extreme form of anxiety[16]—manifests four distinct psychological responses in a time sequence:

Phase I: Victim experiences shock, disbelief, denial, and delusion. There is paralysis of action and denial of sensory impressions;

Phase II: The victim feels hopelessly entrapped. There is a paralysis of affect, a terror-induced, pseudo-calm, noticeably detached behavior—"frozen fright." The isolated and powerless victim takes stock of his/her life and/or keeps him/herself busy in an attempt to cope if the victimization is prolonged;

Phase III: After the acute stage is over, a state of traumatic psychological infantilism sets in with most victims; adaptive response behavior first learned in early childhood resurfaces: compliance, appeasement, submission, and ingratiation toward the terrorists takes place. Empathy and sympathy with the victimizer tends to occur;

Phase IV: If terror continues unabated, pathological transference can set in. Victims no longer focus on an actual death threat but begin to feel that their very lives have been given to them by the terrorist. A process of conversion might set in due to identification of the victim with the aggressor.[17]

In phases III and IV some of the direct victims in a hostage incident might suffer from the regressive "Stockholm Syndrome," and identify with the hostage taker and even end up falling in love with him, as in the original 1973 bank robbery incident in Sweden that gave this phenomenon its name.[18] The conversion of the direct victim might go even further: he or she might join the terrorist group, as was the case with the millionaire heiress Patty Hearst in the 1970s when she became part of the Symbionese Liberation Army.[19] Yet far more serious from an etiological point of view is a finding derived from longitudinal research conducted by Rona Fields in Northern Ireland and Israel. It indicates that crossovers in roles from victim to terrorist are not so exceptional. To quote Rona Fields:

> After a decade of examining torture victims and hostages from several different countries and as many wars, after eight years of testing children aged 6 though 15 growing up in conditions of constant violence, I have been led to conclude that "little victims into big terrorists grow.[20]

There exists also some evidence for intergenerational crossovers from victim to terrorist.

Paradoxically, the victim of some types of terrorism not only fears the terrorist. Hostages also fear becoming victims of those who seek to rescue them. According to one statistical study from the 1970s, almost four out of five hostages who were killed died as a consequence of rescue attempts.[21] Are we to count them as victims of terrorism or as victims of counterterrorism—or of both?

Finally, responders to victimization might also be traumatized, experience burnout, and require assistance. In the literature, these "hidden victims"—ambulance personnel, emergency workers from the five brigades, the police, and the military—are sometimes referred to as "tertiary victims" when they succumb to occupational stress and fatigue in the course of their postdisaster assignments. There might also be possible renewed traumatization of former victims when a state makes peace with the terrorists, grants them amnesty, and even allows them to take political offices as happened, for instance, in Northern Ireland where former terrorists became ministers as a result of the Good Friday agreement.

There are conceptual problems in determining both the quality and the quantity of terrorist victimization. Table 3.1 identifies various categories of victims of terrorism discussed above.

It is clear from this table that, even if it is true that terrorism causes relatively few direct victims, there is a considerable multiplier effect, even more so if the counterterrorist operations of the adversary of the terrorists are

Table 3.1.   Typology of Victims of Terrorism

I. Immediate Victims and Indirect Victims:

I.1. Those killed, tortured, and who disappeared and those who were kidnapped, taken hostage, and who did not reappear;

I.2. Those tortured, mutilated, wounded, and mentally and physically handicapped by terrorism but surviving the assault or captivity;

I.3. Those kidnapped and those taken hostage who survive physically unharmed but suffer from post-traumatic stress disorders;

I.4. Those who are wounded or die in a counterterrorist rescue operation at the hands of the terrorists.

I.5. Those who die in a causal sequence of a terrorist threat or event*;

I.6. Those who report or testify as witnesses on terrorist events and are victimized for it, e.g. journalists.

II. Proximate Victims:

II.1. Those close to human beings in categories I.1–6 (family, friends, dependents, colleagues of victims);

II.2. Those whose names appear on death lists and those who receive credible death threats;

II.3. Those who have otherwise a well-founded reason to fear that they might be the next victims (predictable victims).

II.4. Those who were victimized in the past and, upon learning about another, similar victimization in the media, experience a revival of their own traumatization;

II.5. Those responders who become traumatized by bloody and terrible events in the course of their work;

II.6. Those citizens of countries who experience sanctions due to state-sponsored terrorism by their government.

II.7. Those who experience income loss or property damage or are forced to step up safety measures due to terrorism, e.g. in the tourist industry or the aviation industry.[†]

*An example: In March 1977 the Spanish-Canarian terrorist group Movimiento para la Autodeterminacion e Independencia del Archipelago de las Canarias (MPAIAC) set off a bomb at Las Palmas airport which led to a rerouting of air traffic. As a consequence, two jumbo-jets collided on the tarmac of Tenerife airport with 585 people dying in the accident. J. O. Engene, Patterns of Terrorism in Western Europe, 1950–1995, Bergen: Department of Comparative Politics, 1998: 244.

[†]The economic costs of terrorism can be very substantial. When sixty-eight tourists were killed in Luxor, Egypt, in 1997, the drop in tourism revenues was an estimated $1.5 million. Steve Macko, Tips to Lessen Your Chances of Becoming a Victim of Terrorism, *ERRI Daily Intelligence Report* 4 (September 1998): 251, at www.emergency.com/avoidter.htm.

taken into account. We should not forget that both "Operation Horseshoe" which led to the death of some 10,000 people and the expulsion of 850,000 from Kosovo, and the war in Chechnya (1999–) were originally counterterrorist operations.

What does it mean to have been a victim of terrorism? Those who are killed cannot tell us but here are some symptoms which most survivors experience.

A number of these symptoms are usually referred to as post-traumatic stress disorders (PSTD). The World Health Organization defined post-traumatic stress disorders as follows:

> Delayed and/or protracted response to stressful event or situation (either short- or long-lasting) of an exceptionally threatening or catastrophic nature, which is likely to cause pervasive distress in almost anyone (e.g., natural or manmade disaster, combat, serious accident, witnessing the violent death of others, or being the victim of torture, terrorism, rape, or other crime). Predisposing factors such as personality traits . . . or previous history of neurotic illness may lower the threshold for the development of the syndrome or aggravate its course, but they are neither necessary nor sufficient to explain its occurrence.[22]

Not all who have experienced terror show these symptoms to the same degree. Research has demonstrated that people who manage to minimize traumatic stress disorders tend to share certain characteristics. On the basis of interviews with "successful" survivors of hostage and kidnap situations, the following coping mechanisms, which come into play both during and after the victimization, have emerged, as shown in table 3.4.

Table 3.2.   Victims of Terrorism

Fear, free-floating anxiety, phobias;
Grief;
Shock, apathy, numbness;
Survivor guilt, self-blame;
Anger, hostility, rage, resentment, resignation;
Depression, lack of hope, alienation, and loneliness;
Isolation, interpersonal difficulties;
Physical symptoms of distress: insomnia, startle reactions, nightmares;
Inability to concentrate, memory lapses, sexual problems;
Panic;
Inability to resume normal activity.*

*E. E. Flynn, Victims of Terrorism: Dimensions of the Victim Experience, in *Contemporary Research on Terrorism*, edited by Paul Wilkinson and Alasdair M. Stewart, 350–51 (Aberdeen: Aberdeen University Press, 1987); U.S. Department of Justice, Office of Justice Programs, Office for Victims of Crime, *Handbook for Victims of the East Africa Embassy Bombings* (Washington, D.C.: U.S. Department of Justice, n.d. [1998/99]), 1–4.

Table 3.3.   Post-traumatic Stress Disorder Symptoms (PTSD)

Persistent and intense re-experience of the traumatic event (nightmares, flashbacks, intrusive thoughts of the event);   Major avoidance of situations or people that could remind someone of the event;   Avoidance of emotions in general, including feelings of emotional closeness to others;   Persistent sleep difficulties;   Exaggerated startle response;   Intense need to be aware of everything, hyper vigilance;   Marked loss of interest in activities which were previously rewarding.*

*U.S. Department of Justice. Office of Justice Programs, Office for Victims of Crime. *Handbook for Victims of the East Africa Embassy Bombings*. Washington, D.C.: U.S. Department of Justice, n.d. (1998/99), 1–4.

How can we assess the magnitude of post-traumatic stress disorders that the families of victims—the so-called secondary victims—suffer? What is the price of suffering? What is the worth of a life wasted by terrorists?

These are real questions for which sometimes a monetary answer is given as when courts grant a victim compensation.[23]

RATES OF TERRORIST VICTIMIZATION

Who are the victims of terrorism and what is the role of terrorist victimization?

Terrorism tends to produce an exaggerated fear of victimization. In order to maintain perspective, the risk of terrorist victimization should be balanced against other risks (see table 3.5). Statistics of terrorist victimization are hard to come by.

The neglect of the victim dimension of terrorism is partly due to the inadequate data situation in the field. Terrorism is unevenly covered by the me-

Table 3.4.   Coping Mechanism against PTSD

1. Belief in the innate strength of oneself;   2. Reflections and thoughts of loved ones and friends;   3. Faith in some superordinate power;   4. Hope that captivity will end favorably;   5. Use of calculating powers to interact and plan for possible escape;   6. Physical exercise;   7. Expressions of anger via appropriate self-assertion;   8. Ability to focus attention and become task oriented.*

*Dr. Calvin Jeff Frederick, psychologist at UCLA and the Veterans Administration Medical Center in West Los Angeles; cit. David Jacobson, with Gerald Astor, *Hostage: My Nightmare in Beirut* (New York: Donald Fine, 1991), 279–85.

Table 3.5. Risk of Death from Various Sources (Annual average per million people)

	Political Violence	Homicide	Traffic Accidents
N. Ireland	97.6	11.9	179.0
Italy	0.6	33.7	172.3
Uruguay	1.1	68.5	68.6
Germany	0.1	40.4	251.2

Source: Christopher Hewitt, *Consequences of Political Violence* (Brookfield: Dartmouth Publishing, 1993), 16.

dia. In some countries, e.g., Israel, even small incidents receive ample international publicity, while much larger incidents in places like Burundi, Colombia, Kashmir, or Sri Lanka receive scant international attention. Most acts of terror perpetrated in a context of guerrilla wars and civil war go unreported. In countries where the press is muzzled—and we should not forget that only 21 percent of the world's population lives in countries with a really "free press"[24]—most acts of state terror and many acts of nonstate terror are never revealed.

There exist only a few datasets on terrorism and they are often not even fully comparable, due to different definitions, underlying political and commercial interests, and so on. Some people want to downplay the magnitude of terrorism, e.g., to protect their tourism industry, yet others want to magnify the threat, so that they can sell more antiterrorist services and equipment.

Let us look at some data, starting with the simple question: is terrorism increasing or decreasing? Actually, terrorism can be both: increasing in lethality, but decreasing in the number of incidents. That is one finding that emerges, for instance, from the annual U.S. Department of State figures.

Table 3.6 shows that while the number of registered international terrorist incidents went down to 273 in 1998, the human toll was, in 1998, the

Table 3.6. Decline in Incidents and Rise in Lethality of International Terrorism

	U.S. Dept. of State # of Int. Incidents	U.S. Dept. of State # of Fatalities	U.S. Dept. of State # of Injured
1989	376	411	385
1990	437	218	682
1991	565	102	242
1992	363	91	636
1993	431	109	1,393
1994	322	314	663
1995	440	177	6,277
1996	296	314	2,915
1997	304	221	693
1998	273	741	5,952
1999	392	233	706
2000	423	405	791

Alex P. Schmid

highest since 1985, standing at 741 lives lost while the number of wounded had also jumped from 385 in 1989 to 5,952 in 1998.[25]

On the basis of his own dataset (RAND and St. Andrews), which parallels in many ways the one of the Department of State, Bruce Hoffman also holds that the lethality of international terrorism has been increasing in the last few years.[26] Other data looking at both domestic and international terrorism also confirm such an increase.

While the rising trend in lethality observed by Bruce Hoffman is borne out by this set of statistics as well, the declining frequency in the number of incidents is not evident if one takes international and domestic incidents together and compares them for three, partly overlapping periods (see table 3.8).

If this is true, what are the implications? Since the data in the field of terrorism are so incomplete and hard to compare from country to country, it is difficult to draw conclusions. If terrorist campaigns escalate into war and acts of terror are hidden in the fog of war, one could perhaps notice a reduction in the terrorist crime counted, but one more than made up for in terms of war crimes committed. If terrorism moves, as it were, from areas where such political violence is covered well by the press (like Western Europe) to areas (like the Great Lakes District in Africa) where there is no counting, another distortion can occur. There are other possible distorting factors. Since the 1960s the world population has increased by some two billion people. Other things being equal, bigger crowds make for more victims if bombs explode in their midst.

Yet having said this, it still holds true that in comparison to civil war, genocide, or ethnic cleansing, most nonstate terrorism as recorded since the 1960s has generally not been a major killer. "Terrorists want a lot of people watching, not a lot of people dead," Brian Jenkins said in the 1970s. There is still considerable, thought perhaps diminishing, truth in

Table 3.7. Casualties Caused by International and Domestic Worldwide Terrorism, 1970–93

Period	Number Injured	Number Killed
1970–1983	18,925	28,110
Annual average of deaths		2,007.85
Annual average of injured	1,351,78	
1990–1993	37,010	27,499
Annual average of deaths		6,877.65
Annual average of injured	9,252.5	

Sources: A. J. Jongman, Trends in International and Domestic Terrorism in Western Europe, 1968–1988, in *Western Responses to Terrorism,* edited by A. P. Schmid and R. D. Crelinsten (London: Frank Cass, 1993), 36; Risk Information Services, *Annual Risk Assessments 1990* and Pinkerton's Risk Assessment Services, *Terrorism 1991–93;* cit. P. Chalk, *West European Terrorism and Counter-Terrorism: The Evolving Dynamic* (New York: St. Martin's Press, 1996), 182.

Table 3.8.   Comparative Frequency of International and Domestic Worldwide Terrorist Incidents in Totals and Annual Averages

Period	Totals	Average per Year
Number of incidents, 1968–88	35,150	1,673.8
Number of incidents, 1984–88	16,218	3,243.6
Number of incidents, 1988–93	23,616	4,723.2

Sources: 1989–93 data: Risks Information Services, *Annual Risk Assessments* 1990 and *Pinkerton's Risk Assessment Services, Terrorism 1991–93; 1968–88* and *1984–88;* A. J. Jongman, Trends in International and Domestic Terrorism in Western Europe, 1968–1988, in *Western Responses to Terrorism,* edited by A. P. Schmid and R. D. Crelinsten (London: Frank Cass, 1993), 33; cit. P. Chalk, *West European Terrorism and Counter-Terrorism: The Evolving Dynamic* (New York: St. Martin's Press, 1996), 183.

this. Originally, the Russian terrorists of the late nineteenth century hailed the new method of violence as more humane than civil war since the terrorist's surgical attacks would hit only the most repressive members of the czarist state. They considered the low-casualty rate of terrorism as one of the advantages of what at the time was called "the Russian method."[27] The relative selectivity of terrorism in the nineteenth century has in the twentieth century given way to more indiscriminate violence. Yet the extent of this violence is not as high as one would intuitively guess, with some high-casualty incidents like the September 11, 2001, attack on the World Trade Center in mind.

Jan Oskar Engene, who surveyed 7,743 terrorist incidents in Western Europe over a period of forty-five years (1950–1995) concluded that his database did "not support the assumption that terrorists are out to kill as many people as possible." He concluded, on the basis of his material covering more than 7,700 domestic incidents:

We know already that only one terrorist attack in five in Western Europe kills people. . . . Of these attacks, about 70% kill one person only. And a further 14.6% kill two persons. We are left with 6% of the attacks with a death toll of five people or more. In the entire period under investigation, five attacks caused more than 20 deaths, the worst of which took the lives of 85 people. Though, three of the five most lethal attacks took place in 1980 and another in 1987, there is no clear evidence in the . . . data material to suggest that lethal attacks are becoming more frequent. . . . [T]he number of attacks that caused death fell sharply after 1980. Again the 1970s stand out as the violent decade. In other words, the overwhelming bulk of terrorist attacks do not kill. Those that do kill take the lives of relatively few people. The highly lethal terrorist attacks are known, but relatively uncommon.[28]

The observations by Engene for domestic terrorism in Europe[29] are also reflected in the RAND statistics on international terrorism which cover all continents (table 3.9).

Table 3.9.   Fatalities per Incident of International Terrorism, (RAND–St. Andrews Data Series)

	1994	1996
Number of Incidents:	350	250
of which with fatalities	96	62
with 1 fatality	51	20
with 2 fatalities	20	15
with 3 fatalities	4	5
with 4 fatalities	4	5
with 5 fatalities	4	0
with 6 fatalities	0	2
with 7 fatalities	1	2
with 8 fatalities	1	1
with 10 19 fatalities	5	8
with 20–29 fatalities	3	2
with 30–39 fatalities	1	n.d.
with 40+ fatalities	n.d.	2
with 90+ fatalities	1	
Of total fatalities	n.d.	510

Sources: Bruce Hoffman and Donna Kim Hoffman, *The RAND-St. Andrews Chronology of International Terrorism, 1994* (Santa Monica: RAND, 1997), 225; Bruce Hoffman and David Claridge, The RAND-St. Andrews Chronology of International Terrorism and Noteworthy Domestic Incidents, 1996. *Terrorism and Political Violence* 10, no. 2 (Summer 1998): 143.

Much of the terrorism in Europe in the postwar period served to gain attention and for that terrorists did not usually need large numbers of casualties. Coercive terrorism for extortion and blackmail only produces large numbers of victims if the coerced party does not make concessions to the terrorists. Despite declaratory "no concessions" policies, many governments have in fact given in to terrorist demands, usually secretly. The form of terrorism that produces high numbers of fatalities in order to create public panic or demands for a strong state have been relatively few and have originated mainly with right-wing groups, religious groups, and those engaged in ethnic cleansing. It makes a great difference, then, whether terrorists aim to impress an audience, coerce a government, or intimidate society.

Where attention is the main goal, fatalities are often low. Some 120,000 incidents in six West European countries over a twenty-year period caused "only" some 10,000 direct fatalities and about 20,000 injured as table 3.10 makes clear.

Yet from country to country there are significant differences in the lethality of political violence, as table 3.11 makes clear: The terrorists from ETA and from the IRA are much more lethal than, say, those from the Netherlands or Switzerland.

Table 3.10.   Seven European Countries, 1968–1988

Country	Period	No. of Incidents	Deaths	Injured
Northern Ireland	68–88	43,777	2,672	11,906
Turkey	78–81	40,500	5,241	n.a.
Italy	68–85	14,589	419	>5,000
France	75–84	5,737	130	746
	85–87	2,426	n.a.	n.a.
German Fed. Rep.	67–81		71	1,389
	1980s	12,210	33	n.a.
Spain	68–88	672	n.a.	
Netherlands	1980s	249	7	20
Total		119,488	9,245	19,061

Source: A. J. Jongman, Trends in International and Domestic Terrorism in Western Europe, 1968–1988, in Western Responses to Terrorism, edited by A. P. Schmid and R. D. Crelinsten (London: Frank Cass, 1993) and Special Issue of Terrorism and Political Violence 4, no. 4 (Winter 1992): 47; Christopher Hewitt, Consequences of Political Violence (Brookfield: Dartmouth Publishing, 1993), 15.

Table 3.11.   Deaths Caused by Acts of Terrorism in West European Countries, According to TWEED Database, 1950–1995

Country	Number	Percent
United Kingdom	1,489	53.5
Spain	650	23.4
Italy	298	10.7
France	145	5.2
German Federal Republic	97	3.5
Belgium	31	1.1
Portugal	28	1.0
Greece	27	1.0
Austria	4	0.1
Ireland	4	0.1
Netherlands	2	0.1
Switzerland	1	0.1
Sweden	1	0.1
Denmark	0	—
Norway	0	—
Finland	0	—
Iceland	0	—
Luxembourg	0	—
Total	2,777	99.7

Source: Jan Oskar Engene, Patterns of Terrorism in Western Europe, 1950–1995 (Bergen: Department of Comparative Politics, 1998), 216.

Table 3.12. Characteristics of Those Killed in Political Violence (%)

	Italy	Germany	Spain	Uruguay	N. Ireland
Age					
0–19	12	16	2	11	22
20–39	52	44	56	52	55
40–64	29	27	39	36	20
65+	7	13	3	1	3
Sex					
Male	81	80	96	95	92
Female	19	20	4	5	8

Source: Christopher Hewitt, *Consequences of Political Violence* (Brookfield: Dartmouth Publishing, 1993), 17.

WHO ARE THE VICTIMS?

Most of the fatalities are males from the age cohort of twenty to thirty-nine years, as table 3.12 makes clear. Terror fighters are also mostly from this age group. The age group that is, by and large, most crime-prone is also most terrorism-prone. Most of the victims are male. Yet one terrorist said cynically: "We are so emancipated that we also shoot women."[30]

Broken down by profession, it emerges that the security forces are the largest single victim group, followed by the not gainfully employed and the "unknown" man in the street, as shown in table 3.13.

If we look at various categories of targets of violence in a much larger sample of countries, the following picture emerges, as shown in table 3.14.

Terrorists use a variety of tactics. Most prominent is the hidden bomb that blindly kills bystanders and parties to the conflict alike. It is no accident that terrorism is called "the philosophy of the bomb." (See table 3.15.)

Table 3.13. Occupation of Victims

	Italy	Germany	Spain	Uruguay	N. Ireland
Soldier/Police	23	18	44	38	30
Students	16	4	—	5	—
Blue Collar	15	4	7	4	7
White Collar/ Professional	15	3	8	—	4
Elite	10	13	9	3	—
Not in Paid Employment*	18	42	3	36	4
Unknown**	3	15	29	4	55

Source: Christopher Hewitt, *Consequences of Political Violence* (Brookfield: Dartmouth Publishing, 1993), 17.
* Includes pensioners, housewives, children, criminals, and terrorists without occupation
** Most probably ordinary blue- and white-collar individuals.

Table 3.14. Targets of Violence in 1997 (Domestic and International)

	Number of Incidents
Political Party	625
Other	557
Business, Domestic	533
Police/Military	518
Unknown	450
Government	312
Transportation	239
Media	70
International	69
Business, Foreign	55
Utility	54
Business, United States	33
Other, United States	25
Diplomatic	18
Unknown, United States	10
Diplomatic, United States	8
Government, United States	6
Police/Military, United States	4
Media, United States	1
Transportation, United States	1
Political Party, United States	0
Utility, United States	0
Total	3,588

Source: Pinkerton Global Intelligence Service (PGIS), *Annual Risk Assessment 1997.*

Assassinations

What distinguishes an assassination in conceptual terms from a terrorist killing is that the person murdered has a major value in itself to the killer or his superior. The victim—usually a high-level political figure—is the principle target. Often these are heads of state. Table 3.16 lists a sample of presidents and prime ministers who were targeted, some successfully, others not.

Table 3.15. Total Terrorist Tactics, 1968–1993

Bombing	46%
Attacks	22%
Hijackings	12%
Kidnapping	6%
Hostage	1%

Source: The RAND Chronology of International Terrorism, Responding to Terrorism across the Technological Spectrum by Bruce Hoffman, *Terrorism and Political Violence* 6, no.3 (Autumn 1994): 369.

Table 3.16.　Sample of Assassinations and Attempts of Assassination in the 1990s

India, 21 May 1991: Prime Minister Rajiv Gandhi is assassinated by Tamil Tiger suicide bomber in Madras.

Sri Lanka,1 May 1993: A Tamil suicide bomber, with explosives wrapped around the chest, kills Sri Lankan president Ranasingle Premadasa.

Rwanda, 6 April 1994: The presidents of Burundi and Rwanda are killed by a ground-to-air missile when their aircraft approaches Kigali. The incident sparks a genocide in which some 800,000 Rwandans, mainly Tutsis, are killed.

Egypt, 26 June 1995: Nine Islamic radicals led by Mustafa Hamza, attempt to assassinate Egyptian president Hosni Mubarak in Addis Abbaba by ambushing his motorcade.

Israel, 4 November 1995: Right-wing extremist Yigal Amir kills Israeli prime minister Yitzhak Rabin as latter leaves a peace rally in Tel Aviv.

Cambodia, 29 September 1998: A rocket-propelled grenade narrowly missed the car of Cambodian leader Hun Sen when he was travelling in northern Cambodia.

Pakistan, 3 January 1999: Prime Minister Nawaz Sharif narrowly escaped an assassination attempt when a bomb exploded on a bridge he passed by car, killing three people.

Sri Lanka, 18 December 1999: President Chandrika Kumaratunga survived an assassination attempt by a suicide bomber from the Liberation Tigers of Tamil Eelam (LTTE) at an election rally.

Source: CDISS Database: Terrorist Incidents 1945 to 1998, http://www.cdiss.org/terror_1990s.htm

An assassination is, by the political character of its target, a very visible event. It can unchain social forces, as in Rwanda in 1994, when it led to genocide, or in Sarajevo in 1914, when it triggered the First World War.

Kidnapping

While assassinations receive ample prominence, they are not necessarily terroristic. However, there is a class of terrorist events which are underreported, namely kidnappings. The underreporting is because the release of the victim is often not helped by publicity. Table 3.17 greatly underreports the number

Table 3.17.　Regional Distribution of Kidnappings

Number of People Abducted for Ransom, 1995–1998	
South America	6,755
Asia/Far East	617
Europe	271
Africa	211
Middle East	118
North America	80

Source: Control Risks Group, London.

of kidnappings but probably reflects the regional distribution of kidnappings, especially when it comes to abducted foreigners.

Since Latin America figures so prominently in this table, it is worthwhile to have a closer look at the continent (table 3.18).

According to one analyst, the reporting rate for kidnappings is in some countries estimated to be as low as 10 percent, while the reporting rate worldwide is perhaps 30 percent.[31] This would put the number of kidnappings for political coercion or ransom well beyond 10,000 people per year. Latin America leads the statistics, accounting for more than 80 percent.

These figures in the table are already dated. In Colombia, currently eight persons are kidnapped every day; some 3,000 people were kidnapped from April 1999 to April 2000, 200 of them children.[32] Ruben Dario Ramirez, Colombia's former antikidnapping "czar," estimated that kidnappers in Colombia collect $170,000,000 a year. In Mexico, kidnapping is said to be a $60,000,000 annual industry, and some gangs contract out jobs such as the guarding of the hostages.[33] Guatemala is, after Colombia, Mexico, and Brazil, the fourth most dangerous place in terms of kidnappings in Latin America. No more than 5 percent of the kidnapping cases are resolved.[34]

Table 3.19 identifies the fifteen countries most affected by kidnappings 1992 to 1 April 2000.[35] This table also provides some insights into the length of the ordeal of victims of kidnapping

About one in ten kidnappings worldwide ends in the death of the person abducted, as table 3.20 makes clear.[36]

Did the "negotiations" involve money? Most probably. While local people are the main victims, kidnapping also has an impact on multinational corporations. Sixty to 65 percent of all Fortune 500 companies are estimated to buy kidnap insurance for their executives. Kidnap and ransom insurance policies generate an estimated $150,000,000 a year in premiums, covering ransoms, professional negotiations, and psychological support. While money can save the lives of those kidnapped, every ransom paid is an incentive to further kidnappings. Some organizations—like the Red Cross—refuse to pay a ransom for their people. The following throws some light on the chances of release with or without paying ransom.

Table 3.18.   Estimated Number of Kidnappings in the 1990s

Latin America in 1995	6,500
Colombia, 1989 to mid-1996	7,500
Brazil, 1989 to mid-1996	4,500
Mexico, 1989 to mid-1996	2,300

Source: Ann Hagedorn Auerbach, *Ransom: The Untold Story of International Kidnapping* (New York: Henry Holt, 1998), 435–36.

Table 3.19.   The Fifteen Countries Most Affected by Kidnappings, 1992 to 1 April 2000

Colombia	5,349
Mexico	1,287
Brazil	521
Philippines	501
Former Soviet Union	260
Pakistan	210
Guatemala	180
United States	155
Venezuela	110
India	91
Ecuador	67
Yemen	54
Peru	45
Nicaragua	44
Nigeria	35
Total (all countries)	9,516

Source: Control Risks Group, London. Definition utilized for "Kidnap for Ransom": Abduction of a person with the intent of their detention in an unknown location until a demand is met.

Tadjikistan, 24 December 1996: Twenty-one UN observers kidnapped by guerrilleros loyal to warlord Rizvon Sadirov. Eventually they were all released unharmed.

Chechnya, 3 October 1998: Four Westerners installing a telecommunication system were abducted from a house near Grozny by twenty gunmen. On 8 December, their heads were found in a bag on a road west

Table 3.20.   Fate of Foreign Kidnapping Victims, 1992–1996

Outcome	(N = ?)	(N = 262)
Released after some sort of negotiations/ransom paid	66%	61%
Release without concessions	n.d.	6%
Rescued	20%	21%
Escaped	5%	2%
Killed or died in captivity	9%	10%
Time held		
1–10 days	ca. 50%	
11–50 days	ca. 25%	
More than 50 days	ca. 25%	

Source: Ann Hagedorn Auerbach, *Ransom: The Untold Story of International Kidnapping* (New York: Henry Holt, 1998), 35; Alan Bell, *Kidnap and Ransom Survival,* 1994, at www.terrorism.net/Pubs/Alan2.htm. The statistics in the second column, based on 262 cases of kidnapping, are from A. Bell who, like Auerbach, offers no further details.

of Grozny; their bodies were discovered on 26 December in the village of Chernorechiye. According to the Russian Ministry of the Interior, 1,094 people were kidnapped in Chechnya, or in neighboring areas, between January 1997 (when the last Russian troops withdrew from Chechnya) and August 1999.[37]

Yemen, 28 December 1998: Twelve Britons, two Americans, and two Australian tourists were kidnapped on the main road to Aden. The group demanded the release of its leader, Saleh Haidara al-Atwi. Four of the victims were killed during a rescue attempt the next day.[38]

Colombia, 30 May 1999: About 150 people from a church in the wealthy part of Cali, Colombia, were abducted by members of the National Liberation Army. Eighty-four of them were soon released, the remaining were taken to a jungle hideout. One bodyguard was killed. The last hostage was released on 10 December 1999.[39]

Hostage Taking

Acts of hostage taking differ from kidnapping in that the site of sequestration of those abducted or held is known. In recent years we have seen instances where hundreds and even thousands were taken hostage. Four examples:

Kuwait, 1 August 1990: Saddam Hussein invades neighboring Kuwait and seizes 10,000 Western civilians living in Iraq and Kuwait as human shields against a Western liberation attempt of Kuwait. All hostages are eventually released by the end of the year.[40]

Russia, 14 June 1994: In Budennovsk, Chechen rebels take some 1,000 hostages as they retreat from a hospital. Some 150 are reportedly killed during an abortive rescue attempt by the Russian army. In return for the freedom of the remaining hostages, the Chechen hostage-takers are allowed to escape.[41]

Bosnia, 26 May 1995: More than 360 UN peacekeepers are held hostage by the Bosnian Serb army to serve as "human shields" after NATO airstrikes on their capital Pale. The UN hostages, handcuffed to key military targets, are released during the month of June.

Russia, 9 January 1996: Three thousand civilian hostages are seized in Kizlyar, Dagestan, by Chechen terrorists protesting against Russian military occupation. Russian rescue efforts with helicopters and artillery reportedly result in hundreds of deaths.[42]

The available statistics for recent hostage takings are very incomplete. Table 3.21 lists 175 out of 283 episodes between 1992 and 1 April 2000, for the ten most affected countries.

Table 3.21. Countries Most Affected by Acts of Hostage Taking (1992–1 April 2000)

United States	42
Mexico	30
United Kingdom	19
Brazil	15
Germany	15
Former Soviet Union	14
France	12
Colombia	9
Nigeria	9
Philippines	10
Total (all countries)	283

Source: TPB Database, UN Vienna.

Hijacking

Another coercive tactic, which came into prominence in the 1960s, has recently seen some revival: hijacking of aircraft—sometimes "only" for transport of would-be refugees to a desired destination, sometimes for blackmail and the extraction of concessions. Only in the latter case is a hijacking terroristic in nature.

Between 1992 and 2000, some 173 hijackings of means of transportation (mostly aircraft) have been recorded. Table 3.22 lists the ten countries most affected.

Some examples of recent hijackings are:[43]

Table 3.22. Countries Most Affected by Hijackings, 1992–1 April 2000

Former Soviet Union	21
China	16
Cuba	7
Venezuela	7
Germany	6
Ethiopia	5
Japan	5
Sudan	5
Turkey	5
Algeria	3
Total (all countries)	173

Source: Control Risks Group, London. Definition of "hijacking" utilized: "The majority of cases involve aeroplanes although hijacks of boats, cars, and trains are also included."

May 25, 1998: Three Pakistani students demanding to be flown to India hijacked a Pakistani commercial airliner. The three hijackers belonged to the so-called Baluchistan Students' Federation. The hijackers were captured by Pakistani troops after they had landed in a Pakistani airport, while thinking that they had arrived in India.

October 30, 1998: A Turkish airliner with thirty-four passengers and six crewmembers was hijacked after taking off from Adana, Turkey. The hijacker was a member of the Kurdistan Workers' Party (PKK). The hijacking ended the next day in Ankara when elite Turkish troops stormed the plane and killed the hijacker.

April 12, 1999: Members of the Colombian National Liberation Army (ELN) kidnapped forty-one passengers and five crew members in a hijack of a Colombian domestic airliner flying from Bucaramanga to Bogotá on April 12, 1999. The rebels forced the plane to land and brought the hostages to a remote jungle region. On the same day, six hostages were released near the jungle airstrip, where the plane was found. Nine hostages were released on May 28, 1999, and a U.S. citizen was freed on October 2, 1999.

July 30, 1999: A Venezuelan plane with ten people, two pilots and eight passengers on board was hijacked on July 30, 1999. The Revolutionary Armed Forces of Colombia (FARC), who allegedly had carried out the kidnapping, released the plane and the pilots on August 8, 1999, and freed the passengers on August 10, 1999.

October 19, 1999: Just after it left Istanbul's Ataturk airport for Cairo, an Egypt Air Boeing 737-500 was hijacked on October 19, 1999, by an Egyptian, Khalaf Ahmed Omar, who wielded a cutlery knife. The plane was forced to land in Hamburg where German police ended the hijacking. The hijacker was given asylum in Germany but faced charges for hijacking.

December 24, 1999: An Indian Airlines Airbus with 186 people on board was hijacked on its flight from Katmandu, Nepal, to New Delhi, India, by five armed men on December 24, 1999. After stops in Amritsar, Lahore, and Dubai, where the hijackers released twenty-seven of the hostages and handed over the body of a passenger who had been killed, the plane finally landed in the Afghan city of Kandahar on December 25, 1999. On December 31, 1999, all hostages were freed in exchange for the release of three Kashmiri militants by the Indian government. The hijackers, of whom one was killed by his colleagues, reportedly left Afghanistan for Pakistan together with the released Kashmiri militants.

February 6, 2000: An internal flight of the Afghan company Ariana was hijacked by terrorists on the way from Kabul to Mazar-I-Sharif. After landings in Uzbekistan, Kazakhstan, and Russia, the journey ended in Stansted, London, on 7 February. The hijackers released all their hostages in groups by February 10. Many applied for political asylum.

Behind all these statistics, whether they involve hostages, kidnapping victims, or persons murdered, there are, sometimes, a great number of people. Here are, as a reminder, some of them:[44]

Algeria, 1992–1998: 4,000 women killed in attacks, including massacres of civilians. Another 500 women were kidnapped and 300 women were raped in attacks on villages. Total fatalities of the confrontation between Islamic terrorists and security forces since 1992 range between 60,000 and 100,000 people, some are even higher.

India, 1994: Thirteen near-simultaneous car and truck bombings in reprisal for the destruction of an Islamic shrine, kill 400 persons and injure more than 1,000 others, in Bombay.[45]

United States, 1995: A truck bomb destroys the federal Murrah Building in Oklahoma City, killing 168, and injuring hundreds more. Two militia members, Timothy McVeigh and Terry Nichols, were arrested.

Sri Lanka, 1996: Nearly 100 people are killed and 1,400 injured by a suicide truck-bomb, driven by an LTTE commando into Colombo's Central Bank.[46]

Kenya, 1998: Two hundred ninety-one were killed and approximately 5,000 injured when the U.S. embassy in Nairobi was attacked by a truck bomb from the Islamic Army for the Liberation of the Holy Places.[47] A simultaneous attack took place in Dar es Salaam, Tanzania, causing ten fatalities and injuring seventy-four people.

Russia, 1999: An apartment block in Moscow's Ulitsa Guryanova collapsed after an explosion attributed to Chechens, killed ninety-four people. On September 13, a similar bombing at Kashirskoye Shosse killed 118 people. Similar explosions with fewer fatalities occurred prior to and after those incidents in Buinaksk (sixty-four killed) and Volgodonsk (seventeen dead).

Japan, 1995: The sarin attack killed twelve people and injured hundreds of others.[48]

New York, 2001: Two kamikaze attacks using hijacked American passenger airliners crashing into the Twin Towers of the World Trade Center in New York cause some 3,000 fatalities. The victims came from more than eighty countries.

This partial list of high-casualty incidents supports the thesis that there is an increasing lethality of terrorism. Will we see in the near future terrorist victimization by means of weapons of mass destruction? There is no easy yes/no answer as both capabilities and intentions have to be assessed for dozens of major terrorist and organized crime groups.[49] The risks differ for nuclear, biological, and chemical weapons. CIA director George Tenet told a Senate Foreign Relations Committee hearing that "The CIA has no evidence that any fissile materials have been acquired by a terrorist organization nor any indication that a country has tried to arm terrorist organizations with the capability to use nuclear materials in an attack."

While this sounds reassuring, he also admitted that there was a "high risk" that some such transfers could escape detection. "Biological and chemical weapons," Tenet said, "pose arguably the most daunting challenge for intelligence collectors and analysts."[50]

WHAT ARE THE RIGHTS OF VICTIMS?

The General Assembly Resolution 42/34 (1985) contains seven rights relevant for victims of terrorism.[51]

1. The right to be treated with respect and recognition;
2. The right to be referred to adequate support services;
3. The right to receive information about the progress of the case;
4. The right to be present and to be involved in the decision-making process;
5. The right to counsel;
6. The right to protection of physical safety and privacy;
7. The right of compensation, from both the offender and the state.

These rights presumably reflect general needs of victims; they are not specific to terrorism. The requirements of a terrorist victim service program should incorporate also the following elements:[52]

1. Crisis intervention;
2. Counselling;
3. Advocacy;
4. Support during investigation of a crime;
5. Support during criminal prosecution and trial;
6. Support after case disposition;
7. Training for allied professionals on victim issues;
8. Violence prevention and other prevention services;
9. Public education (including awareness raising campaigns) on victim issues.

Such a program costs money. Already in 1996 several UN member states called for the establishment of a UN Voluntary Fund for Victims of Terrorism (e.g., Angola, Azerbaijan, India). The government of the Netherlands has proposed the establishment of an international fund for the support of victims of transnational crime. It is, however, not specific to victims of terrorism.

With regard to terrorist crimes, a few countries, like France and the United States, have exemplary programs. The French program has been the initiative of a former victim, a survivor of a terrorist attack in Paris in 1986. It is called "S.O.S. Attentats."[53]

Activities of S.O.S. Attentats include:

- Provides information and guidance to victims in their dealings with the authorities and the courts;
- Provides a psychological and social support structure;
- Gives victims an opportunity to meet other people in the same situation and to draw strength from each other;
- Provides financial assistance to those in desperate need;
- Assists victims with medical assessments;
- Provides support to victims throughout the judicial process, from the initial investigative hearings to the trial;
- Helps with legal costs.

S.O.S. Attentats has its offices at the Hôtel National des Invalides and is open to all victims and their families. S.O.S. Attentats has the right to file claims for damages in criminal proceedings on behalf of victims of terrorism. In France, claims for damages incurred from terrorist acts can be filled within a ten-year period. Full compensation is payable in respect to personal injury or death caused by an act of terrorism on French soil, and, for French citizens, also outside France. The program is funded by tax revenues and there is no maximum award limit.[54]

One of the goals of S.O.S. Attentats is to bring to justice all those who order, perpetrate, or aid and abet in the commission of terrorist acts. In 2000, it was involved in twenty-five cases against various sponsors of terrorism.

Terrorist victim-support programs also exist in Colombia, Italy, Israel, the United Kingdom, and the United States.

CONCLUDING REMARKS

The fear of a sudden violent death is what gives terrorism its force. "Will I be next?" is the question in everyone's mind if a community is hit by a campaign of terrorist violence. Terrorists hit a few to frighten the many. Their murder is de-individualized; anybody could be a victim. The anonymity of terrorist killings is an expression of their disrespect for human lives. The most powerful response to this is respect for life, to care for victims so that the moral gap between terrorists and members of the community becomes apparent to all. A community expresses its quality by the solidarity it shows toward the victims in its midst. A cohesive, inclusive community is less likely to face terrorism from inside than one where subgroups live apart from each other, divided by class, color, religion, language, or origin. In this sense, the solidarity with victims not only serves the victims but also enhances the quality of the community as a whole.

NOTES

The opinions expressed in this chapter are entirely those of the author, and have no official status or backing from the United Nations, where the author serves as officer-in-charge of the Terrorism Prevention Branch.

1. Harold J. Vetter and Gary R. Perlstein, *Perspectives on Terrorism* (Pacific Grove, Calif.: Brooks/Cole Publishing, 1991), 77.

2. The modern (Western) state has taken over from the victim and his/her kin the restoration of justice: the victim becomes a third party and often feels left out. Typical is a statement of a victim to the U.S. President's Task Force on Victims of Crime: "Why didn't anyone consult me? . . . I was the one who was kidnapped, not the State of Maryland" (Cit. Margaret DiCanio, *Encyclopaedia of Violence. Origins, Attitudes, Consequences* [New York: Facts On File, 1993], 272). The media also tend to be more fascinated with the criminal than with the (often dead) victim. In cases of terrorism, the direct victim might be randomly chosen and not have the same news value as the ultimate target of the terrorist's violent communication. For a discussion, see A. P. Schmid, *Violence as Communication* (London: Sage, 1982).

3. General Assembly Resolution 42/34, Annex. For full text, see the appendix at the end of this chapter; also available on the Internet under www.victimology.nl.

4. The government of the Syrian Arab Republic, for instance, pleaded for making "a clear distinction . . . between terrorism and acts of national resistance against occupation which we support as the right of every people whose territory has been occupied and whose rights have been usurped, particularly when such actions take place in the actual locality of its struggle" (Syrian president Hafis el-Assad, as quoted by General Ahmed Sobhi Kikhia, head of the delegation of the Syrian Arab Republic to the Tenth United Nations Congress on the Prevention of Crime and the Treatment of Offenders, 10–17 April 2000, at Vienna, Austria.) Document distributed by Vienna, Embassy of the Syrian Arab Republic, 29 March 2000.

5. George Habash, leader of the Popular Front for the Liberation of Palestine: "There are no innocent victims. All share responsibility for society's wrongs. No one is innocent" (R. Reuben Miller, Victims of Terrorism, in *Encyclopaedia of World Terrorism*, vol. 1, edited by M. Crenshaw and J. Pimlott, 250 [Armonk, N.Y.: M. E. Sharpe, 1997]).

6. A. P. Schmid et al., *Zuidmoluks terrorisme, de media en de publieke opinie* (Amsterdam: Intermediair, 1982).

7. A. P. Schmid et al., *Political Terrorism: A New Guide to Actors, Authors, Concepts, Data Bases, Theories, and Literature*, revised, expanded, and updated edition prepared under the auspices of the Center for International Affairs, Harvard University (Amsterdam: North-Holland Publishing, 1988), 28; for legal purposes, a more concise definition has been proposed by Schmid: Act of terrorism = peacetime

equivalent of war crime. See A. P. Schmid, The Response Problem as a Definition Problem, in *Western Responses to Terrorism*, edited by A. P. Schmid and R. D. Crelinsten, 12 (London: Frank Cass, 1999).

8. For a more detailed discussion, see David L. Paletz and Alex P. Schmid, eds., *Terrorism and the Media: How Researchers, Terrorists, Government, Press, Public and Victims View and Use the Media* (Newbury Park, Calif.: Sage, 1992).

9. For a more detailed discussion, see Alex P. Schmid, Goals and Objectives of International Terrorism, in *Current Perspectives on International Terrorism*, edited by Robert O. Slater and Michael S. Stohl, 46–87 (London: Macmillan, 1988).

10. The 1985 Declaration defines "victims" as "persons who, individually or collectively, have suffered harm, including physical or mental injury, emotional suffering, economic loss or substantial impairment of their fundamental rights, through acts or omissions that are in violation of criminal laws operative within Member States, including those laws proscribing criminal abuse of power. . . . The term "victim" also includes, where appropriate, the immediate family or dependents of the direct victim and persons who have suffered harm in intervening to assist victims in distress or to prevent victimization." Victims of abuse of power, in turn, were defined as "persons who, individually or collectively, have suffered harm including physical or mental injury, emotional suffering, economic loss or substantial impairment of their fundamental rights, through acts or omissions that do not yet constitute violations of national criminal laws but of internationally recognized norms relating to human rights" (UN General Assembly Declaration of Basic Principles of Justice for Victims of Crime and Abuse of Power, 29 November 1985).

11. Victor T. Le Vine, On the Victims of Terrorism and Their Innocence, *Terrorism and Political Violence* 9, no. 3 (Autumn 1997): 57.

12. R. Reuben Miller, Victims of Terrorism. In *Encyclopaedia of World Terrorism*, vol. 1, edited by M. Crenshaw and J. Pimlott, 250 (Armonk, N.Y.: M. E. Sharpe, 1997).

13. Cf. Robert Greene and Joost Elffers, *The 48 Laws of Power* (London: Profile Books, 1998), 39: "Nothing is more terrifying than the sudden and unpredictable."

14. David A. Soskis and Frank Ochberg, Concepts of Terrorist Victimization, in *Victims of Terrorism*, edited by F. Ochberg and D. A. Soskis, 106 (Boulder, Colo.: Westview, 1982).

15. Research on torture identified four main purposes: (1) to extract admission of involvement with an opposition group; (2) to learn about the whereabouts of family and friends also involved; (3) to punish and prevent future antigovernment activities, and, most of all; (4) to cause fear through threats of further arrests, ill treatment, or even death (M. Salinsky and C. Miller, *Staying Alive by Accident* [London: Medical Foundation for the Care of Victims of Torture, 1999], 46).

16. Terror has been defined as an "extreme form of anxiety . . . followed by frightening imagery and intrusive, repetitive recollection" (F. M. Ochberg, in response to a questionnaire mailed out by A. P. Schmid). For a more extensive discussion, see A. P. Schmid, *Political Terrorism: A Research Guide to Concepts, Theories, Data Bases and Literature* (Amsterdam: North-Holland Publishing, 1984), 67–72.

17. Martin Symonds, The "Second Injury" to Victims, and "Acute Responses of Victims to Terror," *Evaluation and Change* (special issue, 1980): 36–41; cit. E. E. Flynn, Victims of Terrorism, 343–44.

18. The incident occurred from August 23–28, 1973, in the Sveriges Kreditbank in Stockholm in the course of an unsuccessful bank robbery. Two hostage-takers held four hostages for 131 hours, demanding money and a safe conduct out of the country with the hostages. Twenty-three-year-old hostage Kristin Ehnmark fell in love with thirty-two-year-old bank robber Jan-Erik Olsson. In one telephone call to the Swedish prime minister, one hostage claimed: "The robbers are protecting us from the police." From Sheila Ager, Thera and the Pirates: An Ancient Case of the Stockholm Syndrome, *The Ancient History Bulletin* 12, no. 3 (1998): 86–87.

19. Harold J. Vetter and Gary R. Perlstein, *Perspectives on Terrorism*, 68.

20. R. M. Fields, Research on the Victims of Terrorism, in A. Soskis and F. M. Ochberg, *Victims of Terrorism*, 142.

21. Brian M. Jenkins et al., *Numbered Lives: Some Statistical Observations from 77 International Hostage Incidents* (St. Barbara: RAND, 1977), 27; cit. A. P. Schmid, Force or Conciliation? An Overview of Some Problems Associated with Current Anti-Terrorist Response Strategies, *Violence, Aggression and Terrorism* 2, no. 2 (1998): 157.

22. ICD-10 Classification of Mental and Behavioural Disorders. Geneva: World Health Organization, 1992. <http://www.mentalhealth.com/icd/p22-an06.html>.

23. On March 11, 1998, a U.S. federal judge ordered Iran to pay $247.5 million in damages to the family of a New Jersey student, Alisa Flatow, who was killed in an attack on a bus in Gaza City on April 9, 1995. District Judge Royce Lamberth argued that "The court is seeking to deter further terrorist actions." Islamic Jihad at the time claimed responsibility for the attack but later denied that the movement is funded by Iran (Iran ordered to pay $ 247.5 million to bombing victim's family, *Nando Times*, 11 March 1995, 5:34 p.m. EST, at http://nando.net).

24. Leonard R. Sussman, Press Freedom 1997, Freedom House, at www.fredom/house.org/press97.page1.html, 4; cit. Albert J. Jongman and Alex P. Schmid, Trends in Contemporary Conflicts and Human Rights Violations, 1998, *Terrorism and Political Violence* 11, no. 3 (Autumn 1999): 123.

25. Christopher Marquis and Jonathan S. Landay, World: Today's Terrorist under Attack, *Mercury* (Hobart), 29 December 1999 (electronic version); based on U.S. State Department figures.

26. Bruce Hoffman, *Inside Terrorism* (London: Victor Gollancz, 1998), 204.

27. Nicholas Morozov, a theorist of Narodnaya Volya (The People's Will) held: "All that the terroristic struggle really needs is a small number of people and large material means. This presents really a new form of struggle. It replaces by a series of individual political assassinations, which always hit their target, the massive revolutionary movements, where people often rise up against each other because of misunderstandings and where a nation kills off its own children, while the enemy of the people watches from a secure shelter and sees to it that the people of the organization are destroyed. The movement punishes only those who are really responsible for the evil deed. Because of this the terroristic revolution is the only just form of revolution" (Nicolas Morozov, *Terroristic Struggle* [London, 1880]; reproduced fully in Feliks Gross, *Violence in Politics. Terror and Political Assassination in Eastern Europe and Russia* [The Hague: Mouton, 1972], 106.)

28. J. O. Engene, *Patterns of Terrorism*, 172–73.

29. There are, however, several caveats to be observed with Engene's finding. First, his use of a single source—Keesings Historical Archive—carries the danger that he might have missed a number of incidents. There is indeed evidence of that when one compares his data with others. However, this is not true for the high-casualty incidents which are generally reported in most sources. The second caveat involves the definition of terrorism. If one includes all sorts of political protest acts, including many cases of "violence against objects," in the database, then the more bloody incidents become far and few in a mass of militant action manifestations. Engene defines a terrorist act as "an act that has inflicted personal injury, or attacks against material targets (property) if the act is of a nature that could have led to personal injury or in another way would have a noticeable impact on an audience, while at the same time the act was committed to direct demands of or raise attention from, others than those immediately inflicted with personal or material injury. . . . The following events are counted as violent actions of a terrorist nature: Bombings, explosions, arson, fires, rocket attacks, killings, attempted killings, abductions, kidnaps, shootings, sieges, violent actions, violent attacks, attacks and similar violent actions. The event must be brought about by an actor that has deliberately initiated the action in question. . . . Events in which state authorities (police, secret services, military institutions, etc.) are involved in actions directed against terrorists and terrorist groups, are to be included. Also violent acts of state institutions directed against civilians are to be included, for instance in conjunction with demonstrations, strikes, and the like, when the state institution acts in a way that may put the public or sections of it in a state of fear." J. O. Engene, *Patterns of Terrorism*, 298.

30. Eli, a South Moluccan terrorist in 1975; cit. Frank M. Ochberg, A Case Study: Gerard Vaders, in *Victims of Terrorism*, edited by F. M. Ochberg and D. A. Soskis, 15 (Boulder, Colo.: Westview, 1982).

31. Ann Hagedorn Auerbach, *Ransom: The Untold Story of International Kidnapping* (New York: Henry Holt, 1998), 435–36.

32. BBC World Service, 3 April 2000, 05.06 GMT.

33. Ann Hagedorn Auerbach, *Ransom: The Untold Story*, 435–36.

34. Thomas R. Hargrove, Kidnapped by Colombian Narco-Guerrillas: A Hostage's Experience, and the Kidnap Industry. 32 March 1998, at www.g21.net/narco.html.

35. Control Risks Group, London. Definition utilized for "Kidnap for Ransom": Abduction of a person with the intent of their detention in an unknown location until a demand is met.

36. Kevin Whitelaw. Your Money or Your Life: Strange New Rules in the Global Game of Kidnapping, *U.S. News and World Report* (3 March 1999, electronic version).

37. Whitelaw, Your Money or Your Life; *Moscow Times* (12 October 1999, electronic version).

38. CDISS Database: Terrorist Incidents 1945 to 1998, at www.cdiss.org/ terror_1990s.htm.

39. TPB Database, UN Vienna.

40. TPB Database, UN Vienna.

41. TPB Database, UN Vienna.

42. TPB Database, UN Vienna.

43. CDISS Database: Terrorist Incidents 1945 to 1998, at www.cdiss.org/ terror/htm.

44. CDISS Database: Terrorist Incidents 1945 to 1998, at www.cdiss.org/terror.htm (*Arabic News*, 3 March 1998).
45. Bruce Hoffman, *Inside Terrorism*, 93.
46. Bruce Hoffman, *Inside Terrorism*, 11.
47. U.S. Department of State, *Patterns of Global Terrorism, 1998*, 6.
48. From www.rickross.com/
49. For a discussion, see A. P. Schmid, Terrorism and the Use of Weapons of Mass Destruction: From Where the Risk? *Terrorism and Political Violence* (Spring 2000). A research group on nonproliferation in Monterey identified six characteristics among the groups involved in chemical/biological weapons (CBW) incidents: (1) Charismatic leadership; (2) No external constituency; (3) Apocalyptic vision; (4) Loner or splinter group; (5) Sense of paranoia/grandiosity; and (6) Preemptive aggression. Cit. Steve Bowman and Helit Barel, Weapons of Mass Destruction: The Terrorist Threat, *CRS Report for Congress,* 8 December 1999 (Washington, D.C.: Congressional Research Service, Library of Congress, 1999), 3.
50. Reuters, Washington, 1999, n.d. CIA Director Says Detecting Bio Weapons "Daunting."
51. Cit. United Nations. Tenth United Nations Congress on the Prevention of Crime and the Treatment of Offenders, 10–17 April 2000, at Vienna, Austria (Vienna, UN, 15 Dec. 1999, 3). *(A/CONF.187/8. General Assembly Resolution 42/34, Annex).* For full text, see on the Internet www.victimology.nl.
52. UN Commission on Crime Prevention and Criminal Justice. *Manual on the Implementation of the United Nations Declaration of Basic Principles of Justice for Victims of Crime and Abuse of Power.* Vienna, UN, 25 April 1997 (E/CN.15/1997/CRP.9), 23.
53. Françoise Rudetzki, How to Support the Victims of Terrorism and Crime: Activities and Results of an Association Created by the Victims for the Victims. *Europa 2000* (quarterly newsletter, January 2000): 25.
54. Compensable costs include: Medical and mental health expenses; loss of wages; loss of support; funeral expenses; pain and suffering; disfigurement; any clothing, spectacles, and dental damages; physical therapy; vocational rehabilitation; rehabilitation for disabled victims; services to replace work in home previously performed by the victim. The victims (French citizens in France and abroad; foreigners victimized in France) receive an advance in a minimum of two days and a maximum of one month. (S.O.S. Attentats, Françoise Rudetzki, president, Hôtel National des Invalides, 6 blvd. des Invalides, Paris, France; at www.ojpusdoj.gov/ovc/intdir/france.htm.)

BIBLIOGRAPHY

Ager, Sheila. 1998. Thera and the Pirates: An Ancient Case of the Stockholm Syndrome. *The Ancient History Bulletin* 12, no. 3.
Agger, Inger, and Jensen Soren Buus. 1996. *Trauma and Healing under State Terrorism*. New York: St. Martin's Press.
Antokol, Norman. 1996. *No One Neutral: Political Hostage Taking in the Modern World*. Medina, Ohio: Alpha.

Aston, Clive C. 1982. *Contemporary Crisis: Political Hostage-Taking and the Experience of Western Europe.* Westport, Conn.: Greenwood Press.

Auerbach, Ann H. 1998. *Ransom: The Untold Story of International Kidnapping.* New York: Henry Holt.

Balmer, Desmond.1986. US Tourists React to Terrorism Fear. *New York Daily News,* 2 March.

Bassiouni, Cherif M. 1988. *International Protection of Victims.* Toulouse: Eres.

Belz, M., E. Z. Parker, L. I. Sank, J. Shapiro, and L. Shriber. 1977. Is There a Treatment for Terror? *Psychology Today* (October): 54–56, 108–12.

Buhite, Russell D. n.d. *Lives at Risk: Hostages and Victims in American Foreign Policy.* Published by Scholarly Resources (fax:1-302-654-3871; cf. also www.security-management.com/library/000213.html.)

Chalk, Peter. 1996. *West European Terrorism and Counter-Terrorism: The Evolving Dynamic.* New York: St. Martin's Press.

Cooper, H. H. 1976. The Terrorist and the Victim. *Victimology* 1, no. 2: 229–39.

———. 1978. Close Encounters of an Unpleasant Kind: Preliminary Thoughts on the Stockholm Syndrome. *Legal Medical Quarterly* 2, no. 2: 100–14.

Crelinsten, Ronald D., ed. 1977. *Dimensions of Victimization in the Context of Terroristic Acts.* Montreal: International Centre for Comparative Criminology.

———. 1979. *Hostage-Taking.* Lexington, Mass.: Lexington Press.

———. 1992. Victims' Perspectives. In *Terrorism and the Media,* edited by David L. Paletz and Alex P. Schmid, 208–38. Newbury Park, Calif.: Sage.

Danieli, Yael, Nigel S. Rodley, and Lars Weisaeth, eds. 1996. *International Responses to Traumatic Stress.* New York: Baywood.

DiCanio, Margaret. 1993. *Encyclopaedia of Violence. Origins, Attitudes, Consequences.* New York: Facts On File.

Doerner, William G., and Steve Lab. 1995. *Victimology.* Cincinnati, Ohio: Anderson.

Eichelman, Burr et al., eds. 1983. *Terrorism: Interdisciplinary Perspectives.* Washington, D.C.: American Psychiatric Press.

Elias, Robert. 1995. *Victims Still: The Political Manipulation of Crime Victims.* Newbury Park, Calif.: Sage.

Engene, Jan O. 1998. Patterns of Terrorism in Western Europe, 1950–1995. Bergen: Department of Comparative Politics, 1998. Unpublished manuscript.

Fattah, Ezzat A. 1992. *Towards a Critical Victimology.* London: Macmillan.

Feiler, Stuart I. 1986. Terrorism: Is Tourism Really the Target? *Hotel and Restaurant International* (October).

Fields, Rona M. 1980. Victims of Terrorism: The Effects of Prolonged Stress. *Evaluation and Change* (special issue): 76–83.

Figley, Charles R. 1995. *Trauma and Its Wake.* New York: Brunner/Mazel.

Flynn, E. E. 1987. Victims of Terrorism: Dimensions of the Victim Experience. In *Contemporary Research on Terrorism,* edited by Paul Wilkinson and Alasdair M. Stewart, 350–51. Aberdeen: Aberdeen University Press.

Frederick, C. J. 1987. Psychic Trauma in Victims of Crime and Terrorism. In *Cataclysm, Crises, and Catastrophes: Psychology in Action,* edited by G. R. van den Bos and B. K. Bryant. Washington, D.C.: American Psychological Association.

Guelke, Adrian. 1998. *The Age of Terrorism and the International Political System.* London: I. B. Tauris.

Greene, Robert, and Joost Elffers. 1999. *The 48 Laws of Power.* London: Profile Books.

Harkis, B.A. 1986. The Psychopathology of the Hostage Experience: A Review. *Medicine, Science and the Law* 26, no. 1: 48–52.

Hearst, Patricia. 1988. *Patty Hearst: Her Own Story.* New York: Avon Books.

Hentig, Hans von. 1948. *The Criminal and His Victims.* New Haven, Conn.: Yale University Press.

Herman, J. L. 1992. *Trauma and Recovery.* New York: Basic Books.

Hewitt, Christopher. 1993. *Consequences of Political Violence.* Brookfield: Dartmouth Publishing.

Hoffman, Bruce. 1998. *Inside Terrorism.* London: Victor Gollancz, 1998.

Hoffman, Bruce, and David Claridge. 1998. The RAND-St. Andrew Chronology of International Terrorism and Noteworthy Domestic Incidents, 1996. *Terrorism and Political Violence* 10, no. 2 (Summer).

Hoffman, Bruce, and Donna Kim Hoffman. 1997. *The RAND-St. Andrews Chronology of International Terrorism, 1994.* Santa Monica: RAND.

Iglarsh, Harvey J. 1987. Fear of Flying: Its Economic Costs. *Terrorism* 10, no. 1 (Winter).

Jackson, Geoffrey. 1973. *Surviving the Long Night.* New York: Vanguard.

Jacobsen, David, with Gerald Astor. 1991. *Hostage. My Nightmare in Beirut.* New York: Donald I. Fine.

Jenkins, Brian M. et al. 1977. *Numbered Lives: Some Statistical Observations from 77 International Hostage Incidents.* Santa Monica: RAND (P-3627).

Jongman, A. J. 1993. Trends in International and Domestic Terrorism in Western Europe, 1968–1988. In *Western Responses to Terrorism,* edited by A. P. Schmid and R. D. Crelinsten, 26–76. London: Frank Cass.

Joutsen, Matti. 1987. *The Role of the Victim of Crime in European Criminal Justice Systems.* Helsinki: HEUNI.

Kinchin, David. N.d. *Post Traumatic Stress Disorder: The Invisible Injury.* n.p. (ISBN 0-9529121-1-2).

Kolk, van der, Bessel A. 1989. The Compulsion to Repeat the Trauma: Re-enactment, Revictimization, and Masochism. *Psychiatric Clinics of North America* 12, no. 2 (June): 389–411.

Kuleshnyk, Irka. 1984. The Stockholm Syndrome: Toward an Understanding. *Social Action and the Law* 10, no. 2: 37–42.

Lawson, Don. 1991. *America Held Hostage: The Iran Hostage Crisis and the Iran-Contra Affair.* New York: Franklin Watts.

Le Vine, Victor T. 1997. On the Victims of Terrorism and Their Innocence. *Terrorism and Political Violence* 9, no. 3 (Autumn): 55–62.

Lule, J. 1987. *The Myth of My Widow: A Dramatistic Analysis of New Portrayals of a Terrorist Victim.* Boston: Emerson College, Terrorism and the News Media Research Project.

MacWillson, Alastair C. 1992. *Hostage-Taking Terrorism: Incident-Response Strategy.*

Magee, D. 1983. *What Murder Leaves Behind.* New York: Dodd, Mead.

Mangelsdorff, A. D. 1985. Lessons Learned and Forgotten: The Need for Prevention and Mental Health Interventions in Disaster Preparedness. *Journal of Community Psychology* 13: 239–57.

Miller, Reuben R. 1997. Victims of Terrorism. In *Encyclopaedia of World Terrorism*, vol. 1, edited by M. Crenshaw and J. Pimlott. Armonk, N.Y.: M. E. Sharpe.

Monaham, C. 1993. *Children and Trauma*. New York: Lexington Books.

Montgomery, L. F. 1988. *Media Victims: Reactions to Coverage of Incidents of International Terrorism Involving Americans*. Boston: Emerson College, Terrorism and the News Media Project.

Morozov, Nicolas. 1880/1972. *Terroristic Struggle*. London; reprinted in full in Feliks Gross. *Violence in Politics: Terror and Political Assassination in Eastern Europe and Russia*. The Hague: Mouton.

National Organization for Victim Assistance. 1997. *The Community Crisis Response Training Manual*. Washington, D.C.

New Zealand Police. 1991. *Victim Support Training Manual*.

Ochberg, Frank M. 1978. The Victim of Terrorism: Psychiatric Considerations. *Terrorism* 1, no. 2: 147–68.

———, ed. 1988. *Post-Trauma Therapy and Victims of Violence*. New York: Brunner/Mazel.

Ochberg, Frank M., and David A. Soskis. 1982. *Victims of Terrorism*. Boulder, Colo.: Westview Press.

Paletz, David L., and Alex P. Schmid, eds. 1992. *Terrorism and the Media. How Researchers, Terrorists, Government, Press, Public and Victims View and Use the Media*. Newbury Park, Calif.: Sage.

Paton, D. 1992. International Disasters: Issues in the Management and Preparation of Relief Workers. *Disaster Management* 4, no. 4: 183–90.

Paton, D., and N. Long, eds. 1996. *Psychological Aspects of Disasters*. Palmerston North: Dunmore.

Picard, R. G. 1988. Journalists as Targets and Victims of Terrorism. Boston. Conference paper at Emerson College.

Picard, R. G., and P. D. Adams. 1988. *Characterizations of Acts and Perpetrators of Political Violence in Three Elite U.S. Daily Newspapers*. Boston: Emerson College, Terrorism and the News Media Research Project.

Pollack, Andrew. 1995. Earlier Victims' Horrors Revived. *New York Times*, 22 March.

Pollitzer, Patricia. 1989. *Fear in Chile: Lives under Pinochet*. New York: Pantheon.

Raphael, B. 1986. *When Disaster Strikes: How Individuals and Communities Cope with Catastrophe*. New York: Basic Books.

———. 1986. *When Disaster Strikes: A Handbook for the Caring Professions*. London: Hutchinson.

Ranstorp, Magnus. 1997. *Hizb'allah in Lebanon: The Politics of the Western Hostage Crisis*. London: Macmillan.

Roberts, Albert R. 1990. *Helping Crime Victims*. Oxford: Clarendon Press.

Rose, S., and J. Bisson. 1998. Brief Early Psychological Interventions Following Trauma: A Systematic Review of the Literature. *Journal of Traumatic Stress* 11, no. 4: 697–710.

Rudetzki, Françoise. 2000. How to Support the Victims of Terrorism and Crime: Activities and Results of an Association Created by the Victims for the Victims. *Europe 2000* 23 (quarterly newsletter, January): 25–28.

Sales, Bruce, and Michael Gottfredson et al. 1990. Social Science in Victim Policy. *Violence and Victims* 5, no. 2: 79–140.

Salinsky, Mary, and Christiane Miller. 1999. *Staying Alive by Accident*. London: Medical Foundation for the Care of Victims of Torture.

Saylor, C. F., ed. 1993. *Children and Disasters*. New York: Plenum Press.

Schmid, Alex P. 1988. Force or Conciliation? An Overview of Some Problems Associated with Current Anti-Terrorist Response Strategies. *Violence, Aggression, Terrorism* 2, no. 2: 149–78.

———. 1988. Goals and Objectives of International Terrorism. In *Current Perspectives on International Terrorism*, edited by Robert O. Slater and Michael S. Stohl, 47–87. London, Macmillan.

———. 1999. Terrorism and the Use of Weapons of Mass Destruction: From Where the Risk? *Terrorism and Political Violence* 11, no. 4 (Winter): 106–32.

Schmid, Alex P., and R. D. Crelinsten, eds. 1999. *Western Responses to Terrorism*. London: Frank Cass.

Schmid, Alex P., and Janny de Graaf. 1982. *Violence as Communication: Insurgent Terrorism and the Western News Media*. London: Sage.

Schmid, Alex P. et al. 1982. *Zuidmoluks terrorisme, de media en de publieke opinie*. Amsterdam: Intermediair.

Schmid, Alex P. et al. 1988. *Political Terrorism. A New Guide to Actors, Authors, Concepts, Data Bases, Theories, and Literature*. Revised, expanded, and updated edition prepared under the auspices of the Center for International Affairs, Harvard University. Amsterdam: North-Holland.

Sharif, Idris. 1995. *Success of Political Terrorist Events: An Analysis of Terrorist Tactics and Victim Characteristics, 1968 to 1997*. Lanham: University Press of America, January.

Skurnik, N. 1988. Le syndrome de Stockholm (essai d'etude des criteres). *Annales medico-psychologiques* 146, no. 1–2: 174–79.

Soskis, D., and F. Ochberg. 1982. Concepts of Terrorist Victimization. In *Victims of Terrorism*, edited by F. Ochberg and D. Soskis, 105–35. Boulder, Colo.: Westview Press.

Spungen, D. 1997. *Homicide: The Hidden Victims*. Thousand Oaks, Calif.: Sage.

Staudacher, C. 1987. *Beyond Grief: A Guide to Recovering from the Death of a Loved One*. Oakland, Calif.: New Harbinger Publications.

Strentz, T. 1982. The Stockholm Syndrome: Law Enforcement Policy and Hostage Behaviour. In *Victims of Terrorism*, edited by F. Ochberg and D. Soskis, 149–63. Boulder, Colo.: Westview Press.

Sussman, Leonard R. Press Freedom 1997, Freedom House, at www.freedomhouse.org/press97.page1.html.

Symonds, M. 1980. Victim Responses to Terror. In *Forensic Psychology and Psychiatry*, edited by F. Wright et al., 129–50. New York: New York Academy of Sciences.

Taylor, A. J. W. 1987. A Taxonomy of Disasters and Their Victims. *Journal of Psychosomatic Research* 31, no. 4: 535–44.

Taylor, A. J. W. N.d. *Traumatology: Towards the Classification of Disasters and Victims*, at www.fsu.edu/~trauma/a4v5i2.html.

Taylor, A. J. W., and A. G. Frazier. 1989. *Disaster and Disaster Stress*. New York: AMS Press.

United Nations General Assembly. 1985. *Declaration of Basic Principles of Justice for Victims of Crime and Abuse of Power*. New York: United Nations, 29 November (Resolution 42/34).

U.S. Department of Justice, Office for Victims of Crime. 1996. *International Crime Victim Compensation Program Directory.* Washington, D.C.: U.S. Department of Justice.

———. 2000. Victims' Rights and Services for the 21st Century. Washington, D.C.: U.S. Department of Justice, February.

———. N.d. *Handbook for Victims of the East Africa Embassy Bombings.* Washington, D.C.: U.S. Department of Justice.

U.S. Department of State, Bureau of Diplomatic Security. 1999. *Significant Incidents of Political Violence against Americans.* (10th Anniversary Issue, 1997). Washington, D.C.: U.S. Department of State.

Vetter, Harold J., and Gary R. Perlstein. 1991. *Perspectives on Terrorism.* Pacific Grove, Calif.: Brooks/Cole.

Viano, E. 1989. *Crime and Its Victims.* New York: Hemisphere.

Warden, J. W. 1991. *Grief Counselling and Grief Therapy: A Handbook for the Mental Health Practitioner.* New York: Springer.

Watson, Bruce. 1993. *Sieges: A Comparative Study.* Westwood, Conn.: Greenwood Press.

Webb, N. B., ed. 1993. *Helping Bereaved Children: A Handbook for Practitioners.* New York: Guilford Press.

West, L. J., and P. P. Martin. 1996. Pseudo-Identity and the Treatment of Personality Change in Victims of Captivity and Cults. *Cultic Studies Journal* 13, no. 2: 125–52.

Whitelaw, Kevin. 1999. Your Money or Your Life: Strange New Rules in the Global Game of Kidnapping. *U.S. News and World Report,* 3 March (electronic version).

Williams, M. B., and J. F. Sommers, eds. 1994. *Handbook of Post-traumatic Therapy.* Westport, Conn: Greenwood Press.

Young, M., and J. Stein. 1990. *Coping with the Iraq/Kuwait Crisis: A Handbook.* Washington, D.C.: National Organization for Victim Assistance (NOVA).

Young, M. A. 1996. *Working with Grieving Children after Violent Death: A Guidebook for Crime Victim Assistance Professionals.* Washington, D.C.: NOVA.

Internet Sites

S.O.S. Attentats: www.ojpusdoj.gov/ovc/intdir/france,htm.

U.S. Department of State, Office of the Coordinator for Counterterrorism: www.state.gov/www/global/terrorism/annual_reports.html.

U.S. National Organization for Victim Assistance: www.try-nova.org/

U.S. Office for Victims of Crime: www.ojp.usdoj.gov/ovc/

Victim Assistance Online: A Comprehensive Resource Centre: www.vaonline.org

World Society of Victimology: www.victimology.nl/.

Appendix 3.1

UN Declaration of Basic Principles of Justice for Victims of Crime and Abuse of Power (1985)

The General Assembly,

Recalling that the Sixth United Nations Congress on the Prevention of Crime and the Treatment of Offenders recommended that the United Nations should continue its present work on the development of guidelines and standards regarding abuse of economic and political power,

Cognizant that millions of people throughout the world suffer harm as a result of crime and the abuse of power and that the rights of these victims have not been adequately recognized,

Recognizing that the victims of crime and the victims of abuse of power, and also frequently their families, witnesses and others who aid them, are unjustly subjected to loss, damage or injury and that they may, in addition, suffer hardship when assisting in the prosecution of offenders,

1. Affirms the necessity of adopting national and international measures in order to secure the universal and effective recognition, of and respect for, the rights of victims of crime and of abuse of power;

2. Stresses the need to promote progress by all States in their efforts to that end, without prejudice to the rights of suspects or offenders;

3. Adopts the Declaration of Basic Principles of Justice for Victims of Crime and Abuse of Power, annexed to the present resolution, which is designed to assist Governments and the international community in their efforts to secure justice and assistance for victims of crime and victims of abuse of power;

4. Calls upon Member States to take the necessary steps to give effect to the provisions contained in the Declaration:

a) To implement social, health, including mental health, educational, economic and specific crime prevention policies to reduce victimization and encourage assistance to victims in distress;

b) To promote community efforts and public participation in crime prevention;

c) To review periodically their existing legislation and practices in order to ensure responsiveness to changing circumstances, and to enact and enforce legislation proscribing acts that violate internationally recognized norms relating to human rights, corporate conduct, and other abuses of power;

d) To establish and strengthen the means of detecting, prosecuting and sentencing those guilty of crime;

e) To promote disclosure of relevant information to expose official and corporate conduct to public scrutiny, and other ways of increasing responsiveness to public concerns;

f) To promote the observance of codes of conduct and ethical norms, in particular international standards, by public servants, including law enforcement, correctional, medical, social service and military personnel, as well as the staff of economic enterprises;

g) To prohibit practices and procedures conducive to abuse, such as secret places of detention an incommunicado detention;

h) To co-operate with other states, through mutual judicial and administrative assistance, in such matters as the detection and pursuit of offenders, their extradition and the seizure of their assets, to be used for restitution to the victims;

5. Recommends that, at the international and regional levels, all appropriate measures should be taken:

a) To promote training activities designed to foster adherence to United Nations standards and norms and to curtail possible abuses;

b) To sponsor collaborative action-research on ways in which victimisation can be reduced and victims aided; and to promote information exchanges on the most effective means of so doing;

c) To render direct aid to requesting Governments designed to help them curtail victimization and alleviate the plight of victims;

6. Requests the Secretary-General to invite Member States to report periodically to the General Assembly on the implementation of the Declaration, as well as on measures taken by them to this effect;

7. Also requests the Secretary-General to make use of the opportunities which all relevant bodies and organizations within the United Nations system offer, to assist Member States, whenever necessary, in improving ways and means of protecting victims both at the national level and through international co-operation;

8. Further requests the Secretary-General to promote the objectives of the Declaration, in particular by ensuring its widest possible dissemenination;

9. Urges the specialized agencies and other entities and bodies of the United Nations system, other relevant intergovernmental and non-governmental or-

ganizations and the public to co-operate in the implementation of the provisions of the Declaration.

Part A. Victims of Crime

1. "Victims" means persons who, individually or collectively, have suffered harm, including physical or mental injury, emotional suffering, economic loss or substantial impairment of their fundamental rights, through acts or omissions that are in violation of criminal laws operative within Member States, including those laws proscribing criminal abuse of power.

2. A person may be considered a victim, under this Declaration, regardless of whether the perpetrator is identified, apprehended, prosecuted or convicted and regardless of the familial relationship between the perpetrator and the victim. The term "victim" also includes, where appropriate, the immediate family or dependents of the direct victim and persons who have suffered harm in intervening to assist victims in distress or to prevent victimization.

3. The provisions contained herein shall be applicable to all, without distinction of any kind, such as race, colour, sex, age, language, religion, nationality, political or other opinion, cultural beliefs or practices, property, birth or family status, ethnic or social origin, and disability.

4. Victims should be treated with compassion and respect for their dignity. They are entitled to access to the mechanisms of justice and to prompt redress, as provided for by national legislation, for the harm that they have suffered.

5. Judicial and administrative mechanisms should be established and strengthened where necessary to enable victims to obtain redress through formal or informal procedures that are expeditious, fair, inexpensive and accessible. Victims should be informed of their rights in seeking redress through such mechanisms.

6. The responsiveness of judicial and administrative processes to the needs of victims should be facilitated by:

a) Informing victims of their role and the scope, timing and progress of the proceedings and of the disposition of their cases, especially where serious crimes are involved and where they have requested such information;

b) Allowing the views and concerns of victims to be presented and considered at appropriate stages of the proceedings where their personal interests are affected, without prejudice to the accused and consistent with the relevant national criminal justice system;

c) Providing proper assistance to victims throughout the legal process;

d) Taking measures to minimize inconvenience to victims, protect their privacy, when necessary, and ensure their safety, as well as that of their families and witnesses on their behalf, from intimidation and retaliation.

e) Avoiding unnecessary delay in the disposition of cases and the execution of orders or decrees granting awards to victims.

7. Informal mechanisms for the resolution of disputes, including mediation, arbitration, and customary justice or indigenous practices, should be utilized where appropriate to facilitate conciliation and redress for victims.

8. Offenders or third parties responsible for their behaviour should, where appropriate, make fair restitution to victims, their families of dependants. Such restitution should include the return of property or payment for the harm or loss suffered, reimbursement of expenses incurred as a result of the victimisation, the provision of services and the restoration of rights.

9. Governments should review their practices, regulations and laws to consider restitution as an available sentencing option in criminal cases, in addition to other criminal sanctions.

10. In cases of substantial harm to the environment, restitution, if ordered, should include, as far as possible, restoration of the environment, reconstruction of the infrastructure, replacement of community facilities and reimbursement of the expenses of relocation, whenever such harm results in the dislocation of a community.

11. Where public officials or other agents acting in an official or quasi-official capacity have violated national criminal laws, the victim should receive restitution from the State whose officials or agents were responsible for the harm inflicted. In cases where the Government under whose authority the victimizing act or omission occurred is no longer in existence, the State or Government successor in title should provide restitution to the victims.

12. When compensation is not fully available from the offender or other sources, States should endeavour to provide financial compensation to:

a) Victims who have sustained significant bodily injury or impairment of physical or mental health as a result of serious crimes;

b) The family, in particular dependants of persons who have died or become physically or mentally incapacitated as a result of such victimization.

13. The establishment, strengthening and expansion of national funds for compensation to victims should be encouraged. Where appropriate, other funds may also be established for this purpose, including those cases where the State of which the victim is a national is not in a position to compensate the victim for the harm.

14. Victims should receive the necessary material, medical, psychological and social assistance through governmental, voluntary, community-based and indigenous means.

15. Victims should be informed of the availability of health and social services and other relevant assistance, and be readily afforded access to them.

16. Police, justice, health, social service and other personnel concerned should receive training to sensitize them to the needs of victims, and guidelines to ensure proper and prompt aid.

17. In providing services and assistance to victims, attention should be given to those who have special needs because of the nature of the harm inflicted or because of factors such as those mentioned in paragraph 3 above.

Part B. Victims of abuse of power

18. "Victims" means persons who, individually or collectively, have suffered harm including physical or mental injury, emotional suffering, economic loss or substantial impairment of their fundamental rights, through acts or omissions that do not yet constitute violations of national criminal laws but of internationally recognized norms relating to human rights.

19. States should consider incorporating into the national law norms proscribing abuses of power and providing remedies to victims of such abuses. In particular, such remedies should include restitution and/or compensation, and necessary material, medical, psychological and social assistance and support.

20. States should consider negotiating multilateral international treaties relating to victims as defined in paragraph 18.

21. States should periodically review existing legislation and practices to ensure their responsiveness to changing circumstances, should enact and enforce, if necessary, legislation proscribing acts that constitute serious abuses of political or economic power, as well as promoting policies and mechanisms for the prevention of such acts, and should develop and make readily available appropriate rights and remedies for victims of such acts.

NOTE

This document can be downloaded from the International Victimology Website at http:www.victimology.nl

4

Terrorist Victimization: Prevention, Control, and Recovery, Case Studies from India

Arvind Verma

INTRODUCTION

Terrorist victimization has taken various forms in modern India. Different groups, ranging from extreme left to conservative right, from those seeking secession to those wanting to spread jihad, have been operating on Indian territory. Victimization has ranged from murder, assault, and rape to being an innocent bystander, caught in the battle between the terrorist and security forces. Young, old, and women have been killed in their residences, shops, and offices, in trains, buses, and vehicles blown up by sophisticated explosives. Direct brutal force, violent means, or veiled threats have been used to terrorize the Indian people. Extortion, rape, and kidnapping of young girls for immoral purposes by the militants have also been a common form of victimization in the affected areas. These victims also include those killed, maimed, or harassed by the security agencies for their alleged links to terrorist groups.

Terrorist victimization is not random in nature. It is well known that terrorist violence is aimed at a wider target audience than the immediate victims themselves. Yet, the genesis of terrorism does not occur in a vacuum and is fueled by discontent from government policies, oppression by the state agents, and societal victimization of a segment of people among whom the terrorists find support. Therefore, the need is to understand victimization that occurs *before* and *after* terrorist activities rather than only the latter one. The two groups of victims are inexorably linked to one another. In this tragedy the role of the state, its policies, and its actions are equally blameworthy. Only a comprehensive understanding of the circumstances that promote terrorism in a society can help in developing suitable policies and procedures to aid the victims. In this chapter I will examine two cases of terrorism: left-wing extremism in the state of Bihar and Sikh terrorism in the state of Punjab that have involved victimization of thousands of people. My attempt is to suggest how terrorist victimization must be seen in its entirety: one before formal terrorism becomes active and one after terrorism establishes itself. I will also describe some of the attempts in India to heal these wounds of terrorism and to provide relief to the victims.

TERRORISM IN INDIA: A BRIEF OUTLINE

From the early 1950s, the country faced terror tactics from the Communist Party that was seeking the overthrow of the duly elected government. The "successes" in Soviet Russia, China, Vietnam, and Cuba appear to have encouraged the Indian communists to pursue the line of overthrowing the state through violent means. Their actions led to the victimization of well-off farmers, moneylenders, and, generally, the bourgeoisie, who were described as exploiters of the working people. Around 1967, a powerful movement emerged at Naxalbari and Srikakulam (B. Dasgupta 1974). A number of villages were declared to be liberated by the communist groups functioning in small independent party groups. The threat of these "naxalites," as left-wing groups have been called ever since, assumed a serious dimension after these insurrections. In this region, for almost two to three years, the armed groups, led by Charu Majumdar, Azizul Haq, and Kanu Sanyal, picked and killed the people they considered to be the enemies of the people because of their class status. In many cases, their houses and property were burnt in which many women and children also perished tragically. These leftist groups also began targeting people in the city of Calcutta in the beginning of the 1970s. Many criminal elements also took advantage of this situation in the state and indulged in antisocial activities. Extortion from business people, kidnapping, and rape of women as well as destruction of property were some of the acts perpetuated in the name of overthrowing the state. The state response was equally violent. The police made hundreds of arrests and killed suspects in so called false encounters. Police actions in terms of arbitrary arrests, illegal searches, and seizure of property victimized many innocent people who had nothing to do with violent leftist ideology (S. Dasgupta 1996).

After the failure in Bengal, these radical communist groups managed to organize and establish themselves strongly in the states of Bihar, Orissa, Madhya Pradesh, and Andhra Pradesh. Despite severe police action many leftist guerrilla groups have managed to establish a base for themselves. At present, the People's War Group (PWG), operating in northern Andhra Pradesh (Ramanujan 1997), and the Maoist Communist Center, Communist Party of India (Marxist Leninist) and Party Unity groups in central Bihar are firmly entrenched (Singh 1999). Their victims have been "feudal" elements, landlords, police personnel, and those who have broken away from their party. There are many factions among these left-wing parties based upon ideological and leadership differences as well as territorial supremacy. All these groups are not only in constant combat with the police and landlord supported resistance but have also been battling among themselves. Indeed, this battle for supremacy has assumed alarming trends with one group after another retaliating with brutality. For instance, CPI-ML first staged violent attacks on the landowners in the districts of Bhojpur and Gaya of Bihar state. Their success in terrorizing villagers and targeting the high-caste people, who owned the majority of land, led to the creation of self-defense armies such as Ranbir Sena (Bhelari 1997). These armed groups, consisting of higher caste people, began targeting the lower castes who were aligned with the left-wing groups. In the battle for supremacy, countless atrocities have been perpetuated by both the sides.

Another virulent terrorism emerged in the northeastern region of the country where the Nagas and Mizos formed guerrilla groups and attempted to wage a war of secession. Most of these are tribal areas inhabited by indigenous people with a history of interethnic rivalries. Even during the British period these regions were largely inaccessible and their people difficult to control. After the independence of the country many tribal people demanded a separate country for themselves. In small pockets, terrorist attacks on government establishments, police, and army posts were carried out. Their targets were also the people who did not support their cause, who were aligned with the state, and those who did work for the state. Terrorism in the northeast continued for a long period of time and lasted until the mid-1960s when Lal Denga, the Naga guerrilla leader, accepted peace and joined the political mainstream. This compromise with the government of India finally brought peace to Nagaland and other regions. Subsequently, Manipur and other northeast regions were given autonomy and created as provinces within the Indian union. This political arrangement has brought some peace to the region, though some northeast states continue to be plagued by terrorist attacks carried out by splinter groups (Peace Process 1999).

Since most of these splinter groups function as a regular guerrilla army, the Indian army rather than the police has been used to battle them. Again, in many parts, both sides victimize the local people, suspecting their loyalty to the opposing group. The army has been accused of many kinds of atrocities, including violation of human rights, practice of torture, and killing of suspects. In a celebrated case, *Sebastian Hongray vs. Union of India*, filed before the Supreme Court by public-spirited citizens, it was alleged that two suspects taken away for questioning went "missing." The army authorities maintained that they were released but the villagers denied seeing them again. Despite a habeas corpus petition entertained by the Court, these two could not be traced. The case finally resulted in the award of substantial compensation to the widows as well as the institution of murder cases against the army personnel involved in the case. Naga and Mizo insurgency has subsided considerably although small groups continue to target state officials and those people who refuse shelter or food to the guerrilla bands.

However, other groups like ULFA, operating in the northern part of Assam state, have stepped up their violent methods in fighting against the Indian state. They receive assistance from the neighboring countries of China, Myanmar, and Pakistan, which orchestrates support through their missions in Bangladesh and Nepal. Victimization has been confined not only to the killing of innocent bystanders in bomb blasts or crossfirings but citizens have also been deliberately targeted by these groups. For instance, ULFA kidnapped and killed a social worker Sanjay Ghosh (rediff.com 2001). The victims of these terrorist activities have also been many of the tea planters who have been kidnapped for ransom. In one case, a leading business house of the country negotiated and secured the release of one of its managers by paying a huge sum of money to the ULFA kidnappers. The company also provided medical treatment to some of the terrorist members and their families. This revelation resulted in the prosecution of some of the business managers by the state on ground of collusion with the terrorists (Goswami 1997).

Terrorist activities of a more sinister nature and aided by external agents like Pakistan, China, Myanmar, and Afghan guerrilla groups have created serious problems in the states of Punjab and Jammu and Kashmir (Joshi 1999). Terrorism in Punjab, from 1982 onward, has been a very serious threat and has involved considerable violence with loss of lives. Aided by Pakistan, the Sikh terrorists found it convenient to operate from across the international border and carry out attacks on the police as well as the civilian population. They planted bombs on buses and trains and exploded them in market areas to terrorize the population and cause a breakdown in normal life. Prominent people who dared to write against them, including journalists and newspaper editors, were murdered. Even the family members of police and army personnel were killed to break the morale of government forces and cause panic in the society. These Sikh militants received considerable support, funds, and material resources not only from Pakistan but also from Sikh communities in England, Canada, and the United States. For almost ten years, terrorism continued in Punjab and could only be crushed by a heavy-handed police and army action (Joshi 1993). At present, Punjab is largely at peace; several militant groups lie dormant but have not been totally subdued.

The terrorism in Jammu and Kashmir (J&K) has been more challenging and is still fairly serious. J&K is a predominantly Muslim state and part of it has been occupied by Pakistan since the partition of the country into India and Pakistan. Three wars have been fought over this region and the two armies continue to face each other over the line of cease-fire. The mountainous terrain has also made it difficult to launch strong military operations against these guerrillas, who slip into the country from Pakistan or even from not too distant Afghanistan. The terrorism reached its peak in the mid-1990s when many towns, including the capital city Srinagar, were seriously affected by these mercenary militants. These terrorists used many tactics to spread panic in the society and indulged in violence, killing many prominent civilians. They particularly targeted the Hindu minority population and attempted a form of ethnic cleansing. A very large proportion of Hindus have been driven away to seek shelter in other parts of the country (Kashmir Information Network 2001). These militants also burned down the Hazaratbal mosque, which was considered sacred to Muslims, in order to provoke violent clashes. During the visit of President Clinton, these terrorists killed thirty-nine Sikhs living in Kashmir valley. The threats of further terrorist victimization in the Kashmir valley are still very serious and likely to continue.

NATURE OF TERRORIST VICTIMIZATION IN BIHAR

In this section I will examine the nature of left-wing terrorism in the state of Bihar, where it has caused extreme victimization of a large population. I will briefly explore the genesis of communist insurgency from the early parts of the nineteenth century and its virulent form beginning in the 1970s. I will also comment upon the violent and criminal response by the state that has used illegal and often brutal means to combat left-wing guerrillas. I make the argument that victimization comes from illegality, criminality, and violence, whether coming from ideologically driven revolutionaries or state agents.

Left-wing extremism has its roots in the feudal nature of Indian society that is further segregated in thousands of castes. The state of Bihar was carved out of the old Bengal in 1935 and now comprises roughly 5.4 percent of the land area and 11 percent of the population of India. It is considered the poorest state and ranks almost last in every index of socioeconomic factors (Prasad 1997). It is estimated that more than 60 percent are illiterate among its population and more than three-fourths of residents live below the poverty line. The state is mired in caste that affects every aspect of its society, from politics to education to social conflicts. There are four so-called upper castes that comprise 15 percent of the population, roughly 100 backward castes accounting for 50 percent of the population, and there are 12 percent Muslims, too. The rest are divided among the untouchable castes and indigenous tribes that are largely concentrated in the southern region of the state.

There are significant relations between caste structures and class dominance. The upper castes are generally the rich class, owning most of the land
and well entrenched in the bureaucracy, politics, and business establishments. The untouchable castes, the backward castes, and the tribals are
mostly engaged in agriculture, providing the labor. Most people belonging
to these groups are among the poorest in the world. They have also been the
most exploited by the landlords and state agents and, despite democracy,
have been kept from providing any input into the decisions that affect their
lives.

The Indian state has enacted several well-intentioned laws for an equitable
distribution of the land in order to improve the economic conditions of the
downtrodden people. However, the implementation of these laws has been
half-hearted, as most landlords have considerable influence in the government. Accordingly, Bihar still has many people holding large landholdings,
sometimes in excess of thousands of acres. The Darbhanga Raj, the landowners of Purnea, Bhagalpur, and Mahants of Gaya still occupy large tracts of
land. Most of these owners are not practicing farmers and tend to lease their
lands in exchange for one-third to two-thirds of the produce. Moreover, they
keep changing their tenants so that no claim can be sustained on the basis of
continuing tenancy. Accordingly, despite the richness of the land, Bihar continues to be backward in agricultural production. In terms of the use of fertil-
izers, machinery, and yields per cropped area, Bihar falls far behind the states
of Punjab, Haryana, Andhra Pradesh, Maharastra, Tamil Nadu, and Kerala
(Prasad 1997).

Bihar is plagued by caste-based politics. Caste considerations dominate
the issues of economic policies, agricultural production, education, health,
and shelter for its 90-odd million people. Disputes over language, in particular use of the Maithili language and demand for a separate Jharkhand state
in the south, also frequently cause widespread agitation. The economic
levers of control and the social status accorded by the caste structure have
added to the power of the upper castes even after fifty years of democracy.
Sinha (1986) states that

> the big landlord . . . is virtually a "raja" [king] of his area. He possesses more of
> the total land of his village, . . lives like an aristocrat . . . employs largest num-
> ber of slaves and laborers for domestic and farm work . . . maintains a small pri-
> vate army . . . owns a licensed gun. He also belongs to the caste of the domi-
> nant section. To the social, economic and military power of the "raja"
> democracy . . . added political power. He now commands the Panchayat and
> thus the various executive bodies at the block level. He has the services of an
> obsequious police force in the local [station].

In such a situation the impoverished laborers and small peasants had little
option but to rise in struggle. The uprisings by the Santhals in 1855–56, the

Mundas in 1899–1901, and the struggle against indigo growers led by Gandhi himself in 1917 have been notable features of these class-based uprisings. Many of these struggles were against the British rulers who were seen to be aligned with the British planters and business people. However, in this nationalist fervor, the Congress Party did not support the struggles of the peasants against the local native landlords. This, in spite of the issues of *begar* [forced labor], *abwab* [illegal extraction], use of common public land, right to forest produce, and degrading caste-based practices like untouchability. The failure of the Congress Party to address these issues led to the rise of the Kisan Sabha under the dynamic leadership of Swami Sahajanand Sarasvati, who raised the issue of land ownership and permanent settlement by the British that gave rise to vast land ownership by few landlords. This political group led peasant struggles against the tenancy bill of 1933, the Rewara struggles in Gaya in 1933 and 1938, the Bakasht movement (illegal occupation of public lands by landlords) in Barahiya Tal (Misra 1987). The limited objectives of the Sabha of extracting concessions from the landlords to the total abolition of the landlord system soon made it into a formidable organization championing the rights of the poor, landless, and small farmers. This body ultimately joined the Communist Party of India (CPI) and even after independence raised struggles for the rights of the rural proletariat.

Despite the communist ideology and revolutionary fervor in the name of the poor, the Communist Party of India slowly adopted electoral politics as its strategy. Internal differences among its leaders also led to a split and formation of the Communist Party of India-Marxist (CPI-M) that gained victory in Kerala and formed the first elected communist government in the world. Disillusion of many hard-core communist members led to the creation of yet another party, the Communist Party of India-Marxist Leninist (CPI-ML) that organized the first ever violent movement in the district of Naxalbari in West Bengal in 1967.

The violent movement at Naxalbari has become a legend and its leaders, Charu Majumdar and Kanu Sanyal, have attained heroic stature in India. However, the movement did not last long and was brutally crushed by the police. The methods adopted by the state in meeting this violent movement were repressive and illegal. Many people were killed in suspicious circumstances and a large number arrested on vague charges. The brutal repression crushed the movement but led to an equally powerful reaction by the people targeted by the police. Many of them emerged as the new leaders and many more changed place to focus upon the neighboring state of Bihar.

These people, driven by an extreme form of left-wing ideology, led the first armed struggle at Musahari block of North Bihar. This movement was short-lived and soon collapsed under the onslaught of the police aligned with landlords in the area. However, the movement began to succeed at Bhojpur district when a new leadership, from the ranks of the affected people themselves, took control of the movement. "This was the phase of complete underground and illegal activities, with stress on armed struggle in the form of guerrilla actions against individual landlords and enemy agents as well as police camps for seizure of modern arms" (Misra 1987, 25). Naturally, the movement led to the killing of people alleged to be class enemies, attacks on police, and forcible collection of finances in the name of revolution. Since the movement became a caste struggle, the fight by lower castes against the economic and social dominance of the upper castes, most victims were innocent people killed, assaulted, or hurt because of their caste affiliation rather than because of any specific crimes. The police reaction too became equally brutal. A large number of poor people suspected of harboring the naxalites were arrested, tortured, and forced to flee. Many of the armed members of this movement were also killed in so-called police encounters that were suspect. For almost a decade the district of Bhojpur in North Bihar burned and led to considerable suffering of the people.

A primary reason for the growth of this left-wing extremism in this part of India has been the failure of the government to implement fair and equitable land reforms that could improve the economic conditions of the poor peasants. As stated above, most of the land was usurped by a few powerful landlords who would not invest in agriculture and changed tenants every year to deny them permanent rights. The British had enacted a policy of permanent land settlement that created these landlords who were accepted as owners of the land for which they were required to pay a fixed rent. Initially conceived as collectors of land revenue, these landlords soon became de facto owners and were recognized as such by the British government. The British saw them as close allies who helped maintain their Raj (Yang 1985). This law did not change until the period of independence when the Bihar government passed the Bihar Land Reforms Act in 1950. Through this act the government abolished the private interests in lands, forests, fisheries, mines, and other physical features and placed their ownership in the hands of the state. To avoid the provisions of this act many landlords transferred or fragmented their holdings and had them registered in *benami* [illegal] names, some using even those of their dogs, horses, and fictitious ones. Despite an imposition of ceiling upon the landholding, the upper castes who owned much of the land managed to use legal loopholes to avoid losing their possessions. The government and ruling party, consisting mostly of upper-caste politicians, also displayed considerable apathy toward the implementation of this act and did not use the state power to ensure that the landless gain the fruits of this legislation. For instance, the Ceiling Act came into force on April 9, 1962, but the notices to landlords to show cause for seizure of their land were not served until as late as 1970. In fact, no more than 9,700 acres of an estimated 100,000 to 150,000 acres of surplus land could be collected by the government (Misra 1987).

Similar results ensued when the government made other laws promoting equity, fairness, and the removal of economic inequality. The Minimum Wages Act of 1948 (amended in 1975), the Bihar Consolidation of Holdings and Prevention of Fragmentation Act of 1956 (amended 1970), the Bihar Land Reforms Act of 1970, and the Bihar Money Lenders Act of 1974 were all enacted with good intentions but no serious attempt was made to implement their provisions. Most of the laws were inadequately drafted and left several loopholes for the landed gentry to take advantage of in the courts. There was a clear nexus among the politicians, the government agents, and landed gentry who all saw to the lackluster implementation of these laws. The National Commission on Agriculture stated:

> By their abysmal failure to implement the laws, the authorities in Bihar have reduced the whole package of land reform measures to a sour joke. This has emboldened the landowning class to treat the entire issue of agrarian reform with utter contempt. Elsewhere in the country, the law evaders have a sneaking respect for the law enforcing authority. Their approach is furtive, their method clandestine. In Bihar the landowners do not care a tuppence for the administration. They take it for granted. Their approach is defiant, their modus operandi open and insolent. (Mainstream 1980)

The state also abdicated its responsibility in providing security to the poor who were struggling for their rights. Most of the landless who were employed as agricultural laborers were forced to agitate for higher wages and to obtain land for self-cultivation. However, their agitation and struggles were brutally met by the armed gangs maintained by the landlords who would attack them at the slightest hint of rebellion. These gangs would often surround the hamlets, set them ablaze, loot the property, molest women, and even kill prominent leaders to force them to surrender or flee from the village. In most of these cases the state failed to even prosecute the offenders and the police never came to assist the poor (Balchand 1997). Since most of the bureaucracy and the police come from the upper castes their sympathies have always been with the landlords and they have provided all assistance in suppressing the agitation initiated by the poor for their basic rights. Considering that most of the landlords also own licensed firearms and control economic activities, their position has been very powerful. Caste dominance over hundreds of years has also led to many objectionable social practices, untouchability being a very prominent one. The rise of democratic institutions provided a means for the poor to change the nature of their masters. The so-called backward castes comprise almost 50 percent of the population and they quickly emerged to take advantage of the elections to change the leadership from the upper castes. However, these middle castes, as they have come to be called, adopted the same postures as the upper castes and aligned themselves against the poor, downtrodden lower castes.

A number of serious attacks on the poor were also initiated by the armed gangs of these upper-caste and middle-caste landlords. The carnage at Parasbigha in 1977 saw the killing of many lower-caste people by the upper castes. Another incident at Pipra involved the killing of thirteen people—among them, women, children, and the elderly—some burnt to death by the upper-caste landlords. The list of their atrocities against the poor, landless people is long. In April 1980, Mahendra Singh, the notorious landlord of Amat village of Patna district, went with his armed goons and burned the hamlet of Mushars of Sikandarpur, who were suspected of being sympathetic to the naxalites. In Lahsuna village, the landlord Kishori Singh abducted and raped village women to teach the poor some grim lessons. Nevertheless, he received assistance from the police in the name of being threatened by the naxalites (Misra 1987).

On the other hand, left-wing extremism in Bihar, which initially found support among the downtrodden people, slowly degenerated into random violence. Communist parties comprise four major groups: the CPI-ML, CPI-Party Unity, MCC, and People's War Group and all four have been fighting for control of turf and areas of influence. The infighting has led to killing of members from opposing parties. MCC cadres killed members of CPI-ML and Party Unity and some of their members have been killed in retaliation. Moreover, all the parties collect money for financing their operations by extortion. They particularly target the forest contractors and public works contractors who in turn inflate their prices that the government has to pay. By some accounts this money now runs into millions of dollars and has become very lucrative since the state is unable to protect these contractors (Kurien 1999). Accordingly, these left-wing groups indulge in continuous extortion and there is no proper account of their collections even within their party. The armed cadres maintained by the party now run amuck, indulging in money extraction, levying threats, and generally killing anyone who opposes them. They have even targeted Christian missionaries who are working with the poor in some of these areas. These cadres have arms and act independently of their party line, killing for money and acting as lumpen elements. Left-wing gangs have been accused of robberies, kidnapping, and of course, large-scale extortion. Umadhar Singh, a founding member of the naxalite movement in this part of Bihar, says, "The fight between MCC and Liberation (CPI-ML) is not on ideological one but a gangland war" (Ahmed 1994).

On the other hand, the upper castes have violently reacted to the attempts of the communists to organize the people against them. In particular, they have organized private armies for the protection of their interests and to combat the guerrilla bands of the communists. Private armies such as Bhoomi Sena, Lorik Sena, Brahmarshi Sena, Shoshit Dalit Samajvadi Sena, and Shoshit Mukti Sena have gained considerable notoriety (Bhelari 1997).

Largely, these consist of lumpen rural elements supported by the landlords and those whose farms and income are threatened by the communists. Moreover these are caste-based, in support of the upper castes and ranged against the lower castes. For instance, Brahmarshi Sena was organized by Sardar Krishna Singh, an upper-caste Bhumihar; while upper-caste Anand Mohan Singh has organized his Krantikari Samajvadi Sena. "Seemingly enjoying the support of their caste men, these ring leaders are in constant touch with the landed nobility, readily lending a helping hand whenever such necessity arises" (Misra 1987, 71). Among the most notorious of these Senas has been the so-called Bhoomi Sena that has killed more than 200 people, 38 in one carnage at Poonpoon, set more than 300 houses ablaze, and have driven more than 100 families from their villages. They have also not spared their caste brethren, extorting massive levies in the name of protection, forcing them to provide shelter, food, liquor, and even women.

Both sides choose soft targets and mass killings have taken place in the affected central plains of Bihar. Mass killings indulged by the communist gangs have targeted upper-caste people in the villages of Paras and Jaitun Bigha where not even young children and women were spared. They similarly targeted another village of Bhumihars, cutting throats in an orgy of violence. The upper-caste gangs have victimized lower-caste village hamlets and individuals on a seemingly random basis. Thus in April 1985 they killed a Paswan caste person of Korthu village and looted his house. On August 30, 1985, they shot to death Munna Thakur and Potari Dom of Naima village. In September, they ransacked the entire hamlet of Mandachh village belonging to the lower castes. In October these upper-caste gangsters raped a poor woman, hacked a person to death, and set fire to ten houses in Masarh and Sikandarpur villages (Misra 1987). Most of their victims were randomly targeted and only because they belonged to the lower castes, who were seen to be aligned with the communist groups.

Table 4.1 lists the various massacres ascribed to the forward caste goons against suspected sympathizers of communist groups in this part of India

In retaliation, one of the strong communist parties running its own armed bands selected an isolated forward caste village called Senari and massacred thirty-four men by slitting their throats on March 3, 1999 (Baweja and Jha 1999). In none of the cases could the police arrest the offenders and ensure

Table 4.1. Massacres Ascribed to Forward Caste Goons

Site	Date	# Killed	Terrorist Party
Bathe	12/1/1997	59	Ranbir Sena
Shankar-Bigha	1/25/1999	23	Ranbir Sena
Narainpur	2/11/1999	11	Ranbir Sena

Source: Baweja and Jha 1999

security to the people. Indeed, the Bihar police have been accused of siding with the upper castes and targeting the lower castes with vengeance. For the past twenty-five years, the rule of law and the state of Bihar have been the most mismatched entities of Indian democracy. In contrast to norms, institutions, and fair play, Bihar has seen anarchy, strife, mismanagement, corruption, and killing fields. The state appears to be sliding uncontrollably down the road of regression. There are a multiplicity of scams involving misappropriation of nearly $500 million of public funds, about 1,200 judicial strictures, and 2,186 pending contempt cases (NCRB 1997). The terrorists are running parallel administrations where any challenge to their authority is met with swift murderous assault (Yadav 1997). In the last year, 5,327 people were killed, 2,472 abducted, and 342 kidnapped for ransom in the state. The state police have been prevented from acting against the extremists and the politicians who support them. Twenty-four ministers who are facing criminal charges still continue to function while notorious criminals have been released from prison on political considerations. The state is falling behind every other state in the country on every socioeconomic index of development. It is considered the most backward state and totally unable to prevent victimization of the people from terrorism, both by left-wing extremists and by state agents.

Moreover, the state has not learnt any lessons and has not taken any steps to aid and assist the victims. In a bankrupt state, hospitals and medical facilities are in short supply and most of the people are extremely poor. Consequently, none of the victims of terrorism appear to be getting any support from the state for their rehabilitation. In many cases, the government, under pressure to do something for the victims of large-scale massacres, has announced ex-gratia payments to the surviving family members, but the corrupt administration has generally failed to deliver even these amounts smoothly and without siphoning a portion. The victims, traumatized by their oppressors and ignored by the state, have felt betrayed and in some cases have sought revenge. Several instances have come to light where young children whose family members were killed by one or the other terrorist groups have grown up bitter and angry. Some of them have joined the opposing terrorist groups to seek revenge and they have indeed participated in killings, unfortunately of innocent people belonging to the other group. This seems to have set up a spiral of revenge and counter revenge in a continuing orgy of violence.

In order to prevent and control victimization from left-wing extremism, it is necessary that the government reform its style of functioning and evolve a rule of law based on human rights and fairness. The government also needs to ensure an equitable distribution of wealth by pursuing socioeconomic transformation. There is an urgent need to give the fruits of development to all the people and involve everyone in sustainable economic activities. The present situation in which a large number of people feel alienated and discriminated against is a major reason for pushing people into supporting the violent ideology propagated by the communists. They are able to exploit the situation by playing upon the misrule and indifference of the government. The state is perceived as alien, uncaring, and incapable of coming to the rescue of the marginalized people. In such a state, growing dissatisfaction with the government and loss of faith in its fairness and sincerity are going to push people toward violence and terrorists who are seeking to overthrow the state. The response of the police in resorting to illegal means in combating the terrorists and its own corruption further alienates the people. Thus the need to provide justice through legal means is a paramount consideration. People have to realize that violence does not pay and this will only come when the state itself displays faith in the rule of law and employs proper means in administration and law enforcement.

SIKH TERRORISM AND ITS VICTIMIZATION

Beginning from early 1980 onward the state of "Punjab was tormented by a virulent campaign of terror," says K. P. S. Gill (1997, 5), the police officer who eventually succeeded in defeating the terrorists and bringing the state back to peace. Terrorism in Punjab emerged in the name of religion, namely, the Sikh religion, and the avowed goal of the terrorists was to establish Khalistan, the land for the the Sikhs. Nevertheless, this faith and the majority of the Sikh community had little to do with the savagery and killing of innocent people. The genesis of terrorism lies in the logic of fundamental aspects of democracy, the cultivation of a vote bank. It is this pursuit of the lowest common denominator that makes politicians use religion as a tool for political mobilization and attempt to drive a wedge between different communities so that their hold, in the name of threats to the particular community, can be maintained. The ability of a vociferous, violent, and small minority to silence dissent, stifle the search for alternatives, and force adoption of rigid postures creates a situation in which the majority loses its hold. The Sikh terrorism emerged from the attempts of a small minority religious group that could not attain power through the ballot box to adopt mechanisms that evolved into a major confrontation in the country. The role of Pakistan in fomenting these troubles, supplying arms and ammunition and giving shelter to the terrorists, was also crucial in keeping this terrorism going for a long period of time.

The scriptures, especially the Guru Granth Sahib, are a living voice for the Sikhs and recordings of Gurubani, the hymns, are found in every Sikh home. The Gurudwara, the holy temple of the Sikhs, is not only a place of ritual visitations but a gathering of the community where the religion is practiced through various means until it becomes an integral part of the community. Therefore, for every Sikh, whether in Punjab or Canada or the United States, the practice of religion, its symbolism in terms of the headgear, the uncut hair, the carrying of Kirpan (a small dagger), are all a necessary part of who they are, rather than mere symbols to be discarded at will. The Punjab countryside is also dotted with small *deras* [abode] of preachers who sing and pray for the community and are seen as an integral part of any Sikh gathering. It is here that songs of valor, of righting the injustices against the community by kings and emperors of the past are recited. These stories in fact are manipulated to create a sense of heightened sentiments that are then used for political objectives. The tyranny and hardships inflicted in the past are cleverly converted into the present to make the community turn away from the present political establishment against whom these *granthis*, the preachers and religious leaders, are unable to compete in a free democratic election. Gill writes: "in an atmosphere surcharged with religious fervor and a deep sense of injury, preachers and religious activists harangue the assembled faithful on the wrongs of the present regime," against those "who seek to destroy the Faith." In these speeches made from the religious dais, "no evidence is needed, no concrete cases of prosecution, no martyrs. All the emotions aroused by the preceding drama are simply transferred to the present; ambiguous, but strangely tangible wounds suppurate in the mind; and when the time, the opportunity, and the final prompting come, explode in putrefying violence" (1997, 34–35).

This tirade began right after independence. Master Tara Singh, the chief of the Shiromani Gurudwara Prabandak Committee (SGPC) alleged that "under the garb of democracy and secularism our Panth, our liberty and our religion is being crushed" (Singh 1953). Pritam Singh Gill, another prominent Sikh religious leader, alleged that partition resulted in cheating of the rights of the Sikh community. The Muslims got Pakistan and Hindus got India but the Sikhs got nothing. Those who could arouse the masses reaped rich harvest in terms of political power. Political parties wooed them, they got nominated to elected bodies and increased their bargaining powers. Kapur Singh, who was dismissed from the Indian Civil Service, harangued against Nehru saying that he had ordered the police to treat every Sikh as a criminal. Despite such false utterances, he managed to get elected to the assembly and then to the Parliament.

Another factor in the genesis of Punjab's terrorism has been the role of the SGPC. Constituted as a religious body for the maintenance of Sikh shrines in the country, it controls enormous funds through its control of over 700 Sikh shrines. The SGPC is a well-organized bureaucracy, has a large number of preachers, priests, musicians, and *sewadars* (workers), and it functions as an autonomous body. Despite a system of elections, a small coterie has continued to hold to all the offices and that has given them control over funds, material resources, and political power. The Akali Dal, the political wing of SGPC, has overt political ambitions and has not hesitated to use religious sentiments for political objectives. "The more extreme, or 'fundamentalist' positions have tended, over time, to prevail" over this body. "It was precisely this spiral that culminated in terrorism; and it is precisely for these reasons that the Gurudwaras [Sikh temples] were the centers of militancy, and among them, the Golden Temple its axis" (Gill 1997, 37).

The Akali leaders succeeded in arousing Sikh sentiments to the point that the central government was forced to concede to their demands. The state of Punjab was bifurcated into Punjab, Haryana, and Himanchal Pradesh, which made Sikhs the majority community in Punjab. The Akalis wanted this division, hoping that this majority would enable them to gain political power in the state. Furthermore, it also led to a Hindu backlash. The Jan Sangha and Arya Samaj, two fundamentalist groups, exhorted people living in Punjab to register as Hindus and give Hindi as their language in order to provoke the Sikhs. Even decades of these political maneuvering did not get Akalis the majority that they were seeking. The moderate Sikhs, who outnumbered the small minority turning toward fundamentalism, voted otherwise and forced Akalis to go for coalitions. These temporary groupings did little to bring stability to the state, further enabling extremists to allege conspiracies and indulge in growing violence. The role of other political parties was no different and they too supported their own goons to settle scores or embarrass the ruling party. These struggles resulted in the escalation of fundamental rhetoric and the rise of Bhindranewale, the leader of the Damdami Taksal group. In 1978, a clash took place between Nirankaris, a sect within Sikhism, and the Damdami Taksal group, which resulted in the killing of more than ten people on either side. Bhindranewale utilized this clash for his own advantage and entered a phase of murder, extortion, and intensifying extremist propaganda. The whole of Punjab was pushed into anarchy with agitation, "do-or-die" calls, recruitment of suicide squads, and obstructions to the functioning of the state.

In 1982 Bhindranewale moved his headquarters to the inner chambers of the Golden Temple where the police, for fear of arousing the sentiments of Sikhs, did not enter. This gave Bhindranewale the opportunity to operate with impunity from the precincts of the temple and virtually become a state within the state. For almost two years the government waited impotently, letting his goons kill Hindus and Sikhs suspected of not sympathizing with the terrorist cause. Thousands were killed, the state agencies were neutralized, and a reign of terror ruled supreme. In April 1983, Atwal, senior police officer of Punjab, who had gone to pray at the temple, was gunned down in front of his men and scores of people. "Such was the terror of these days, so great the demoralization of the police—crippled and constrained as they were by the political leadership—that his bodyguards fled and the rest of the policemen hid in the shops outside the temple" (Gill 1997, 86).

It was only in April 1984 that Mrs. Gandhi, the prime minister, sent the Indian army to flush out the militants hiding in the temple in operation Blue Star. However, the army action was badly planned, its reasons not explained to the people, and this provoked the Sikhs. Although Bhindranewale and some of his associates were killed, many more managed to escape to Pakistan from where they continue to operate. A few months later, a Sikh bodyguard shot and killed Mrs. Gandhi, which in turn provoked Hindu goons to attack innocent Sikhs caught in this senseless violence.

It was perhaps the large-scale killing of Sikhs, especially in Delhi, that gave impetus to Sikh terrorism. A large number of disgruntled youth joined different gangs and many Sikhs too began to sympathize with them. Pakistan took full advantage of this situation by giving arms, shelter, and money to escalate this terrorism. For the next ten years, Punjab was engulfed in an orgy of violence that almost threatened the existence of the Indian state.

The dithering Akali party could not control the extremists within its ranks and the chief minister, ignoring the gravity of the situation, released en masse over 2,000 terrorists accused of heinous crimes. These released militants quickly regrouped and, by 1986, the militants once again captured the Golden Temple. They hoisted Khalistani flags, brought back the guns, and indulged in killing, torture, and even rape. "A large number of kidnapped women were kept captive in the temple, to be 'used ' when and how the warriors of Khalistan pleased; and then be killed in cold blood; almost without exception, these were Sikh women" (Gill 1997, 98).

After operation Black Thunder in 1988, in which the terrorists who had captured the premises of the Golden Temple were encircled and forced to surrender, the nature of victimization from Sikh terrorism came to light. The rooms occupied by the terrorists were found to have been converted into torture chambers where apparatus to deliver electric shocks, sharp-edged weapons, leather straps, and rubber spatulas covered with dried blood were recovered. The recovered evidence suggested that at least seventy-five suspected "police informers" and "government agents," violators of militant code, were tortured in these chambers. Forty-one mutilated bodies were recovered from the debris that had been treated with salt to arrest the decomposition and stench. "All the evil they did was in the name of God. And they did all that was evil. The murder of innocents, torture, rape, extortion, the desecration of temples, the abuses of sanctuaries and a limitless host of other crimes that do not bear mention next to these" (Gill 1997, 75).

The movement had by then lost its ideological moorings and a number of splinter groups emerged led by various leaders. However, aided by Pakistan, some of the prominent leaders kept trying to give the movement a religious tone. Thus when the killers of Mrs. Gandhi, Satwant Singh and Kehar Singh, were hanged after a lengthy court trial in which they were found guilty, ten innocent Hindus were hanged in "retaliatory action" in Batala, Taran Taran, and Ferozpur in January 1989. However, these attempts further alienated most of the Sikh population that had itself become the target of these terrorists. The death toll inflicted by the terrorists between 1988 and 1992 was 9,693 and, of these, 6,280 (close to 65 percent) were Sikhs. "So many Sikh families had witnessed the gratuitous and senseless brutal murder of their loved ones that the myth of a war for the defense of Sikhism and Sikh interests was wearing thin" (Gill 1997, 101).

This was not all. The fear of death was pervasive and terror reached every house as terrorists sought shelter in the homes of common Sikhs. The terrorists not only demanded food, shelter, and liquor but forced sex on the young women of the families. Abduction and rape became commonplace. Furthermore, extortion and land grabbing by the terrorists and their family members became rampant. The media also began reporting about the pornographic literature, medicines to promote sexual prowess, love letters found in the terrorist's possession that displayed their depravity, sexual adventurism, and illegal acquisition of property. Babbar Khalsa's Sukhdev Singh Babbar was discovered living in a palatial house with his paramour. Two more palatial buildings were traced to his ownership. His associate Sakhira raped two sisters in village Sirhali and forcibly married yet another sister. This was his own third marriage. Bhuri, the "Lt. General" of the Khalistan Commando force, abducted an eighteen-year-old girl from Maochal village and kept her in captivity for over four months, using her to satisfy his gang members. So-called General Labh Singh, the KCF chief, forced a married woman to become his partner and, suspecting her, tortured her and set her house on fire. His nephew Panjwar and another associate Billa, suspecting this woman of going to the police, killed her in October 1989.

Panjwar himself became the chief of KCF, acquired a large bungalow in Delhi, invested money in a transport company, and occupied twenty acres of land in Jhabal village. Chinna, the chief of the BTFK terrorist group, acquired fifty acres of land in Purampur village, constructed a large house at Delhi, kept two wives, and maintained illicit relations with scores of women. Sukhinder Singh "Gora," a particularly brutal character, raped and killed two married women of Enkot village, abducted and raped the daughter of a retired army officer in Dialgarh village, and kidnapped two girls from Bhjian Wali village and another from Manan village. Another prominent terrorist, Balwinder Singh, the chief of Dashmesh regiment, reportedly ravished more than fifty girls in Sathiala Batala area alone (Gill 1997, 102–103).

In 1991, a survey of the socioeconomic profile of the terrorists indicated that the majority had joined for the lure of easy money and the "benefits" attached to being a terrorist. Families of hard-core terrorists, such as Gurbachan

Singh, Manochahal, Panjwar, Thande, Dehriwal, and others amassed great fortunes. Heads of their families were respectfully addressed as Baba in the villages and they were approached for settling disputes. Some set up an independent business of extortion, mediation, and others acts of coercion. They also became beneficiaries of forcible acquisition of lands and other properties. Even if their sons died, they acquired the halo of martyrs and were called *Shaheedi Parivars* [martyrs' family] and received substantial financial support from the people. According to a study by three sociologists from Guru Nanak University (Judge, Puri, and Sekhon 1997), at least 180 out of a study sample of 300 terrorists joined out of fun. They were interested in acquiring a motorcycle, guns, and women. A judge asserts that he knew of a doctor who terminated at least ten to fifteen pregnancies every week (cited in Gill 1997, 104). The majority of terrorists died within a year, but during this period they would have access to fifty to fifty-five women.

Among other victims, the family members of police and army officers were special targets of the terrorists. The police paid a terrible price for their duties. "To wear a police uniform in the era of militancy in Punjab was to proclaim yourself a willful target for preferential terrorist attack" (Gill 1997, 106). Between 1988 and 1992, 1,566 policemen were killed by the terrorists. However it was their families who bore the most vicious brutal attacks. In a few days of special targeting, more than sixty members of police officers' families were murdered, which also included women and children. In the village of Barnala, eighteen family members were herded into a small enclosure and shot at point-blank range. Furthermore, those who attempted to shield the victims were also targeted. In June 1989, terrorists hijacked a bus and separated the ten Hindu passengers near Talwandi Ghuman. As the terrorists prepared to execute them, two Sikh passengers, Avtar Singh and Rajwant Singh, resisted. They too were immediately murdered (Gill 1997).

The killings were done by the state too. In dealing with this virulent terrorism, the police and paramilitary forces unleashed their own terror. Suspects were routinely picked up, tortured, and often killed in custody. In order to combat the terrorists, police pitted the same caste people, often victims of terrorists, against their killers. Punjab police created the rank of Special Police Officers (SPO), who were given training and arms to fight the terrorists. Most of these SPOs were Majhabi Sikhs, the low-caste Sikhs who had been particularly targeted by the Jat Sikh terrorists. At the rate of 35 rupees per day (around 1 dollar) they became the extended arms and eyes of the police and played a major role in putting terrorism to an end. By the time terrorism peaked in 1992 and began to abate in its virulence, more than 25,000 people had died in Punjab in terrorist-related violence (Sandhu 1993). From a low of sixty-three civilians, eight policemen, and two terrorists in 1985, in 1992, the casualties were 1,518 civilians, 252 police officers, and 2,113 terrorists (Gupta and Sandhu 1993, 37).

The victimization has not ended. The victims suffer because of the killings of their family members or for attacks on themselves. Medical reports suggest that such victims undergo a physiological stress that is intense and prolonged and has important health consequences. "They experience their victimization as a personal affront to their pride, compounded by perceived indifference to their plight. They tenaciously hold on to their feelings of rage and injustice, seeking only reparations and revenge for their victimization and thus remaining physiologically disabled" (Symonds 1982: 96–97). Soskis and Ochberg (1982, 109) suggest that terrorist victimization includes "grief, death imagery, encounters with bloody or terrible events, and the [horrible] experience of rape victims."

The government and police also need to consider the case of providing assistance to the victims. The large number of orphans, widows, and shattered families need assistance to rebuild their lives. Menon (1993) has drawn attention to the many child victims of terrorism, arguing that this silence of the lambs may be broken by revenge that these children harbor in their minds. Many have seen their close family members assaulted and killed in front of their eyes. A social reformer, Baba Balkan Singh of Anandpur Sahib, has started the Baba Ajit Singh Jhanjhar Academy, where children whose parents and guardians have been killed by terrorists are being sheltered and taken care of. The Punjab police have also started an operation "Healing Touch" in which police, former terrorists, and family members publicly come together in a spirit of reconciliation (Sandhu 1993, 51).

CONCLUSION

The two types of terrorism described above suggest many lessons for those seeking to understand and heal the wounds of terrorist victimization. First of all, terrorism is directly linked to state policies and the inability of the state to devise suitable remedial measures within the framework of its laws. The Indian state has been almost criminal in its dealings with terrorism. In the case of left-wing terrorism that emerged as early as the 1950s, the government failed to see that inequitable distribution of wealth, the failure to integrate the poor and downtrodden people, would provide the communists with the means to extend their violence-ridden ideology. In the state of Bihar, the successive governments have only treated this form of terrorism as a matter of law and order and have not addressed the basic underlying economic causes. Despite the fact that higher castes have usurped vast amount of land through illegal means, the government has failed to take action. The government machinery has often sided with the rich landlords and thus destroyed its neutrality. The poor no longer trust the police and the government agents to provide them justice. Indeed, the victimization of the poor and downtrodden has been so serious that Bihar has come to be known as the dark state of the country. From the blinding done by the police to the un-provoked firing and killing of the poor demanding their civil rights, the state has almost invariably attempted to crush the attempts of the poor to organize themselves against their exploitation.

It is this victimization of a large number of people that has created the opportunities for left-wing extremists to find fertile ground. Most of the poor, unable to find justice and even secure a fair hearing from the state authorities, have been forced to go to the terrorists or at least sympathize with them. On the other hand, attacks upon the higher castes and forcible seizure of their lands and property have driven them to organize their own armed bands for protection. The police, largely composed of people from the upper castes, sympathized with them and used illegal means and brute force to combat the naxalites and their sympathizers. At present, both parties, left-wing extremists supported by lower caste sections and the higher castes supported by state police, are locked in a fierce combat. Severe victimization is taking place on the sides and is affecting everyone else, too. The state has largely become inactive; there is virtually no worthwhile economic activity in most of the affected areas, a sense of insecurity is escalating, and criminal incidents are also rising.

Thus, the only way to prevent further victimization in Bihar from left-wing extremism is to evolve prudent and fair policies that can assure the people of economic and social justice. Only a government that understands these victims and is prepared to cope rationally with what they experience, say, and do can bring some relief to the region. Any kind of overreaction or outrage precipitates harsh counterterrorist actions that further cause victimization of the people caught in the middle. Only a government that is representative, prepared to educate the people, and inform itself about the senseless victimization will be able to evolve prudent policies and develop appropriate means for dealing with terrorist victimization. The police in particular also need to be modernized and trained so that they can become a democratic force, accountable to the people rather than remaining a colonial legacy of the British Raj.

A large number of people have been traumatized on both sides and have not been given any attention. The cases of actual victims mentioned in the chapter suggest severe attacks on the human psyche that are likely to have long-term effects. These people have undergone stress, tragedy, and grief that one cannot even imagine. How they have reacted to their problems, what means they are using to react to these constant stressors, both on a short-term and long-term basis, need detailed examination. Quite likely the people of that area are undergoing long-term effects on their psychological and physical functioning that are likely to extend to the second and even third generation. The problems of child victims, who have seen their family members killed before their eyes, young girls kidnapped and gang-raped, women widowed in their young lives, are all cases that have not received any attention in India.

Moss (1972, 240) has argued that "often it is not until the guerrilla threat has emerged that the ruling elite becomes conscious of the urgent need for reform." Before the period of crisis, the vested interests and governments brush aside pleas for adaptation and try to hold on to them and avoid compromises. The state emphasizes socially destructive repression as an instrument rather than social adaptation. This creates a conflict between human rights and political-economic domination by the ruling elite. The present situation in Bihar still looks chaotic and depressing. The continuation of terrorism, the infighting among the leftist groups, the criminalization of the state apparatus, and the political process all are continuing. There seems to be little development of any enlightened policy that will soon end this terrorist victimization of a large number of people.

Similarly, Sikh terrorism, though contained though some brilliant police action, needs to be watched carefully. There are small pockets of resistance and terrorist groups who operate occasionally and continue to get support from Pakistan. The ideology of Khalistan is also being artificially being kept alive by some active groups of nonresident Indians living in Canada, the United States, and the United Kingdom. The flow of propaganda and financial support remains despite peace in the state. Subversive activities spearheaded by these groups include use of pamphlets and letters, displaying little regard for truth but high on emotion and an invented history of persecution directed to the governments of Western nations (Khalistan.net 2001). A number of militant coordinators still operate from the United States, Canada, Pakistan, Nepal, Thailand, Singapore, and Dubai. Pakistan continues to provide shelter and substantial support in terms of arms and finances to keep terrorism alive in Punjab. The government has to maintain vigilance and ensure that past mistakes are not repeated. Above all, politicians must not use violence and deceit to further their agenda. Also, the state forces should not be compromised and should be permitted to operate independently though remaining accountable to the rule of law and beholden to the judiciary. This alone can prevent future terrorist victimization in Punjab.

Terrorist victimization remains a serious problem in the country. Even though Punjab has quieted, serious terrorism has emerged in Kashmir, the northeastern states, and Andhra Pradesh. It continues its violence in the state of Bihar where almost every day one or the other terrorist group is killing people. Fortunately, Punjab has provided some lessons that suggest ways in which to deal with even extreme form of terrorism. By empowering the state agents, by focusing upon the victims rather than the offenders alone, it is possible to evolve some form of prevention and control over victimization. However, the need is to ensure that the state follows policies that provide all segments of the population a say in running their own affairs. The state also needs to understand that despite competitive politics, inevitable in a democratic state, the urgent need is to disassociate from those who advocate violence. It is also necessary to ensure that state agencies are not compromised and, more important, that these agencies do not go beyond the purview of legal boundaries. Only a state dealing fairly, ensuring the rule of law, and concerned about victimization can bring about the desired recovery of the people who alone suffer grievously.

BIBLIOGRAPHY

Ahmed, Farzand. 1994. Let a 1000 Guns Boom. *India Today* (31 May 31): 51.

Balchand, K. 1997. Wanton Killings on the Rise. *The Hindu Online* (7 April) at www.hinduonline.com/, accessed 10 April 1997.

Baweja, Harinder, and Sanjay Kumar Jha. 1999. Inside the Bloodland. *India Today* (5 April): 20–24.

Bhelari, Kanhaiah. 1997. Waking Up to Death. *The Week* (14 December).

Dasgupta, Biplab. 1974. *The Naxalite Movement.* Monograph, Centre for the Study of Developing Societies, no.1. Bombay: Allied Publishers.

Dasgupta, Swapan. 1996. Face of Liberal Conformism: Recalling Naxalite Terror. *Indian Express* (29 June).

Gill, K. P. S. 1997. *Punjab: The Knights of Falsehood.* New Delhi: Har-Anand Publications.

Goswami, Sabita. 1997. Tata Buy-Buy. *The Week* (26 October).

Gupta, Shekhar, and Kanwar Sandhu. 1993. K.P.S. Gill: True Grit. *India Today* (15 April): 36–40.

Joshi, Manoj. 1993. Combating Terrorism in Punjab: Indian Democracy in Crisis. *Conflict Studies* 261 (May).

———. 1999. *The Lost Rebellion.* New Delhi: Penguin.

Judge, Paramjit Singh, Harish Puri, and Jagrup Singh Sekhon. 1997. A Socio-Psychological Profile of Terrorists. Cited in *Sunday*, 16–22 February.

Kashmir Information Network. 2001. The Invisible Refugees, at www.kashmir-information.com/Refugees/index.html (accessed 6 February 2001).

Khalistan.net. 2001. www.khalistan.net (accessed 6 February 2001).

Kumar, Satyendra. 1999. Naxal Groups Get Bogged Down in Caste War. *Times of India* (23 March) at www.timesofindia.com (accessed 25 March 1999).

Kurien, J. 1999. Banned Bihar Outfit Prepares Its Own "Budget." *The Times of India* (1 February).

Mainstream. 1980. *A Field Study: Agrarian Relations in Two Bihar Districts* 11, no. 40 (2 June): New Delhi.

Menon, Ramesh. 1993. Silence of the Lambs. *India Today* (15 April): 49–53.

Misra, Vinod. 1987. *The Flaming Fields of Bihar: A CPI(ML) Document.* Calcutta: Prabodh Bhattachrya Publisher.

Moss, Robert. 1972. *The War for the Cities.* New York: Coward, McCann, and Geoghegan.

National Crime Records Bureau. 1997. *Crime in India, 1995.* Faridabad, India: Government of India Press.

Peace Process Receives a Major Boost. *Oriental Times* 2, issue 3–4 (22 May–6 June) at www.nenews.com (accessed 15 June 1999).

Prasad, K. N. 1997. *Bihar Economy: Through the Plans—In Comparison with All-India and Other States.* New Delhi: Vedam e-Books.

Ramanujan, Anand. 1997. No Sign of Political Settlement with PWG. *Times of India* (13 January) at www.timesofindia.com (accessed 16 January 1997).

Rediff.com. 2000. Sanjay Ghosh's Killer Shot Dead in Encounter. *Rediff.com* at www. rediff.com/news/2000/sep/11assam.htm (accessed 14 September 2000).

Sandhu, Kanwar. 1993. Punjab: Picking up the Pieces. *India Today* (15 June): 46–53.

Saxena, N. S. 1987. *Law and Order in India.* New Delhi: Abhinav Publications.

Singh, K. K. 1999. The Killing Fields of Jehanabad. *Times of India* (19 March) at www.timesofindia.com (accessed 26 March 1999).

Singh, Tara. 1953. Presidential Address. All India Akali Conference, 28 March, Armistsar, India: Shriromani Akali Dal.

Sinha, Arun. 1986. Class War, Not Atrocities against Harijans. In *Agrarian Movements in India: Studies on 20th Century Bihar*, edited by Arvind N. Das. London: Frank Cass.

Soskis, David A., and Frank M. Ochberg. 1982. Concepts of Terrorist Victimization. In *Victims of Terrorism*, edited by Frank M. Ochberg and David A. Soskis, 105–135. Boulder, Colo.: Westview Press.

Symonds, Martin. 1982. Victim Responses to Terror: Understanding and Treatment. In *Victims of Terrorism*, edited by Frank M. Ochberg and David A. Soskis. Boulder, Colo.: Westview Press.

Yadav, J. P. 1997. Parallel Powers in Bihar Outshine the Ill-equipped Rabri Devi. *The Asian Age* (28 September 28).

Yang, Anand A.,ed. 1985. *Crime and Criminality in British India.* Tucson, Ariz.: Association for Asian Studies by the University of Arizona Press.

5

Trends and Threats in the Terrorism of the New Millennium: A Perspective from Israel

Ely Karmon

This chapter was presented almost two years ago at the United Nations Ancillary Meeting on Terrorist Victimization: Prevention, Control, and Recovery. Since then the world has witnessed the dramatic events of September 11, 2001, and for the first time in history terrorism has provoked the killing of thousands of people, victims of a single mass destruction attack. This is not a completely updated version of the original essay, as most of the directions and mode of operation of the terrorist attacks were already anticipated. However, it includes a new section analyzing the operational and strategic implications of the September 11 attacks.

This chapter analyzes the main characteristics of international terrorism in the 1990 decade and evaluates the main trends for the near future. The dramatic events and changes of the 1980s and 1990s in the international system have taught us that it is unrealistic and dangerous to voice evaluations and predictions for the long term. This evaluation can help establish the main foci of terrorist activity, the countries and the populations involved, the direct and indirect victims affected, and the amount of human and material damage provoked by the various modi operandi employed by the terrorist organizations and groups.

ASSESSMENT OF THE MAIN CONTEMPORARY TRENDS

On the whole, international terrorism in the 1990s has not changed as dramatically as the media or some researchers affirm. According to many researches and the report *Patterns of Global Terrorism* issued annually by the

U.S. State Department, international terrorism in the second half of the 1990s has diminished in quantity of incidents but the quality of the attacks and their lethality has increased dramatically.[1]

But if we look back to the 1970s and 1980s we should remember many attacks with sophisticated barometer or time bombs against airplanes, mainly of Western countries: Swissair, Austrian Airlines, Air India, TWA, Pan Am (in Honolulu, and not only at Lockerbie) which produced hundreds of innocent casualties. Fortunately many more attacks were foiled by the security services or by sheer luck and thus saved many other lives.[2]

Among the reasons given by researchers for the increased lethality of terrorist attacks is the appearance of new terrorist organizations with more amorphous religious and millenarian aims, organizations with less clear nationalist or ideological motivations.[3]

But again, looking back to the 1980s, the two bombings of the American embassy in Beirut in 1983 and 1984, as well as the suicide bombings against the headquarters of the American Marines and French troops in October 1993 in Beirut, which caused hundred of casualties, were also the result of attacks by so-called amorphous religious organizations, as the organization responsible for them, Hizballah, was seen at that time as a kind of mysterious umbrella organization known by its telephone statements as "Islamic Jihad."

It is true that the role of the religious movements and groups responsible for terrorist activities has greatly increased in the 1990s and that this has influenced the new tactics and patterns of terrorism. One of the reasons for this change is the neutralization by security forces and the extinction as a result of the crumbling of the communist block of ideological groups and organizations of the extreme left in Western Europe and South America.

The radicalization of religious groups is very clear in the Muslim world, and the assassination of the late Israeli prime minister Itzhak Rabin shows that the trend could involve radical Jewish groups as well. It is less obvious in the Christian world, although some radical right-wing terrorists are also influenced by Christian fundamentalist motivations.

One of the main strategic modi operandi used by such organizations has been the suicide terrorism or the indiscriminate bombing of civil or public targets: in Sri Lanka and in India by Tamil terrorists of the Liberation Tigers of Tamil Eelam (LTTE), in Lebanon and Israel by Islamic radicals of Hizballah and Hamas, but also in Turkey by the Kurdish rebels of the Kurdistan Worker's Party (PKK) and lately in Africa in the bombings of the American embassies in Kenya and Tanzania by al-Qaed'a, the international radical Islamic group of Osama bin Laden.[4] The United States has been struck by such attacks perpetrated in 1993 by Islamist radicals, in the case of the bombing of the World Trade Center in New York, and in 1994 by extremist right-wingers in the Oklahoma City bombing.

The suicide attacks are strategic because they have huge political reper-cussions, as in the case of the disruption of the political process between Is-rael and the Palestinian Authority in 1995–96 and the ensuing sufferings of both the Israeli and Palestinian populations. Until now there is no opera-tional answer to them.

The suicide terrorism and the bombings of civil or public targets are ex-tremely malicious because in most of the cases dozens or even hundreds of innocent people are killed or wounded along with those who, according to the terrorists, are the "legitimate" targets. In the case of the bombings by al-Qaed'a activists of the American embassy in Nairobi, for instance, hundreds of Kenyan citizens were killed or wounded besides the twelve American cit-izens.[5] The other danger is the possibility of imitation by other organizations, stimulated by what they see as the success of such operations. It seems that this is the case with the Kurdish PKK, although its suicide operations were less successful than those of the Islamic or Tamil groups which served them as examples.[6]

This kind of terrorism poses also the problems of treatment and indemni-fication for the numerous victims involved. In the case of the bombings of the American embassies in Africa, the U.S. government has provided much needed financial and material support, but who has taken care of the Indian citizens killed along with their ex-prime minister by Tamil terrorists, or the Pakistani victims of the suicide bombing of the Egyptian embassy by Islamist radicals?[7]

Looking at the second half of the 1990s, we can see two conflicting trends in international terrorism. On the one hand, there is indeed a trend of radi-calization. But the center of gravity of the intense terrorist activity has moved from parts of the Middle East and Europe to Afghanistan and Pakistan, the Caucasus, and Central Asia. This is a result of the dismembering of the Soviet empire, the aftermath of the Afghanistan war against the Soviets, and the po-litical instability in Afghanistan and Pakistan.

These two last countries, Afghanistan and Pakistan, have replaced Lebanon as hotbeds of terrorist organizations and playgrounds for the train-ing of groups and individuals from Muslim and non-Muslim countries. As a consequence of this trend, the major international activity has been staged this decade by the radical Islamist organizations. Osama bin Laden, his al-Qaed'a organization, and the World Islamic Front for the Struggle against Jews and Crusaders that he created have grown on this foundation.

In the Middle Eastern arena it should be noted that terrorism has had ma-jor negative strategic consequences: The suicide terrorism of Hamas and the Palestinian Islamic Jihad (PIJ) has been responsible for the interruption of the negotiation process between Israel and the Palestinian Authority;[8] Hizballah's terrorism and guerrilla activity has served not only this organization's goal of destroying Israel but also Iran's strategic regional interests and Syria's goals in negotiations with Israel. The danger is that intense terrorist activity will continue to exist in this area as long as the negotiating process is not finalized, with the prospect of more Israeli citizens suffering from them and more Palestinians affected physically and economically by the Israeli retaliatory measures.

However, it is important to stress that we are witnessing a counter current—the shift of important organizations to the political process and negotiations as a means to achieve their strategic goals. This is true for the Irish Republican Army (IRA) in Northern Ireland, the Basque Fatherland and Liberty (ETA) in Spain, the PKK in Turkey, Revolutionary Armed Forces of Colombia (FARC) in Colombia, and also the Front Islamique du Salut (FIS) in Algeria and the al-Jihad and Gama'a al-Islamiyya in Egypt.[9] It is important to be attentive to this trend, understand the motivations behind it, and learn from them the mechanisms that can be used on other fronts.

This trend is most likely the result of the failure of the armed struggle to bring the central strategic results expected by the organizations involved, and the example they saw in the achievements won by the Palestinian Liberation Organization (PLO) through negotiation and the political process. But as in the case of the political process between Israel and the Palestinians, there are difficulties and crises in all the negotiating processes opened by these organizations.[10]

It is of note that, contrary to many expectations, the wars in Bosnia and Kosovo have not produced significant terrorist activities. The support that the democratic countries and the international community have given to the Muslim populations of these two countries has proved to many Muslims around the world that the West is not the demonized enemy described by the radical Islamists, and thus prevented the use of this front by radicals such as Osama bin Laden.

Far-right terrorism has also changed location: from Europe at the end of the 1980s and beginning of the 1990s it has emerged as a dangerous threat in the United States. The Oklahoma City bombing in 1993 has proved that this indiscriminate terrorism, using the new leaderless resistance strategy, can be as lethal as the radical religious one. It is characterized by the fact that the perpetrators and the victims of the bombings were citizens of the same country and of the same ethnic origin, the motif behind the attack being mainly ideological. If this trend continues, it can provoke a polarization and exacerbation in the social and political fabric of society.

The only significant change in the 1990s has been the appearance of cults in the arena of terrorism and the breaking of a taboo in the use of nonconventional terrorism, which is in itself connected to the activity of one cult, the now famous Japanese Aum Shinrikyo.

The threat of the millenarian and apocalyptic groups exists, although in this field we are quite in the dark in identifying the potential terrorists because of political, moral, and legal constraints in the control activity of the security forces.

The Aum Shinrikyo cult, the most remarkable example in this category, must be considered not only as an apocalyptic cult but also as a religious/ideological organization: it had an anti-American, anti-Western, and anti-Semitic ideology, a political and strategic plan for taking power in Japan (it even ran in the general elections), and it had an organizational pattern similar to a government. What characterizes it most strikingly is the kind of dictatorship wielded by the guru and his total influence on his followers, which is found in many cults and new-religion groups.[11]

The latest example, the massacre on March 17, 2000, of several hundred followers of the Movement for the Restoration of the Ten Commandments of God in Uganda, although probably of criminal origin, illustrates the enormous danger for thousands of credulous people, in advanced and rich societies as well as in the poorest countries, who can become themselves victims of unscrupulous leaders, or executioners of other innocent people.[12] In these cases some of the executioners are indeed no less victims than those victimized.

THE EMERGING RADICAL ISLAMIST SUNNI TERRORISM

As a result of the Afghan's and their Arab allies' victory over the Soviet Union, the Gulf War, the increased military American and Western presence in Saudi Arabia and the Gulf area, and the consequences of the Western military activity against Iraq, the already existing Sunni radicalism has developed as the main terrorist threat in the region.

The victory of the extremist religious Taliban in the internal struggle in Afghanistan and the increased instability and radicalization of the Pakistani Islamist movements and of the regime itself have given to these Sunni movements and groups the necessary territory to organize, train, make sorties, and take refuge in case of necessity. The investigations following the bombing of the World Trade Center in New York and those of the American embassies in Africa have brought these trends to light.

THE GRAY ZONES AND NEW BATTLE ZONES

The existence and expansion of the so-called gray zones, countries and territories under control of anarchic fighting groups without the presence of moderating democratic or international forces, have become another dangerous hotbed for terrorist groups. Somalia, Chechnya until lately, Central Africa, and parts of Afghanistan and Pakistan have become the exclusive territories of such uncontrollable and violent forces. Bin Laden and his allies, like the splinter groups of Egyptian Islamists, can find refuge for their followers in these faraway corners of the world.

This trend is enhanced by the appearance of new battle zones for the Islamist radicals: Russia, the Central Asian Muslim republics, and possibly parts of Indonesia in the near future.

The human sufferings and the number of people involved in these religious or ethnic conflicts are exacerbated by the terrorist or guerrilla activity of the fighting factions, which tend to escalate their stakes. Thus the Chechen rebels have taken hostages and endangered the lives of hundreds of people in a civil hospital of a small town and have threatened to use radiological devices and even atomic bombs against the population of Moscow.[13] They were also probably responsible for the bombings of populated apartment buildings in Russia's capital.[14]

THE DANGER OF NONCONVENTIONAL TERRORISM

The evaluation of the threat represented by nonconventional terrorism (chemical, biological, radiological, and nuclear) as presented in this chapter is based on research led at the International Policy Institute for Counterterrorism (ICT) at the Interdisciplinary Center in Herzliya, Israel.[15] The research has not dealt with cyberterrorism, a relatively new modern threat.[16]

Based on publicly available reports of incidents, ICT has built a large database, although the very definition of nonconventional terrorism and the significance of each incident is a matter of controversy among researchers. This is not a complete or exhaustive database, but it surely includes most of the known and significant ones.

The incidents were classified by the period of occurrence (divided into three decades), the continent and country of occurrence, and by their degree of severity.[17]

Categories and Period of Occurrence (Annex I):

The incidents of nuclear terrorism have sharply declined over the past three decades: from 120 incidents during the 1970s to only fifteen in the 1990s. In contrast, the incidents of chemical and biological terrorism are showing a gradual but stable rise. In the 1970s there were fourteen incidents of chemical terrorism and ten incidents of biological terrorism; in the 1980s, there were thirty-four incidents of chemical terrorism and thirteen incidents of biological terrorism; whereas in the 1990s there were thirty-six reported incidents of chemical terrorism and eighteen incidents of biological terrorism.

Severity (Annex II):

The incidents were classified into seven categories according to their degree of severity:

- Threats to use weapons of mass destruction
- Threats against facilities of weapons of mass destruction
- Attempts to acquire weapons of mass destruction
- Possession of weapons of mass destruction
- Attempted use of weapons of mass destruction
- Action against facilities of weapons of mass destruction
- Actual use of weapons of mass destruction

Thirty-four percent of the incidents were threats against facilities of weapons of mass destruction, all threats against nuclear reactors and installations. The threats to use weapons of mass destruction in terrorist attacks make up 17.5 percent of the incidents. In this category the threats to use chemical terrorism comprise the majority of the incidents (55 percent).

Thirty percent of the incidents relate to an actual terrorist attack, from which 16 percent refer to action against facilities of weapons of mass destruction and 14 percent refer to actual use of weapons of mass destruction. Eighty-three percent of the incidents of actual use of weapons of mass destruction were incidents of chemical terrorism.

From the data it appears that most of the terrorism involving nuclear targets happened during the 1970s and diminished dramatically in the next two decades. Even so, the great majority of the incidents refers to threats (98) or involved mainly actions against facilities (43). These actions were due mainly to the activity of extremist left-wing organizations, which opposed the American and Western nuclear armament and deployment of nuclear missiles, especially in Europe, and decided to attack mainly civil nuclear facilities empty of fissile materials. With the disintegration of the antinuclear movement in the middle of the 1980s and parallel with the elimination of the violent extremist leftist groups in Europe and the fall of the Soviet Union, which had a strategic interest in supporting the antinuclear movement, the antinuclear violent activity almost disappeared.

Chemical and biological terrorism developed in the 1980s and 1990s, after the war between Iraq and Iran and again after the Gulf War of the U.S.–led coalition against Iraq.

The indiscriminate use of chemical weapons by the Iraqis and the fear that the Gulf War could provoke a large chemical-biological conflict and a wave of nonconventional terrorism brought about the feeling that this kind of terrorism is inevitable. The attacks perpetrated by the Japanese cult Aum Shinrikyo in March 1995 generated surprise only because of the place where they happened and the magnitude of the infrastructure at the disposal of the organization. Today it is known that the Gulf War influenced the decision of Aum's leader (Shoko Asahara) to produce and use chemical and biological weapons.

Between the two types, the chemical terrorism has a clear advantage, not only in the number of incidents involved but also in their seriousness and lethality.

Location (Annex III):

Almost 55 percent of the incidents have occurred in the United States. Of those, 75 percent were incidents of nuclear terrorism. Nearly 28 percent of the incidents have occurred in Europe (53 percent of the incidents were of nuclear terrorism). But again it must be stressed that most of these incidents did not present a real danger of nuclear explosion or contamination.

The incidents that took place in the Middle East represent only 4 percent of the total; of those, ten out of twelve were incidents of chemical terrorism and two were of a biological nature. However, it should be noted that Middle Eastern countries (Egypt, Iraq, Iran, and possibly Sudan) have made relatively massive use of chemical weapons. Elsewhere, 10.5 percent of the incidents have occurred in Asia (mainly in Japan) and some 1 percent took place in South America and Africa each.

These findings may indicate that nonconventional terrorism is not common where conventional terrorism is a major factor, such as the Middle East and South America.

From the existing data it results that the developed, industrial world (United States, Europe, and Japan) was the main ground for nonconventional terrorism, the United States leading the targeted countries. This means that the industrial-technological infrastructure is necessary for the development of a nonconventional capability in a terrorist organization. The facilities that are targeted (nuclear or chemical plants, military weapons, etc.) are also usually found in these countries. But with the expansion of nuclearized states, like Pakistan and India, and the political instability in parts of the ex-Soviet Union republics, the danger of proliferation of such weapons and materials to terrorist groups has been enhanced.

One of the main conclusions of the research is that it is imperative to differentiate between what could be called limited nonconventional and extreme nonconventional terrorism, or terrorism which could produce mass casualties, in contrast to terrorism leading to the extermination of entire populations or settlements or the contamination of land for a long period.

According to the evaluation by ICT, none of the known terrorist organizations and groups has the capability to perpetrate nonconventional extermination attacks, today or in the near future.

Some of the bigger organizations, and some of the smaller ones with the assistance of state sponsors, can carry out less lethal, limited attacks. But it is clear that even such limited attacks will have enormous political and psychological effect with strategic consequences. But at least for the foreseeable future, nonconventional terrorist attacks will not be able to exterminate or to endanger entire populations, as some researchers have threatened.

Chemical terrorism seems to be the main threat in the use of nonconventional weapons for the short and medium term. Chemical agents are more stable and more containable, easily dispersed and controllable, inasmuch as they are not contagious; posing less danger to their users and being less likely to cause unintended damage, thus allowing for more precise and discriminate attacks. Chemical agents are also more readily available commercially. Most of the known terrorist organizations, especially the more advanced technologically and financially wealthiest, have good chemical specialists in classic explosives and developed quite suitable techniques and modi operandi in the field of chemistry for terrorist use.[18]

Biological terrorism could be considered the second threat in order of priorities. BW agents can be hundreds to thousands of times more potent than chemical agents and provide a much cheaper route. As international controls are strengthened on nuclear and chemical weapons materials, biological weapons become more attractive. Few terrorist groups have attempted to acquire biological agents, and even fewer have actually attempted to use the agents. The number of incidents involving use or attempted use of biological agents, although on the rise, is extremely small and there are no known fatalities.[19]

Nuclear terrorism: although it was the most feared menace, the past thirty years experience has shown that most of the incidents were threats, hoaxes, or attacks against inactive nuclear facilities. For the foreseeable future the production by a terrorist organization of a real nuclear weapon must be discarded. The sabotage of a civil nuclear site or facility or the capture of a nuclear material shipment is plausible, but again it poses serious operational and safety problems for the group involved.

Radiological dispersal: although there have been surprisingly few incidents of this kind to date, the opportunities for this form of nuclear terrorism are perhaps more numerous than any other form of nuclear material terrorist threat, and therefore the most plausible.

There is also a dreadful suicidal aspect in the use of nonconventional terrorism. The successful use by an organization of chemical or biological terrorism could produce such a severe military reaction by the country attacked as to endanger the life of a large fraction of the population, the constituency that this organization claims to represent. It would in fact amount to a collective suicidal attack. For this reason it is obvious that any serious organization takes into account this danger and this could be one explanation for the minor number of incidents and alerts that we have experienced until today in the field of nonconventional terrorism

GROWING INTERNATIONAL COOPERATION

However, there is an optimistic aspect in the prevention of terrorism. During the last decade, and more so during the last two to three years, we have witnessed a growing readiness and interest on the part of more countries to cooperate in the fight against terrorism, in the local, regional, and global arenas.

The regional agreement reached by the countries of the Arab League to commonly fight radical Islamic movements has already had positive effects for Egypt's fight against al-Jihad and Gama't Islamyya.

The United Nations itself is more and more involved in this battle: the embargo on Libya and the opening of the trial in the Lockerbie affair, or the sanctions against Afghanistan for the extradition of Osama bin Laden, would not have been possible some years ago. The creation of the Terrorism Prevention Branch, as part of the larger Office for Drug Control and Crime Prevention in Vienna, is the best example of the growing awareness and readiness of the international community to actively cooperate in the fight against terrorism.

This international cooperation has resulted also in the decrease in state sponsorship of international terrorism. Today only Iran, Syria, and Afghanistan can be considered real sponsors or supporters of terrorist organizations and even they are constrained to more caution and cover in their activity.

THE IMPLICATIONS OF THE SEPTEMBER 11 ATTACKS

Although the U.S. administration feared a major terrorist attack against American targets during the year 2001 by the network of Osama bin Laden and his allies in the Islamist camp, the strikes against the World Trade Center towers in New York and the Pentagon building in Washington (and possibly the intent to attack the White House or the Capitol)—symbols of American economic and military power—surprised the security and political authorities:

- The expectations were of attacks against American targets abroad and not against the heart of the U.S. territory.

- This was indeed a unique terrorist operation: simultaneous hijackings of four planes, the use of trained pilots to arrive at the chosen target, multiple teams of suicide terrorists ready to act in concert and sacrifice their lives (although if looked at more closely, the various elements of this complex, precise, and coordinated attack seem quite familiar to the terrorism specialist and have been already applied or planned in the past, albeit disjointedly).[20]
- The security systems of the U.S. aviation infrastructure (airports, planes, training, personnel) proved to be completely inadequate to the necessities of a superpower confronted with a continuous and relentless anti-American terrorist offensive.
- The subsequent anthrax campaign by simple letters mailed through the federal postal structure also proved the unpreparedness of the concerned authorities, considering that the country invested a large amount of money and technological effort in preparing itself for WMD attacks since the mid-1990s.
- The anthrax attacks also point, according to the last official estimations, to the potential threat of domestic radical elements which could be involved in this plot, allied, at least objectively, to the external enemies of the nation.

The United States has considered the attacks as a declaration of war against the American nation, comparable or even worse than the Pearl Harbor Japanese attack in World War II. Therefore, it has declared a "War on Terrorism," without defining clearly all its goals and stages, but asserting that it will be a long, complex, and arduous campaign. In order to wage this global war against terrorist networks and the states supporting and sponsoring them, the United States has formed a coalition comprising most of the European states, Pakistan, Russia, Muslim countries in Central Asia, Turkey, India, and others.

The first stage in the war on terrorism has been to destroy the Taliban regime and the al-Qaed'a infrastructure in Afghanistan. This goal has been largely and, surprisingly, quickly achieved, although the arrest or killing of Osama bin Laden and his main deputies and Mullah Omar, the Taliban leader, has not yet been attained. It is clear that the United States will continue relentlessly the pursuit of these leaders and of the remnants of the huge Islamist networks connected with al-Qaed'a.

The next months will witness the continuation of the war, mainly against the states that harbor Islamist terrorist networks or cells, like Somalia, Yemen, Sudan, Syria, Lebanon, and also Iraq and Iran, two states that present an enhanced strategic threat because of their efforts to achieve nuclear capability, besides the existing chemical and biological weapons they already possess. The war will include also the fight against Islamist terrorists and guerrillas in the Philippines, Indonesia, Chechnya, Kashmir, and others.

The war will be waged on different parallel levels: diplomatic, economic, financial, political, and also military moves or strikes, depending on the conditions and the necessities of the moment or the arena involved. One of the main problems facing the planners of this war is the sensitivity of Muslim and Arab countries, which could be threatened by internal instability and turmoil as a result of the concentrated effort against the Islamist radicals. Countries such as Egypt, Saudi Arabia, Pakistan, Indonesia, and Malaysia will find it difficult not only to participate in this campaign but also even to support it verbally.

Therefore, it can be predicted that in the near future we will witness attempts by the remnants of the al-Qaed'a networks to avenge the Afghanistan debacle and strike at U.S., Western, and other coalition targets and assets. The opening of new fronts by the coalition against Somalia, Hizballah, or Iraq will provoke the appearance of new radical elements ready to strike back and try to stop or retaliate against what they will consider the "aggressors."

In light of the "high standards" and challenge put forward by the September 11 terrorists, it can be posited that the future attacks could attempt to reach the same operational and destructive level or even to surpass it. In this sense, the main targets could be:

- Civilian chemical or nuclear facilities (one of the most frightening scenarios)
- Aviation infrastructures and civil planes (the planes becoming themselves a weapon in the hands of terrorists, as demonstrated by the September 11 attacks and Richard Reid's attempt to blow up an American Airlines plane in the air)
- Governmental buildings and embassies (several plans to bomb American embassies have been foiled lately in Europe and Singapore; see also the suicide attack on the Indian Parliament)
- High buildings and public places, such as stadiums or malls
- Military facilities and targets (like the suicide bombing against the USS *Cole*)
- The sarin attack in Tokyo and the recent anthrax campaign prove that low-level chemical, biological, or radiological attacks could also be waged against some of the above targets, although as already proved by the last events, the limited physical damage will be greatly enhanced by their psychological, moral, and political effects.

CONCLUSION

The September 11 attacks confirmed the evaluation that terrorist organizations, and, mainly the radical Islamist ones, would continue to strike with extreme conventional means at U.S., Western, and other targets and will try to escalate their assaults, although the exceptional al-Qaed'a operation surprised even the more pessimistic observers.

The subsequent anthrax campaign also confirmed the expectations for a limited low-level biological or chemical attack, but with huge psychological, moral, and socioeconomical consequences.

The next months and years will see the continuation of the campaign against terrorism and its state supporters on a global level, accompanied by internal and regional instability in the Middle East, Central and Southeast Asia, with possible direct implications on the Muslim communities in the Western world.

International terrorism, mainly by Islamist radicals, will continue to present a serious tactical and strategic threat to the United States, the Western democratic world, and countries with large concentrations of Muslim communities or confronting ethnic and religious conflicts with Muslim populations. The terrorist attacks will try to achieve mass destruction and casualties and there is the potential for limited use of WMD.

It is possible that some local ethnic or ideological conflicts outside the Muslim world, like those in Northern Ireland, Spain, Colombia, or Peru, will be more easily solved within the context of the ongoing campaign against terrorism, as it appeared from the agreement of the IRA to decommission its weapons or the FARC acceptance of a government ultimatum to retreat from occupied zones in Colombia and to restart the peace negotiations.

The last months have again demonstrated the unique importance of good inside intelligence on all levels—tactical, operational, and strategic—based on all possible sources. They have also brought forth the absolute necessity of close international cooperation in the fight against the single terrorist individual or cell and against the military infrastructure of states sponsoring international terrorism.

Above all, the murderous attacks against the WTC in New York, as well as the subsequent military actions against the al-Qaed'a infrastructure and the Taliban regime in Afghanistan, have proven that terrorism is not actually a tool for the weak to wage a psychological and political struggle against a stronger enemy, but a potential threat to humanity and its future peaceful development. In the event terrorist organizations or rogue states would be allowed to produce, achieve control over, and use chemical, biological, or nuclear weapons, whole cities, populations, and cultures could become victims of this blind desire for conquest and destruction.

NOTES

1. There were 273 international terrorist attacks during 1998, a drop from the 304 attacks recorded in 1997 and the lowest annual total since 1971. Yet, the total number

of persons killed or wounded in terrorist attacks was the highest on record: 741 persons died, and 5,952 persons suffered injuries. See *Patterns of Global Terrorism–1998*, U.S. State Department.

2. During the 1980s, several American planes had explosions on board but landed safely with a minimum of casualties on board and, in at least three or four cases, attacks against Israeli airplanes were foiled or aborted for technical failures.

3. See Brian Jenkins in the forward to *The New Terrorism: Changing Terrorism in a Changing World*, RAND Publications (1999), p. vii.

4. Founded in 1976, the LTTE is the most powerful Tamil group in Sri Lanka. The LTTE began its armed conflict with the Sri Lankan government in 1983 and relies on a guerrilla strategy that includes the use of terrorist tactics. The group's elite Black Tiger squad conducts suicide bombings against important targets. The Tigers control most of the northern and eastern coastal areas of Sri Lanka but have conducted operations throughout the island.

The Hizballah (Party of God) is an umbrella organization of various radical Shi'ite groups and organizations in Lebanon led by religious clerics, who see in the adoption of Iranian Khomeinist doctrine a solution to the Lebanese political malaise. This includes the use of terror as a means of attaining political objectives. The organization was established following Israel's 1982 war in Lebanon and an increased Iranian presence and influence there.

Hamas as an acronym that stands for Harakat almukaawamat al-islaamiya (Movement of Islamic Resistance). The movement was founded by Sheikh Ahmad Yassin in Gaza in 1987. The Hamas is a radical Islamist organization which became active in the early stages of the first Palestinian *intifada* (uprising), operating primarily in the Gaza Strip but also in the West Bank. The Hamas has played a major role in violent fundamentalist subversion and radical terrorist operations against Israel. It defined its highest priority as jihad (Holy War) for the liberation of Palestine and the establishment of an Islamic Palestine "from the Mediterranean Sea to the Jordan River."

The PKK was born out of the leftist student organizations in Turkey in the 1960s with the goal to set up an independent Kurdish state in southeastern Turkey. In keeping with its Marxist ideology, the PKK initially saw itself as part of the worldwide Marxist revolution. Its founding and ideological base was primarily the work of one man, Abdullah Ocalan, who established the group and laid down its goals, strategy, and structure. Although the PKK was born in Turkey, it operated out of Syria and the Beka'a valley in Lebanon under Syrian control from 1980 until it was ousted in 1998 under heavy Turkish pressure.

Al-Qaed'a is a multinational support group which funds and orchestrates the activities of Islamist militants worldwide. It grew out of the Afghan war against the Soviets, and its core members consist of Afghan war veterans from all over the Muslim world. It was established around 1988 by the Saudi militant millionaire Osama bin Laden. Based in Afghanistan, bin Laden used an extensive international network to maintain a loose connection between Muslim extremists in diverse countries. The organization's primary goal is the overthrow of what it sees as the corrupt and heretical governments of Muslim states, and their replacement with the rule of *Sharia* (Islamic law). Al-Qaed'a is intensely anti-Western, and views the United States in particular as the prime enemy of Islam.

5. In Nairobi, where the U.S. embassy was located in a congested downtown area, 291 persons were killed in the attack, and about 5,000 were wounded. In Dar es Salaam the blast killed ten Tanzanians, including seven local embassy employees, and injured seventy-seven persons, including one U.S. citizen.

During the violent *intifada* of 2001, dozens of Israeli civilians have been killed by numerous suicide attacks waged by the radical Islamist Hamas and Palestinian Islamic Jihad. The retaliatory Israeli military strikes to these attacks have raised the already high number of Palestinian civilians killed or wounded during the violent events of the last year and a half.

6. The Tamil extremist organization LTTE is responsible for the largest number of suicide attacks (some 170 from a total of some 280 recorded all over the world). For instance, at the end of December 1999, a woman suicide bomber attempted to kill Sri Lankan president Chandrika Kumaratunga at an election rally. The president escaped with relatively minor injuries, but at least twenty-six people were killed and more than 100 wounded by the blast. A week later, a suicide bomber killed herself and twelve others in front of the prime minister's office in the Sri Lankan capital. At least twenty-nine people were injured in the explosion. The prime minister was not in the building at the time of the blast.

The PKK used mainly women in its suicide operations. Since the arrest of PKK leader Ocalan and his trial in Turkey in February 1999, this mode of operation has been practically abandoned by the organization.

7. In the assassination of Rajib Gandhi, eighteen Indians were killed. On November 19, 1995, a suicide bomber of the Egyptian Al-Gama'a al-Islamiyya (The Islamic Group, IG) drove a vehicle into the Egyptian embassy compound in Islamabad, killing at least sixteen persons and injuring some sixty others. The bomb destroyed the entire compound and caused damage and injuries within a half-mile radius.

8. The PIJ (Harakat al-Jihad al-Islami al-Filastini) has in recent years become the most prominent Palestinian terrorist group to adopt the Islamic Jihad ideology. It views Israel, the "Zionist Jewish entity," as the main enemy and strives for the liberation of all of Palestine. This is to be accomplished by guerilla groups, led by a revolutionary vanguard, which carry out terrorist attacks aimed at weakening Israel.

9. The IRA (Provisional Irish Republican Arm, The Provos) is a radical terrorist group formed in 1969 as the clandestine armed wing of Sinn Fein, a legal political movement dedicated to removing British forces from Northern Ireland and unifying Ireland. The organization has a leftist orientation, and is organized into small, tightly knit cells under the leadership of the Army Council.

The ETA (Euskadi ta Askatasuna—The Basque Fatherland and Liberty) group was founded in Spain in 1959 by a group of student activists dissatisfied with the moderate nationalism of the traditional Basque party. The group's aim is the creation of an independent homeland in Spain's Basque region. The group has a loose commitment to Marxism.

The FARC (Fuerzas Armadas Revolucionarias de Colombia) is the largest, best trained, and best equipped guerrilla organization in Colombia. Established in 1966 as the military wing of Colombian Communist Party its goal is to overthrow the government and ruling class. It has been anti–United States since its inception. FARC operates mainly in Colombia, with occasional operations in Venezuela, Panama, and Ecuador. They have approximately 6,000 to 7,000 armed combatants.

The FIS (the Islamic Salvation Front) was created in February 1989 in Algeria as a network of small, informal groups which grew rapidly, filed for legal recognition, and was certified as a political party. Algerians went to the polls in December 1991 to vote in their first multiparty democratic election. The FIS won a clear-cut victory, but the army resumed its historic role, took power, and outlawed the FIS. As a result, the FIS began a terrorist and guerrilla war against the military government which degenerated into civil war, fragmentation of the Islamist movement, and the appearance of even more radical organizations, like the Groupe Islamique Arme (Islamic Armed Group—GIA), responsible for a series of massacres of innocent civilians and for the internationalization of terrorist activity toward Europe and North America.

The al-Jihad is an Egyptian Islamist group active since the late 1970s. The movement is divided into two factions: one led by Ayman al-Zawahiri—in Afghanistan—and the Vanguards of Conquest (Talaa' al-Fateh) led by Ahmad Husayn Agiza. Al-Zawahiri is a key leader in terrorist financier Osama Bin Laden's al-Qaed'a. Like al-Gama'at al-Islamiyya, the Jihad factions regard Sheikh Omar Abd-al Rahman, imprisoned in the United States, as their spiritual leader.

Al-Gama'a al-Islamiyyah (the Islamic Group) emerged during the 1970s as a phenomenon rather than an organized group, mainly in Egyptian jails and later on in some of the Egyptian universities. The phenomenon of the Islamic Group was mainly affected by the militant ideology of Sayyid Qutb (executed in 1966), who paved the way for the establishment of several Islamic militant branches in Egypt and the Arab world.

10. Since October 2001 the Palestinian Authority, under the direct guidance of Chairman Yasser Arafat, has waged the so called "al-Aksa Intifada," an already year and a half long terrorist and guerrilla war against Israel, transforming the nationalistic conflict between the Palestinian and Israeli nations into a religious war using suicide terrorism as the extreme weapon of destruction.

11. For an understanding of the dogma, ideology, and operational activity of Aum Shinrikyo, see Shimazono Susumu, "In the Wake of Aum: The Formation and Transformation of a Universe of Belief," *Japanese Journal of Religious Studies* 223/3 (1995): 381–415; Manabu Watanabe, "Religion and Violence in Japan Today: A Chronological and Doctrinal Analysis of Aum Shinrikyo," *Terrorism and Political Violence* 4 (Winter 1998): 80–100; Ely Karmon, "Aum-Shinrikyo, the Anti-Semitic Doomsday Cult: A Dangerous Comeback," in *Anti-Semitism Worldwide 1998/1999*, (Stephen Roth Institute for the Study of Contemporary Anti-Semitism and Racism, Tel Aviv University, distributed by the University of Nebraska Press), pp. 5–15.

12. See the section on this cult at CESNUR (Centro Studi sulle Nuove Religioni, Torino, Italy) website at www.cesnur.org/testi/uganda_002.htm.

13. In March 1995 Shamil Basayev's men, one of the leaders of the Chechen dissidents, put a small container with radioactive isotopes in a park in Moscow and threatened a nuclear attack on the city's population. In June 1995 a commando under the leadership of the same Basayev seized more than 1,500 hostages in the hospital of the city of Budionovsk.

14. In the first half of September 1999 more than 200 people were killed in two bombings of apartment blocks in Moscow, 64 in a small town in Daghestan, and 17 in the town of Vokgodonsk. As a consequence more than 11,000 ethnic Chechens have been expulsed from Moscow.

15. ICT is a research institute and think tank dedicated to developing innovative public policy solutions to international terrorism. The institute applies an integrated, solutions-oriented approach built on a foundation of real-world and practical experience. ICT is part of the Interdisciplinary Center in Herzliya, the first private university in Israel.

16. See "Weapons of Mass Destruction: The Threat from Terrorist Organizations," several articles on the subject, in the framework of an international research project during the years 1998–99, by ICT, the Interdisciplinary Center for Technological Analysis and Forecasting at Tel-Aviv University (ICTAF) and the Fondation de la Recherche Stratégique (FRS) in Paris (unpublished).

17. See "Trends in Contemporary International Terrorism" in *Countering Suicide Terrorism: An International Conference* (The International Policy Institute for Counter-terrorisms, Herzliya, 2001): 37–41.

18. Terrorist organizations have produced or acquired liquid and ceramic explosives in the 1970s and 1980s, fertilizer explosives in the World Trade Center attack, suicide belts, etc.

19. The Aum Shinrikyo tried to produce and use biological agents, but it failed and passed to the production of chemical agents, mainly sarin, which was used in the 1995 attack in the Tokyo underground.

20. A coordinated hijacking of four planes had already taken place. In September 1970, the Popular Front for the Liberation of Palestine diverted a Pan Am airliner to Cairo while three others—TWA, Swissair, and BOAC planes—were diverted to Dawson airport in Jordan. All were blown up on the ground.

Based on intelligence, the hijacking of a plane in order to crash it in a populated area has been feared in Israel since the mid-1970s. On May 24, 2001, a small Lebanese civilian plane was shot down north of Tel Aviv by Apache attack helicopters because it was feared to be part of a Hizballah suicide operation. In December 1994 an Air France Airbus was hijacked by Algerian GIA terrorists, landed in Marseille for refueling, and was stormed by French counterterrorist teams when it became clear that they were planning a suicide mission over Paris.

Ramzi Yussef, the planner of the first truck-bomb attack on the WTC in 1993, was known to have planned in 1994 the hijacking of twelve U.S. civil planes and their simultaneous explosion in midair.

6

Challenges of the Terrorist Phenomenon in the Twenty-first Century

Ashraf Mohsen

Terrorism has always been a deadly and perilous phenomenon; the technological advances that occurred in the last few decades resulted in the creation of new and much more lethal challenges for human civilization from the terrorist phenomenon. These new challenges arise mainly from the increase in the lethality of terrorist attacks, the new modes of organization of terrorist elements. This unfortunately will lead to increased victimization from terrorism, and when the international community addresses the issue of the victims of terrorism, it should give particular attention to the indirect victims of terror. However, it is essential to correctly identify the danger of the terrorist phenomenon, namely, whether it is a tactical or indeed a strategic threat. The importance of this assessment is that it will determine the best way to effectively and efficiently combat terrorism. For if terrorism is simply a tactical threat, then the best way to combat it will be through limited (or even extensive) security means. However, if we correctly identify terrorism as a strategic threat, then the best way of trying to limit the numbers of victims of terrorist crimes will have to be through political as well as security means. Policymakers will have to realize that combating terrorism should be a long-term policy that will have to address the issue of eradicating the causes as well as the manifestations of the terrorist phenomenon.

In addition, the international cooperation that is badly needed to combat terrorism is still hampered by the same problems and obstacles that prevented the creation of a viable international regime against terrorism. Even worse, some international efforts aimed at combating terrorism have created an atmosphere that hampers the efforts aimed at ridding the world of this deadly phenomenon.

INCREASED LETHALITY AND VICTIMIZATION OF TERRORISM

Increased Lethality of Terrorist Acts

The technological and scientific advances that one may say characterized the last century—advances that increased the standard of living, improved the quality of life and the quality of medical care—meant among other things a marked increase in life expectancy in most nations. However, and as if Nature is determined to keep Earth's population under control, the same technological and scientific advances also included monstrous advances in the field of manufacturing radical weaponry (conventional as well as weapons of mass destruction) able to inflict colossal damages and the loss of lives. Thus, despite the obvious decrease in the number of terrorist acts committed annually, the number of fatalities resulting from terrorist acts has drastically increased.[1]

A simple review of terrorist attacks and the weapons seized from terrorist elements in the last decades shows the proliferation of immensely lethal weapons in the hands of criminal elements, especially terrorists. From this perspective, each and every terrorist attack by almost any terrorist group has the potential for inflicting a great number of fatalities on any nation in the world today.

Furthermore, there is the growing risk that some terrorist group or another may acquire weapons of mass destruction. The use or even the threat of use of such weapons by any terrorist group will blow the number of fatalities arising from terrorist acts to unfathomable proportions. The fact that there has already been a terrorist attack using weapons of mass destruction only highlights the danger and indeed the possibility that other terrorist groups may indeed attempt the use of weapons of mass destruction.[2] Such a threat is no longer valid only in fiction, as the proliferation of the technology and expertise needed to manufacture almost all kinds of weapons of mass destruction—whether chemical, biological, or nuclear—meants that these weapons can be produced by an increasing number of existing terrorist groups.

The increase in the numbers of fatalities and the the growth in the number of terrorists who thrive to maximize the number of their victims is motivated by a rational and logical reason, not necessarily by an irrational desire to shed blood. The fact that there are two major elements of terrorism, the use of violence and the desire to obtain publicity or propaganda, is an accepted axiom. For terrorist groups to be able to get the media attention that they crave, there is an added competition to commit yet more grotesque and spectacular crimes, and the measure of their success unfortunately has become the number of their victims. Furthermore, the advances in telecommunications technology increased the reach and the effectiveness of terrorist acts. It became much easier for terrorist attacks to receive maximum exposure for high profile acts no matter where such acts were committed. The significance of this development lies in the fact that terrorists gained the ability to terrorize and spread fear and panic to virtually all areas of the globe. Any terrorist attack, no matter how far away it occurs, will shock and terrorize the public around the world who will witness the devastation firsthand on their television screens in their homes.

In addition, it can be expected that terrorists will seek to attack "soft targets," especially given the marked increase in the quality of protection that most world leaders enjoy, as well as the protection of governmental and other sensitive installations. By definition, "soft targets" means unprotected and unsuspecting civilian groups, or indeed tourists, who are not necessarily in need of a specialized counterterrorism protection or security. The risks and costs of attacking such groups can be minimal for a terrorist organization while at the same time it will ensure such an organization the maximum number of fatalities, and thus full media attention.

The reasons for the increased fatalities in terrorist attacks can be summarized as follows:

- The increased abilities of terrorist elements to obtain more destructive arsenals.
- The increase in terrorist acts committed by extreme religious groups and cults, the operations of which are characterized by high numbers of casualties.
- The surge of reliance of terrorists groups on "amateurs" who have no scruples in using deadly methods without full appraisal of the consequences.
- The increase in organizational capacities, effectiveness of the leadership of terrorist groups, and acquisition of the know-how to manufacture deadly weapons and methods of concealment.
- The perception by terrorists that international public opinion has become less sensitive to limited terrorist acts, and thus they began to seek to commit more spectacular and deadly acts.
- The increased technological abilities of terrorist groups, which allowed them to use cheap and legal materials to manufacture highly destructive explosives that can inflict costly damages.[3]

Increased Victimization of Terrorist Acts

When the issue of increased fatalities is addressed, it is pertinent to address the issue of the victims of terrorism. Insufficient attention has been given to the plight of victims of terror. One explanation for this partial neglect is that most direct victims of terrorist acts are innocent bystanders. Their plight in most cases had nothing to do with whatever action that they might have taken, but rather with their being in the wrong place at the wrong time. Another explanation is the fact that the attention span of the media is rather short, and it gradually dissipates after the terrorist incident. Moreover, it is perceived by some that the continued media attention to the victims of a particular terrorist incident manages to perpetuate the attention given to the criminals who committed the terrorist act. Regardless of the reason, the plight of the victims of terror should be addressed. United Nations specialized agencies, such as the World Health Organization, should sponsor programs aimed at training specialists in post-traumatic stress and other related effects.

However, more important, there has been almost no attention given to the problem of the "Indirect Victims of Terrorism." This problem relates to innocent people who were severely affected by the aftermath of terrorist acts though they were not physically hurt by the act itself. The most pertinent examples in this regard are the indirect victims of the Luxor attack in Egypt in 1997.[4] The indirect victims of this terrorist act were the tens of thousands of people in the south of Egypt who were dependent on the tourist industry for their livelihood. The loss of revenue that Egypt incurred due to this incident exceeded US$2 billion in 1997–1998 alone. The al-Gama'a al-Islamiyya which waged this heinous crime intended for those indirect victims to suffer as much as those direct victims who were killed. And just as the murders were indiscriminate, the fallout of the attack was also indiscriminate; almost all categories of people were affected: travel guides, hotel workers, drivers, shop owners, doctors, etc. The entire economic activities of several Egyptian regions were severely affected after the attacks in Luxor. Several factories that supplied goods to these areas went bankrupt due to the drastic fall in demand for their products. The terrorist rationale for the atrocities they committed in Luxor was their desire to deal a severe and deadly blow to the Egyptian tourism industry, which is a major source of foreign currency for the Egyptian economy. They hoped that their actions would result in denying the Egyptian people revenues from tourism and to prevent the flow of foreign investments to Egypt, so as to lower the standard of living and heighten discontent and poverty. Thousands of Egyptian families found themselves, almost overnight, without any means of subsistence.

Thus, when the plight of victims is addressed, the indirect victims of terrorism should be taken into account. The wave of terrorist acts that plagued Egypt from 1992–1997, and which was successfully combated by the Egyptian government and people, did not result solely in the death of around 400 innocent civilians. It created a state of poverty and impoverishment for tens of thousands of Egyptian families who were severely hurt by the loss of over US$8 billion in lost revenues. In case the international community decides to establish funds for the victims of terrorism, the plight of the indirect victims of terrorism should not be ignored.

INTERNATIONAL RESPONSE TO TERRORISM

Despite the fact there is an almost universal awareness that no country alone can successfully eradicate terrorism, and that international cooperation is a necessary prerequisite to combat terrorism, the level of international cooperation that exists leaves much to be desired. The obstacles that blocked the path of the international community to reach a consensus on the definition of terrorism and its underlying causes or to agree on the strategy needed to combat this phenomenon are still very much in evidence. In addition, some of the policies adopted by some states have adverse effects even though the policies are designed to make the world inhospitable to terrorism.

Counterterrorism Conventions

It is important to note that the international community showed an early interest in cooperation to combat terrorism as far back as 1926. One of the recommendations of the First International Conference of Penal Code in 1926 was related to the need to conclude an international convention to combat terrorism. In fact, the issue of international terrorism was discussed in conferences of the international association for unifying the penal code that were held in 1931, 1934, and 1935. And though these efforts were unsuccessful in concluding a comprehensive international instrument, they nevertheless contributed in crystallizing the international legal thought in that field. The first formal proposal to conclude such a comprehensive agreement to combat terrorism was submitted by Romania to the League of Nations in 1926. This drive gained an additional momentum toward the end of 1934, when France submitted a proposal to the League of Nations after the assassination of King Alexander I and the French foreign minister in Marseilles earlier that year.

The efforts of the League of Nations resulted in the conclusion of the Convention for the Prevention and Punishment of Terrorism in Geneva in April 1937, which was the first international legal instrument to combat terrorism. And though twenty-four states signed that convention,[5] it never went into force because of the outbreak of the Second World War, and the ultimate demise of the then-existing international regime (the League of Nations). As a matter of fact, only one state managed to ratify that convention.[6]

The search for an international legally binding instrument to combat terrorism has been continued by the United Nations since its inception. There proved to be, however, an insurmountable difficulty in that regard, namely, the absence of a unanimously approved definition of terrorism and the inability of the international community to reach a differentiation between terrorism and legitimate national struggle for liberation from colonialism and foreign occupation. The work of the first ad hoc committee on terrorism was hampered by the existing ideological and political differences between states—differences that manifested themselves in heated arguments over issues such as the definition of terrorism, the differentiation between terrorism and legitimate armed struggle, the causes of terrorism as well as the issue of state terrorism. These problems prevented the committee[7] from submitting a viable plan of action that the international community could adopt to combat terrorism in its report.[8] The deliberations of the above-mentioned committee simply exposed some of the differences between the member states of the United Nations over the issue of international terrorism. It is perhaps noteworthy that the First Ad Hoc Committee on International Terrorism was comprised of only thirty-five states.[9] A report was finally submitted to the Thirty-Fourth General Assembly of the United Nations in 1979. The UN General Assembly adopted the recommendation of the ad hoc committee related to practical measures of cooperation for the speedy elimination of the problem of international terrorism. The General Assembly merely took "note" of the study contained in that report of the underlying causes of international terrorism.[10]

The failure of the international community in reaching a definition of terrorism, or a comprehensive convention to combat terrorism, led to the adoption of a totally different approach. Instead of working toward reaching a definition of terrorism in the context of a comprehensive international convention, the international community concentrated its efforts on criminalizing the different acts that constitute the terrorist crime—"the corpus delicti" approach. The aim became one of reaching thematic conventions that dealt with specific terrorist acts, such as hijacking planes, interference with civil aviation or maritime transport, the taking of hostages, or the assassination of internationally protected persons, as well as other manifestations of terrorist offenses. These legal instruments were always in reaction to waves of terrorist criminal acts that compelled the world community to conclude thematic conventions were useful to combat terrorism.

Four conventions and/or protocols criminalized the hijacking of aeroplanes and the destruction of or interference with airport operations and civil aviation. The first of these conventions was concluded in Tokyo in 1963 and the latest was concluded in Montreal in 1988. These conventions came about as a response to the favorite modus operandi of terrorist groups in the 1960s, 1970s, and 1980s, namely, hijacking airplanes and attacking the infrastructure of civil aviation.

Two conventions related to terrorist attacks targeting maritime navigation and fixed maritime platforms were held in response to some terrorist operations in the mid-1980s, in particular the attack on the passenger ship *Achille Lauro*.

A convention to mark plastic explosives to aid in their detection came in response to the increased use of such weapons by terrorist groups and the ease with which they can be smuggled. The increased desire by the international community to conclude that agreement was a result of the attacks on Pan Am flight 103 over Scotland on August 21, 1988, and UTA flight 772 in Niger on September 19, 1989. The purpose of such an act by its nature and context, is to intimidate a population or to compel a government or an international organization to do or to abstain from doing an act.[11] Needless to say, this particular article consumed a major part of the deliberations of the second Ad Hoc Committee on Terrorism (established under UN resolution 51/210 of 1996).[12] These deliberations, which took place in March and late September and early October 1999, clearly show the decrease in the differences between the positions of the different member states of the United Nations over how to deal with the problem of international terrorism. There were still marked divisions between the different states over this issue. However, these deliberations should be compared with the deliberations of the First Ad Hoc Committee established under GA Resolution 27/3 034.[13] Such a comparison will show the positive development that took place in the international community's awareness of the need to resolve the existing differences.

In addition to the international conventions to combat and eliminate international terrorism, five regional organizations succeeded in concluding regional conventions to combat terrorism, namely, the Organization of American States, the European Union, the South Asian Union for Regional Cooperation (SAARC), the Arab League, and the Organization of African Unity. The latest of these conventions, the Convention of Organization of African Unity on the Prevention and Combating of Terrorism is among the best legal instruments in the field of combating terrorism.

There is a great potential for the role of regional and subregional organizations in combating terrorism. Regional organizations can agree on joint solutions to fight the infrastructure of terrorism. Furthermore, the member-states of such organizations can agree on practical policies to prevent the movement of terrorists and the illegal arms traffic.

Some Negative Aspects of International Efforts in Counterterrorism

It should be acknowledged that the international community made significant progress in the fight against international terrorism, despite the lack of consensus on a universally accepted definition of terrorism, and the political and ideological differences between states that do not help efforts to stem the terrorist phenomenon.

In this regard, the "corpus delicti" approach adopted in international conventions in the field of counterterrorism is particularly important. More important, one should appreciate the contributions made by the General Assembly of the United Nations in condemning terrorism in all its forms and manifestations. In this context one should mention that since 1969 the General Assembly of the United Nations adopted over twenty-seven resolutions that deal with the issue of international terrorism, whether directly or indirectly, starting with GA Resolution 24/2551[14] and ending with the latest of these resolutions, namely, GA Resolution 54/110.[15]

It is correct to consider GA Resolutions 49/60,[16] which contained "The Declaration on Measures to Eliminate Terrorism," and Resolution 51/210,[17] which attempted to embark on a plan of action for the international community against terrorism and contained "The Declaration to Supplement the 1994 Declaration on Measures to Eliminate International Terrorism," as the most important of the above mentioned GA Resolutions.

Nevertheless, these significant efforts not only fall far short of the necessary work that is needed but, more important, were accompanied by individual actions of some states and unacceptable media coverage that undermined some of the efforts and contributions undertaken. Even worse, they created waves of sympathy with terrorist elements and even led to an increasing number of people identifying themselves with some of the menacing terrorist elements, even if they disapproved of their methods. Due to the rise of extremist terrorist elements that unjustifiably claim that they are "Islamic," there occurred, in some reports, outrageous and unjustifiable statements that link the godly and holy Islamic religion and culture to the heinous crime of terrorism. Misguided media reports, and some ill-willed actors, tried to link a whole religion and its culture to this crime. This is as dangerous an endeavor as terrorism itself. No religion or culture should be linked to this crime; otherwise, the international community will not be fulfilling its goal of ostracizing terrorism and the terrorist elements—as they should—but on the contrary, it will be inadvertently alienating hundreds of millions of Muslims from the legitimate and necessary fight against the crime of terrorism. States should always be aware of the danger that their actions might be ill perceived by the public in other nations. Such misperceptions might certainly contribute to the failure of the counterterrorism policy deployed. One should always remember that the fight against terrorism is not only to prevent terrorist elements from doing harm but more important, to also alienate terrorists from the public so that they shall not be successful in their endeavors to destabilize either internal regimes or regional or international alliances.

In addition, some member states of the international community, under the guise of the sacred duty to protect human rights, offer the right of abode to criminal and terrorists elements who use the territories of such states as safe havens to wage terrorist crimes against other nations. Even worse, some states abuse the 1951 Geneva conventions related to the rights of refugees, which prohibit granting political asylum to the perpetrators of criminal offenses. As a matter of fact, article I(F) of the Refugee Convention enables states to ensure that asylum is not extended to perpetrators of violence and other inhuman acts such as genocide. The Office of the United Nations High Commissioner for Refugees on October 7, 1997, stated that "with regard to terrorism in particular, article I(F)(b) requires exclusion from refugee status of a person with respect to whom there are serious reasons for considering that . . . he [or she] has committed a serious nonpolitical crime outside the country of refuge."[18]

NEW TRENDS IN THE TERRORIST PHENOMENON

There is no evidence that suggests that the terrorist phenomenon will decrease; on the contrary, there are reasons that suggest quite the opposite. Furthermore, it is expected that the mode of terrorist organizations will develop so that it will be harder for relevant agencies to successfully contain them.

Reasons for the Continued Surge of Terrorism

International terrorism will unfortunately increase, especially in light of the following:

- Terrorism remains the ideal weapon of the weak; it has an increasing appeal for racist, religious fanatics as well as minorities who lack the military capabilities to confront their opponents.
- This holds especially true for states that are unable to confront their opponents in a conventional warfare paradigm. Such states may resort to waging indirect war by proxies. The best weapon in such a pseudo-war paradigm is terrorist organizations.
- Through increased links between terrorists and organized crime, some terrorist organizations have begun to have access to immense sources of funding through the trade in narcotics.
- Terrorism remains as a way of asserting identity and attracting attention to the extent that for some elements waging terrorist acts has become an end in itself.
- Terrorism holds a special appeal to religious extremists who believe in the destruction of existing regimes to create a future world order based on their convictions.

Development of the Terrorist Phenomenon

The organizational structures of terrorist groups are becoming increasingly flexible, and decentralized cells that do not follow classic modes of organizations (such as the Abu Nidal organization) are becoming the norm. Furthermore, such organizations are becoming transnational rather than national cells.

Terrorists groups are increasing their reliance on high-tech equipment, especially in the fields of weaponry and communications. This is evident by the increased use of the Internet by terrorist organizations, whether to disseminate their political message, for incitement, or as a method of communications between the various transnational cells.

In addition, new terrorists organizations are in command of higher resources, whether in terms of funding or in human resources. An example of the above is the fact that the Bin Laden organization[19] is reported to have between four and five thousand fighters dispersed in different countries around the world. This should be compared to other classical terrorist organizations such as the Japanese Red Army, whose basic structure contained between thirty to fifty persons, or the Abu Nidal organization, which had less than 500 active members.

We must consider the rise of new and much more lethal religious terrorist organizations that will actively seek the acquisition and use of weapons of mass destruction, and the rise of new forms of terrorism, namely, those that engage in what is called "Netwar," which is based on loose terrorist structures waging and coordinating their attacks through the Internet.

In addition to the new forms of terrorism, traditional terrorist organizations (such as ethnic separatist or leftist organizations) will continue with their methods of using grenades, explosives, and handguns, albeit with a marked improvement in these weapons (such as the increased explosiveness of bombs and the detonation devices).

CONCLUSION

Despite the progress that has been achieved in combating terrorism, there is still much more that can be done. It is indeed necessary to view—from this perspective—the Egyptian initiative to convene an international summit conference, under the auspices of the United Nations, that would formulate a unified international strategy to combat this crime in all its forms, manifestations, dimensions, and sources. The gathering of all world leaders to combat terrorism will provide an excellent chance to add the necessary weight to this issue and will demonstrate the solidarity of all states—regardless of their ideological, religious, or ethnic compositions—in condemning and combating this deadly phenomenon.

One should be aware that combating terrorism cannot succeed if it is perceived as a security concern or endeavor. For, though terrorism is indeed a crime, it is a strategic and not a tactical threat; therefore, it requires political and strategic solutions. Historical experiences from the dawn of civilization have proven to us, time and time again, that a crime such as terrorism can be eradicated only through a political strategy and not just security measures.

There are two final points that should be emphasized. All countries of the world should cooperate to make the world inhospitable to terrorism. If we do not cooperate closely, then the terrorist danger will certainly threaten us not only with the loss of the lives of victims comparable in number that we have seen in past decades but it will threaten our entire way of life, and it will affect plans for development and raising the standard of living of our peoples as well. The increase in the terrorist threat will have to lead to an increase in security measures that will affect our civil liberties and will force us all to divert much-needed funds from essential development projects to security needs. Moreover, we all have to be prepared that, while all should aim for the elimination of the terrorist threat, one has to be realistic in one's expectations. We should try to contain the danger of terrorism; however, terrorism, like other forms of crime, will never entirely disappear by security means alone. To successfully contain this threat we must also concentrate on the elimination of the underlying causes of terrorism by raising standards of living, educating publics, and promoting democracy around the world. Only such a comprehensive and broad-minded policy may have any hope in successfully tackling the problem of international terrorism.

EPILOGUE

This chapter was written in the beginning of the year 2000, to be submitted to the Ancillary Meeting on Terrorism Victimization: Prevention, Control, and Recovery at the Tenth United Nations Congress on the Prevention of Crime and the Treatment of Offenders on Crime and Justice: Meeting the Challenges of the Twenty-First Century. Apart from some editorial revisions, I have not made any substantial change to the material. Nevertheless, the events of September 11, 2001, which brought the world a great deal of distress, have unfortunately supported the findings and the views reflected in this chapter. The fact is that the plight of the indirect victims of terrorism which I tried to highlight in this chapter outweigh by a huge distance, both qualitatively and quantitatively, those of the direct victims who were injured or killed by any terrorist crime. The sufferings of the people employed in the airline and hotel industries and their families who have lost their means of subsistence or who have lost their livelihood becomes even more apparent. The tragedy perhaps lies in the fact that the numbers of people who were badly affected goes far beyond those who were actually the target of the terrorist crimes. Though New York and Washington were the unfortunate targets of the 11th of September attacks, nevertheless, people in all industries and walks of life in other parts of the United States were seriously and negatively affected. However, this is not the whole picture: economies around the globe were direly affected due to the slump in tourism and airline travel as people from around the world became naturally afraid to travel. The damage that occurred to the people of the United States was also shared by ordinary and innocent people from around the globe as people lost their means of subsistence due to the consequences of these acts.

More important, the events of September 11 and the negative ramifications have proven that terrorism is indeed a strategic and not a tactical concern. The crime committed in September 2001, as well as the international response, proved yet again that only a long-term political and strategic solution can combat terrorism with any reasonable chance of success.

NOTES

The views expressed in this chapter are solely those of its author in his capacity as an individual expert. They should not be construed as portraying the views or positions of the Ministry of Foreign Affairs of the Arab Republic of Egypt.

1. The number of terrorist acts that are committed annually diminished significantly from 484 acts in 1991, to less than 273 act in 1998, which is the lowest number committed since 1971. The number of persons killed or wounded in these attacks was the highest on record where over 700 persons were killed and over 5,000 were wounded.

2. The sarin nerve gas attack on the Tokyo subway system in March 1995 was performed by the "Aum Supreme Truth" (also known as Aum Shinrikyo), which is a Japanese religious cult that was established in 1987 by Shoko Asahara.

3. Perhaps the best example of this is the fact that the cost of manufacturing the bomb that exploded in the World Trade Center on February 26, 1993, in New York was less than US $400; the damages, however, exceeded US$550 million.

4. This relates to the attack by a group of terrorists (belonging to al-Gama'a al-Islamiyya) using assault rifles on a group of Egyptians and tourists in the courtyard of the Temple of Hatshepsut in the city of Luxor in the south of Egypt. There were sixty-eight fatalities in that incident.

5. The Convention for the Prevention and Punishment of Terrorism was signed by the following states: Albania, Argentine Republic, Belgium, Bulgaria, Cuba, Dominican Republic, Egypt, Ecuador, Spain, Estonia, France, Greece, Haiti, India, Monaco, Norway, Netherlands, Peru, Romania, Czechoslovakia, Turkey, Union of Soviet Socialist Republics, Venezuela, and Yugoslavia.

6. On January 1, 1941, India ratified the Convention for the Prevention and Punishment of Terrorism.

7. Established by United Nations General Assembly Resolution 27/3034 in 1972.

8. "Report of the Ad Hoc Committee on International terrorism," Official Records of the General Assembly: Thirty-Fourth Session. Supplement no. 37.

9. The Ad Hoc Committee on International Terrorism was composed of thirty-five states appointed by the president of the General Assembly under the terms of paragraph 9 of General Assembly Resolution 27/3034 of 18 December 1972.

10. United Nations General Assembly Resolution No 34/145 of 17 December 1979.

11. United Nations General Assembly Resolution No 34/145 of 17 December 1979, Article 2: 3–4.

12. United Nations General Assembly Resolution No 51/210 of 17 December 1996.

13. United Nations General Assembly Resolution 27/3034 of 18 December 1972.

14. United Nations General Assembly Resolution No 24/2551 of 12 December 1969.

15. United Nations General Assembly Resolution No 54/110 of 9 December 1999.

16. United Nations General Assembly Resolution No 49/60 of 9 December 1994.

17. United Nations General Assembly Resolution No 51/210 of 17 December 1996.

18. United Nations, Economic and Social Council, Commission on Human Rights, Fifty-fourth session, Item 9 of the provisional agenda: Human Rights and Terrorism. Note by the Secretary General E/CN.4/1998/48, 24 December 1997.

19. Al-Qaed'a

7

Victims of the Sarin Gas Attack at Tokyo Subway

Ayako Uchiyama

INTRODUCTION

At approximately 8 A.M. on March 20, 1995, an incident of "daymare" occurred. Sarin gas was released from containers wrapped in newspapers and
left inside the trains of three subway lines (Hibiya, Marunouchi, and Chiyoda
lines). This attack was centered on Kasumigaseki, through which all of the
subway lines run and where many national central government buildings are
located. The sarin gas was released in several cars, killing twelve persons
and injuring more than five thousand.

Sarin gas (methyl phosphonofluoride isopropyl) was discovered in Germany before World War II in the process of manufacturing an organic phos-
phorus insecticide. Sarin gas is highly volatile and colorless and is heavier
than air. In people, it is absorbed through respiratory organs and the skin,
causing vomiting, contraction of the pupils, headaches, dizziness, respiratory
difficulty, and other complications.

Sarin gas is an extremely lethal substance used in chemical weapons; it has
no recognized purpose other than to wound or kill human beings. The use
of this antisocial chemical weapon for indiscriminate killing in public transport at rush hour is an atrocity unprecedented not only in Japanese but also
in international criminal history.

Who conducted this incident and why was this incident implemented?
Based on evidence that emerged gradually, the police investigation suggested that this crime was conducted by the religious group Aum Shinrikyo.
Many articles and books on Aum Shinrikyo already exist worldwide.[1] Although their crimes are too numerous to describe in one article, below is a
brief description of crimes by Aum Shinrikyo as understood by the author

based on the literature and what she observed during court proceedings in this case.

CRIMES OF AUM SHINRIKYO

In all, 484 people of the Aum Shinrikyo Group were arrested for violations of the penal code and various other special codes after the sarin gas attack. Asahara, the top planner, is still in court for committing seventeen crimes, including ten homicides and attempted homicides. The first crime by Aum Shinrikyo was conducted in 1988, which was the cremation of a trainee who died by accident; his body was burned and his powdered bones were sprayed into a lake near their buildings in Kamikuishikimura. This is the crime of abandoning a body. The group's leaders thought that the accidental death of a monastic in an Aum-owned building might prevent the Aum group from being recognized as a religious group by the Tokyo metropolitan government. A series of crimes by members of the Aum Shinrikyo showed that once they committed a crime without being arrested, they did not seem to hesitate to commit additional ones.

In Kamikuishikimura, Aum Shinrikyo had built many of buildings for training followers, a residential area for staff members, and an area for research with a military purpose for staff members

The trigger case of police investigation toward Aum Shinrikyo was the kidnapping of an old man. Aum members kidnapped Kiyoshi Kariya, whose sister used to be a monastic and had separated from this group on his suggestion. The Aum group targeted him, kidnapped him (February 25, 1995), and finally killed him. This information was known to the police early in March 1995, then the police started an investigation cryptically.

Among the crimes Aum committed, the following three crimes are the major ones.

Murder of Lawyer T. Sakamoto and His Family in November 1989

The ways of Aum, which compelled the monastics to donate all their possessions to Aum and prevented the monastic from contacting his/her family, were criticized by people such as lawyers and journalists. Asahara and his executive staff discussed this problem and decided to eliminate Sakamoto, a lawyer who took a leadership role in criticizing Aum Shinrikyo. They planned to kill Sakamoto on his way home by injecting him with potassium chloride. Unfortunately, on the day that six Aum members tried to attack lawyer Sakamoto, he was at home because of a national holiday. The attack team decided to break into his unlocked house about 3:00 A.M. when the lawyer, his wife, and his fourteen-month-old son were sleeping. All the

Sakamoto family members were killed and buried in different boondocks and were not recovered until the autumn of 1995.

Matsumoto Miasma in June 1994

At midnight on June 27, 1994, in a residential area in downtown Matsumoto, five people were dead and a few hundred were injured without manifest cause. Later it was identified that sarin gas caused this incident. This was the first recorded incidence of sarin gas use in Japan.

The Health Center in Matsumoto assessed the effect of sarin gas by conducting a follow-up survey on the physiological effects of sarin six months after the incident.[2] At the time, the offender was unknown; however, on January 1, 1995, *Yomiuri Shimbun* carried a report that a soil sample taken from the Aum complex at Kamikuishiki contained an organic compound, a byproduct of the sarin manufacturing process, which was exactly the same compound found in soil samples taken from the site of the Matsumoto gas poisoning in June 1994. Later it became clear that the sarin gas produced by the Aum group was used to attack the apartment house where the judges and the court staff of Matsumoto lived. Their main objective was apparently to examine the effect of the sarin they had succeeded in producing.

Sarin Gas Attack on the Tokyo Subway

Details of the process of this incidence are still being discussed in court, even at the beginning of 2002; however, an outline of the incident follows.

The sarin gas attack incident was a well-organized crime. Almost all executive members of Aum were anxious about a police raid and investigation because they had committed many crimes, though the majority of monastics were not aware of them. The idea to release sarin nerve gas in the Tokyo subway to postpone a police raid occurred to the guru. Early in the morning on March 18, he told H. Murai, minister of Science and Technology in his Aum organizational structure that replicated the Japanese government, to produce sarin. He gave this instruction while in a limousine on the way to Kamikuishikimura after a small party in Tokyo; for this reason, the plot became known as the Limousine Conspiracy. Asahara, Murai, Endo, Aoyama, and two other members were present in the car. Their roles are defined below.

Top Planner

Asahara Shoko (Guru; autonym: Chizuo Matsumoto). He was the organizer and planner of this incident and selected and nominated members to spray sarin.

Leader

Hideo Murai (minister of Science and Technology). He ordered T. Nakagawa to produce sarin to help S. Endo under the guru's direction.

Sub-leader

Yoshihiro Inoue (minister of Intelligence). He organized and arranged details. For example, he insisted that drivers were necessary to take the members to spray the sarin to the station and bring them back afterward. He identified five pairs of individuals (one sarin releaser and one driver) after he had prepared the cars they would use.

Work of Sarin Producing

Seiichi Endo (minister of Health and Welfare), Tomomasa Nakagawa (director of Household Agency), Masami Tsuchiya (minister of Second Health and Welfare), and Endo and Nakagawa were the main producers of sarin; Tsuchiya analyzed the finished product. Around 11 P.M. on March 19, they succeeded in making sarin that was not of high purity. Endo asked the guru if they could wait one day for more pure sarin. The guru replied that the less pure sarin might be adequate, because they did not have time. Had they used purer sarin, more victims would almost certainly have died. Then Endo and Nakagawa packed the sarin into eleven plastic bags, so that four people could release two bags of sarin each and the fifth could release three bags.

The Assault Team

The guru ordered selected members to spray sarin to make the victims *poa* or *phowa*, which means that Aum members (the winners of Truth) could eliminate all the "evil karma of people" through death, and they could ascend the killed to a higher realm. The selected members believed they were releasing sarin to save people with evil karma who did not recognize these truths.

The assault team consisted of five pairs of individuals: one who released the sarin and the other who drove the getaway vehicle. Four of the five sarin gas sprayers were the Aum's vice ministers of science and technology, Yasuo Hayashi, Kenichi Hirose, Masato Yokoyama, and Toru Toyoda. The last member was Dr. Ikuo Hayashi, head of Aum's Medical Treatment Ministry. They were busy preparing for the attack on March 19 and 20. At 3:00 P.M. they went to Tokyo to practice a dry run of the sarin spray attack and to identify where to get on and off the train. Then they went back to the Kamikuishiki area to get the sarin. Around 11.00 P.M., the eleven sarin bags were ready.

The assault team trained by practicing puncturing with umbrella tips plastic bags filled with water. This was to simulate the release of sarin fluid through the bag. They returned to Tokyo at 3:00 A.M. and they prepared to get the train early in the morning. They did not sleep for two nights. All members of the assault team left the house to get to the targeted trains by car around 6:00 A.M. carrying sarin bags and umbrellas. Each prepared to take a sarin antidote pill and an injection filled with PAM. The attacks occurred at the following sites and were perpetrated by the associated pairs of accomplices.

Hibiya Line (for Nakameguro)—Yasuo Hayashi & Shigero Sugimoto

Y. Hayashi took the train for Nakameguro at Ueno Station and got off at Akihabara just after poking three bags of sarin. Seven persons were killed and 2,475 (this number is on the list of opening statements of prosecutor in the beginning of the court, as below) were injured.

Hibiya Line (for Tobu Zoo Park)—Toru Toyoda and Katsuya Takahashi

T. Toyoda took the train for Tobu Zoo Park at Nakameguro at 7:59 A.M. and got off at the next station, Ebisu, killing two persons and injuring 532 persons.

Marunouch Line (for Ogikubo)—Kenichi Hirose and Koichi Kitamura

K. Hirose took the train at Ikebukuro at 7:47 A.M. and got off at Ochanomizu, killing one person and injuring 358 persons.

Marunouch Line (for Ikebukuro)—Masato Yokoyama and Kiyotaka Tonozaki

M. Yokoyama took the train at Shinjuku and got off at Yotsuya after bursting one sarin bag, injuring 200 persons.

Chiyoda Line (for Yoyogi-Uehara)—Ikuo Hayashi and Tomomitsu Niimi

I. Hayashi took the train at Kitasenju and got off at Shin-ochanomizu after bursting one sarin bag, killing two persons and injuring 231 persons.

(An additional person died several months later. The line ridden was not identified.)

Thus, Tokyo was full of victims and the sounds of emergency ambulances. The numbers of victims vary at each point of the report. Almost 5,600 victims were treated at hospitals, 5,311 victims reported their victimization to the police, and the prosecutor's office was informed of twelve dead persons and 3,794 injured victims. It opened the case with these numbers. Later the prosecutor's office focused only on the twelve dead and fourteen injured victims to simplify the court process.

FIRST SURVEYS ON VICTIMS

The sarin gas attack incident was the biggest such incident Japan had ever experienced, with thousands of innocent victims. This incident forced the public to develop an awareness of victimization in Japan, an issue that had hitherto received little attention. In 1998 the National Police Agency decided to conduct a survey of the victims, with the cooperation of the National Research Institute of Police Science. The survey was supported by a governmental grant as a part of a research project on victim assistance in the National Research Institute of Police Science. The author was responsible for the entire survey process and managed the survey procedure.

Procedure

Two surveys of victims of the sarin gas attack have been conducted. The first survey was conducted in April 1998; three years after the incident occurred, and the second survey was conducted in 2000.

An initial request for victim response to the questionnaire was conducted in two stages. In the first stage, victims were asked whether they were willing to respond to the two questionnaire surveys. The first survey analysis was completed just after their replies were returned and the second survey was conducted two years later. The subjects of this initial request were all individuals (5,311 persons) who reported that they had been victims of the sarin gas attack to the police.

If victims responded "yes" at this stage, they were sent the first questionnaire. The request to respond to the second survey, which would be conducted two years later, was solicited simultaneously. Most of those who agreed to participate in the first survey also agreed to the second one.

The questionnaire involved the situation of the criminal scene, degree and syndromes of injury, psychological influence, and impressions about Aum Shinrikyo members, involved sarin releasers, and demands for government action.

Results of First Survey

Of the 5,311 victims, 1,677 replied. The respondent rate was 37.9 percent from among victims who got request letters; those who had moved to another address were not included. Of these, 1,545 victims agreed to the survey (92.1 percent of respondents), and were distributed the questionnaire; 1,268 returned the first survey questionnaires. The overwhelming majority of the respondents, 1,247, were victims themselves. The remaining number was composed of family members of the victims.

The self-reports of the victims were analyzed (1,247 subjects) according to demographic characteristics and these are presented in table 7.1.

Attributes of Respondents

Age Distribution

The age distribution is presented in table 7.1 and reveals that the ages of male subjects differed from that of females: forties (26.9 percent) and fifties (26.2 percent) were the majority in male respondents, twenties (44.5 percent) and thirties (31.1 percent) were the majority in female respondents. Female respondents were much younger than males.

Occupation

Table 7.2 shows the distribution of occupation. Almost all subjects were white-collar businessmen and office working women (76.7 percent); some were self employed (3.6 percent), and some were unemployed (11.4 percent).

Victimization Process

Place of Victimization

The places respondents were victimized were in the subway trains, on the platforms, and in the subway stations. Most of the victims were victimized in the train cars (52.4 percent) or on platforms of subway stations (38.7 per-

Table 7.1. Age Distribution of Subjects

Number of Subjects	Total		Males		Females	
	1247		709		528	
	N	%	N	%	N	%
Under 29	300	24.1	65	9.2	235	44.5
30–39	310	24.9	146	20.6	164	31.1
40–49	239	19.2	191	26.9	48	9.1
50–59	228	18.4	186	26.2	42	8.0
60+	156	12.5	119	16.8	37	7.0
unknown	13	1.0	2	0.3	2	0.4

Table 7.2.   Occupation of Subjects

	Total		Males		Females	
Number	1247		709		528	
of Subjects	N	%	N	%	N1	%
Workers	956	76.7	591	83.4	364	68.9
Self-employed	44	3.5	32	4.5	12	1.3
Students	14	1.1	8	1.1	6	1.1
No job	142	11.4	50	7.1	92	17.4
Others	41	3.3	13	1.8	28	5.3
Unknown	50	4	15	2.1	26	4.9

cent). They recognized their victimization through physical symptoms (40.1 percent), or by the atmosphere and the experience of people around them who were suffering (40.7 percent).

Transportation of Victims from the Scene to Hospitals

The majority of the victims were conscious as they went to the hospital; only 23 persons (1.8 percent) were unconscious. Only a segment of the victims went to the hospital directly from the scene of the attack (17.0 percent); others went to hospitals after going to the office (68.5 percent) or going back home (11.6 percent) when they received the information about sarin through the media or they felt sick. Ambulances were used for only a few victims (11.5 percent); others went to hospitals by themselves (60.7 percent) either on foot or by taxis or other vehicles, including police cars. When victims went to the hospital directly from the scene, ambulances were used more frequently (34.3 percent). For more than half of the victims, the medical charge was covered by workers' compensation (57.0 percent); the modal average (34.0 percent) medical charge was less than Y10,000 (about US$83); however, some victims paid the medical expense themselves. The highest cost of emergency medical care was Y750,000 (US$6,250). At the time of the survey, some victims were still hospitalized and in need of twenty-four-hour care.

Physical Victimization: Degree of Injury

The degree of physical injury was classified into three categories: seriously injured (more than a month to recover), medium level of injury (more than a week and less than a month to recover), and slightly injured (less than a week to recover). The proportion of victims for each category was 14.5 percent, 35.4 percent, and 30.1 percent, respectively; the rest were unknown.

Physical Victimization: Physical Disorder

A list of physical signs and symptoms was developed so that subjects could check for their presence both at the time they were exposed to sarin gas and again at the time of the survey three years later. The results of each response under categorized physical condition are shown in table 7.3. As in previous studies,[3] eye syndromes such as myosis and eye pain were prominent (91.0 percent of respondents checked at least one item in this category), which is the main effect of mild exposure to sarin. Also, they showed "disorder in throat and nose" (58.2 percent), such as runny nose and dyspnea, "pain or ill-being in a part of the flesh" (52.4 percent), such as headaches, "general disorder"(45.9 percent), such as general ill health, and "a feeling of malaise" (54.5 percent), such as languor, just after the exposure. Though the physical condition of respondents became better three years later, particularly in respect to myosis and eye pain, more than half of the subjects still suffered from some physical disorder such as eye strain, decrease of eyesight, or ill-health, which differed from the replies concerning the victim's symptoms directly after the exposure. In comparing males with females, for almost all syndromes except eye syndromes, a much higher percentage of female victims suffered adverse effects than did males. Comparison by age revealed no difference in eye syndromes; however, the younger victims showed more malaise or neurological problems than did those over the age of fifty.

Psychological Influence

Literature indicates that victims of various crimes often suffer from post-traumatic stress disorder (PTSD) syndromes. The victims of this report were exposed to dying people and many severely harmed people in the train cars or stations; they were also threatened by death, even though they did not know what caused it.

The survey included a checklist of both behavioral and conscious (emotional) PTSD characteristics; thus, subjects reported both the behavioral and the emotional effects about which they were aware. Tables 7.5 and 7.6 show the list of questionnaire items and categories checked here, which involve:

- "Reexperiences" such as flashbacks and nightmares (four items in emotional level, one item in behavioral level),
- "Avoidance" such as avoidance behavior of thoughts and places which related to the trauma (two items in emotional level, two items in behavioral level),
- "Numbing of General Responsiveness" such as passive attitude to social activities or loss of interests (eight items in emotional level, two items in behavioral level),

Table 7.3. Physical Signs and Syndromes of Subjects

Categories	Question Items	Just After the Incidence			Three Years Later		
		% Total	% Males	% Females	% Total	% Males	% Females
Eye Symptoms	myosis	77.6	80.4	74.2	5.1	5.2	5.1
	eye pain	48.5	47.2	50.2	8.1	7.3	8.9
	congestion	41.6	40.1	43.8	5.9	4.9	7.4
	eye strain	51.1	50.2	52.1	33.5	33.7	33.3
	tearing	30.1	30.6	29.0	7.5	8.3	6.6
	glary	37.7	36.0	40.0	10.3	8.5	12.9
	eye decrease	38.0	40.5	34.8	26.3	27.4	25.2
	blurred vision	27.6	25.5	30.1	10.3	11.0	9.7
	flicker	36.2	33.7	39.4	8.5	7.6	9.8
Disorder in Throat and Nose	running nose	27.7	24.5	31.8	6.8	7.5	6.1
	cough	23.8	17.6	32.2	5.1	4.2	6.4
	throat pain	21.4	15.0	30.1	4.2	4.1	4.4
	dyspnea	31.3	24.1	40.9	3.3	2.1	4.9
	nosebleed	1.0	0.7	1.5	0.6	0.3	1.1
	salvation	3.1	3.0	3.2	1.0	1.3	0.6

Disorder in a Part of Flesh	stiff shoulder	11.9	9.6	15.3	15.8	13.7	18.9
	extremity pain	4.1	3.4	5.1	3.2	2.8	3.8
	diarrhea	5.8	5.1	6.8	1.7	2.0	1.3
	headache	37.4	31.3	46.0	9.6	7.1	13.3
	tachypnea	9.9	7.1	13.4	7.5	5.2	10.8
	difficulty of walking	5.1	4.1	6.4	0.3	0.1	0.6
General Disorder	numbness	11.4	9.2	14.4	3.5	3.9	3.0
	convulsion	7.0	5.9	8.5	2.3	2.4	2.3
	out of curl	14.8	11.4	18.6	1.8	1.4	2.5
	rigor	3.5	2.5	4.9	1.8	1.6	2.1
	nausea	26.5	24.1	30.1	1.6	1.1	2.3
	vertigo	21.3	17.8	25.9	4.5	3.4	6.1
	sweat	4.5	5.5	3.2	5.9	5.9	6.1
Malaise or Neurological	loss of appetite	15.6	10.9	22.2	1.1	0.6	1.9
	fever	13.6	10.0	18.8	1.8	1.0	3.0
	lungour	29.3	24.1	36.4	8.4	7.2	10.2
	easy fatigability	22.3	19.5	26.3	19.9	16.6	24.2
	catch cold	4.7	2.4	7.8	8.8	6.8	11.7
	sleepless	19.4	16.8	23.3	9.1	7.5	11.4
	decrease of consciousness	8.3	7.6	9.3	1.3	1.6	0.9
Others		5.2	3.7	7.0	4.1	3.5	4.5
No Signs		6.7	6.6	6.8	46.0	46.0	46.0

Table 7.4. Psychological Influence in Consciousness Level

Categories	Question Items	Just After the Incidence			Three Years Later		
		% Total	% Males	% Females	% Total	% Males	% Females
Reexperiences	flashback	33.0	30.6	36.0	17.5	15.8	19.9
	intrusive recollection	25.0	19.0	33.1	9.6	6.5	13.6
	nightmare	17.2	14.8	20.5	7.4	7.3	7.4
	distress at exposure to events that symbolize trauma	17.2	11.7	24.6	12.8	10.2	16.3
Avoidance	avoid thought associated with the incidence	13.5	8.9	19.7	15.1	14.4	16.3
	avoid the place of incidence	18.4	11.8	27.5	10.2	6.8	14.8
Numbing of General Responsiveness	inability to recall the incidence	3.5	3.5	3.6	3.1	3.0	3.4
	diminished interest	2.6	1.6	4.2	2.2	1.1	3.6
	social withdrawal	4.9	1.4	9.7	1.1	0.4	2.1
	restricted range of feeling	1.9	2.0	1.9	2.9	3.8	1.7
	foreshortened future	4.3	2.4	7.0	3.8	2.5	5.7
	forgetfulness	6.7	7.2	6.3	15.0	15.0	15.3
	stupefaction	6.0	3.8	8.7	5.1	2.7	8.1
	derealization	16.0	12.3	21.2	14.0	11.3	17.8

Alienation, Isolation, Loss of Self-esteem						
no one understands me	4.3	3.0	6.1	3.9	3.5	4.5
vanity	4.1	3.5	4.9	4.4	3.5	5.7
depressed	10.2	6.3	15.3	7.3	4.2	11.2
absurdity	8.5	7.6	9.8	7.9	7.9	8.1
desire to die	1.1	0.3	2.3	1.0	0.1	2.1
fear to be alone	5.7	2.1	10.6	2.0	0.8	3.6
feel myself as worthless	1.4	0.6	2.5	1.8	1.3	2.7
dependency	6.2	2.7	11.0	3.8	2.3	5.9
distrust	5.2	3.1	8.1	3.9	2.7	5.7
Arousal Symptoms						
fear of recurrence	23.7	16.4	33.7	18.4	14.1	24.4
fear of subway	30.1	19.9	43.8	13.9	10.9	18.0
ill-tempered	7.5	7.3	7.8	7.6	6.2	9.5
difficulty concentrating	10.4	10.3	10.6	6.5	6.6	6.3
irritability	6.2	3.2	10.2	1.6	0.7	2.7
Others	4.1	3.8	4.4	3.8	3.7	3.8
No Response	30.3	36.1	22.2	43.3	45.7	39.6

- "Alienation, Isolation, Loss of Self-esteem" such as depression or vanity (nine items in emotional level, one item in behavioral level),
- "Arousal Symptoms" such as cautious attitude or irritability (five items in emotional level, one item in behavioral level),
- "Addict" such as alcoholic (three items in behavioral level), and
- "Adaptation" (two items in behavioral level).

Results are shown in table 7.4 (emotional level) and table 7.5 (behavioral level). Among them, in emotional and behavioral levels, they indicated "Reexperiences" most frequently (53.6 percent), and "Arousal Symptom" (50.8 percent), "Feeling of Alienation" (35.9 percent), "Numbing of General Responsiveness" (33.2 percent), "Avoidance of Related Stimuli" (31.4 percent). Females felt more psychological damage in every aspect than did males.

Next, the survey analyzed psychological damage by degree of injury as measured by the length of time taken to recover. This variable was divided into three categories: one month and more, more than one week and less than a month, and less than a week. As the results in table 7.6 show, the more seriously the victims were injured, the more serious was the psychological damage.

Influence of the Incident

Reactions of Other People to Victims

The victims were asked what kind of reactions they received from other people. The results are shown in table 7.7. Those who supported the victims were family members (81.8 percent), officemates (64.8 percent), and friends (62.2 percent). However, some victims experienced negative reactions from people. For example, some officemates joked about them, naming victims "Mr. Sarin" or "Miss Sarin" [Sarin-chan], leading to additional victimization (23.2 percent).

Impression about Aum Members

How do victims feel about the offenders? They were asked their impression of three types of offenders: Asahara, the executive staff, and the sarin releasers, respectively. When some victims gave evidence at court, everyone chose capital punishment for Asahara.[4] However, victims had different impressions about each offender among the sarin releasers. For the medical doctor, Ikuo Hayashi, for a variety of reasons, including his remorse, several of those bereaved would not support capital punishment because the resolution of this sarin gas attack incident investigation was based on his confession. In the process of the police investigation, medical doctor Ikuo Hayashi

Table 7.5. Psychological Influence in Behavior Level

Categories	Question Items	Just After the Incidence			Three Years Later		
		% Total	% Males	% Females	% Total	% Males	% Females
Reexperiences	feel fear in getting train	29.5	23.0	38.4	17.6	14.4	21.8
Avoidance	change the route for office	24.2	17.9	33.0	7.6	5.5	10.6
	avoid the place of incidence	12.9	8.2	19.3	4.2	2.3	6.8
	avoid the media information related to the incidence	10.6	6.5	16.1	9.3	6.6	12.7
Numbing of General Responsiveness	inability to do daily deeds	1.4	0.3	2.8	0.6	0.1	1.1
	feeling of estrangement from others	5.9	4.2	8.1	5.9	4.1	8.3
Alienation, Isolation, Loss of Self-esteem	distressed to be alone	6.4	3.1	11.0	3.0	1.7	4.9
Arousal Symptoms	lack of concentration	6.9	5.9	8.0	3.7	4.4	2.8
Addict	hyperphagia	4.3	3.0	6.1	4.2	2.5	6.4
	taste alcohol	4.3	5.5	2.8	5.3	6.2	4.0
	sleeping pill	3.5	3.2	4.0	2.0	2.0	2.1
	workerphoric	2.6	2.7	2.3	1.4	2.3	0.4
Adaptation	behave as usual	14.0	12.6	15.7	8.6	8.3	8.7
	positive contact to media	49.8	50.8	48.7	55.3	56.4	54.2
	No Response	26.7	31.5	20.5	27.6	28.9	25.4

Table 7.6. Psychological Influence by Degree of Injury

Category	Items	Just After the Incidence			Three Years Later		
		1 Month More %	1 Week–1 Month %	Less Than 1 Week %	1 Month More %	1 Week–1 Month %	Less Than 1 Week %
Re-experiences	flashback	51.4	34.6	26.9	19.9	18.3	16.3
	intrusive recollection	35.4	29.4	18.4	13.8	10.0	6.9
	nightmare	28.7	20.4	10.1	11.6	7.9	5.9
	distress at exposure to events that symbolize trauma	32.6	18.1	13.6	23.8	12.0	9.1
	mean	37.0	25.6	17.3	17.3	12.1	9.6
Avoidance	avoid thought associated with the incidence	23.2	13.3	9.3	25.4	15.8	9.9
	avoid the place of incidence	30.4	20.8	11.5	19.9	10.2	6.1
	change the route for office	30.4	26.2	19.7	9.9	7.2	6.4
	avoid the media information related to the incidence	19.3	10.2	8.3	17.7	9.3	6.7
	mean	25.8	17.6	12.2	18.2	10.6	7.3
Numbing of General Responsiveness	inability to recall the incidence	4.4	4.8	1.3	3.9	2.9	1.9
	diminished interest	4.4	2.0	2.7	4.4	1.8	1.9
	social withdrawal	9.9	5.7	2.9	1.7	0.7	1.3
	restricted range of feeling	1.7	1.1	1.9	3.9	1.8	2.7
	foreshortened future	6.1	5.0	3.2	7.2	1.4	3.5
	forgetfulness	16.6	5.7	4.3	26.5	12.9	11.5
	stupefaction	12.2	5.7	4.0	7.2	3.8	4.3
	de-realization	19.3	16.1	13.9	14.4	16.3	10.9
	feeling of estrangement from others	7.7	6.1	4.8	7.7	4.8	6.1
	inability to do daily deeds	3.9	1.4	0.8	0.6	0.7	0.3
	mean	8.6	5.4	4.0	7.8	4.7	4.4

Alienation, Isolation, Loss of Self-esteem	no one understands me	8.3	3.4	4.0	9.9	3.2
	vanity	6.6	3.6	3.5	7.2	3.5
	depressed	21.0	11.5	5.1	14.4	4.3
	absurdity	12.7	8.6	7.2	12.2	5.3
	desire to die	2.2	1.4	0.5	0.6	1.1
	fear to be alone	9.9	7.2	2.7	2.2	1.3
	feel myself as worthless	1.1	1.4	1.6	2.8	1.9
	dependency	8.8	7.7	4.8	5.5	3.5
	distrust	7.7	6.3	3.7	5.0	3.7
	mean	8.7	5.7	3.7	6.6	3.1
Arousal Symptoms	fear of recurrence	33.7	24.4	19.7	19.9	16.8
	fear of subway	39.2	32.8	24.5	18.8	11.5
	ill-tempered	16.0	7.7	4.5	14.4	4.8
	difficulty concentrating	26.0	9.3	5.3	11.0	5.3
	irritability	9.4	7.5	4.0	2.2	1.9
	lack of concentration	18.8	6.1	2.9	5.0	1.6
	mean	17.6	7.7	4.2	8.2	3.4
Addict	hyperphagia	3.9	3.6	3.7	4.4	4.0
	taste alcohol	5.5	4.3	4.3	10.5	4.8
	sleeping pill	5.0	4.8	1.3	2.2	0.8
	workerphoric	6.6	1.4	2.4	3.9	0.5
	mean	5.3	3.5	2.9	5.3	2.5
Adaptation	behave as usual	24.3	13.1	10.1	14.9	5.6
	positive contact to media	47.0	51.6	50.4	56.4	50.7
	mean	35.7	32.4	30.3	35.7	28.2

Table 7.7. Reactions of People Surrounding Victims

	Positive Reactions			Negative Reactions		
	Total %	Males %	Females %	Total %	Males %	Females %
Family members	81.8	79.4	85.6	5.8	3.4	9.3
Officemates	64.8	63.8	66.4	23.2	16.5	32.4
Neighbors	27.2	27.4	27.3	2.9	2.4	3.6
Friends	62.2	53.4	74.5	7.1	3.7	11.7
Lovers	21.0	9.6	36.6	2.3	0.4	4.9

was arrested in April 1995 for the offense of harboring criminals and suppressing evidence, as well as for the offense concerning improper evasion of execution. He confessed his crime as a member of the team that had sprayed sarin gas in the subway in May when he heard that his actions caused the death of two station officers who were attempting to save subway passengers. He had kept silent until this time for two months after his arrest. Soon the police were able to retrieve information about most of the process of the gas attack on the Tokyo subway. But for the other sarin releasers, the bereaved would choose capital punishment. These results shown in table 7.8 are the average perceptions of the victims concerning Aum members. Victims felt anger against them and needed apologies and compensation. These feelings were a little bit stronger with respect to the guru than to other executive members of Aum Shinrikyo or sarin releasers. Victims thought the guru was most responsible for these crimes.

Impressions of Incident among Victims

The impressions about the incident are shown in table 7.9. The victims felt a fear of the recurrence of the same type of crimes by Aum members (89.1 percent). Around 40 percent of victims felt a lack of comprehension of their being victimized (41.5 percent). However, half of the victims accepted the

Tables 7.8. Feeling against Aum Members

	Asahara %	Executive Staff %	Releaser Sarin %
Feel anger	94.9	89.8	88.1
Offenders should admit their crimes	92.1	87.2	87.4
Offenders should cooperate with other staff for the quick court procedure	86.8	80.9	79.5
Victims keep watching the court	82.8	75.1	75.7
Offender should tell the truth	82.4	77.1	77.9
Offenders should apologize	78.1	73.1	72.7
Offenders should compensate	60.2	56.5	55.3

occurrence of the incident, recognized the importance of life (48.5 percent), and made a resolution to restart and enjoy their lives.

Demands on the Government

There were various expectations held by victims and these are shown in table 7.10. The top demand for the government was the "prevention of a recurrence of the same type of crimes" (71.6 percent), a "quick proceeding of judgment for defendants" (71.2 percent), and an "investigation of the incident" (61.6 percent). As it is not clear what kind of effect sarin has after exposure, victims worried about the influence of sarin gas in the future. They therefore expected the government to "clarify the influence of sarin" (65.0 percent) and "establish a new hospital for treatment" (21.5 percent). They also required that the government "understand the situation of victims properly" (59.7 percent) and provide financial (37.1 percent) and emotional (26.0 percent) support. They hoped that these expectations would be met through government policy. They appealed to the public "not to forget the incident" (62.6 percent).

Results of Open-Ended Questions

A blank space on the questionnaire allowed victims to describe their feelings or what they thought. The following categories were described.

- physical and psychological disorder without clear causes
- the demand for long-term health care supported by the government and free medical treatment or cure for victims

Table 7.9. Impression of the Incidence

Category Items		Total	Males	Females
Number of Subjects		1247	709	528
Negative Attitude or Anxiety	why was I victimized	41.5	42.3	40.9
	anxiety for physical disorder	11.1	10.6	11.7
	fear for future	14.2	11.1	18.4
	recurrence of activities of			
	Aum members	89.1	88.4	90.5
	compensation	22.6	26.5	17.8
Positive Attitude	better physical condition	14.8	11.1	19.9
	recognize the reality	9.5	9.7	9.3
	enjoy being alive	56.0	53.3	59.8
	positive way of life	12.5	11.1	14.4
	restart my life	10.9	10.2	11.9
	feel the importance of life	48.5	46.1	52.1

Table 7.10.   Demands for the Government

	Contents	Total	Males	Females
For the Government	prevention of recurrence	71.6	70.4	73.7
	early judgment of court	71.2	74.8	66.5
	clarify the influence of sarin	65.0	63.3	67.2
	investigation on the incidence	61.6	58.7	65.9
	understand victims	59.7	57.0	63.6
	treatment for victims	45.1	43.6	47.0
	financial support	37.1	37.4	36.7
	psychological support	26.0	22.3	30.7
	special hospital for treatment	21.5	19.6	23.9
	compensation	15.5	15.0	16.3
For the Public People	not to forget the incidence	62.6	58.7	68.0

- the demand for a governmental policy to prevent the recurrence of the same type of crimes
- compassion for other victims
- recurring traumatic flashbacks
- demand for quick progress of the law enforcement process
- demand for control of the activities of Aum Shinrikyo
- a desire that others understand the situation of victims
- strong anxiety about pregnancy among young female victims

THE SECOND SURVEY OF VICTIMS

Attributes of Respondents

Two years after the first survey was conducted, the second survey questionnaire was distributed to the 1,536 victims who had agreed to reply in 1998. Most respondents were the same subjects as those of the first survey. One to two percent of subjects (30 persons) have differed in the two surveys because someone completed only the first or second survey. To the second questionnaire, 910 subjects replied (respondent rates, 61.7 percent), victims (837 persons—509 males and 328 females) and family members (34 persons, including the bereaved: spouses, 22; children, 19; parents, 11; brothers or sisters, 5; others, 2).Thirty-nine respondents' demographic characteristics were unknown. Although the age distribution of respondents were almost equal in every age bracket, male respondents were older (forties, 27.5 percent; fifties, 24.2 percent) than were females (twenties, 30.0 percent; thirties, 43.3 percent). Two-thirds were white-collar workers (males, 75.6 percent; females, 61.6 percent) and, among females, 22.9 percent were without jobs.

Table 7.11.   Age Distribution of Subjects of Second Survey

Age	Total		Males		Females	
	N	%	N	%	N	%
Total	837	100.0	509	100.0	328	100.0
<29	122	14.6	30	5.9	92	28.0
30–39	235	28.1	93	18.3	142	43.3
40–49	158	18.9	120	23.6	38	11.6
50–59	167	20.0	140	27.5	27	8.2
60+	151	18.0	123	24.2	28	8.5
NA	4	0.5	3	0.6	1	0.3

Physical Disorders

As a whole, they felt better since the incident (38.4 percent), although 10 percent of the subjects felt worse than before. Subjects checked each item and specified whether it had improved or was retrogressive. Table 7.12 shows the details of physical conditions.

Subjects felt most of the symptoms had improved. In particular, those problems that stemmed from sarin poisoning, such as myosis or eye pain had almost disappeared; however, different problems such as deterioration of eyesight and eyestrain were seen much more frequently. Physical disorder items were categorized into five groups: Eye Symptoms, Disorder in Throat and Nose, Disorder in a Part of the Body, General Disorder and Malaise, or Neurological Difficulty. Results showed eye syndromes such as myosis and eye pain were prominent (56.0 percent of respondents checked at least one item in this category), which is the main effect of mild exposure to sarin. Also, they showed "disorder in throat and nose" (25.7 percent) such as runny nose and dyspnea, "pain or ill-being in a part of the flesh" (37.4 percent) such as headache, "general disorder" (26.2 percent) such as general ill health, and "a feeling of malaise" (38.1 percent) such as languor just after the exposure. Table 7.3 shows a comparison of the results of the first and second surveys by category. The percentage of those who experienced these items decreased from the previous survey in each category.

Table 7.12.   The Change of Physical Condition

Number of Subjects	Males	Females	Total
	509	328	837
	%	%	%
Better	35.6	42.7	38.4
No change	24.2	23.2	23.8
Worse	11.0	7.3	9.6
Can't tell	24.4	19.8	22.6
NA	4.9	7.0	5.7

Table 7.13. Physical Situation (5 years later)

Categories	Signs	Percent of People with Signs			Percent of Worse Change		
		Males	Females	Total	Males	Females	Total
Eye Symptoms	eyestrain	43.6	42.1	43.0	70.5	70.8	70.6
	eye decrease	37.5	36.3	37.1	74.3	78.3	75.8
	blurred vision	20.2	17.1	19.0	57.5	48.7	54.1
	glary	17.9	19.8	18.6	43.5	45.5	44.3
	tearing	15.1	17.4	16.0	45.5	39.3	43.1
	flicker	15.7	12.8	14.6	41.8	38.5	40.4
	congestion	10.8	13.5	11.8	29.4	33.1	30.9
	eye pain	10.0	13.5	11.3	27.0	29.3	28.0
	narrowed vision	10.6	7.0	9.2	21.1	13.6	18.1
Disorder in Throat and Nose	running nose	16.5	17.1	16.7	56.4	48.3	52.8
	cough	10.0	8.8	9.5	42.9	31.5	37.9
	throat pain	5.9	8.0	6.7	33.3	32.9	33.1
	dyspnea	6.5	9.1	7.5	33.3	30.0	31.7
	nosebleed	2.4	3.6	2.8	36.4	50.0	42.1
	salvation	2.6	1.2	2.0	35.1	18.2	28.8

Disorder in a Part of the Flesh	stiff shoulder	23.0	35.3	27.9	74.5	84.1	79.0
	extremity pain	9.6	8.5	9.2	60.5	62.2	61.1
	tachypnea	12.5	17.1	14.4	66.0	62.2	64.2
	headache	9.5	18.6	13.0	34.5	42.4	38.5
	diarrhea	4.7	3.9	4.4	42.9	31.0	37.8
	difficulty of walking	1.2	0.9	1.0	17.6	15.0	16.7
General Disorder	vertigo	8.9	14.7	11.1	42.1	46.6	44.3
	sweat	12.3	9.1	11.1	58.3	58.8	58.5
	numbness	8.2	5.8	7.3	45.2	33.3	40.7
	out of curl	5.7	7.0	6.3	36.7	33.8	35.4
	rigor	5.0	4.3	4.7	41.7	45.2	42.9
	convulsion	5.6	3.0	4.5	42.4	34.5	40.0
	nausea	2.4	6.7	4.1	15.0	27.8	21.4
Malaise or Neurological	easy fatigability	27.5	29.9	28.4	67.6	73.7	70.0
	languor	13.7	20.8	16.5	44.3	52.7	48.1
	catch cold	13.0	20.1	15.8	64.1	71.7	67.7
	sleepless	10.7	13.8	11.8	49.1	49.5	49.3
	decrease of consciousness	3.9	4.9	4.3	34.5	34.8	34.6
	fever	3.2	5.5	4.1	20.5	26.9	23.4
	loss of appetite	1.6	2.7	2.0	14.3	15.0	14.7

Table 7.14.   Change of Physical Disorder

	1st Survey	2nd Survey
Eye Symptoms	91.0%	56.0%
Throat/Nose	58.2%	25.7%
A Part of Flesh	52.4%	37.4%
General Disorder	45.9%	26.2%
Malaise or Neurological Signs	54.5%	38.1%

Psychological Influences

Items that measured psychological influences are divided into five categories. Results are shown in table 7.15. The results show that reexperiences (53.6 percent in the first survey, 29.4 percent in the second survey) and avoidance of stimuli associated with trauma (31.4 percent in the first survey, 20.0 percent in the second survey) decreased, but hypervigilance (50.8 percent in the first survey, 57.8 percent in the second survey) did not change. Numbing of general responsiveness (33.2 percent in the first survey, 52.2 percent in the second survey) and alienation or loss of self-esteem (35.9 percent in the first survey, 63.7 percent in the second survey) increased. Thus, although physical disorder decreased gradually, psychological effects such as hypervigilance and alienation did not disappear for a long time.

Causes of Change in Social Attitudes among Victims

Attitudes toward this incident differed among respondents. Some subjects were pessimistic about physical disorders and the attitudes of the public, including mass media, and others were quite optimistic. One of the factors affecting such attitude formation might be human relations; some victims experienced support and advice from family, officemates, friends, and neighbors. However, some victims got bullied by those around them. Those who recognized their change as positive thought that time passing, positive thinking, a change in their environment (marriage, birth of child, moving), and the support of people who helped them were beneficial. Aging, intrusion into the memories of the sarin incident, slow progress of the prosecu-

Table 7.15.   Change of Psychological Disorder

	1st Survey	2nd Survey
Reexperiences	53.6%	29.4%
Avoidance	31.4%	20.0%
Hypervigilance	50.8%	57.8%
Numbing of General Responses	33.2%	52.2%
Alienation, Isolation and Loss of Self-esteem	35.9%	63.7%

tion of the perpetrators, and reflection on the incident (inadequate treatment at the hospital, insufficient rest) recalled bad memories.

The majority of the demands made of the government by the subjects as specified in the first survey were left unresolved.

Supplement

The summary of the results of the two surveys was disseminated to the public through mass media such as TV news and newspaper articles. This led the public to recognize the seriousness of victimization of not only this incident but other types of victimization as well. Also many related authorities in the government might recognize the necessity of providing support or assistance to victims of crime.

Simultaneously, the leaflet summarizing the results of the two surveys was distributed to the individuals who agreed to respond to the questionnaire. This was useful as it helped them to understand their own physical and psychological condition.

CONCLUSION

The airplane crashes at the World Trade Center in New York and the Pentagon in Washington, D.C., on September 11, 2001, reminds the Japanese of the "daymare" of the sarin gas attack on March 20, 1995. Both are the crimes of terrorists. The sarin gas attack at Tokyo Subway destroyed the myth that "Japan is the safest country in the world." The results of the survey of the victims of the sarin gas attack makes clear that many victims are still suffering from physical and psychological disorder after five years. In the second survey, a majority of respondents (except those among the injured who are still hospitalized) became better after the time of the first survey. However, psychological effects have longer lasting effects than physical harm. Also, as of the beginning of December 2001, judgment had yet to be passed on seven defendants. Table 7.16 shows, to date, the court rulings on the sarin gas attack defendants. The slow progress of the law enforcement and judicial processes is highly disturbing and irritating to the victims.

The survey presents a dilemma. It has been useful in providing an understanding of the effects on victims; however, it also brings to light the only slight improvement in their situation from the period of the first survey. Perhaps additional time will show greater change and help develop a clearer understanding of the long-term effects on the victims.

The top demand made on the government by victims was prevention of recurrence of the same type of crime, and, at the same time, the public also expects more from the government because Japan had lost the safety myth

Table 7.16. Results of Judgment for Offenders of the Sarin Gas Attack

Role of Incident	Name of Defendants	Result of Judgment	Notes
Top Planner	MATSUMOTO Chizuo (ASAHARA Shoko)	On court	
Leader	MURAI Hideo		Killed by accident
Sub-leader	INOUE Yoshihiro	Life sentence	Appeal from prosecutor
Sarin Producers	ENDO Seiichi	On court	
	NAKAGAWA Tomomasa	On court	
	TSUCHIYA Tomomi	On court	
Sarin Releasers	HAYASHI Ikuo	Life sentence	Determination
	YOKOYAMA Masato	Death penalty	Appeal from defendant
	HAYASHI Yasuo	Death penalty	Appeal from defendant
	TOYODA Toru	Death penalty	Appeal from defendant
	HIROSE Kenichi	Death penalty	Appeal from defendant
Getaway Drivers	KITAMURA Koichi	Life sentence	Appeal from defendant
	TONOZAKI Kiyotaka	Life sentence	Appeal from defendant
	SUGIMOTO Shigero	Life sentence	Appeal from defendant
	NIIMI Tomomitsu	On court	
	TAKAHASHI Katsuya		Not arrested

that Japan was the safest country in the world. The government enacted the "group regulation law" for the group that committed indiscriminate homicides in 1999; also the group has been monitored by the police since 2000. Aum Shinrikyo was deprived of its certification as a religious group and was ordered to disband.

Later, Aum Shinrikyo was born again as group "Aleph," and apologized about a series of crimes.

The newness of the Japanese victim support program may also be a factor in the slow progress as it began only after this incident. The sarin attack incident, nevertheless, played a very important role in informing the Japanese government of the necessity of establishing programs for victims of crimes. Such victim assistance programs might not have come into existence had it not been for the widespread effect of the sarin attacks. The mass media raises awareness of the sufferings of victims, and there is a growing recognition of the importance of support for victims not only at an official level but also by the general public.

For the purposes of this study, in addition to reviewing the available literature, the author observed the court proceedings. Some issues are still under discussion, and some judgments are still pending. Most of the offenders arrested indicated that they had not committed the crimes willingly. They committed these crimes because the guru ordered them to do so. In the court, on June 20, 2001, with Asahara as defendant, T. Nakagawa, who conducted almost all the major crimes committed by Aum Shinrikyo, gave evidence as a witness. Finally he burst into tears shouting, "I didn't join Aum Shinrikyo to produce sarin or to spray sarin." This outburst was highly symbolic of the entire sarin incident. He committed a series of crimes because he unconditionally obeyed the guru. A mentally deranged man, Chizuo Matsumoto (a.k.a. Shoko Asahara) created many offenders. Even inside the Aum organization, there might be many victims like T. Nakagawa. To some degree, there is a similarity between Japanese traditional organized crime groups Boryokudan (70 percent of sampled Boryokudan members agreed with the premise of absolute loyalty to the boss, 52.4 percent of them agreed with the opinion that they could devote their lives to the boss)[5] and Aum Shinrikyo, with the crime lords wielding immense power over the thoughts and actions of their members.

NOTES

1. D. W. Brackett, *Holy Terror* (New York: Weatherhill, 1996); Robert Jay Lifton, *Destroying the World to Save It* (New York: Henry Holt, 1999); Rei Kimura, *Japan's Unholy Sect Press* (Catskill, NY: Tige Publishing, 1999); K. Furihata, *Aum Houtei* [Courts on Aum], Vol. 1: Followers of the Guru (Asahi-Bunko, 1998); K. Furihata, *Aum Houtei* [Courts on Aum], Vol. 2: The Guru vs. Believers (Asahi-bunko, 1998); K. Furihata, *Aum Houtei* [Courts on Aum], Vol. 3: Ikuo Hayashi, Minister of Medical Treatment (Asahi-bunko, 1998); K. Furihata, *Aum Houtei* [Courts on Aum], Vol. 4: Statements of Chizuo Matsumoto (Asahi-bunko, 1999); K. Furihata, *Aum Houtei* [Courts on Aum], Vol. 5: Who Told a Lie? (Asahi-bunko, 2000); K. Furihata, *Aum Houtei* [Courts on Aum], Vol. 6: Sentence to Capital Punishment (Asahi-bunko, 2000); K. Furihata, *Aum Houtei* (Courts on Aum), Vol. 7: The Queen Hisako Ishii (Asahi-bunko, 2001); Ian Reader, *Religious Violence in Contemporary Japan: The Case of Aum Shinrikyo* (Honolulu: University of Hawaii Press, 2000); Tetsu Okumura, *Kinkyushoshu (Stadt Call)?* Kawade Shobo Shinsha.

2. N. Yanagawa, ed., *Report for Toxic Gas Attack in Matsumoto* (Matsumoto: Matsumoto Local Medical Council, 1995)

3. Hiroshi Morita, Nobuo Yanagisawa, Tamie Nakajima, Mikio Shimizu, Hidemitsu Hirabayashi, Hiroshi Okudera, Masahiko Nohara, Yoko Midorikawa, and Shohei Mimura, "Sarin Poisoning in Matsumoto," *Japan Public Health* 346: 290–93; Y. Okumura, N. Takasu, S. Ishimatsu, S. Miyanoki, A. Mitsuhashi, K. Kumada, K. Tanaka, and

S. Hinohara, "Report on 640 Victims of the Tokyo Subway Sarin Attack," *Ann Emerg Med* 28 (August 1996): 129–35.

4. *Asahi Shimbun*, April 2001.

5. A. Uchiyama and K. Hoshino, A Study on the Conformity of Boryokudan Members to the Boryokudan Sub-culture, *Report of NRIPS* 34, no. 2 (1993): 27–35.

8

The Forgotten Victims of Narco-Terrorism in Latin America

George Millard

INTRODUCTION

All the ingredients for producing highly profitable illicit drugs can be found in Latin America. Ecuador, Peru, Bolivia, and Colombia provide the coca plantations. The chemicals come from Brazil. The powerful criminal organizations and their laboratories can be found in Colombia. In the narcotics context, there is not a great deal of difference between these countries; practically all of them in Latin America are involved to some degree or other. Each country participates with its own specific contribution: from cultivation to transformation, to processing and finally to distribution.

Latin America is also a melting pot for criminal organizations such as the drug cartels, the Italian- and USA-style Mafia, Lebanese and Nigerian syndicates, and even the newcomers from Eastern Europe.

These activities are performed by nationals of virtually all of these countries, which, in association with those involved in each stage of the production process, strive to achieve the securest trafficking routes to the consumers.

Notwithstanding that considerable drug enforcement efforts have been invested in reducing the areas of coca plantation, the final balance demonstrates that cultivation has in fact increased. There are new areas being planted, and even new varieties of drugs being developed, such as poppies for the production of Latin American heroin.

The efforts invested in reducing the areas of coca plantations had, by the end of 1999, shown a change in this pattern, with the continuous and steady decline in the Andean crops. These totals are now at a new low. The most dramatic decline occurred in Peru and Bolivia, formerly the world's two principal coca producers. They now rank in second and third place behind Colombia. The bad news is that Colombian coca cultivation, in compensation, increased by 20 percent in 1999.

This is not surprising, but rather a predictable consequence following the successful eradication efforts in Peru and Bolivia. The loss to the major producers had to be compensated, and the Colombian coca cultivation has consequently expanded from 101,800 hectares to a currently estimated 122,500 hectares. And despite the above efforts, the potential for processed cocaine will be in the region of 765 metric tons for this year.

Thus the drug trade continues to flourish with intensity, and as stated in the 1999 International Narcotics Control Strategy Report (INCSR), generating extraordinary revenues.

Definitions

Within the context of the narcotics topic, of such danger to society, a complicating factor appears in practically all regions of the planet, where drugs or substances which cause dependence are produced. It is a new activity which is fast gaining space: Narco-Terrorism.

It is comprised of two species—one, the terrorist activity, without any political connotation but destined to protect criminal activity, and the other, which for its own political objectives takes advantage of the vast resources available that are generated through drug trafficking.

The definition of terrorism refers to political violence that targets civilians deliberately and indiscriminately. More than guerrilla warfare, terrorism is a shadowy world of faceless enemies and irregular tactics marked by extreme brutality. The purpose of terrorism is to demoralize a civilian population in order to use their discontent as leverage on national governments or other parties to enter into conflict.

Narco-terrorism is conducted to further the aims of drug traffickers. It may include assassinations, extortion, hijackings, bombings, and kidnappings directed against judges, prosecutors, elected officials, and law enforcement agents, and the general disruption of a legitimate government to divert attention from drug operations.

CHRONOLOGY

Because all terrorist organizations need to raise funds to sustain their violent objectives and resort to illegal means to finance their crimes, drug trafficking comes at the top of the list of illegal money-raising activities.

At a given moment in the past, the descriptions of narco-traffic and narco-terrorism and their links start to be revealed with frequency. It was the evidence of these connections which became part of official documents and terminology from then on.

Back in 1988, the United Nations Convention against Illicit Traffic in Narcotics Drugs and Psychotropic Substances referred to the relationship between illicit drug traffic and other organized criminal activities which undermine the stability, security, and legitimacy of sovereign states.

In 1992, the United Nations Control Board reported, "illicit cultivation of narcotics plants and illicit trafficking in drugs continue to be a threat to the political, economic and social stability of several countries. Links appear to exist between illicit cultivation and drug trafficking, and the activities of subversive organisations in some countries."[1]

In 1993, attention was drawn to the organic connections between drug cartels and terrorist organizations (INCB).

The 49th Session of the General Assembly of the United Nations underlines concerns about the growing and dangerous links between terrorist groups, drug traffickers, and their paramilitary gangs, which have resorted to all types of violence.

Links with Organized Crime

The enormous amount of money generated by the commercialization of drugs, principally cocaine, indicated to countless terrorist organizations the path to take for obtaining financial resources, in the context of Latin America. Unconfirmed numbers, which incidentally are used by all those who refer to statistics that give an account of the worth and earnings from narco-traffic, suggest that cocaine will be responsible for earnings of US$120 billions per annum in Latin America.

The link started out in a very limited way, with the guerrillas establishing themselves in a way to provide protection for the cultivation areas. Little by little their activities extended to charging tolls for the use of clandestine airstrips, and also for providing escort and protection during transportation. These were parallel activities, as seen in the Alto Huallago valley in Peru at the time of the Sendero Luminoso actions.[2]

While in Colombia, we apparently had a situation of agreement between the interested parties, with the Colombian syndicates steadily moving cultivation to the conflict-ridden south and southwest of the country. That was the only way to protect and have a guaranteed source of coca plants at the same time

The convergence of interests has led to an expansion of cultivation in guerrilla-dominated territory, where, as mentioned in the International Narcotics Control Strategy Report of March 2000, security conditions make it difficult for the central government to conduct eradication operations.

The same report also states that the Colombian drug trade has been rushing to make up for the shortfall by the two Andean producers (Peru/Bolivia), "realizing that the only way to have a guaranteed source of coca was to plant it in lands under their immediate control."[3]

The INCSR/99 country report indicates that the government's talks with the FARC, which earns substantial funds from the drug trade, particularly from protection and taxation (tolls), have shown few gains thus far. Like the guerrillas, the paramilitaries are also involved in the drug trade, and are competing for an ever-greater share.

The situation today is the same as in 1998, when guerrillas protecting the drug trade increased their attacks on Colombian security forces and hampered counter-narcotics operations, particularly in the coca growing regions of southern and southeastern Colombia, at the same time as Colombia struggles to climb out of its worst economic crisis since the 1930s. The Colombian government is hard pressed to commit the resources necessary to combat the powerful combined threat of drug traffickers and guerrilla elements involved in the drug trade.

The collaboration of transnational criminality with terrorism has always been a motive for concern, since in Latin America powerful drug groups have established ad hoc mutually beneficial arrangements with insurgent or terrorist groups, such as Sendero Luminoso in Peru or the Revolutionary Armed Forces of Colombia (FARC).

While the relationship between drug dealers and these groups has been contentious at times, insurgents are sometimes paid to provide security services for drug traffickers, where they often "tax" drug operations in areas they control and, in some instances, they are directly involved in narcotics cultivation.[4]

More recently, a little after the collapse of the communist bloc, a new situation has arisen. Analysis of seized military equipment, revealing armaments for exclusive military use of Russian origin, leads one to believe the existence of links between Russian organized crime and Colombian guerrillas.

Indeed, during hearings on the threat from international organized crime and global terrorism before the House of Representatives Committee on International Relations, it was made clear that there is a link between the Colombian drug cartels and the Russian Mafia.

The Mafia provides weapons and ammunition for the emerging smaller drug cartels that stepped in to replace the enormous Medellín and Cali cartels. Russian organized crime has amassed large quantities of weaponry. The Colombian narco-guerrillas, such as the FARC and ELN, have used drug proceeds to purchase weapons such as heavy machine guns, mortars, surface-to-air missiles, and high-tech communications equipment, often from Eastern Europe. Russian organized crime elements have become virtual arms bazaars for the purchase of weapons by Colombian narco-guerrillas. Starting in Colombia, the drug traffic moves to Eastern Europe and Russia, returning to Colombia in the form of weapons of death that feed, in a continuous cycle, the violence in that country.

It was further declared that "about the links between the terrorists and drugs: the influx of ill-gotten drug money means that the boundaries between the FARC, drug traffickers and organized crime have merged in a pool of terror and bloodshed that has dramatically increased violence in Colombia."[5]

It is interesting to observe the analysis proposed with respect to the change in the nature relative to organized crime and terrorism, when Ward notes:

> One of the most perplexing aspects of the changing crime problem throughout the world is an increasing network of criminal activities which crosses traditional boundaries, and merges heretofore separate offences in pursuit of common goals. The joining of narco-trafficking and terrorism . . . contribute to what has been loosely termed the grey phenomenon.
>
> Referring to the grey area phenomenon as conflicts ranging from terrorism, insurgencies, mass illegal drug trafficking to warlordism, militant fundamentalism, ethnic cleansing and civil war to other transnational threats and consequences of instability. And Narco-terrorism has become a part of the underworld dictionary.[6]

As a consequence, new mechanisms are developing through optimizing the level of relationships between these organizations by fully utilizing the specific vocations of each one. Although having said that the activities continue in determined geographic areas, the expansion of the relationships will depend on international connections for the placing of the illicit products and the obtaining of arms. By reason of such actions, although being realized in a determined territorial context, they end up reflecting in a whole region or extrapolating their effects, and will affect and victimize communities in a totally aleatory manner around the globe. In other words, it is a question of wide-scale victimization.

VICTIMIZATION

The Latin American countries, through the increase in the narco-traffickers' firepower, together with the natural difficulties which hamper and make it almost impossible for an effective repression of drug trafficking, are victimized in a differentiated manner. Nevertheless, it is certainly impossible to really separate, with respect to the participation of guerrillas as one portion in narco-traffic, the entire productive criminal activity as a whole from the cultivating, processing, refining, and international distribution of the drug.

But it is also correct to imagine the appreciable participation of the various insurgent groups and terrorists who gravitate around the easy money obtained under their cloak of protection, in global terms, in the drug economy.

It is also true that, in one way or another, during the past decade this relationship of exchange of interests has resulted in the capacity to continue to increase production levels, despite governmental activities aimed at eradication of the plant and elimination of the narco-traffickers.

The so-called guerrilla zones, transformed into war zones, where the domination of the area comes under the control of the insurgent groups, have passed the stage of independent territories. This situation is seen today in part of the Colombian territory.

Peru

This situation is nothing new on the continent. For years we have been seeing this same scenario in Peru. The saga through which the Colombian communities have passed takes on the same characteristics today as in the past. Peru has faced nearly twenty years of civil disobedience by several Marxist insurgency movements.

The Tupac Marau Revolutionary Movement, along with the Sendero Luminoso, or Shining Path, have used peasants to grow illegal coca plants in an effort to fund their guerrilla armies. The Marxist insurgency movements have additionally allied themselves with such powerful narco-trafficking organizations as Colombia's Medellín Cocaine Cartel as well as the Cali Cartel.

The Shining Path's People's Guerrilla Army was formed in March 1983. This was the means, in May 1984, for the fanning out of the rebel actions beyond the departments of Ayacucho and many other parts of the Andes and jungle regions.

While the security forces tried to oblige the peasant communities in northern Ayacucho to form self-defense groups (*las rondas*) and treated them brutally if they showed resistance, Shining Path responded by crushing the *rondas* with all the savagery they could muster. There were relatively few direct clashes between the rebels, the soldiers, or police. Instead, each side concentrated on punishing the people for whose hearts they were supposedly fighting.

The communities found themselves in a no-man's land where death came from within and on every side.[7] With the capture in 1992 of Shining Path leader Abimael Guzman, the leadership became crippled.

Peru's second insurgency movement, the Tupac Amaru Revolutionary Movement (MRTA) is almost contained. With the successful ending of the

MRTA hostage takeover of the Japanese embassy in the capital, Lima, MRTA's credibility as a strong terrorist force was destroyed.

Both groups, Shining Path and MRTA, use peasants to harvest coca to fund their armies. Once the coca has been farmed and harvested by the peasants, the insurgent groups sell the coca to Colombian drug cartels.

Colombia

From the clashes between the constituted authorities and the revolutionaries, direct and immediate victims resulted. These are the ordinary people who suffer the consequences of simply finding themselves being where the confrontation takes place. And further, there is the victimization engendered, as mentioned before, by exposing the peasants to the pressures and violence of the opposing groups. As a result, there was by the end of 1999 an enormous contingent of more than 1 million, or perhaps 1.5 million, displaced persons living on the edge of civilized society.

While displacement is a national problem in Colombia, the poorest are the most affected. In rural regions where paramilitary actions are frequent, the small farmer, in trying to avoid the violence, becomes displaced.

These people are concentrated in the capital, Bogotá, in that city's poorest areas. Apart from the poverty the displaced have to face, they also suffer the loss of nonmaterial possessions that make life meaningful: family, friends, regional culture, familiar surroundings.

The roots of all this can be found in the civil war between the Liberals, Conservatives, and Communists, which lasted between 1948 and 1966. This was *La Violencia* during which an estimated 200,000 people were killed.

The perpetrators of today's violence and displacement also espouse conflicting political views, though they are battling less for ideological reasons than for land, money, and power. There are left-wing guerrillas who torture villagers suspected of sympathizing with the government, right-wing paramilitaries who are paid by wealthy landowners to push small farmers off their land, and dangerous narco-traffickers who will kill those who get in their way.

Also in Colombia, thirty-five massacres cost the lives of 272 individuals in the first months of 1977, during which period more than 450 were assassinated for political reasons. The biggest massacre, according to Human Rights Watch/America, was attributed to paramilitary groups who generally operate with the collusion of the military.

Further, according to the 1988 Global Report, the Colombian Commission of Jurists declared that of human rights violations in 1977, 76 percent were committed by paramilitaries, 17 percent by guerrillas, and 7 percent by government agents.

Lamentably, in that country the classification *the forgotten victims of narco-terrorism* proves, in what can be considered as in no uncertain terms, to be true.

Without going back in history, a simple look at the recent past shows us another facet of terrorist violence linked to drugs.

As a matter of fact, this is not the preserve of the Colombian cartels, where actions of extreme violence to intimidate and perpetuate the pursuit of criminal activities are carried out. These were also practiced in other countries, such as in Italy.

There was the example of Sicilian Mafia terrorism, where terrorists placed a bomb on a Naples-Milan train, which caused the death of fifteen passengers and the wounding of another 230. And in 1992, the Mafia assassinated the magistrates Giovanni Falcone and Paolo Borselino, who had become the symbols of the struggle against the Cosa Nostra.

These attitudes of terrorism without political connotation started to appear in Latin America after 1983, when Rodrigo Lara Bonilla was appointed minister of justice in Colombia. He launched a campaign against the drug trade, which was supported by one of the leading Bogotá newspapers. In early 1984, fourteen tons of cocaine were seized, and the police confiscated a number of airplanes, vehicles, and chemicals at the premises of the largest laboratories operated by the Medellin Cartel.

War was declared on the drug lords Pablo Escobar, Jorge Luis Ochoa, Gonzalo Rodriguez Gacha, and Carlos Lehder. That same year, Minister of Justice Rodrigo Lara Bonilla was assassinated.

The government's response was to implement an extradition treaty with the United States, where drug traffickers would be judged under American legislation. In 1987, Carlos Lehder was extradited to the United States.

To demonstrate their power of intimidation, the traffickers responded with a campaign of terror: bombing banks and burning down farms in the Antioquia department and newspaper offices and private homes in Bogotá, Cali, Medellín, and Barranquilla.

To further demonstrate what we should understand as narco-terrorism as being apolitical, it is simply unleashed by terrorist actions sponsored by criminals linked to drug trafficking. Its power of destruction and the sacrifice of people are in the same proportion as those acts which are politically motivated.

It is worth recording two acts carried out in Colombia, which exemplify the intensity of damage and similarity to other outrages by groups of terrorists spread out throughout the world. The first was in September 1989, when a mid-air bombing killed all 101 passengers and six crewmembers of an Avianca flight from Bogotá to Cali. In December that same year, a huge truck bomb ripped into the lower floors of the National Police Agency headquarters.

These terrorist actions were attributed to Gonzalo Gacha, "El Mexicano," one of the leaders of the Medellín Cartel, this cycle only ending with his death. This motivated the leaders' remaining at that time to negotiate with the government.

The legacy of violence is clearly shown by the data available from Medellín, where the proportion of fifteen- to nineteen-year-olds and twenty- to twenty-four-year-olds who die is much higher relative to the national totals. Also, 78 percent of the deaths registered in Medellín are due to violence.[8]

In Colombia, the violence reached world records during the 1950s and 1960s, where guerrilla warfare, paramilitary groups, and paid political assassinations were all part of the population's way of life.

Even so, there was a tremendous increase in violence during the last decade, when drug trafficking and the dirty war prospered. Today the homicide rates are three times higher than they were ten years ago.[9]

As well as all the aforementioned problems, it must also be borne in mind the insecurity caused by the loss of billions of dollars in foreign investments in the country, according to the Colombian Ministry of Foreign Trade. Through internal conflicts over the last decade, in which left-wing guerrillas, ultra right-wing paramilitary death squads, and government forces have taken part, at least 35,000 civilians have been killed and around 1.5 million displaced.

Colombia, a country of 40 million inhabitants, is facing the oldest conflict in the continent. This conflict has caused all kinds of damages, including ecological, such as those carried out by the National Liberation Army (ELN) by rupturing oil pipelines. Between 1994 and 1997, proven damages by guerrillas, according to government data, have caused the spillage of more than 1 million barrels of petroleum. Damage caused to the environment, in rivers, woods, and the jungle itself is practically irreparable, and forms one more part of the forgotten aspects of this enormous problem.

Brazil

The financial movement in drugs in Brazil is estimated to be US$10 billion, an amount which while difficult to prove, gives a fair view of the importance of the country in the context of Latin America. Brazilian gangs have always specialized in the transport of drugs, by virtue of the natural corridor established by the international markets.

The operations traditionally paid for as a percentage of the drug transported, in the order of 10–20 percent, contributed to the increase in the local supply side. For this reason the number of users has been increasing in alarming proportions. Lately, new criminal activities have started to be identified by the police. Investigations by Brazilian police show that the laboratories are leaving Colombian territory and coming to Brazil, because the guerrillas are increasing the "taxes," the toll charged to give the criminals cover. Groups specializing in refining (transforming the cocaine paste into the powder form ready for consumption) are installing themselves in the remote regions of the Amazon and in the Mato Grosso state (in the west of Brazil).

Control over the area of refining enriches the trafficker most, and signifies an evident rise in the direction toward the top of the organization. In the case of the industrialization of the drug, because of the amount of people involved, it is obvious that some sort of organization is required.

The country therefore becomes pervaded with the influx of an organized and violent criminality, which, in order to achieve its production needs, has fully integrated the whole process, occupying a place in society through corruption and intimidation, and thus destabilizing that society.

The migration of laboratories to the country, together with the traffic, produced an enormous impact on the economies of the cities in the region.[10] This generates untold sources of wealth, and brings in tow financial criminality through the need to establish the mechanisms for money laundering. The penalization of the country, by the influx of this specialized criminality, is a long way from the real victimization, which affects the user.

Crack, a cocaine derivative, is chosen by 61 percent of drug dependants in São Paulo, compromising a whole generation. This type of cocaine, in rock form and smoked in improvised pipes, has produced 150,000 victims in São Paulo alone.

The crack victims, who now cover the whole spectrum of society, when they are from the middle class, lose their jobs or abandon school, selling everything they own to buy the drug. In about six months they start to hallucinate, very often become mortally aggressive, and this normally leads to a life of crime. With respect to the lower classes, they abandon home and start living rough in the streets, in the most miserable conditions, forming a contingent of youngsters without futures, the targets for all kinds of violence, and with the prospects of a very short and extremely hard life span.

The data on the increase in violent crime in the 1980s are irrefutable. The violent crime that is linked mostly to the drug gang warfare is homicide. Generally the young violator's participation in violent crimes is evident.

The relatively large participation of young males as agents and victims of violence in Brazil follows an international trend on the American continent. Because these deaths follow the same patterns as elsewhere on the continent, it is most probable that they are due to the fact that drugs and arms enter the country easily.[11]

These are perhaps the most terrible effects of the ominous business of drugs, which would certainly be combated against more efficiently and less onerously if it weren't linked to terrorism—the same terrorism that protects the trafficking of drugs on the one hand and promotes its use on the other, in order to obtain the benefits upon which it feeds and guarantees its well-being.

CONCLUSION

There is a growing significance of apolitical groups that resort to terrorism in pursuit of financial gain as a part of the criminal enterprise. While a number of these groups may, in part, justify their actions under the rubric of political rationalization, their major goal will relate to maximizing the profits through coopting, corrupting, and neutralizing the authority of the states in their respective countries and regions of operations. These groups, which include narco-terrorists, are particularly difficult to counteract given the vast resources gleaned by illicit trade in drugs or weapons, and because of their ability to influence, control, and demoralize governments in countries where they operate. This new criminal order can engage in operations with the kind of violence that makes the old Mafia seem pacifistic by comparison.[12]

The resort to terrorism by apolitical terrorists who are engaged in violence and intimidation will be particularly threatening since, as a result of their illegal trade in drugs and other criminal enterprises, they may have access to vast funds. What could make those groups especially dangerous may be the fact that their threats and acts of terrorism would not necessarily be meant to achieve publicity or dramatize their cause.

The threats of narco-terrorism, whether of a political basis or not, are a reality. One could even say that they cannot be confronted separately. Various declarations have been made in the sense that "one cannot fight drug trafficking in Latin America without fighting the guerrillas."

Perhaps this is true; in concluding the analysis as a whole, it can be seen there is immense suffering by the people, inestimable loss of life, and widespread social instability. This could yet attain other levels which we cannot imagine, such as damage to the ecology and irreparable economic disorder, which would affect communities independent of their frontiers.

In the same way as governments engage in the unremitting task of attacking transnational criminality, organized crime should be prosecuted at all costs, irrespective of its bogus alliances with insurgents, terrorists, or guerrillas, and all possible efforts to do so must be exerted.

Obtaining this objective calls for, inclusively, the fullest cooperation between countries, embracing popular awareness and political volition at the national level.

Finally, and who knows even in a utopian way, the governments may pursue negotiations with the guerrillas as a possible solution, aimed at minimizing the impacts of suffering across the whole continent, absorbing the same through political integration.

NOTES

1. United Nations Control Board, *Report of the International Narcotics Control Board,* United Nations Office for Drug Control and Crime Prevention, 41st Plenary Meeting, July 30, 1992: 1.

2. George Millard, "Drugs and Corruption in Latin American." *Dickinson Journal of International Law.* 15, no. 3: 533.

3. U.S. Bureau for International Narcotics and Law Enforcement Affairs, International Narcotics Control Strategy Report 1999, Washington, D.C.: U.S. Department of State, March 2000: 1.

4. *Ibid.*

5. Committee on International Relations, House of Representatives, *The Threat from International Organized Crime and Global Terrorism,* October 1, 1997: 1.

6. Richard H. Ward, "Gray Phenomena: The Changing Nature of Organized Crime and Terrorism," *Crime and Justice International,* March/April 1995: 37.

7. Simon Strong, *Shining Path.* London: Fontana, 1993.

8. Alba Zazular, *Violence Related to Illegal Drugs: "Easy Money" and Justice in Brazil—1980/1995,* Discussion Paper Series, no. 35. MOST–Management of Social Transformations Control Program, United Nations Educational, Scientific, and Cultural Organization, 1999.

9. *Ibid.*

10. Lia Osorio Machado, "Financial Flows and Drug Trafficking in the Amazon Basin," Discussion Paper Series, no. 22. MOST–Management of Social Transformations Control Program, United Nations Educational, Scientific, and Cultural Organization, 1998.

11. Alba Zazuar, *Violence Related to Illegal Drugs: "Easy Money" and Justice in Brazil—1980/1995,* MOST/United National Drug Control Program (UNDCP), 1996.

12. Stephen Sloan, *Terrorism: How Vulnerable is the United States?* The Strategic Studies Institute of the U.S. Army College, May 1995.

9

The Targets and Intended Victims of Terrorist Activities in the United States

Kelly R. Damphousse, Brent L. Smith, and Amy Sellers

Little empirical information has been available on the actual targets and/or the intended victims of terrorist groups. For the current analysis, the authors extracted actual targets and intended targets of terrorists indicted in the United States between 1980 and 1999. Using data from the American Terrorism Study, the authors identified the top three actual targets (completed acts) and the top three intended targets (prevented acts) of over 400 terrorists from about fifty terrorist groups. Information was extracted from the federal criminal indictments of the terrorists. Analyses of the data suggest that targeting typically falls into one or more of four categories: (1) efforts to obtain funding for the terrorist organization; (2) "ideological revenge" against specific persons who have been vocal in their opposition to the group or its goals; (3) "ideologically symbolic" targets that epitomize the group's stance on specific political issues; and (4) internal targeting of wayward members for security purposes. While one would expect "ideologically symbolic" targets to dominate such an analysis, the number of crimes committed by terrorists in the other categories suggests that the criminal activities of terrorist groups are much more varied and unpredictable than most persons realize.

Although significant efforts have been made in recent years to provide a variety of services to the victims of terrorism (Office for Victims of Crimes 2002), this type of victim has received little attention in the empirical literature. This is due to a variety of reasons. First, the number of victims of terrorist attacks in a given population available for study has been relatively small until recently. The infrequent occurrence of terrorist incidents precluded the identification of a large sample of victims until the Oklahoma City bombing in 1995 and September 11, 2001, attacks. Second, like the study of terrorism in general, the study of the victims of this phenomenon is mired in conceptual difficulties. Our inability to adequately define and apply a universally acceptable definition of terrorism adversely affects our ability to study the victims of these crimes as well.

Finally, the explicit assumption that terrorism is characterized by "indiscriminate violence" has, in many ways, diminished the study of the victims of terrorist acts. Other than studies of the adequacy of victim services and how victims psychologically adapt to victimization, a major focus of victim research has been to learn about the interactions that take place between victims and offenders. The study of these interactions can help us learn how to minimize the risk of victimization, as well as help us learn more about the dynamics that led offenders to select these victims in the first place. On the other hand, if these offenders select their victims randomly and indiscriminately, as we assume that terrorists do, then the study of the victims of terrorism has somewhat limited utility in this regard.

The extent to which this is the case is unclear. An important question, therefore, is: Are the innocent victims of terrorism actually randomly selected? Despite the argument that one of the salient characteristics of terrorism is its "indiscriminate nature," the ideological blinders that terrorists wear suggests closer scrutiny of this issue. To answer such a question requires that we examine the "terrorist targeting" literature. However, once again, we are faced with methodological problems that have inhibited the study of this phenomenon. For example, when operationalizing the victims or targets of terrorist attacks, does one code the building that was bombed as the target or the people who were injured as the victim or target of the attack? One might easily argue that the building was the target and the people were the indiscriminate victims, but such an explanation belies the complexity of the relationship between terrorist groups, their ideology and organizational structure, and the targets or victims they choose.

These difficulties have precluded our ability to progress beyond simply listing broad categories of terrorist targets and/or their victims (e.g., Patterns of Global Terrorism Annual Reports, U.S. Department of State). In this chapter, we propose the quantification of terrorist targeting/victimization data in such a way that empirical testing of hypotheses can be conducted. Due the limited literature on this subject and the exploratory nature of this effort, however, our results merely set the stage for future analyses. To begin this endeavor, a review of the somewhat sparse literature on the targets and victims of terrorism is necessary.

RELEVANT LITERATURE

Terrorists engage in a variety of criminal conduct prior to the commission of any terrorist acts (Smith and Orvis 1993; Smith 1994). The crimes that these terrorists commit as part of their group activities also have targets and victims. Sometimes these crimes are related to the creation of false identities for group members, the maintenance of internal security, or the procurement of funding to purchase weapons or explosives. These behaviors ultimately culminate in acts of terror. Previous empirical research on terrorism, however, has focused almost exclusively on the terrorist incident itself. Most terrorism databases are "incident-driven," with data singularly focused on the characteristics of the terrorist incident. Consequently, these databases contain little information about other crimes committed by terrorist groups or the crimes committed in preparation for the terrorist incident.

As the literature review below suggests, an examination of the antecedent criminal conduct of terrorist group members places the subsequent terrorist incident in context, providing an opportunity to potentially identify patterns of conduct that might lead to intervention prior to the commission of actual terrorist incidents. In essence, only examining the victims or targets of the ultimate terrorist incident limits our understanding of the complex dynamics associated with target and victim selection.

The focus of the proposed study requires attention to the literature in two specific areas: (1) research on the political (primary) targets of terrorist groups, and (2) research on antecedent or ancillary terrorist targets and victims and the criminal conduct associated with each. Empirical research in both of these areas is scant. The scarcity of quantitative data on terrorism has been the Achilles' heel of efforts to improve the quality of terrorism research (Blumstein 1996; Crenshaw 1992; Hoffman 1992; Wardlaw 1989). Despite this scarcity, some theoretical literature has emerged during the past twenty years on "targeting" by terrorist groups.

For discussion on antecedent and ancillary criminal conduct, extrapolation will have to be made from the general criminological and organizational theory literature. Generalization from the general criminological literature, it should be noted, is somewhat risky. The demographic characteristics of traditional offenders are substantially different from those persons indicted for terrorism-related crimes here in the United States.

Terrorists tend to include a disproportionately higher percentage of females and white persons than nonterrorist criminals. Terrorists also tend to be slightly better educated and they include more persons from middle- and upper-class backgrounds than the conventional criminal population (Smith and Morgan 1994; Smith 1994). Most important, they are significantly older than traditional offenders, indicating a pattern of career criminality uncharacteristic of common criminals. These demographic variations reflect the motivational differences between terrorists and traditional criminals (Schafer 1971). In other words, the causes of traditional criminality appear to be fundamentally different from the causes of terrorism, thereby making generalizations from one to the other tenuous at best.

Terrorist Targeting

Studies of terrorist targeting have typically been limited to anecdotal information or descriptive analyses of U.S. Department of State reports. Most databases that exist linking terrorist groups to targeting data are encyclopedic in nature (e.g., Mickolus 1980, 1989, 1993). Although this method has been useful in chronicling terrorism over the years, only marginal quantification of data has been available to either test hypotheses or identify statistical relationships that might aid in the development of public policy (see Drake 1998; e.g., the RAND-St. Andrews Chronology of International Terrorism). The ITERATE (International Terrorism: Attributes of Terrorist Events) database developed by Edward Mickolus, for example, has been one of the few quantitative databases available that allowed even rudimentary empirical examination linking terrorist groups to their targets. The ITERATE database, however, focused primarily on international terrorism and is, therefore, of somewhat limited utility for an analysis of American terrorism.

Despite these limitations, theoretical efforts to predict the targets of terrorism emerged. The most obvious factor influencing target selection and which has formed the basis of most theorizing about the subject focuses upon ideology. Traditionally, most interpretations of targeting behavior describe terrorism as a means to an end—the intent being "to produce a change in the government's political position" (Crenshaw 1988, 13). Consequently, ideology has been the most prevalent predictor of targeting behavior (Drake 1998). Crenshaw contends that scholars using this method of analysis view terrorism as "instrumental"—that the "targets of terrorism are symbolically related to the organization's ideological beliefs" and are, therefore, fundamental to an assessment of targeting behavior (Crenshaw 1988, 15).

While this rather obvious relationship can help us predict the targets of terrorist groups, Crenshaw also notes that other factors may influence this process. In particular, she contends that an alternate framework may explain more of the variance in target selection. "Organizational process" theory assumes that the "fundamental purpose of any political organization is to maintain itself" (Crenshaw 1988, 19). From this perspective, the selection of terrorism targets is analyzed not as ends in themselves (i.e., to attain specific political goals), but as the outcome of efforts to maintain the integrity of the terrorist organization. For example, targets may be selected so that "leaders [can] maintain their position by supplying various tangible and intangible incentives to members" (Crenshaw 1988, 19). Examples might include allowing group members to seek vengeance on a personal enemy, because he/she had castigated them publicly, as in the 1984 killing of Alan Berg by members of the Order.

A second hypothesis emerging from this perspective suggests that "the older the organization, the more its behavior is explained by organizational imperatives" (Crenshaw 1988, 21). Hence, the longer a terrorist group survives, the more likely its targets will reflect a concern for maintaining the group and its organizational structure. Conversely, the longer the group continues, "the less concerned it becomes with the achievement of political goals" (Crenshaw 1988, 21). Rapoport (1992) contends that well over 90 percent of terrorist organizations have a life expectancy of less than one year. For maturing terrorist organizations capable of surviving beyond infancy, the politically symbolic targets that serve as the basis of much group discussion may, in reality, be replaced by targets that reflect social relations or financial reward. In this manner, Crenshaw contends that terrorism becomes self-sustaining for many organizations. During the mid-1980s, for example, members of the Order and the United Freedom Front became more concerned with the financial rewards associated with bank and armored truck robberies than they were with the commission of actual terrorist incidents (Smith 1994).

In more recent literature on terrorism, theorists have begun to acknowledge that ideology is merely the tip of the iceberg in our understanding of the selection of terrorist targeting. In a recent analysis, Hoffman (1998) reached the conclusion that "the tactics and targets of various terrorist movements, as well as the weapons they favor, are therefore ineluctably shaped by a group's *ideology*, its internal *organizational dynamics* and the *personalities of its key members*, as well as a variety of internal and external factors (Hoffman 1988, 157, emphasis added). Hoffman notes, however, that other factors may also play a significant role in the selection of targets or victims. In particular, he contends that the need to appease the terrorist group's constituency is an overriding feature of target selection. Frequently, Hoffman argues, the "target audience" may not be the opposition government, but the particular populace the terrorist group is trying to accommodate to maintain support and recruitment.

A dominant theme that has emerged in the evolution of the terrorism literature is the acknowledgment that the criminality of terrorists is more widespread and complex than previously discussed. Crenshaw (1988) expanded terrorist targeting to include "organizational maintenance" crimes while Hoffman (1998, 158) argued that the overriding tactical imperative of many terrorist groups "has been the deliberate tailoring of their violent acts to appeal to their perceived constituencies." This suggests the need for an empirical assessment of these propositions.

Antecedent Preparatory and Ancillary Targets

Although the causes of traditional criminality may be fundamentally different from the causes of violent political crimes like terrorism, recent studies of traditional criminality link a variety of antecedent crimes to the ultimate objectives of many types of offenders. The literature on drug use is replete with links to the use of antecedent preparatory crimes to fund an offender's addiction (e.g., Inciardi, Horowitz, and Pottieger 1993; Kaplan 1995). Wright and Decker's (1997) analysis of armed robbers characterizes armed robbery as an antecedent to the procurement of illicit drugs and alcohol. Similarly, the organized crime literature is saturated with descriptions of both legitimate and illegitimate ancillary activities related to the maintenance of crime cartels (Abadinsky 2000; Albanese 1996).

Many of the victims of terrorist groups were victimized not during an "officially" recognized terrorist incident, but were targeted in support of the terrorist group's planning or maintenance activities. Recent analyses of terrorism prosecutions reveal that terrorists are seldom prosecuted for the commission of actual terrorist incidents, but instead are charged and convicted of a wide variety of more traditional offenses (Smith 1994; Smith and Damphousse 1996; 1998; Smith and Orvis 1993). Many of these crimes have real victims. But they have not traditionally been considered when examining the targets and victims of terrorist groups.

Research Questions

We will not be able to address all of the issues and hypotheses outlined in the above discussion. For the purposes of this exploratory analysis, we are interested in several basic research questions. First, what have been the "actual" and "intended" targets of American terrorist groups during the past twenty years? Terrorist groups are precluded from actually carrying out most of their planned terrorist actions. The FBI routinely identifies in its annual report a larger number of "preventions" than "actual" terrorist incidents each year. The inclusion of these intended targets (e.g., preventions) will provide a more thorough examination of victim and target selection.

Second, have these targets and intended victims changed over time? For example, have new security measures by the government or advances in technology and training by terrorists in the 1990s caused terrorist groups to modify the types of targets and victims selected?

Third, can we empirically demonstrate variations in terrorist targets and victims by type of terrorist group? For example, have the rise of right-wing extremism in the 1990s and the decline of leftist terror during this decade significantly altered the types of persons or facilities targeted by terrorist groups?

METHODOLOGY

Efforts to study terrorism in America have been difficult at best. Little national-level data has been available for analysis. Subsequently, scholars have been forced to collect data independently, using definitions of terrorism that frequently reflect the ideological persuasions of the researcher and employing empirical methods that are suspect at best. The data in the current study are derived from the American Terrorism Study,[1] a project that began monitoring federal prosecutions of terrorists in 1988 (dating back to 1980) and continues to the current time. The American Terrorism Study attempts to overcome some of these deficiencies by adhering strictly to the Federal Bureau of Investigation's definition of terrorism.[2] Despite criticism regarding the FBI's application of the definition (see Carlson 1995, for example), FBI data on terrorism provides the greatest continuity over time. Furthermore, the study ensures adherence to the practical application of the definition by restricting itself to data collection only on cases that occurred as a result of an indictment stemming from a federal "domestic security/terrorism investigation." These investigations, conducted by the FBI in accordance with the *Attorney General Guidelines on General Crimes, Racketeering Enterprises, and Domestic Security/Terrorism Investigations*, "set forth the predication threshold and limits for investigations of crimes . . . in support of terrorist objectives" (FBI 1999, 2).

The FBI conducts hundreds of investigations regarding suspected terrorist activities each year. Many of these crimes are investigated through the FBI Joint Terrorism Task Forces. Occasionally, the crimes committed indicate a pattern or suspected pattern that involves the continued threat of political violence from an individual or group. When that occurs, the FBI may open a "domestic security/terrorism" investigation (in lieu of a "general crimes" investigation). During the 1990s, the FBI routinely was investigating between eight and twelve terrorist groups under these guidelines at any one time. The exact number of groups being investigated and the names of groups under active investigation are classified.

Once an indictment is issued, however, these cases become a matter of public record, retained in the federal criminal case files at the federal district courts where the cases were tried. Although the court cases are public record, the FBI is precluded from *collating* data or creating lists for private individuals that would identify these cases. Consequently, the U. S. House of Representatives Judiciary Subcommittee on Crime has acted as a sponsor for the project. The subcommittee requests the collated data from the FBI, and once collated, it can be submitted to the principal investigator for further data collection.[3] In November 1997, data collection began on terrorists indicted in federal criminal court from 1990–1996 as a result of an official terrorism investigation. These data were supplemented with persons indicted in 1997–1999 in 2001. Information in the current study is compared with data from Smith's 1980s database of federally indicted terrorists.

The 1980s sample includes approximately 75 percent of the known terrorists indicted in federal courts during that decade. It includes information on some 210 "indictees"[4] from over twenty terrorist groups. They were charged with nearly 1,400 federal counts. The 1990s sample includes over 90 percent of the terrorists indicted in federal court from 1990–1998. These 220 indictees, representing nearly thirty terrorist groups, were indicted for over 1,300 violations of federal criminal law.

The dataset includes information on approximately eighty variables divided into four major categories: (1) demographic information such as the age, race, and sex of the defendant; (2) information about the terrorist group to which the individual belongs including types of preferred and actual targets of the group; (3) prosecution and defense data, which includes precise identification of the charges, method of prosecution, and other variables reflecting defense strategies such as types of motions filed; and (4) count/case outcome and sentencing data for each defendant. The "common denominator" for all cases in the sample is the *count*. All subsequent data on individuals, terrorist group affiliations, prosecution/defense strategies, and sentencing data are replicated for each count. Consequently, analyses can be conducted on variables using any of the four major units of analysis.

For the current study, project personnel reread each of the indictments and associated materials relevant to each criminal case from 1980–1998. Each target or victim was identified and coded, linking the target data to specific groups. These targets were divided into "actual" and "intended" categories. Actual targets include completed offenses in which a building was damaged, person injured, or the specific target was actually hit. Actual targets also include the targets of "antecedent" or "ancillary" criminal activities by terrorist groups. These may include internal targets (wayward members) as well as facilities or personnel victimized in planning for future terrorist incidents.

Intended targets include those targets or victims identified in the indictments and other case materials that were planned, but resulted in intervention by law enforcement personnel before an actual terrorist incident could take place. In addition to these "inchoate" terrorist crimes, intended targets include those "desired" targets or victims mentioned by members of the terrorist group in court testimony or documents.

RESULTS

Over seventy-five specific victims and targets or categories of each were identified from the federal court records. Among them, 220 of these targets or victims were "actual targets," while 120 were "intended targets." In all, some 340 targets or victims were identified. Two issues should be noted at this point regarding the coding strategy. The 220 actual targets or victims are not a measure of the number of terrorist incidents in the United States during the past two decades. There are a number of factors that render the two incompatible, the most important being that our measure of targets includes "antecedent" and "ancillary" victims and targets. We have not distinguished between "terrorist targets" and "antecedent or ancillary targets" in the current analysis. Second, there is always some confusion regarding whether the target was a "facility" or a "person." For example, although there were hundreds of victims in the Oklahoma City bombing and scores of persons aboard Pan Am Flight 103, these are coded as two targets, not a separate target for each of the victims. In contrast, individuals were coded as targets or victims if they were specifically identified by the terrorists as the intended target (e.g., Alan Berg).

The seventy-five or so categories of victims/targets were collapsed into nine broad categories for the current analysis. Both personnel and facilities are included in each of the nine major groupings. Government personnel

Table 9.1.   Type of Target for All Terrorists, 1980–1998

Type of Target	Intended		Actual		Total	
	F	%	F	%	F	%
Government[1]	49	40.83	43	19.55	92	27.06
Military[2]	19	15.83	14	6.36	33	9.71
Hate Crime[3]	15	2.50	30	13.64	45	13.24
Defense-Related/Public Retail[4]	2	1.67	47	21.36	49	14.41
Economic Establishments[5]	11	9.17	54	24.55	65	19.12
Media/Outspoken Opposition/ Group Affiliate[6]	15	12.5	14	6.36	29	8.53
Utilities (Gas/Power/Water)[7]	2	1.67	5	2.27	7	2.06
Transportation Systems[8]	6	5.00	5	2.27	11	3.24
Farms/Animal Labs[9]	1	0.83	8	3.64	9	2.65
Total	120		220		340	

[1]Government targets include the following: federal courthouses/buildings, federal law enforcement facility, United Nations, foreign government facility, other government facility, U.S. embassy, U.S. prison, IRS, Department of State, Department of Commerce, U.S. Customs, Department of Human Services, Department of Treasury, Department of Agriculture, Department of Natural Resources, federal law enforcement personnel, foreign official, other government personnel, judge, New World Order, other.

[2]Military targets include the following: military base/fort, recruiting station, British military helicopters, reserve centers, training centers, other military building, military personnel, U.K. military, British military soldiers, other.

[3]Hate Crime targets include the following: Jewish facility, Black facility/NAACP, Israeli embassy, Jewish person, Black person, U.S. person, White person, Israeli person, gay facility (nightclubs, etc), abortion facility, church, adult movie theater, gay person, abortion provider.

[4] Defense-related/public retail targets include the following: defense-related corporation, retail store, performing arts center, tobacco company, restaurant, weapons retailer, ski resort, theater.

[5]Economic establishment targets include the following: bank, armored truck–bank, armored truck–casino, armored truck depot, World Trade Center, drub dealers.

[6]Media/outspoken opposition/group affiliate targets include the following: media crew, Spokane Review Building, magazine office, radio/TV station, Morris Dees, Southern Poverty Law Center, Anti-Defamation League, opposition leader, group affiliate.

[7]Utilities (gas/power/water) targets include the following: gas/power/water facility.

[8]Transportations systems targets include the following: Pan Am flight 103, airliner, airport, public roads/tunnels/bridges.

[9]Farms/animal lab targets include the following: fur farm, university with animal research units.

and facilities were the dominant target of terrorist groups in the United States, accounting for slightly over one-fourth (27.1 percent) of the total targets. While the federal government may be a favorite target of terrorist groups, an alternative explanation is also possible. Specific types of targets may be more likely than others to trigger the opening of an "official" terrorism investigation. Consequently, an overrepresentation of government targets may be as much an indicator of governmental application of the definition of terrorism as it is an indicator of the distribution of terrorist activities. This is reflective of Black's (Black and Reiss 1970) description of arrest records as being better indicators of "police activity" than an accurate measure of the volume of criminal activity.

Economic establishments, defense contractors and public retailers, and hate crime victims round out the top four target categories. With the exception of the World Trade Center (which was coded as an economic establishment), the overwhelming majority of economic establishments were targeted not for terrorist acts, but as means of procuring funding for their respective terrorist groups. When comparing actual versus intended targets in table 9.1, one noticeable pattern emerges. Although government and military targets are the most desired, the proportion of intended targets to actual targets is considerably lower for the government and military categories than all other categories. For example, forty-three of the ninety-two government targets (47 percent) identified by terrorists in court documents were carried out. In contrast, forty-seven of the forty-nine defense-related or retail corporate targets (96 percent) and fifty-four of the sixty-five economic targets (83 percent) were actually targeted. The most obvious explanation for this pattern is that government and military targets have substantially better security than private companies. These patterns suggest that "target hardening" at government facilities and military installations have probably had a significant impact on either reducing terrorism or diverting it to other targets.

Tables 9.2 and 9.3 compare terrorist targets and victims for the 1980s and the 1990s. In terms of total targets, the decades are fairly consistent. One hundred eighty-four targets were identified for the 1980s, while 156 emerged in the 1990s. Similarly, government and military targets/victims accounted for 38 percent of the total targets in the 1980s and 35 percent in the 1990s. There are substantial differences, however. Although the total number of military and government targets identified remained about the same in both decades, the number of actual targets (completed acts against the government and the military) declined substantially. Forty military and government targets were actually hit during the 1980s compared with only seventeen in the 1990s. This pattern is reflected in the overall statistics: the number of actual targets declined substantially while intended targets increased. Although not a precise measure, these statistics suggest that federal intervention efforts have become more successful in recent years. Cases in the 1990s are charac-

Table 9.2.   Type of Target for All Terrorists, 1980–1989

Type of Target	Intended F	Intended %	Actual F	Actual %	Total F	Total %
Government	23	52.27	26	18.57	49	26.63
Military	7	15.91	14	10.00	21	11.41
Hate Crime	2	4.55	9	6.43	11	5.98
Defense-Related/Public Retail	1	2.27	47	33.57	48	26.09
Economic Establishments	3	6.82	30	21.43	33	17.93
Media/Outspoken Opposition/ Group Affiliate	6	13.64	6	4.29	12	6.52
Utilities (Gas/Power/Water)	0	0.00	5	3.57	5	2.72
Transportation Systems	2	4.55	3	2.14	5	2.72
Farms/Animal Labs	0	0.00	0	0.00	0	0.00
Total	44		140		184	

terized by inchoate conspiracies, while 1980s criminal cases were more likely to involve a greater proportion of completed terrorist acts. Federal law enforcement agencies appear to have been playing "catch up" in the 1980s, while the 1990s experienced a pattern of early federal intervention. The exception to this pattern appears to be an increase in terrorism related to animal rights.

Tables 9.4 through 9.6 summarize target selection by type of group— whether left-wing, right-wing, or international. The most obvious pattern that emerges in table 9.4 is the level of efficiency exhibited by leftist terrorists in America over the past twenty years. Of the 101 targets identified, they carried out attacks on eighty-four of them. One reason for the small number of "intended" as opposed to actual targets may be due to the inability of law

Table 9.3.   Type of Target for All Terrorists, 1990–1998

Type of Target	Intended F	Intended %	Actual F	Actual %	Total F	Total %
Government	26	34.21	17	21.25	43	27.56
Military	12	15.79	0	0.00	12	7.69
Hate Crime	13	17.11	21	26.25	34	21.79
Defense-Related/Public Retail	1	1.32	0	0.00	1	0.64
Economic Establishments	8	10.53	24	30.00	32	20.51
Media/Outspoken Opposition/ Group Affiliate	9	11.84	8	10.00	17	10.90
Utilities (Gas/Power/Water)	2	2.63	0	0.00	2	1.28
Transportation Systems	4	5.26	2	2.50	6	3.85
Farms/Animal Labs	1	1.32	8	10.00	9	5.77
Total	76		80		156	

Table 9.4. Type of Target for Left-Wing/Environmental Terrorists, 1980–1998

Type of Target	Intended		Actual		Total	
	F	%	F	%	F	%
Government	6	35.29	14	16.67	20	19.80
Military	5	29.41	12	14.29	17	16.83
Hate Crime	0	0.00	13	15.48	13	12.87
Defense-Related/Public Retail	0	0.00	13	15.48	13	12.87
Economic Establishments	1	5.88	18	21.43	19	18.81
Media/Outspoken Opposition/ Group Affiliate	3	17.65	3	3.57	6	5.94
Utilities (Gas/Power/Water)	0	0.00	2	2.38	2	1.98
Transportation Systems	1	5.88	1	1.19	2	1.98
Farms/Animal Labs	1	5.88	8	9.52	9	8.91
Total	17		84		101	

enforcement agencies to infiltrate these groups during the early 1980s when they were at the peak of their activities. Both the United Freedom Front and the May 19th Communist Organization were active in the years immediately prior to the creation of the federal terrorism task force concept and implementation of new Attorney General Guidelines in 1983. During this period, these two groups committed over forty bombings and bank robberies. By 1986, the FBI had neutralized the threat from these groups through numerous arrests. Most of these persons were arrested not for crimes they were planning to commit, but for crimes they had already committed from the late 1970s through the mid-1980s. The one exception is, once again, the rash of environmental terrorism that targeted university research laboratories using animals.

Table 9.5 reveals that right-wing groups identify a lot more targets than they actually carry out. Despite this, they are similar to leftist groups in that

Table 9.5. Type of Target for Right-Wing Terrorists, 1980–1998

Type of Target	Intended		Actual		Total	
	F	%	F	%	F	%
Government	29	46.03	16	21.33	45	32.61
Military	3	4.76	1	1.33	4	2.90
Hate Crime	8	12.70	12	16.00	20	14.45
Defense-Related/Public Retail	1	1.59	1	1.33	2	1.49
Economic Establishments	10	15.87	35	46.67	45	32.61
Media/Outspoken Opposition/ Group Affiliate	10	15.87	7	9.33	17	12.32
Utilities (Gas/Power/Water)	2	3.17	3	4.00	5	3.62
Transportation Systems	0	0.00	0	0.00	0	0.00
Farms/Animal Labs	0	0.00	0	0.00	0	0.00
Total	63		75		138	

both left-wing and right-wing groups targeted (1) military and government personnel and facilities and (2) economic establishments more than any other category. Although ideological rationales are provided by both groups for targeting economic facilities, in both cases, the primary reason seems to have been to obtain funding for their respective organizations. One notable difference between leftist groups and right-wing groups has been the greater tendency on the part of right-wing groups to target persons or organizations for their lifestyle, ethnicity, or outspoken opposition to the ideology espoused by the terrorist group.

Table 9.6 provides a similar breakdown for targeting by international terrorists. International terrorists indicted in federal courts have been, in many ways, much more discriminating. About 60 percent of the total number of targets identified and about 75 percent of the total number of targets actually hit were in only two categories: (1) government personnel or facilities and (2) defense-related and retail corporations. Whereas left-wing and right-wing groups frequently target economic facilities (banks and armored trucks, primarily) to help fund their terrorism, international terrorists apparently are funded from other sources. The World Trade Center was the only economic institution in our sample targeted by international terrorists; yet, it was targeted for its symbolic value rather than for the procurement of funds.

Table 9.7 provides a comparison of the total number of targets (both intended and actual) among left-wing, right-wing, and international terrorists. The total number of targets attributed to each category of terrorists is similar; right-wing terrorists accounted for the most, but they were also the least likely to carry out their threats. Right-wing terrorists contributed significantly to the two leading targets of terrorists' threats and actions—the government and economic establishments. They were also the leading contributors to hate-related offenses and retributive actions against the media or ideological

Table 9.6.   Type of Target for International Terrorists, 1980–1998

Type of Target	Intended F	Intended %	Actual F	Actual %	Total F	Total %
Government	14	35.00	13	21.31	27	26.73
Military	11	27.50	1	1.64	12	11.88
Hate Crime	7	17.50	5	8.20	12	11.88
Defense-Related/Public Retail	1	2.50	33	54.10	34	33.66
Economic Establishments	0	0.00	1	1.64	1	0.99
Media/Outspoken Opposition/ Group Affiliate	2	5.00	4	6.56	6	5.94
Utilities (Gas/Power/Water)	0	0.00	0	0.00	0	0.00
Transportation Systems	5	12.50	4	6.56	9	8.91
Farms/Animal Labs	0	0.00	0	0.00	0	0.00
Total	40		61		101	

Table 9.7. Type of Target by Type of Terrorist Group, 1980–1998

Type of Target	Left-wing/Environmental[1]		Right-wing[2]		International[3]		Total
	F	%	F	%	F	%	F
Government	20	21.74	45	48.91	27	29.35	92
Military	17	51.52	4	12.12	12	36.36	33
Hate Crime	13	28.89	20	44.44	12	26.67	45
Defense-Related/Public Retail	13	26.53	2	4.08	34	69.39	49
Economic Establishments	19	29.23	45	69.23	1	1.54	65
Media/Outspoken Opposition/Group Affiliate	6	20.69	17	58.62	6	20.69	29
Utilities (Gas/Power/Water)	2	28.57	5	71.43	0	0.00	7
Transportation Systems	2	18.18	0	0.00	9	81.82	11
Farms/Animal Labs	9	100.0	0	0.00	0	0.00	9
Total	101	29.71	138	40.59	101	29.71	340

[1]"Left-wing" includes members of the Macheteros, FALN, El Rukn, May 19 Communist Organization, United Freedom Front, New African Freedom Fighters, Provisional Party of Communists, Yahweh, and Prairie Fire Organizing Committee. "Environmental" includes members of EMETIC/Earth First and Animal Liberation Front.

[2]"Right-wing" includes members of the Aryan Nations, Arizona Patriots, Covenant, Sword and Arm of the Lord, Order, Sheriff's Posse Comitatus, Ku Klux Klan, Order II, White Patriot Party, Washington State Militia, Phineas Priests, Montana Freemen, Oklahoma Constitutional Militia, Patriots Council, Ohio Unorganized Militia/Mountaineer Militia, Aryan Resistance Army, Oklahoma City bombing, Washington based Freemen, 1st Mechanical Kansas Militia, New Order, Colorado 1st Light Infantry, 3rd Continental Congress, and Republic of Texas.

[3]"International" includes members of the Provisional IRA, Japanese Red Army, Omega 7, Libyans, Palestinians/Syrians, World Trade Center bombing, Abu Nidal Organization, Lockerbie Scotland bombing, CNPZ, El Salvador, and Letelier bombing/Cuban National Movement.

critics. Predictably, right-wing terrorists seldom targeted the military. Perhaps the large number of veterans filling their ranks as well as their own sense of patriotism inhibited the targeting of American military personnel and facilities. International terrorists led in only one category of terrorist targeting: they recorded the largest number of threats against defense-related and public retail corporations.

DISCUSSION

The foregoing presentation leaves much to be desired methodologically. An intended threat—one that terrorists thought about and perhaps planned for—is not the same as one that is carried out. Similarly, incidents such as the bombings in Oklahoma City (1995) and at the World Trade Center (1993) are quantitatively and qualitatively different from the rather improbable written threats made against the director of the FBI by members of the Republic of Texas. Yet, our coding strategy fails to distinguish between the severity of the threat, the likelihood of it being completed, and the extent of the damage inflicted.

Despite these flaws, this exploratory analysis is revealing. The data shed light on commonly held beliefs about the influence of various factors on the target selection of various types of terrorist groups. Left- and right-wing groups both had ideological complaints about the federal government and targeted it according. Similarly, they both targeted economic establishments as a means of funding their terrorist activities. International terrorists, in contrast, seldom used bank or armed truck robberies to fund their activities.

The data suggest that the "efficiency" of leftist terrorist groups in the 1980s was probably due to inadequacies in federal intervention policies during that period. Similarly, data from the 1990s suggest that the FBI has become much more aggressive, and successful, in infiltrating terrorist groups and intervening prior to the commission of terrorist incidents. This pattern is particularly apparent among right-wing terrorist groups.

Our preliminary analyses raise a number of important theoretical and methodological questions. We noted that many of the targets of terrorist groups had nothing to do with actual terrorist incidents. Many of these targets reflected efforts to obtain funding for the organization, while others merely reflected efforts to maintain order or improve group morale and cohesion. What is the relationship between these antecedent preparatory and ancillary offenses and the eventual acts of terrorism committed by extremist groups?

Finally, how long do terrorist groups typically plan a terrorist incident before actually committing it? A "preparatory act," in addition to discussion of the commission of a terrorist act, is typically required to initiate a conspiracy.

Do terrorist groups vary in the length of time they take in preparation for an incident depending upon the organizational or tactical structure of the group? For example, right-wing white supremacy groups modified their tactics in the early 1990s to minimize civil and criminal liability of group leaders. The move to an "uncoordinated violence" strategy (in this case, "leaderless resistance") was intended to reduce the ability of law enforcement agents from infiltrating terrorist groups and cells. In addition to modifications in the structure of terrorist groups, are they also modifying the length of time in preparation as a tactical measure to avoid detection? These and other questions can be assessed empirically through the use of targeting data if methodological standards can be met.

NOTES

Support for this research was provided by a grant from the Memorial Institute for the Prevention of Terrorism (MIPT grant # 106-113-2000-064) and the National Institute of Justice (grant #1999-IJCX-0005). Any opinions, findings, conclusions, or recommendations expressed herein are those of the authors and do not necessarily reflect the views of the funding agencies.

1. The American Terrorism Study was conducted with the cooperation of the Federal Bureau of Investigation's Terrorist Research and Analytical Center and was sponsored by the U. S. House of Representatives Judiciary Subcommittee on Crime.

2. The FBI defines terrorism as "the unlawful use of force or violence against persons or property to intimidate or coerce a government, the civilian population, or any segment thereof, in furtherance of political or social objectives" (Federal Bureau of Investigation).

3. The procedure for release of the data was evaluated and approved by the Office of General Counsel at both FBI Headquarters and the U. S. House of Representatives.

4. An "indictee" is distinguished from a "person" since a few of our terrorists were indicted more than one time. When providing demographic characteristics, we use the "person" as the unit of analysis; when describing case outcomes, such as whether someone pleaded guilty or went to trial, we use the "indictee" as the unit of analysis.

BIBLIOGRAPHY

Abadinsky, Howard. 2000. *Organized Crime, Sixth Edition*. Belmont, Calif.: Wadsworth Publishing.

Albanese, Jay. 1996. *Organized Crime in America, Third Edition*. Cincinnati, Ohio.: Anderson Publishing.

Black, Donald, and Albert Reiss. 1970. "Police Control of Juveniles." *American Sociological Review* 35: 63–77.

Blumstein, Alfred. 1996. "Comments before the Committee on Law and Justice, National Research Council, Planning Meeting on Terrorism, Hate Crime, and Anti-Governmental Violence." 20 March, at Washington, D.C.

Carlson, Joseph. 1995. "The Future Terrorists in America." *American Journal of Police* 14, no. 3/4: 71–91.

Crenshaw, Martha. 1988. "Theories of Terrorism: Instrumental and Organizational Approaches." In *Inside Terrorist Organizations*, edited by David C. Rapoport, 13–31. New York: Columbia University Press.

———. 1992. "Current Research on Terrorism: The Academic Perspective." *Studies in Conflict and Terrorism* 15, no. 1: 1–11.

Drake, C. J. M. 1998. *Terrorists' Target Selection*. New York: St. Martin's Press.

Federal Bureau of Investigation. 1999. *Terrorism in the United States: 1997*. Washington, D.C.: U. S. Government Printing Office.

Hoffman, Bruce. 1992. "Current Research on Terrorism and Low-Intensity Conflict." *Studies in Conflict and Terrorism* 15, no. 1: 25–37.

———. 1998. *Inside Terrorism*. New York: Columbia University Press.

Inciardi, James, Ruth Horowitz, and Anne Pottieger. 1993. *Street Kids, Street Drugs, Street Crime: An Examination of Drug Use and Serious Delinquency in Miami*. Belmont, Calif.: Wadsworth Publishing.

Kaplan, Howard B. 1995. *Drugs, Crime, and Other Deviant Adaptations*. New York: Plenum Publishing.

Mickolus, Edward F. 1980. *Transnational Terrorism: A Chronology of Events, 1968–1979*. Westport, Conn.: Greenwood Press.

———. 1989. *International Terrorism in the 1980s: A Chronology of Events, Volume I: 1980–1983*. Ames: Iowa State University Press.

———. 1993. *Terrorism, 1988–1991: A Chronology of Events and Selectively Annotated Bibliography*. Westport, Conn.: Greenwood Press.

Office for Victims of Crimes. 2002. "Terrorism and International Victims Unit." *OVC Fact Sheet*. Washington, D.C.: Department of Justice.

Rapoport, David. 1992. "Terrorism." In *Routledge Encyclopedia of Government and Politics, Volume 2*, edited by Mary Hawkesworth and Maurice Kogan, 1160–80. London: Routledge.

Schafer, Stephen. 1971. "The Concept of the Political Criminal." *Journal of Criminal Law* 62, no. 3: 380–87.

Smith, Brent L. 1994. *Terrorism in America: Pipe Bombs and Pipe Dreams*. Albany: State University of New York Press.

Smith, Brent L., and Kelly R. Damphousse. 1996. "Punishing Political Offenders: The Effect of Political Motive on Federal Sentencing Decisions." *Criminology* 34: 289–322.

———. 1998. "Terrorism, Politics, and Punishment: A Test of Structural-Contextual Theory and the 'Liberation Hypothesis.'" *Criminology* 36: 67–92.

Smith, Brent, and Kathryn Morgan. 1994. "Terrorists Right and Left: Empirical Issues in Profiling American Terrorists." *Studies in Conflict and Terrorism* 17, no. 1: 39–57.

Smith, Brent L., and Gregory Orvis. 1993. "America's Response to Terrorism: An Empirical Analysis of Federal Intervention Strategies during the 1980s." *Justice Quarterly* 10: 661–81.

Wardlaw, Grant. 1989. *Political Terrorism*. 2nd ed. New York: Cambridge University Press.

Wright, Richard, and Scott Decker. 1997. *Armed Robbers in Action: Stickups and Street Culture*. Boston: Northeastern Press.

10

The Psychological Impact of Terrorism: Lessons from the U.K. Experience

Andrew Silke

Serious concerns exist over the psychological impact on individuals and communities who are exposed to terrorist violence. This chapter reviews the impact of terrorism in the United Kingdom over the past thirty years. In that timeframe, the United Kingdom has experienced thousands of violent terrorist incidents, most of which have been connected to the dispute over Northern Ireland. Since 1969, terrorist violence has resulted in some 4,000 deaths and over 50,000 injuries. Together with such physical casualties, there has also been the issue of the psychological impact of the violence. The manner in which terrorism can impact psychologically is outlined. Significantly, initial fears that terrorism would have a prolonged and deeply deleterious psychological effect on the wider population have proved unfounded. Even within the more troubled regions of the United Kingdom, the overall impact of terrorism in these terms has been surprisingly mild. Why terrorism has not had a more obviously debilitating impact is explored and possible lessons to be taken from the U.K. experience are outlined.

How seriously does terrorist violence undermine a society? In the wake of high-profile terrorist attacks such as those seen on September 11, it is easy to imagine that terrorism is capable of causing great damage to the fabric of entire countries and of fundamentally undermining the way of life for hundreds of millions. Faced with such profound loss of life as seen in New York and Washington and destruction on such immense scale, it is often easy to forget that many countries have been contending at close range with obdurate campaigns of terrorism for many years, and that the experience of these countries has much to tell us about the impact terrorism will have today and in the future.

The United Kingdom is one such country and for over thirty years the U.K. has had to grapple in particular with the consequences of terrorist violence emerging from the troubles of Northern Ireland. Violence connected to the province has claimed the lives of nearly 4,000 people and has maimed and injured at least a further 50,000 people. Most of these casualties have been contained within the relatively small population of Ulster, but terrorist attacks have frequently spilled into the U.K. mainland in general, and England and its cities in particular. The advent of the paramilitary cease-fires in 1994 and the groundbreaking progress of the current peace process have thankfully heralded a dramatic reduction in the level of violence emerging from the conflict. However, this is not to say that the terrorist threat has ended. On the contrary, a number of dissident terrorist groups continue relentlessly with their campaigns of violence and the single most destructive bombing of the past thirty years occurred in the cease-fire era: a bombing which left 29 people dead and over 200 wounded.

Nearly eight years after the first round of cease-fires was declared, the current relative calm provides an opportunity for reflection and assessment, useful commodities when the wider world finds itself transfixed with the fight against terrorism from other quarters. Many commentators have argued that the populations of liberal democracies are the ones most vulnerable to the ravages of terrorist violence: independent media coverage of terrorist activity, unfamiliarity with acts of extreme violence, the possibility that anyone could become the victim of terrorist violence, and the fight to maintain civil liberties in the face of pressures to ensure wider security, are issues not seen in other regimes. Terrorism then has its widest and generally least-hardened audience in liberal democracies. One then would be forgiven for expecting the worst.

THE RELATIVE IMPORTANCE AND
UNIMPORTANCE OF TERRORISM

A prevailing belief exists that terrorism is one of the most dangerous and threatening problems facing the modern world. The events of September 11 have served forcefully to reinforce and ingrain this perception, as have the sporadic acts of bioterrorism made in the aftermath. Yet, set within broader schemes, such a view is probably unjustified. This may seem a harsh and cold comment when one considers the thousands of lives tragically lost in the New York and Washington attacks. But this is only because human suffering at the hands of other forces can be so much greater. In the past ten years somewhere in the region of 3,500 Americans have lost their lives as a result of terrorism. This loss is heartbreaking, but it pales in comparison to the death toll inflicted by other causes. In the last ten years in the United States, over 210,000 people have been the victims of criminal murder, over 300,000 people have taken their own lives, 420,000 people have been killed in automobile accidents, 5,400,000 Americans have died of cancer, and nearly 7,500,000 have died as a result of heart disease. Recognizing this massive discrepancy in scale, Walter Laqueur (1987) has commented that the fiercely malignant reputation which terrorism enjoys is largely a myth (and one of many myths to surround the subject). At the heart of such a reputation is the expectation that the casualties of terrorism are many and that terrorist attacks are both frequent and highly lethal. In the eyes of some commentators, terrorism is as great a threat to civilization as full-scale warfare, and this encourages a pervasive belief that terrorism is also as debilitating as warfare. The reality though is very different. While it is often difficult to make such points in the sensitive periods following shocking attacks, it deserves to be noted that most of the more experienced researchers and experts accept that terrorism is not the overwhelming problem or threat that it is perceived to be (rare consensus indeed when the experts often agree on so little else) (Wilkinson 1987).

"If it bleeds, it leads" is the operating maxim of the world's media, and with high coverage on television and in the press we are all painfully aware that terrorist attacks occur with disheartening regularity. We are painfully aware too that the casualties of such attacks can be very high and very innocent. The destruction wrecked on the lives of those caught up in terrorist events is obvious and immediate. Yet terrorism is also attributed with a powerful destabilizing effect on society. Terrorism distinguishes itself from other forms of political violence in that for the perpetrators it is often more about the unharmed world watching events than about those victims who are killed and maimed in attacks. "Kill one, frighten ten thousand" goes the Chinese saying and when terrorism is directed against innocent civilians it has the ability to impact on innocent civilians everywhere. People know that as they travel to work, attend school, stay at home, go on holiday, or go to religious service, the potential is there that they could become the victim of terrorist aggression borne from issues and conflicts of which they potentially have no involvement and little awareness. The expectation of many is that such fear and uncertainty cannot help but have deleterious effects on even large and otherwise prosperous and safe societies. However, after over thirty years of study, the picture emerging from research is a little more optimistic. Laqueur (1987) noted that terrorism's influence on society is not as profound or as long lasting as is commonly believed. He and others have argued that in the wider scheme the direct victims of terrorism are few and the effects on wider society are actually quite limited.

This, however, is not the perception of popular imagination. The victims of terrorism, like the activity, are high profile. The death of 100,000 people in a country at war does receive media attention but sometimes surprisingly little compared to a small number of people killed in a bombing in a country at peace. While September 11 catches in the mind when one now attempts to think of terrorist violence, the vast majority of terrorist attacks result in either very few fatalities or else none at all. The media focus, however, can work to distort this perception. A good example of this is provided by the bombing of Centennial Park during the 1996 Atlanta Olympics. This bomb killed one person and a second man died shortly afterward at the scene from a heart attack. Media coverage of the incident was intense, drowning out all other news stories for days. Lost in the wake of the bombing, for example, were accounts of heavy fighting in Sri Lanka occurring at the same time which left around 1,500 people dead (Keesing's Record of World Events 1996). Yet, an American observer in particular would be hard pressed to realize that the violence in Sri Lanka was far more serious simply in terms of raw human suffering. Most people in the Western world are familiar with the Atlanta bombing and can describe the basics of the event. Very few though are aware that simultaneous to the death of two people in Atlanta, 1,500 people were being killed that month in Sri Lanka.

In an atmosphere where terrorism attracts such attention, the statistic that a person is generally more likely to be struck by lightning than to be killed in a terrorist attack seems preposterous (Schmid 1992, 101). Yet—in the Western world, at least—it is true. Media attention has negated such reassuring facts and fostered a widespread belief that terrorist attacks are both common and very dangerous. Worse, this biased media focus plays right into the hands of terrorists.

For the professional criminal, as with the terrorist, the victim is often incidental. But the needs of the perpetrators for the two types of victimization are quite different. The criminal's motivations are local and personal. In contrast, the terrorist seeks to send a wider message, and because of this his actions will have a relevance and impact on society in a way quite different from that of any other crime. Victims of terrorism are not simply victims of violent crime, and the threatening effects on society cannot be expected to be simply on a par with those of crime.

Ultimately, the reason for the extra media attention is the similarity the audience feels it has with terrorist victims. For example, this chapter has already alluded to the political violence which has ravaged the island of Sri Lanka. A terrorist campaign has been raging in that troubled country since 1975, and in recent years this violence has sporadically escalated to the level of a de facto civil war. In two decades of fighting the conflict has claimed over 60,000 lives. Military violence in Sri Lanka then is not especially surprising. But in the United Kingdom, the United States, and other stable countries of the world, civilians are not exposed to such conflict. There is a common and justified expectation that danger will not come from explosives and deliberate violence. So when deaths emanate from such causes they compel special attention because of this incongruity *and* because of the realization that everyone in such peaceful societies is at risk to this threat.

Indeed, research has shown that it is factors relating to the victims and not the terrorists that affect media attention given to terrorist incidents (e.g., Nelson and Scott 1992). For example, the number of terrorists taking part in an attack does not affect the depth of media coverage, but the number of victims involved does. Not surprisingly, the more victims the greater attention. Following on from this, the seriousness of the victims' injuries increases coverage also, with the death of victims attracting a six-fold increase in media attention compared to if the victims are wounded but not killed. The nationality of the victims is important too, with domestic victims attracting over 100 times more attention than foreign victims. Importantly, while increased media attention does not lead to increased levels of terrorism, the effect on victims and on society of this increased coverage has only recently been explored. In the United States, after the bombing of the Murrah building in Oklahoma City in 1995, an attack which claimed 169 lives, media coverage of the aftermath was intense. Understandably, this was particularly the case for the Oklahoma region itself. Psychologists later found this intense media coverage had some damaging impact, with some adults and children appearing to suffer serious psychological problems as a result of long exposure to media coverage of the attack. They often had trouble sleeping, suffered from nightmares, had anxiety problems, or suffered depression. Yet, these people had not been at the scene when the attack occurred and they were not connected to victims of the bombing. They had not lost family members, friends, neighbors, or colleagues in the devastation, but they had witnessed a great deal of media coverage. Researchers found that in some groups of schoolchildren, media exposure alone seemed to be a primary cause of post-traumatic stress disorder (PTSD)[1] in the aftermath of the bombing (Pfefferbaum et al., 1999).

If the death of a compatriot attracts so much attention in domestic media, it must inevitably increase awareness of terrorism and lead to heightened (and almost certainly unrealistic) expectations of the threat from terrorism. While it is true that terrorism attracts more attention than it truly warrants, we are nevertheless painfully aware of its victims. What then is the real effect of terrorism? In particular, considering the psychological and social impact attributed to this form of violence, what is its toll on the few direct, and many indirect, victims?

THE IMPACT ON INDIVIDUALS

There is a widespread belief that individuals caught up in terrorist incidents will invariably suffer psychologically because of the experience. Consider the following comment dating from the 1970s:

> Victims of terrorist attacks suffer extreme psychological and physiological stress. The effects of stress may be immediate or delayed. Extreme stress may result in disease or even death for the victim, quite apart from any injury di-

rectly inflicted by the terrorist. The effects of captivity by terrorists may last
for years. Studies of concentration camp survivors show that they had higher
rates of mortality and morbidity for many years after their release. (Roth 1977,
45–47)

Yet the degree of stress felt by individuals varies hugely, as does their ability to cope and respond to it. The evidence that terrorism will always have a
negative effect is far more patchy then might be expected and this is certainly
the case with regard to research which has emerged from the United Kingdom's lengthy experience. In particular, few regions experience terrorism to
the extent Northern Ireland has, or for as long. It has been said of the
province that it is "the most heavily researched area on earth" (Whyte 1990).
Consequently, one would expect that if terrorism does have an impact on
wider populations, such effects will have been recorded in the copious body
of research conducted on the troubles.

Some of the early research on terrorism indicated that most of the people
who have been caught up directly in terrorist events, as victims or bystanders, would suffer significant psychological harm. For example, Lyons
(1974) found that 92 percent of bystanders at terrorist bombings suffered "serious affective disturbance," while Hadden et al. (1978) in a review of over
1,500 victims of terrorist bombings, found that over 50 percent suffered
"emotional shock" even though most had received no physical injuries.
Loughrey et al. (1988) conducted a study looking at the incidence of PTSD
in a wider range of terrorist victims including survivors of assassination attempts, knee-cappings, hostage-takings, as well as witnesses and bystanders
of bombings. Taking a sample of 499 victims, the study found that 23 percent
of the victims suffered from PTSD in the wake of a terrorist incident. A later
study by Allen, Cassidy, and Monaghan (1994) also looked at a similar range
of victims but found that far more of their victims (55 percent) could be diagnosed as suffering from PTSD.

Even those victims who did not display PTSD could still be very strongly
affected by their experience. In Allen, Cassidy, and Monaghan's study, the 45
percent of victims who did not display signs of PTSD were still found to be
suffering psychologically. Other researchers have noted that sleep disturbances are reported by virtually all terrorist victims and exaggerated startle
responses are also extremely common. Intrusive imagery and to a lesser extent, nightmares are also frequent features. Loughrey notes that such reactions "are to be expected as they are a universal finding in the aftermath of
severe stress."

Depressive syndromes were diagnosed in many terrorism victims during
follow-up visits with medical personnel. Assessments with people suffering
PTSD showed that they were also three times more likely to suffer depression compared to other victims. In the case of Allen's work, up to 80 percent

of the victims needed to be prescribed antidepressant drugs. (Interestingly, substance abuse and incidents of attempted suicide are remarkably low among terrorist victims, something which distinguishes them from other populations of PTSD sufferers.)

These findings indicate clearly that significant numbers of individuals will experience serious psychological responses to violent terrorist situations. However, the extent of this response may have been overstated in much of the early research. We now know, for example, that there are a number of risk factors associated with PTSD. For instance, people with good psychological health are less likely to show signs of PTSD after a catastrophic event (though the more appalling the event, the less likely that they will be protected). Family background can also influence a person's susceptibility to PTSD. For example, in Israel it has been found that soldiers whose parents were concentration camp survivors were much more likely to develop PTSD after combat than their comrades (Rosenhan and Seligman 1995). It is also now recognized that there is a genetic component to PTSD. Still, PTSD found in response to terrorism (at least within the United Kingdom and Northern Ireland) has arguably been relatively low. This can be illustrated with regard to one of the more serious terrorist incidents to occur there in recent decades.

There have been tens of thousands of individual acts of terrorist violence in the United Kingdom in the last thirty years and these have included a number of mass casualty bombings. One of the more notorious of these incidents was the bombing of Enniskillen town center by the Provisional IRA in 1989. A bomb planted by the IRA was detonated in the town during a public celebration. Eleven people were killed and more than sixty were seriously injured, making it one of the worst terrorist attacks of the troubles in terms of casualties. Curran et al. (1990) reported on the psychological impact of the bombing. Thirty-three survivors of the attack, twenty-six adults and seven children, were referred to Curran's hospital department for psychological assessment. He found that within the first six months after the bombing, 50 percent of these survivors had developed PTSD, with the remaining victims displaying strong negative stress reactions. Even a year after the bombing, this group of survivors was still clearly suffering badly. Their scores on the General Health Questionnaire (GHQ)—a widely used measure of psychological distress—were twice those typically found in local samples. The findings gave a strong impression that the bombing was responsible for a severe psychological impact on survivors, including many who had received no physical injuries in the attack.

This finding suggested that major terrorist attacks will have serious long-term effects on those caught up in them, including those who emerge unscathed and physically unharmed. However, there is a problem with such a conclusion for the Enniskillen bombing. Curran found that only thirty-three people were referred to him or his colleagues as needing psychological assessment or help. Yet there were at least 500 people standing within thirty meters of the bomb when it exploded that day in Enniskillen. Eleven of these people died, sixty were seriously injured, and as we have seen from the above, thirty-three were diagnosed as suffering significant psychological problems afterward. Yet what of the remaining 400 or so survivors? Why did they not seem to suffer any clear long-term effects? The next section tries to answer this question.

THE WIDER IMPACT OF TERRORISM

In Northern Ireland itself, some 3,700 people have been killed in thirty-two years of fighting and most of these victims have been civilians. At least a further 45,000 people, again mainly civilians, have been maimed, many horrifically, and tens (if not hundreds) of thousands more have directly witnessed terrorist violence and associated civil disturbances. The result is that most long-term residents of Northern Ireland have personally experienced terrorist violence to some degree, and/or have family members, friends, or work colleagues who have been directly exposed to terrorist violence. What then, has the cumulative effect of all this experience been?

While an incident undeniably has an impact on those in the immediate vicinity, whether physically injured or not, it is far less certain whether terrorist violence has a long-term detrimental impact on wider society as a whole. A considerable body of work has looked at Northern Ireland with this question in mind.

Curran (1988) reviewed studies on hospital referrals and admissions, parasuicide and suicide rates, psychoactive drug prescriptions, and community-based studies. He found there were no significant increases in any of these measures which could be correlated with terrorist violence. This finding was supported by Cairns and Wilson (1992), who also concluded that "only a very small proportion of the population not directly involved in the civil violence in Northern Ireland have become psychiatric casualties as a result of the political violence."

However, Curran stressed that while the findings indicated that Northern Irish society on a whole seemed to have escaped relatively unscathed from the violence, there were specific communities which did show signs of suffering. For example, he noted Fraser's 1971 study which found that within urban areas especially badly affected by violence (as is the case with certain areas of Belfast) there was a considerable increase in tranquillizer consumption, with an accompanying risk of long-term dependency. Curran noted though that within these high-risk areas there were other factors which are also considered to lead to high levels of tranquillizer consumption, such as overcrowding and high unemployment. (It is worth noting again that dependency for prescribed drugs in terrorist victims seems to be lower than that found for victims of other types of violence.)

Curran cites a number of reasons to explain the low impact of the violence on the wider society apart from standard human resilience and adaptability. He gives special emphasis to what he calls *cohesion*. Curran notes that the psychological ill effects felt by the direct victims of terrorism could be "buffered by a state of rebound psychological well-being in the rest of the community." He quoted research in America which found that after incidents of serious rioting, significant proportions of the local populations actually reported a long-term improvement in their mental well-being. This research showed that "A certain number of people develop psychological distress as might be expected of those who witness terrifying situations or tragedies or catastrophes, but remarkably, a larger number may actually improve psychologically" (Curran 1988).

This remarkable effect has been noted in a number of different places and areas. Extra-normal violence—and the threat of such violence—can work to bind communities together with a sense of common purpose and common outrage. Combined with the perception that there is a shared enemy out there, terrorist attacks bolster an individual's ties to the local community, deepening the sense of belonging and the identification with others living in the area. This is a powerful social effect which has been witnessed many times before. For example, during the London Blitz in World War II, many people noted the widespread camaraderie and closeness of what became known as the Blitz Spirit. Some aspects of this effect have already been seen in the United States after the dreadful events of September 11. While many commentators talked about the sense of fear and panic sweeping the country, it was equally clear that there was a massive and widespread sense of shared community. Sales of American flags rocketed and millions of homes flew flags in a very public display of shared identity.

Social psychologists have long understood that a strong sense of community in a population is associated with a wide range of positive benefits, including better physical and psychological health. In fostering a greater sense of community, terrorism can actually end up working to improve the ability of most people to cope and respond positively to it. While recognizing that individual victims can still be profoundly affected by their experiences, the overall reality is that the psychological impact of terrorism on wider communities has been surprisingly mild even in countries where terrorist attacks are very common.

THE IMPACT ON CHILDREN

If society in general seems resilient to the effects of terrorism, does this also apply to more vulnerable groups such as children? There has been considerable speculation on what impact the terrorist campaigns have had on the children of Northern Ireland. Most commentators during the 1970s expressed a belief that the violence and social disruption of the troubles would inevitably produce generations of psychologically and morally damaged youth. This concern was widely felt by all sections of the North's disparate communities. Within psychological circles, the picture painted in the early years of the conflict was very depressing. Consider the bleakness of the following assessment from one local psychologist in 1979:

> Trauma induced stress . . . is the condition of children in Northern Ireland. . . . The children there have suffered severe disruption in the development of moral judgment—a cognitive function—and are obsessed with death and destruction about which they feel helpless, and against which they feel isolated and hopeless. . . . [The children's] anger, frustration, fear and confusion are finally articulated through their vision of others in terms of "symbol quality." Members of another group become targets of hatred for their "symbol value" and are never viewed as human beings or as having any relationship to the self. This form taken by the fear-into-hatred-into-violence cycle is the road map of childhood in Northern Ireland." (Fields 1979, 73–74)

Fields based her beliefs on her own experience with children living in Northern Ireland, and a considerable amount of research activity has since focused on this relatively accessible dimension of the conflict. Certainly a few early research studies did seem to justify the widespread fears for the fate of the province's children. For example, Fee (1980, 1983) reported the results of two surveys which asked teachers to rate how emotionally disturbed pupils were in schools in Belfast. Using random samples, the results indicated that about 15 percent of children were judged to be emotionally disturbed when the survey was first done in 1975 and a lower figure of 9 percent when it was repeated in 1981. These figures were considerably higher than levels reported from elsewhere, including other parts of the United Kingdom (6.8 percent), as well as foreign countries such as New Zealand (6.0 percent) and Norway (5.0 percent). Taken at face value, such research seemed to indicate that terrorist violence was having a discernable negative impact on children living in the region.

However, a great deal of other research has not supported this view. Indeed, much to the surprise of the early speculators, a large series of ongoing studies have consistently failed to vindicate Field's fears and have not found clear indications that Northern Ireland has or is producing damaged young generations. For example, Joseph, Cairns, and McCollam (1993) found that children in areas strongly affected by violence were no more likely to suffer depression than children living in peaceful areas. Examples of similar findings are plentiful and a general overview of this and related work is provided by Trew (1995), who concluded that the vast majority of children were emerging psychologically healthy from the troubles.

Interestingly, Trew also concluded that there was plenty of evidence to suggest that the moral development and moral standards of children in the province were the same as that of children in neighboring regions. Significantly, there was no indication that the Northern Irish children found violence more acceptable, had lower moral standards, or were more likely to become involved in illegal activities than their counterparts elsewhere. Indeed, several of the studies found that the North's children scored higher on a number of measures of morality when compared with children in neighboring regions.

The most remarkable feature to emerge from this wealth of research is the sheer lack of detrimental effect on the North's children. While reassuring, this in itself has been a cause of concern for some researchers. This can be seen for example in some comments made by Professor Ed Cairns at the University of Ulster, who is one of the most experienced researchers into the psychological impact of political violence in the region. He has voiced concern that the pendulum of belief which had previously held that there would be widespread maladaptive responses among children to a terrorist environment has now swung too far in the other direction, and rests on a belief that children's ability was such as to overcome or simply ignore the ravages of terrorist violence around them (Cairns 1996). While research such as Fee's (1983) discussed above does provide some grounds for Cairn's cautionary warning, it should be said that the overwhelming majority of Cairn's own research work seems in general to support a more resilient view (e.g., Cairns 1987; Cairns and Conlon 1985). A few of his studies though have had more worrying findings. For example, in one research project Cairns noted that particularly high levels of terrorist violence in an area seemed to be linked to an increase in aggression among young children living in that community (Wilson and Cairns 1992). Some support for this particular finding came from foreign research, with Liddell et al. (1994), for example, finding that South African children living in areas suffering high levels of political violence also displayed more violent behavior than children in other areas.

However, such findings (at least with regard to Northern Ireland) are relatively isolated and are not well supported by other research work. Indeed, several studies have indicated no such impact, with Lorenc and Branthwaite (1986), for example, finding that the attitudes on the use of violence among Northern Irish children were the same as their English counterparts, while other evidence cited by McQuoid (1994) seemed to provide strong support for the view that Northern Irish juveniles were actually *less* violent than their European contemporaries.

Ultimately the story to emerge from Northern Ireland and the rest of the United Kingdom with regard to the impact of terrorism on children is one of surprising resilience. Unquestionably, terrorist violence has had a profound detrimental effect on some individual children, but it is also clear that the overwhelming majority who have been exposed to terrorism here in the past three decades have emerged from the experience without suffering long-term distress. Neither do the majority seem to show evidence of any significant psychological harm. While the debate continues over exactly how resilient children are to the effects of terrorism, what is certainly clear today is that as a group they are nowhere near as vulnerable as was once feared.

CONCLUSION

Ultimately, research on the impact of terrorism has found that even widespread and long-lasting campaigns of terrorist violence can have a surprisingly limited detrimental impact on the overall psychological health of the society. Even with apparently vulnerable groups such as children, the evidence emerging from the United Kingdom's experience strongly suggests that in most cases terrorist violence has not impinged in any significant manner on normal moral and psychological development.

When one considers that if terrorism has failed to seriously undermine the mental health and ability to cope of populations in deeply troubled regions such as Northern Ireland, it is unlikely then that it would easily be able to do so in other societies which experience comparable or more limited campaigns of violence.

This, of course, is not to suggest that the impact of terrorism is entirely benign or negligible. All authors agree that, for a small minority, terrorism is psychologically highly destructive and damaging. However, it needs to be emphasized that such victims are the exception and not the rule. Largely, these unfortunate souls are the direct victims of terrorist violence and suffer physical injuries to accompany their mental scars. Most of the rest are either immediate witnesses to such violence, or else are closely connected to the original victims as family members or friends. Very few outside these intimate circles will suffer significant long-term effects. Fortunately, many within such circles—and especially among the witnesses—will prove remarkably resilient and will quickly recover from the experience to lead a normal existence.

Terrorism does destroy individuals but it rarely truly threatens entire societies. There exists a widespread perception though that terrorism is one of the great evils of our time and that it has a significant malignant impact on large numbers of people. The reality, however, is that terrorism is a small evil committed by a handful who wish their desperate violence to appear more threatening and more incessant than it actually is. Understandably, we sometimes succumb to this message but it is a false one. We do no service to ourselves, or honor to fallen victims, to believe it for long. Parallels inferred between populations experiencing terrorism and populations who have experienced genocide or ethnic cleansing are unrealistic and unjustified. Terrorism does not even begin to match the malevolence of those evils and suggesting otherwise is paying homage to a false fear that it does. Realizing this truth is the task we now face.

NOTES

The views expressed in this chapter are those of the author and do not necessarily represent the position of the Home Office or the government of the United Kingdom.

1. Post-traumatic stress disorder is an anxiety disorder which results from having experienced or witnessed situations involving or threatening death or injury. Typical symptoms of the condition include emotional numbness, flashbacks, nightmares, and extreme anxiety. These symptoms can last for months or even years after the event (Rosenhan and Seligman 1995).

BIBLIOGRAPHY

Allen, J., C. Cassidy, and C. Monaghan. 1994. "A community mental health team in Northern Ireland: New referrals as a result of civil disorder." *Irish Journal of Psychological Medicine* 11, no. 2: 67–69

Cairns, Ed. *Caught in Crossfire: Children and the Northern Ireland Conflict.* 1987. Belfast: Appletree Press and Syracuse University Press.

———. 1996. *Children and Political Violence.* Oxford: Blackwell.

Cairns, E., and L. Conlon. 1985. "Children's moral reasoning and the Northern Irish violence." Unpublished paper. Coleraine: University of Ulster.

Cairns, E., and R. Wilson. 1992. "Stress, coping, and political violence in Northern Ireland." In *International Handbook of Traumatic Stress Syndromes,* edited by John P. Wilson and Beverley Raphael. New York: Plenum Press.

Curran, P. S. 1988. "Psychiatric aspects of terrorist violence: Northern Ireland 1969–1987." *British Journal of Psychiatry* 153, no. 5: 470–75.

Curran, P. S., P. Bell, A. Murray, G. Loughrey, R. Roddy, and L. G. Rocke. 1990. "Psychological consequences of the Enniskillen bombing." *British Journal of Psychiatry* 156: 479–82.

Dillenburger, K. 1992. *Violent Bereavement: Widows in Northern Ireland.* Aldershot: Avebury.

Fee, F. 1980. "Responses to a behavioural questionnaire of a group of Belfast school children." In *A Society under Stress: Children and Young People in Northern Ireland,* edited by J. Harbison and J. Harbison. Somerset: Open Books.

———. 1983. "Educational change in Belfast school children 1975–81." In *Children of the Troubles,* edited by J. Harbison. Belfast: Stranmillis College Learning Resources Unit.

Fields, R. M. 1979. "Child terror victims and adult terrorists." *Journal of Psychohistory* 7, no. 1: 71–75.

Hadden, W. A., W. H. Rutherford, and J. D. Merrett. 1978. "The injuries of terrorist bombings: A study of 1532 consecutive patients." *British Journal of Surgery* 65, no. 8: 525–31.

Joseph, S., E. Cairns, and P. McCollam. 1993. "Political violence, coping, and depressive symptomatology in Northern Irish children." *Personality and Individual Differences* 15, no. 4: 471–73.

Keesing's Record of World Events. 1996. "News digest for July." *Keesing's Record of World Events* 42, no. 7/8: 41174–212.

Laqueur, Walter. 1987. *The Age of Terrorism*. London: Little, Brown.

Liddell, C., K. Kvalsig, P. Qotyana, and A. Shabalala. 1994. "Community violence and young South African children's involvement in aggression." *International Journal of Behavioral Development* 17, no. 4: 613–28.

Lorenc, L., and A. Branthwaite. 1986. "Evaluation of violence by English and Northern Ireland schoolchildren." *British Journal of Social Psychology* 25, no. 4: 349–52.

Loughrey, G. C., P. Bell, M. Kee, R. J. Roddy, and P. S. Curran. 1988. "Post-traumatic stress disorder and civil violence in Northern Ireland." *British Journal of Psychiatry* 153: 554–60.

Lyons, H. 1974. "Terrorist bombing and the psychological sequelae." *Journal of the Irish Medical Association* 67: 15.

McQuoid, J. 1994. "The self-reported delinquency study in Belfast, Northern Ireland." In *Delinquent Behaviour among Young People in the Western World: First Reports of the International Self-Report Delinquency Study*, edited by J. Junger-tas, G. Terlouw and M. Klein. Amsterdam: Kugler.

Nelson, P. S., and J. L. Scott. 1992. "Terrorism and the media: An empirical analysis." *Defence Economics* 3, no. 4: 329–39.

Pfefferbaum, B., S. Nixon, R. Krug, R. Tivis, V. Moore, J. Brown, R. Pynoos, D. Foy, and R. Gurwitch. 1999. "Clinical needs assessment of middle and high school students following the 1995 Oklahoma City bombing." *American Journal of Psychiatry* 156, no.7: 1069–74.

Rosenhan, D., and M. Seligman. 1995. *Abnormal Psychology*. 3d ed. London: Norton.

Roth, Walton. 1977. "Psychosomatic implications of confinement by terrorists." In *Dimensions of Victimization in the Context of Terrorist Acts*, edited by R. Creslinsten. Montreal: International Centre for Comparative Criminology.

Schmid, A. P. 1992. "Terrorism and the media: Freedom of information vs. freedom from intimidation." In *Terrorism: Roots, Impact, Responses,* edited by L. Howard. London: Praeger.

Trew, K. 1995. "The psychological and social impact of the troubles on young people growing up in Northern Ireland." In *Growing through Conflict: The Impact of 25 Years of Violence on Young People Growing Up in Northern Ireland*, edited by W. McCarney. Belfast: IAJFCM.

Whyte, John. 1990. *Interpreting Northern Ireland*. Oxford: Clarendon Press.

Wilkinson, Paul. 1987. "Pathways out of terrorism for democratic societies." In *Contemporary Research on Terrorism,* edited by P. Wilkinson and A. Stewart. Aberdeen: AUP.

Wilson. R., and E. Cairns. 1992. "Trouble stress and psychological disorder in Northern Ireland." *The Psychologist* 5: 347–50.

III

PREVENTION, CONTROL, AND RECOVERY FROM TERRORIST ACTIVITIES

11

Antiterrorism Strategy in the Arab Gulf States

Mamdooh Abdelhameed Abdelmattlep

This chapter deals with the issue of terrorism. It examines whether it exists or if there are even indications of its existence in the Arab Gulf States. If it is existing, then what is its size? And does it at this size constitute a phenomenon calling for attention? At the outset, the chapter endeavors to find a realistic definition for terrorism, taking into consideration several previous definitions given either through collective or individual efforts in accordance with the concept of their specialization, interest, or objective of the definition.

The chapter then investigates the existence and trends of terrorism in the Arab Gulf States. It is worth mentioning in this regard that neither a definition is given in the legislations of these states nor a separate incrimination is stipulated for the crime under the name "Terrorist Crimes," resulting in the absence of any statistics on them. It is therefore assumed that—if these crimes do exist—they have certainly been classified as violent crimes or crimes affecting state security and consequently have been included within the general statistics of crime.

Despite the absence of accurate statistics, certain incidents that have taken place in the Gulf States may be designated—though limited—as terrorist crimes. Examples are the explosions of Bahrain and Al Khubar (in Saudi Arabia) as well as certain remote instances of aircraft hijacking, explosions, and armed attacks in both Kuwait and the United Arab Emirates.

Although all the Arab Gulf States recently ratified the Arab Antiterrorism Convention, it is evident from the research that no security agreement on prevention of terrorism exists among these states, despite the exigency and availability of the main components and factors therefor. However, the research has shown that understanding and cooperation prevails among most of these states in the field of prevention and follow-up of the terrorist crimes that take place from time to time.

Through the examination of these exigencies as well as the components and features characterizing the Arab Gulf States, the present chapter attempts to lay down the concepts and scope for an antiterrorism strategy in the Arab Gulf States.

INTRODUCTION

Is mankind approaching, in an unperceived manner, a terrorism era? Statistics, which endeavored to determine the size of terrorism worldwide, is not deemed as the only means for outlining the features of the present age. Though the number of people who lose their lives in causes other than terrorism outnumber those lost in terrorism incidents in the various parts of the world, the main explanation for the public concern about these incidents of terrorism is that the violence exercised in terrorist attacks has been given considerable publicity. Nowadays, terrorists resort to violence and other overwhelming scenarios such as kidnapping, explosions, murder, and hostage taking. The press and visual media, on the other hand, have greatly contributed to this by putting the terrorists in the spotlight. These violent and emotional scenes are usually telecasted via satellites to the various parts of the world where they are viewed by millions who are targeted by terrorist propaganda. Actually the media has, through such keen interest in presenting their activities and feats, bestowed upon the terrorist an importance equal to that of national leaders.

However, the public will eventually acquire immunity against the dissonance of violence. This may explain a more terrifying aspect in the pattern of contemporary terrorism and public concern. The random nature of violence is the only factor causing such panic. The relatively smaller groups of terrorists have a destructive power that is disproportionate to their actual power. This is actually where the core of the threat in modern terrorism lies. It is unreadable. Cooperation on the international scale for counteracting and prevention of terrorism continues to be of concern.

Despite the fact that terrorism has become a reality with which we have to coexist, a controversy, though limited, still exists among the experts as to its definition. The term terrorism has traditional, pragmatic, and revolutionary definitions according to the person using it and whether he is perpetrator of an act thereof or a victim. The person participating in guerilla warfare for liberation of his country is deemed a commando rather than a terrorist. Other experts use the term terrorism to describe any act involving disturbance of the public functions of society involving various types of violence.

It is, therefore, impossible to arrive at a uniform approach or definition covering these various types. Such ambiguity in the usage of the term is deemed a main reason for misunderstanding the nature of terrorism and the consequential threats posed by it. The disagreement has, on the other hand, lead to an exaggeration of the statistical data in a manner which made it appear bigger than its actual size.

However, for the purpose of the present research, we will endeavor to solve the problem by defining terrorism in a convenient manner. To do this it is essential to distinguish between terrorism and the other forms of violence in order to assess the real size of the phenomenon and be able to propose a strategy for its prevention.

The term strategy in its abstract sense means "the best utilization of material and moral resources available as per a perfect and accurate plan for facing an existing situation or problem with a view of achieving specified targets and objectives." This definition was actually adopted by the Council of Arab Ministers of Interior at its second session held at Baghdad, Vice Resolution No. 18 dated July 2, 1983, calling for a definition for the Arab security strategy enabling implementation of the same for achieving the required objectives of internal and foreign stability for each of the member states.

In this research, strategy refers to the scientific method mainly based on security planning and characterized with reality, aiming at the achievement of certain objectives, utilizing all subjective data and information in all fields of knowledge. Strategy is also characterized with maneuverability because the extent of its success depends on its ability to achieve the element of surprise to the source of security disturbance in addition to the degree of confidentiality being applied. Strategy usually builds on the lessons learnt from past experiences and embodies a great deal of measures, steps, and solutions, giving it the flexibility to adapt to existing circumstances. Moreover, it is characterized by "impressionism," which is the ability to be influenced by all circumstances prevailing in the society, whether at the preparation or implementation stages. A major factor for the success of a strategy is the necessity of continuous coordination with all other sectors, whether within or outside the society in order to contain any phenomenon or security risk.

The Arab and Gulf strategy depends on following major constituents that should be made available:

- Spreading of ideological values and proper Islamic guidance in addition to the rationalization of the Arab penal policy through the adoption of Islamic *Sharia* for formulating its principles.
- The modernization and updating of the Arab security institutions so as to enable them to play a more effective role.
- Adoption of the scientific methodology as a basis for the joint Arab security efforts.

- The development and upgrading of the Arab penal and conventional institutions to enable them to effectively undertake the rehabilitation and correction of the convicts.
- Provision of support to the civil protection and rescue institutions in the Arab world and assess their status.
- Activation of the public role in crime prevention in order to protect states and their societies from its consequences.
- Enhance Arab cooperation in the security field and reformulate it on an integral basis characterized with efficiency and flexibility.
- Enhance the international cooperation in the field of crime prevention through the exchange of expertise and assistance for countering crime.

These concerns were dealt with in the Arab security strategy adopted by the Council of Arab Ministers of Interior in 1983. They may be summarized in three main aspects: the ideological values, the soundness of the Arab-Islamic approach, the efficiency of the enforcement agencies as well as the effectiveness of the penal laws, and the reinforcement of international and Arab cooperation.

The establishment of an antiterrorism strategy necessitates a statistical analysis to be carried out for determination of the size and trends of the phenomenon in the Arab Gulf States. The statistical investigation plan depends on the data collection, sorting, analysis, and interpretation. Although the security statistics may not explain this criminal phenomenon, it still contributes to its interpretation. All countries of the world (including advanced countries) suffer from organizational and statistical analysis problems due to the variations in concepts and meaning at the stage of statistical data collection. The most important difficulties affecting the validity of statistics are:

- The special difficulties in data collection as a result of mistakes, negligence, and lack of uniformity of concepts and meanings.
- The unreliability of the penal statistical resources in general, as it is usually derived from reports in which either an acquittal judgment is passed or the investigations are not completed for insufficiency of evidence. On the other hand, certain incidents which have either actually taken place or are not officially detected are not reported to the concerned authorities. This type of data is referred to as "dark figures of crime."
- The categorization of the crimes according to legal definitions may be significantly changed during the investigation and decision stages to a lower or higher crime. Moreover, some officers may underestimate the significance of serious crimes which are committed in their area of jurisdiction so as to downplay their responsibilities.

- The incomplete recording of crimes such as listing several crimes under one case and designating it as the most serious. Moreover, there is a possibility for multiple entry of the same crime when several reports are received on it.

The statistics of the criminal justice institutions as represented by police statistics in addition to judicial, penal, and conventional statistics are the main sources for any researcher investigating crime in any particular modern community.

The strategy also requires analysis of the factors that lead to violent acts, such as the motivations behind terrorism, characteristics of the population, types of culture, economical and social status of the society, level of police efficiency, and suitability of the criminal policy adopted for countering terrorism as well as the available technical capabilities.

The outcome of this analysis will facilitate the drafting of plans for the prevention of violence and terrorism, which would consequently contribute to the solution of the problem. These plans are variables covering economic, social, legal, administrative, and police areas and will eventually assist in outlining the antiterrorism strategy in the Arab Gulf States.

In view of the above, the antiterrorism strategy of the Arab Gulf States shall be discussed, taking into consideration their geographical location, since neighboring countries may be taken as the basis of their cooperation. This historical reality has given these states a common interest toward the expansion of their markets, social exchange, and confinement of their regional conflicts to a minimum. Such a reality becomes more significant when something in common is shared, such as language, history, culture, religion, and destiny—which is actually the situation in the Arab Gulf States and Iraq.

THE DEFINITION OF TERRORISM

Terrorism is a rather recent term in the Arabic language. Terrorism is the origin of the Arabic verb "terror" and to terrorize carries the meaning of "making somebody feel frightened." In the Holy Quran, the term bears several meanings. One meaning is "love and reverence to God," as in the verse "These were ever quick in emulation in good works; they used to call on Us with love And reverence." Another meaning is fear, as in the verse "and draw thy hand Close to thy side (To guard) against fear." A third meaning resembles deterrence, which is currently used in military balance of forces, as in the verse: "Against them make ready Your strength to the utmost Of your power, including Steeds of war, to strike terror Into (the hearts of) the enemies, Of Allah and your enemies, And others beside, whom Ye may not know, but whom Allah doth know."

According to *Al Mujim Al Waseet* Arabic dictionary, a terrorist means whoever practices violence and terrorism for realizing a political objective. *Al Munjid* Arabic dictionary defines a terrorist as one who resorts to terrorism for assuming power, while *Al Raed* Arabic dictionary defines terrorism as the panic created as a result of violent acts such as murder, explosions, and sabotage.

To summarize, the term terrorism linguistically denotes fear and panic. However, upon the approval of the Arabic Lingual Academy of these meanings as synonyms for terrorism, they acquired a technical meaning as well.

To arrive at a technical meaning for terrorism it is deemed better to adopt a subjective approach rather than a material one. Jurists have in this regard adopted two methodologies: the first depends on the selection of several elements of the phenomenon which ultimately yield a definition thereof. So terrorism can be defined in term of its scope without paying attention to the words forming the definition. The other method is through the establishment of a comprehensive and restrictive definition for the terrorism concept. This would give it an abstract and subjective character and tackles the various aspects of the phenomenon without leaving out any of them. A scholar once endeavored to quote about 200 definitions of terrorism developed by several scientists in the various disciplines of the social sciences. Yet arriving at a standard definition is still a dream to most researchers. The main subjective criteria to be adopted by the compiler of the definition is the one applicable when defining the concept of terrorism.

The term *terrorism*, as the author of this research defines it, means the exercise of force in a regular, continuous, and illegal manner with the intention of achieving certain objectives of a political nature resulting in a breach to the concept of public order in the state at its three levels: public security, public health, and public tranquility. The characteristics of terrorism in terms of this definition are explained hereunder; terrorism is the exercise of force in a regular, continuous, and illegal manner.

This comprises all forms of force in its broad material and moral senses involving the element of threat within them. This abstract sense aims at giving the psychological effect which leads to the achievement of the terrorism objective. A main feature of force is the exercise of violence as one among other means.

It is worth mentioning here that many researchers are confused over the terms violence and terrorism and deem them to be synonymous. Actually, violence is one of the most important features of force constituting the acts of violence. The word *violent* reflects the sense of toughness and cruelty and is thus deemed as an actual behavior, whereas the Latin root of the word in the English language refers to the use of force to inflict harm on others, which is deemed a material behavior.

The exercise of force in general should not be interpreted as terrorism unless it is organized, continuous, and illegal, which are deemed as major features for judging whether the exercise of force is legitimate or otherwise.

Though force may be exercised in an individual or collective criminal plan, the two elements of organization and continuity may not be seen to exist in the absence of a local or international organization or body.

The organized exercise of the illegal force distinguishes terrorism from personal incidents of limited effect. Whatever the consequences of exercising force on the national and international levels, it is still ineffective for establishing a state of threat and panic unless it represents part of the organized activities of a terrorist group. The word "organized" here denotes the persistence of terrorist operations leading to a state of panic. The assassination of President Kennedy, for example, was not a terrorist incident whereas the assassination of President Sadat is deemed so because a series of organized operations followed the assassination and created a state of instability for a long period of time.

Therefore, a characteristic feature of current terrorism is that its existence is unanticipated unless an organization capable of undertaking its activities is found. The terrorist activities nowadays require planning, financing, armament, and personnel with vast experiences and skills at both the preparation and execution levels.

The exercise of force must also be continuous besides being organized (i.e., having an entity governed by administrative rules). The activity of such an organization must persist for an extended period of time sufficient to cause the required psychological effect. On this basis, the criminal acts perpetrated by some persons may not be deemed as terrorist activities unless they adopt an organized and persistent pattern for inflicting the intended effect on the public order of the state.

Persistent exercise refers to the series of unobstructed operations involving force in such a way that the public is practically, psychologically, and mentally kept preoccupied with the follow-up of said operations. This does not, of course, mean that the operation has to take place on a daily basis, but it is sufficient to take place at time intervals that give the required effect.

Finally, the continuous and organized exercise of force must be illegitimate. Legitimacy here refers to the constitutional legitimacy of the legal system of the state. The exercise of force must represent an act contravening the law in its broad sense in order to include it under the incriminating scope.

On this basis, the different forms of legitimate force exercised by a state (which is sometimes referred to as "official violence") as represented in political arrests or instruction of the security forces or the army to quash the violent acts directed against the political regime or constitutional machineries, are all excluded from terrorist activities. In our opinion such activities should not be described as terrorist, as the main constitutional role of the state is to protect its legal and social entity, whether its constitutional bodies or the provision of security to its subjects. The presumption of negligence by a state of such a role is certainly unperceivable; otherwise, it would seem to be destroying its own constitutional entity.

On the other hand, the mere description of such acts as terrorist may encourage power-seekers in the modern Western democratic or social systems to adopt force for overthrowing the existing regimes, which is in contradiction to democratic principles. Democracy is a means through which the people mutually manage state affairs in a peaceful manner. It is not associated with violence or the exercise of force.

Further, the nonrecognition of the use of force in acts of terrorism as legitimate would unfortunately stigmatize those activities of armed opposition of liberation movements seeking their country's independence as illegitimate. This is of course in contradiction to the UN charter, which has recognized the legitimacy of these movements as long as they observe the Geneva conventions and supplementary protocols thereto as issued in 1977.

On this basis, the armed struggle against occupation or racial dominance as a feature of the established rights of self-determination is deemed a legitimate struggle from the point of view of international law as long as the members of these national liberation movements abide by international law as provided for in the Geneva conventions of 1949 and 1977.

Terrorism Aims at the Realization of Political Objectives

At the outset, we would like to explain the issue of the association of legitimacy or legality with terrorism. The resort to force as a means of political understanding between ruler and subjects is not recommended, due to the consequences that may follow, such as disorder, insurrection, damages, instability, and insecurity. If the state has the legitimate right of exercising force to keep order, it must be based on a prevailing state of order, security, and law for the state and subjects. In other words, the resort to violence by a state becomes in this case both legitimate and legal as it is deemed to be within the acceptable limits and restrictions already laid down in its legal and constitutional systems.

Accordingly, terrorist operations often aim at achieving objectives of a political nature and not material benefits. Usually these activities are intended to influence political decisions and compel the state either to adopt or withdraw a certain decision which it would not otherwise do.

The method of terrorism in this regard assumes several patterns, such as spreading of terror, threatening the lives of the public, or endangering their freedom and safety, causing damage to the environment, a facility, a public or private property, the natural resources, or otherwise attempt to occupy or seize them.

It is the political objective that distinguishes terror from other crimes, particularly those involving violence, which should not be classified within terrorist activities unless they affect the political decisionmaker.

Terrorism Leads to the Breach of the Public Order Concept in the State

Another characteristic of terrorism is that its activities pose a public threat to the state and eventually disturbs the public order whose responsibility lies with the security agencies. The public order is defined as the group of legal rules that must be observed. It is usually derived from law, customs, or traditions and is flexible and proportional varying both in time and place according to the existing regime in the state.

The elements comprising public order are: (1) public security, which refers to all acts that make the individual feel secure in his life, honor, and property; (2) public health, which refers to all measures adopted to preserve the health of the people through their protection against fatal diseases and prevention of epidemics, and (3) public tranquility, which refers to all measures taken for preserving peace and prevention of nuisance within residential areas and public roads.

Therefore, the threat to the public order and/or breach thereof, whether committed by an individual or a group, is deemed a terrorist act if it involves the other factors such as the exercise of force in an organized, persistent, and illegal manner for the purpose of achieving a political goal.

THE SIZE AND TRENDS OF THE TERRORIST CRIMES IN ARAB GULF STATES

The Arab Gulf States comprise the states of the Gulf Co-operation Council (that is, Kuwait, Bahrain, Qatar, U.A.E., Saudi Arabia, Oman) in addition to Iraq, who share in common certain geographical, social, political, religious, and national characteristics that necessitate some sort of interrelationship for ensuring success in any efforts exerted for countering terrorism.

However, the efforts required to counter terrorism initially call for the determination of the size and trends of the terrorism phenomenon (if it is yet so) in the Arab Gulf States. Such an approach would certainly enable the establishment of a common antiterrorism strategy within a supplementary coordination context with the Arab, Islamic, and international strategies.

At the outset, a lot of methodological arguments are being raised as to the validity of the criminal statistics in the Arab states as well as the other states of the world. Nevertheless, the scientific determination of the size and trends of any crime requires a statistical investigation and analysis to be carried out over a specified period of time. It is worth mentioning here that the United Nations prepared a guide for developing the criminal statistics of member states as well as a database on the crime trends based on the survey investigations undertaken by the UN every five years. The statistical data obtained during these surveys from the member states are then compared to assess the size of interstate cooperation achieved, and accordingly are used to propose the methods for reinforcing the states' capabilities for effectively dealing with crimes.

Unfortunately, many states—including some Arab states—have either not responded to the UN surveys or furnished only limited and incomplete data. Consequently, the preliminary sources of Arab criminal statistics (i.e., those recorded in annual reports issued by the ministries of interiors under various names) had to be consulted.

Apparently, some of the statistical reports (to which we have referred) do not deal with terrorist crimes separately in the form discussed earlier in the introduction. They are usually found dispersed here and there under various subtitles, such as violent crimes dealing with property or human beings or crimes entailing a public risk or affecting state security and interests or religious beliefs, or those falling under the punishments stipulated in the laws supplementing the penal code.

As a matter of fact, the statistical reports issued by the Arab Gulf States classify crime according to their legal definition in the penal codes. Apparently, this explains the absence of any reference to the crime of terrorism in these statistics. The Arab Antiterrorism Convention enumerated certain forms of terrorist crimes: assault on kings, presidents, and the like or persons enjoying international protection; murder crimes; robbery crimes; sabotage and damage crimes; or crimes involving the manufacture, smuggling, and acquisition of weapons, ammunition, and explosives. However, the statistical investigation under this classification lacks accuracy, as a statistical breakdown will be required in order to know whether such crimes could be identified as terrorist crimes as above mentioned, or as merely criminal. In the absence of the said breakdown, the statistical reports of the Arab Gulf States will continue to refer to the terrorist crime in a generalized form.

Examples for the abovementioned are quoted hereunder from the statistical reports of U.A.E. and Bahrain.

In view of the above, it may be concluded that statistics on terrorism are lacking an accurate definition. This is, in our opinion, due to the nonadoption by most of the Arab States, particularly the Arab Gulf States (subject of the current study) of a clear and accurate concept for the crime of terrorism so as to be incorporated under the relevant punishments in their penal codes. Had these steps been undertaken, it would have certainly been reflected in their statistical reports, thereby enabling an actual and practical investigation to be conducted by scientific method.

Table 11.1. A Statistical Statement of the Crimes Punishable under the Penal Code in the U.A.E. (1996)

No.	The Legal Definition of the Crime	Total
1.	Crimes affecting State Security and Interests (Clauses 149–233)	297
2.	Crimes relating to the Public Function (Clauses 234–252)	180
3.	Crimes disturbing the justice process (Clauses 253–287)	137
4.	Public Risk Crimes (Clauses 288–311)	223
5.	Crimes affecting the religions believes and rites (Clauses 312–236)	15
6.	Crimes affecting the family (Clauses 227–330)	3
7.	Crimes on persons (Clauses 321–380)	4,306
8.	Crimes on Property (Clauses 381–434)	15,825
9.	Crimes under Drugs Control Act	596
10.	Crimes under Alcoholic Drinks Act	45
11.	Crimes under Immigration and Residence Act	10,288
12.	Crimes under Labors Act	1,226
13.	Crimes under the Municipality Rules and Regulations	54
14.	Crimes under Fire Arms and Explosives Act	55
15.	Crimes under Communication Equipment Act	5
16.	Crimes under the Organization of Hunting of Birds and Animals Act	2
17.	Crimes under other Acts	12
	Total	37,359

The earlier studies, which endeavored to investigate the size and trends of the terrorism phenomenon, confined the terrorist crimes to incidents like hijacking of aircrafts, assassinations, terrorist threats, demonstrations, insurrections, riots, strikes, and coups d'état. Obviously, not all of these crimes on which the said studies were based are considered as terrorist crimes. For example, the demonstrations which take place for wage increases or to protest the result of a football game may not be classified as a terrorist crime. Another example is that the violations under a firearms act may be misleading as it may be due to the expiration of the licensing period as well as the acquisition of a firearm or weapon with the intention of committing a crime.

In view of the above, it is evident that the statistical reports in their present form do not tell us much about the existence of the crime of terrorism and/or its significance as compared to other crimes in the Arab Gulf States.

It is worth mentioning here that certain terrorist crimes have been reported in some Arab Gulf States and that it has assumed an organized form in one of these states recently. Unfortunately, these types of crimes were listed under the various crime categories, rendering their identification impossible. Interestingly enough, depending on the security intimation alone, the terrorism phenomenon may not be readily established as existing in the Arab Gulf States. This may be attributed to the nature of their social structure or stable

Table 11.2. The Numerical Distribution of Crimes Committed in the State of Bahrain (1996)

Crime	No.
Murder	8
Attempted murder	3
Fatal ballry	
Assaults	3,151
Threats	488
Sexual assault	225
Thefts	6,612
Breaches of trust	92
Fraud	238
Burning	2,638
Damage to property	2,862
False representation	26
Issurance of bad checks	2,007
Falsification of documents	53
Bribery	1
Misappropriation	53
Acquisition of spurious currency	5
Adultery	16
Lewdness and prostitution	222
Breach of public conduct	468
Gambling	16
Utilization of title	—
Drug cases	332
Violation of liquor act	1,563
Committing suicide	34
Attempted suicide	163
Suspected death	6
Total	21,294

political regimes or the economic prosperity of their peoples or all of these factors together.

MEASURES OF PREVENTION AND COUNTERACTION OF TERRORIST CRIMES IN THE ARAB GULF STATES

Though terrorist crimes still do not represent a phenomenon in its plain scientific sense, according to the trends detected, their size is escalating internationally and the Arab Gulf States, despite their rather stable condition, are no exception in this regard. Therefore, strategic planning calls for an overall antiterrorism strategy comprising the several criteria for countering crime in general—on the assumption that terrorism is actually a crime—in addition to other criteria pertaining to the crime of terrorism in particular.

It is not deemed convenient to discuss in the present study the basis of criminal strategy and its security applications, whether in terms of its components, objectives, characteristics, elements, categories, and types or on the basis of the standards of the strategy and the associated strategic plan phases, the progress of implementation, difficulties of forecasting, or the extent of timely strategy implementation.

In view of this, we will concentrate on the crime of terrorism only, as regards the measures being adopted to prevent and counteract it, taking into consideration its rather typical characteristics. Despite the absence of any joint conventions in this regard among and between the Arab Gulf States, still the said measures are actually being implemented whether within the framework of emergency plans or crisis management.

The measures for countering terrorism are clearly reflected in the mutual undertakings by the Arab Gulf States not to organize, finance, or commit terrorist activities or take part therein in any form whatsoever, and the consequential prevention of utilizing their territories as a scene for the planning, organization, or execution of terrorism crimes, attempting the execution of the same, or taking part therein. Further, the Arab Gulf States undertook to prevent the infiltration of terrorist elements across their boundaries or their residence and prevent the acquisition of facilities in any of the said states.

Cooperation and coordination among the Arab Gulf States covered the selection and development of certain systems for the detection of firearms, explosives, murder, destruction, and other means of assault in addition to the securing of boundaries and check points, through the reinforcement of surveillance measures for preventing the infiltration of terrorist elements.

The antiterrorism measures call for the reinforcement of security and protection systems of VIP personnel, public structures, and other potential targets. They further require the establishment of a database for the collection, collation, and analysis of data on terrorist elements, groups, movements, and organizations as well as the close follow-up and updating of data pertaining to terrorism and the successful experiences and means for countering the same, provided the said data is given to the concerned authorities within the Arab Gulf States, as is permissible by the internal laws and procedures adopted in each state.

In this context, it has been agreed to enhance the role of the security agencies assigned with antiterrorism functions as well as counteraction of organized crime in member states. The said enhancement could be realized through the provision of support to concerned agencies along with the intensification of meetings for direct exchange of intelligence. Moreover, the senior officials in charge of these agencies and organizations assigned with antiterrorism duties should be instructed to develop the existing measures as appropriate according to the degree of the threat posed by terrorism.

The ratification of Arab conventions for countering terrorism by the Arab Gulf States (April 1998) marked the adoption of general standards for Arab cooperation for counteraction and prevention of terrorist crimes, constituting an outline for formulating the Arab Gulf States' strategy according to their internal laws.

The general outline of the said strategy included the information as shown in table 11.3. The general outline of the proposed strategy includes measures calling for extradition of persons accused of practicing terrorist activities, as well as protection measures for witnesses and experts.

Table 11.3. Arab Gulf States' Strategy

- Exchange of Intelligence
  Enhance the exchange of intelligence among themselves as regards the activities of terrorist groups, their leadership, elements, areas of concentration, training, means, sources of finance and armament, as well as types of firearms, ammunition, explosives, and other means of assault, murder, and destruction used by them.

  Examine the means of communications and propaganda used by the terrorist groups, their style of work, the movements of their leaderships, and elements and type of travel documents used by them.

  To undertake to immediately convey to any other state any available intelligence on any terrorist crimes committed on its territories but targeting the interests or citizens of that state. The details of all the risks involved in the crime and the circumstances, victims, losses resulting thereof, and the means and methods used in its perpetration should be provided unless it affects the good progress of investigations.

  To undertake to cooperate among themselves as regards the exchange of intelligence on the counteraction of terrorist crimes. They further undertake to immediately notify the concerned state or other signatory states of all available intelligence and data that could assist in the prevention of an anticipated terrorist crime on the territory of that state or pose a threat to its citizens, residents, or interests.

  To undertake to provide any of the Arab Gulf States with all available intelligence or data that may (1) assist in the arrest of any person or persons accused of committing a terrorist crime threatening the interests of that state, or accused of attempting to commit or take part therein, whether through provision of assistance, acquiescence, or instigation, or (2) lead to the detection of any firearms, ammunition, explosives, tools, equipments, or funds used or made ready for use in a terrorist crime.

  To observe the confidentiality of the intelligence exchanged among themselves and undertake not to expose it to any other state or agency without the prior permission of the source state.

- Investigations
  To enhance cooperation among themselves and assist in the investigations and arrest measures taken against any fugitive accused or convicted in terrorist crime pursuant to the laws and regulations applicable in each state.

- Exchange of Expertise
  To cooperate among themselves in the completion and exchange of studies and researches on the counteraction of terrorist crimes making use of the available expertise in the filed.
  To extend cooperation, within capabilities, to other member states by making available technical assistance for organizing private or joint training courses to be undertaken by a single state or a group of states. These training courses shall be organized when and as necessary for law enforcement officers assigned with antiterrorism duties with a view to developing their scientific and practical capabilities and upgrading their performance standards.

- Extradition of Criminals
  To undertake to extradite persons accused of or convicted of terrorist crimes upon the request of the member state, in accordance with the rules and conditions stipulated.

- Requests for Legal Assistance
  Any of the Arab Gulf States may request any of the other member states to undertake on its behalf any legal procedure pertaining to a case arising out of a terrorist crime and in particular:
  Hear the testimony of witnesses and take statements for evidence fact finding, serve summons and notices, carry out searches and attachments, and conduct inspections.

- Judicial Cooperation
  Each member state shall provide the others with all possible assistance in the investigations or trial procedures pertaining to terrorist crimes when and as deemed necessary.

- The Proceeds of the Crime
  In case a decision is taken to extradite a wanted person, any of the Arab Gulf States hereby undertakes to seize and hand over to the requesting state all items and proceeds of the terrorist crime whether they were found with the wanted person or with any third party.
  To hand over the items referred to in the above paragraph even if the extradition of the wanted person was not finalized due to his escape or death or for any other reason. The hand over of the items shall only be effected after duly ascertaining their connection with the terrorist crime without prejudice to the good faith or any state rights.

- Exchange of Evidence
  To undertake, either through its concerned authorities or the authorities of another state, the examination of the evidences and traces resulting from any terrorist crime. It further undertakes to take all measures necessary to preserve these evidences and traces in addition to any proof of their legal significance. It shall solely have the right to furnish the state against whose interest the crime was committed with the result of the examination upon its request. The state/states that provided the technical assistance should be instructed not to disclose such results to any other state.

Finally, it should be pointed out that the adoption of this strategy by the Arab Gulf States requires the incorporation of the following general and protective measures in the national policy of each of state:

General Measures

Each state shall adopt effective and strict measures for countering terrorist crimes of different forms and types through the following:

To undertake not to organize or attempt to organize or participate in any way whatsoever in the organization of terrorist activities or their financing nor to instigate others to do so or assist in their organization or perpetration.

To prevent the use of its territories as a scene for the planning, organization, or execution of terrorist crimes or attempt to do so nor to participate therein in any form whatsoever. It further undertakes to prevent individual and collective infiltration into, or their accommodation within, its territories and shall neither receive and accommodate them nor train, arm, or provide them with any sort of facilities which may enable them to achieve their goals.

To guarantee the arrest, trial, or otherwise the extradition of terrorist crime perpetrators.

To adapt its internal legislation to the antiterrorism conventions to which it is a party.

To provide protection and security services to the diplomatic and consular personnel and missions accredited thereto under the relative international conventions.

Protective Measures

The protection from terrorism crimes may be realized through the following:

Extension of support to the family by the state to ensure the proper upbringing of children.

Incorporation of the ethnic, moral, and educational values derived from the Islamic *Sharia* in the educational curricula.

Explanation of the correct concepts and methods of Islamic belief and *Sharia* by the religious institutions.

Enhancement of national public awareness through intensive audiovisual and printed mass media campaigns, highlighting the role of the dedicated, loyal, and peaceful citizenship and soliciting, at the same time, public support. The campaigns should also endeavor to explain the correct concepts of Islam.

Undertaking of an investigation by the appropriate governmental organizations of the motives behind the phenomenon of social protest and other troubles prevailing among young people in particular and drafting effective measures for dealing therewith.

Support by the political organizations and institutions for democratic practices and observance of human rights principles in accordance with the provisions of Islamic *Sharia* and international conventions.

Updating of Legislation

Criminal laws and procedures should be updated and measures taken to achieve the following:

Incorporation of criminal legislation to criminalize terrorism activities and prescribe deterrent punishment to their perpetrators.

Adoption of procedures and policies aiming at the provision of efficient protection for the judiciary and law enforcement personnel.

Establishment of suitable means, enactment of appropriate legislation, and allocation of sufficient resources for assistance and rescue of terrorism victims.

Adoption of appropriate measures and policies to provide an effective protection for witnesses in terrorist crimes against violence during the criminal investigations and trial procedures and exchange of expertise in this regard on an international scale.

Enactment of a special act organizing the acquisition, import, export, storage, and transport of firearms, ammunitions, explosives, and all other dangerous materials with a view to co-coordinate their monitoring by the custom authorities at the boundaries to prevent their transport from one state to another except for absolutely lawful purposes.

Expand the administrative powers vested in public authority officials assigned with the deportation of foreigners suspected of constituting a security risk, and deny them entry into the country.

Updating the Security Institutions and Development of Its Working Plan

The required updating and development may be achieved through the following:

Formation of a higher antiterrorism committee comprising representatives of the concerned bodies to be charged with prescription and supervision of the necessary antiterrorism programs as well as the coordination of intelligence exchange with other concerned security agencies.

Establishment of a specialized unit equipped with the latest technical equipment to undertake the collection, collation, analysis, utilization, and storage of intelligence on terrorism and exchange the same with other concerned security agencies.

Establishment of a special antiterrorism squad with high efficiency and properly equipped for dealing with terrorism situations, making use of international expertise and training programs in this regard.

Introduce improvements in training programs in order to upgrade the qualifications and skills of security staffs, paying special attention to the inclusion therein of a program on terrorist crimes.

Establishment of advanced programs for the safeguarding and protection of very important personnel utilizing modern equipment in the field.

Augmentation of the protection systems of vital structures, public transport means along with the development of the performance standards of the security elements assigned with their protection responsibilities.

Development of private security-guard systems in order to enable them carry out their self-protection functions.

Employment of modern technologies for detecting explosives planted in sensitive areas, mail parcels, or passenger luggage.

Strengthening of surveillance operations in frontier areas, airports, and seaports to prevent the infiltration of terrorists.

Adoption of the Scientific Methodology
The scientific methodology may be achieved through:

Encouragement of research dealing with investigation and analysis of terrorism with a view to identifying its causes, means and techniques, and identifying resulting consequences. The required research should propose the approach to be adopted for curbing or minimizing the said consequences to the lowest level as well as other means and measures for countering terrorism.

Employment of modern technologies in security work and follow up the latest development in this regard.

These are the general outlines of the antiterrorism strategy to be adopted in the Arab Gulf States. Though GCC states have not actually concluded a convention in this regard, the effective coordination existing among them as well as that with the Arab League has kept this region from suffering from the terrorism that has devastated many other nations.

CONCLUSION

In order to achieve a more effective and beneficial counteraction of terrorism, which represents a concern not only to the developing countries but also the advanced ones, it is imperative to adopt a regional, Arab, Islamic, and international strategy comprising security as well as economic, social, religious, political, and cultural measures.

A close examination of the above reveals the importance of countering terrorism through an integrated strategy in all legal systems, regardless of the variations in ideologies on which these systems are based in the various parts of the world. At its inception, this strategy should involve enactment of preventive legislation on terrorism, which defines its concepts and nature. Further, it should clearly draw a distinction between terrorists on one hand and religious persons and politicians on the other hand. Terrorism injects fear and panic whereas religion and politics invite mercy and wisdom. Consequently, it can be concluded that the rights and freedoms enjoyed by a religious person, even if he exaggerates or holds an extreme view on religious precepts (whatever the religion in which he believes) as well as those enjoyed by a politician even if he exaggerates or holds an extreme view on his country's policy, should not be enjoyed by terrorists. The main rights referred to include the right of asylum and the right of nonextradition. The first step, therefore, is to draw a distinction between terrorism as a criminal act punishable by penal law and deeds motivated by religion and politics that are based on moral and intellectual beliefs. How different is crime (and terrorism being one of its forms) from vice and morals (and religion and rational politics being one of its concepts).

To conclude, the right of asylum should be confined to all persons holding a different view on the political ideology adopted in their country as long as such difference has not amounted to the exercise of force, provided the interpretation of the same should be left to an international court specialized in the settlement of political refugee extradition. On the other hand, there is a need to incorporate a legislative definition to the crime of terrorism in addition to the extradition of perpetrators of terrorism in the laws of all states on the basis of designating them as criminals in both internal legislation and bilateral and multilateral conventions.

In view of the above, there is obviously an urgent need for cooperation on the international, as well as the Arab regional levels. The cooperation on the regional level may be effected either at the Arab League level, which recently succeeded in the conclusion of an Arab Antiterrorism Convention, or at the level of the GCC countries, which are already committed to an implemented strategy for countering crime in all forms.

Finally, we would like to point out that although the measures proposed are predominated by security features, the impact of the other measures, such as cultural, social, political, educational, and economic on the restriction of terrorism should not be overlooked. Actually these measures play almost the major role in antiterrorism strategies on both the local and international levels.

BIBLIOGRAPHY

Besides the references referred to in the text and the foreign references, we enlist hereunder the major references used for conducting of this research.

Abdul Aziz Ahmed Al-Hajiri. 1997. *Al Irhab* [Terrorism]. Research Presented to the Police College-Officers Training Institute, Abu Dhabi, U.A.E.

Abdul Hadi Al Shireedah. 1995. *The Arabian Gulf Co-operation Council.* Cairo, Egypt: Madpooli Bookshop.

Ahmed Dayaa Al Din Al Wakeel. 1992. *Usos Al Istratigia Al-Jannia wa Tatbiqatiha Al Amnia* [The Criminal Strategy Principles and Their Security Applications]. Riyadh, Saudi Arabia: Publishing House of the Arab Security Studies and Training Center.

Ahmed Jalal Izzaldin. 1986. *Al Irhab wa Al Onf Al Seyasi* [Terrorism and the Political Violence]. Cairo, Egypt: Dar Al Hurria Printing and Publishing House.

Annual Statistical Reports of the GCC States for 1995 and 1996.

Hassan Doah. 1993. *Al-Irhab Al-Marfood wa Al-Irhab Al-Mafrood* [The rejected and the imposed terrorism]. Cairo, Egypt: Dar-Al-Itism for Islamic Printing.

Hassnain Tawfeeq Ibrahim. 1992. *Zahirat Al Onf Al Seyasi fi Al Nuzum Al-Arabia* [The Phenomenon of Political Violence in the Arab Regimes]. Beirut, Lebanon: Arab Unity Studies Center.

Kamal Shukri. 1992. *Aqniat Al Irhab* [Terrorism Masks]. Cairo, Egypt: The Public Book Authority.

Mamdouh Abdul Hameed. 1992. *Al Wazeefa Al-Idaria lil Shurta, Al Dabt Al-Idari* [The administrative functions of the Police, Management Control]. Cairo, Egypt.

Mohammed Al Samak. 1992. *Al-Irhab wa Al Onf Al-Seyasi* [Terrorism and Political Violence]. Beirut, Lebanon: Dar Al Nafayes.

Mohammed Aziz Shukri. 1991. *Al Irhab Al Dowli* [The International Terrorism]. Beirut, Lebanon: Dar-Al Ilm lil Malayin' for Editing Translation and Publishing.

Mohammed Farooq Al Nabhan. 1989. *Naho Istratigia Arabia Muwahada li Mukafahat Al-Ijram Al-Munazum* [Toward an integrated Arab Strategy for countering organized crime]. Riyadh, Saudi Arabia: The Publishing House of the Arab Security Studies and Training Center.

Morris, Eric, and Alan Who. 1991. *Terrorism: The Threat and Response,* translated by Ahmed Hamdi Mahmoud. Cairo, Egypt: Public Arab Book Authority.

Odnis Al Akkra. 1993. *Al-Irhab Al Seyasi* [Political Terrorism], 2nd ed. Beirut, Lebanon: Dar Al Talab Printing & Publishing.

Papers presented to the Conference on the Development of the Arab Police and Security Cooperation during the period 1972–1992; Achievements and Prospects. Sharjah Police Publications, UAE, 1992.

Plus, Thomas, et al. 1990. *Violence and Man,* translated by Abdu Hadi Abdul Rahman. Beirut, Lebanon: Dar Al Taleeah.

Tened Henderson. 1986. *The Political Violence.* 1st ed. Translated by Abdul Karim and Eisa Tanoos. Cairo, Egypt.

12

Terrorism and Human Rights Violations: An Assessment of Protective Measures in Uganda

Steven Kasiima Munanura

INTRODUCTION

Terrorism is back with a vengeance. After being subdued internationally and within most Western countries in the late 1980s, it has returned in ferocious and fearful new forms.[1]

From the early 1990s up until today, Uganda has experienced several terrorism activities. These activities have claimed many lives, left several injured and others destitute. They have not only brought untold suffering but have also violated people's human rights.

Terrorism has been a traditional tactic for the weak. Terrorism in the form of assassinations, kidnapping, and hostage taking has been employed with varying degrees of success since the beginning of civilization.

To understand its present-day use, it is necessary to understand the evolution of terrorism. Throughout history, many people have employed terrorist tactics. This fascination with terrorism and political violence can be traced practically to the dawn of history. Since before the birth of Christ, the assassination of a tyrannical ruler was not only condoned but often glorified, praised, and revered.[2]

The assassins of Persia and Assyria appeared in the eleventh century and spread fear and terror throughout the Islamic Empire.[3] During the French Revolution, Robespierre used terrorism to destroy much of the French aristocracy. During the American Revolution, terrorism was used against the British and their colonial sympathizers.[4] An American group, the Ku Klux Klan, used violence to terrorize blacks and their sympathizers after the end of the American Civil War in 1865.

The origins of contemporary terrorism are traced from the nineteenth and early twentieth centuries, in particular from Czarist Russia.[5] The works of Mikhail Bakunin, Sergei Nechayev, Morzov, and Frantz Fanon appeared in Europe. They had their foundation on terror.[6] Since then, they have been translated into modern languages and have served as the basic primers of many terrorist movements.

In the 1960s terrorist groups like the Red Brigades in Italy and Red Army factions in West Germany surfaced. Both groups sought the destruction of the existing political and economic systems in their home countries and the development of new systems.[7]

In Israel, in the 1940s, before her independence, a terrorist Jewish group used terrorism to end British rule in Palestine and so create a Jewish homeland.[8] Since 1945, terrorism has been an important factor in the subversion of many newly emerging countries and was also a form of surrogate warfare waged against democratic societies.[9]

Contemporary terrorism can be traced to the swell of unrest of the 1950–1970 era. Violence to make a political statement or to arouse social conscience became a popular strategy.

During the later part of this century, terrorism spread across national boundaries to become a major form of political expression. It has been used to further political goals, to attack enemies, or as a cheap and effective tool of foreign policy, to instill fear, seek to destroy the confidence of the people, harm social relations, damage public order, build feelings of distrust and hostility toward governments, and cause physical damage to civilians, security officers, and property.[10]

THE PHENOMENON OF TERRORISM
NATIONALLY AND INTERNATIONALLY

Definition of Terrorism

Consensus as to the definition of terrorism remains as the source of much disagreement. The problem of definition is raised again when an individual, who is labeled as a terrorist by one segment of society, is revered as a freedom fighter by another segment of society. Thus it is no surprise that there are problems defining terrorism.

An act can be defined as terrorism if it meets the following criteria:

The act is unlawful, as it involves the use or threatened use of violence or force that is directed against individuals or property and is designed to coerce government or society. Such an act often undermines a government's political, ideological, or religious objectives.[11]

Factors That Contribute to Terrorist Activities

Many factors contribute to the rise of terrorism. These include unpopular, repressive, or corrupt governments, gross discrimination, extreme poverty, high unemployment, violent opposing political philosophies, religious strife, and foreign support of dissident activities, among several others.

Acts of terrorism are directed against noncombatants, with a goal of terrorizing a wider audience than the immediate victim, thereby attempting to achieve a political, economic, or social objective. Terrorists aim to advertise their existence and goals, intimidate and coerce the public into supporting their cause, undermine and seek the overthrow of the existing order, provoke government overreaction, and impose excessive and unpopular, repressive countermeasures.

Operations

Terrorist operations are increasingly well executed. They are usually carried out by specially trained and organized clandestine elements. Strict security techniques are followed by terrorist groups after a target is selected or the area is designated.

For further security, the team members are not brought together until the final rehearsal phase and just before departure to the target site. To increase security, reconnaissance will likely be conducted in depth. Reconnaissance is always done by a special intelligence member who is tasked only for that role in the operation. To make detection and prevention difficult, many more attacks are planned than conducted. Terrorists normally seek to exploit vulnerabilities. They often attack targets which are not defended or have weak security. Terrorist operations are characterized by violence, speed, and surprise.[12]

Theoretical Framework

Terrorism as a crime is located in two major theories. These are the religious theory and the psychological theory.

Religious Theory

The religious theory asserts that terrorism has a central role in religious conflicts. This theory states that religion has several characteristics that make terrorism a very potent form of violence.

Simon Jeffrey advanced the theory that there is a moral justification for committing the seemingly immoral acts of killing people; believing that God is on one's side is a powerful incentive to action.[13] The sacred terrorist believes that divine authority, which humans have no right to alter, sanctioned their ends and means.[14]

The majority of terrorists see religion as a *homegrown answer to disorder, corruption, and inequality*.[15] It has also brought comfort and peace of mind to countless millions of men and women. However, as already pointed out, this theory does not address and account for the terrorist incidents that do not have any fundamental religious connotations. Such a theory is not merely incomplete, it is misleading.

Psychological Theory

One of the myths about terrorism is that it is perpetuated by irrational people. This is a logical conclusion for people to reach when they see on television or read about planes blown up in mid-air, suicide attacks on buildings, and a host of other seemingly senseless violent acts.

Some public officials, as noted earlier, foster this myth with statements about terrorism being the work of barbarians, madmen, and sick individuals. But the terrorist who kills for his cause sees himself as no different from the soldier who kills for his country or the guerrilla or freedom fighter who kills for his group. All believe they are on the just and moral side of a conflict.[16]

Among the more extreme psychological theories on terrorism is that terrorists suffer from faulty vestibule functions in the middle ear or from inconsistent mothering resulting in dysphoria. Another view is that while terrorists do not fit into a specific psychiatric diagnostic category, individuals with particular personality dispositions are drawn to the path of terrorism. According to Jerrod Post, terrorists rely on "externalization and splitting which are psychological mechanisms found in individuals with narcissistic and borderline personality disturbances."[17]

The main problem with psychological explanations for terrorist behavior is that they obscure the ethnic-nationalist, political-ideological, religious, and other reasons that motivate the vast majority of terrorists into action.[18] However, we must not fall prey to Jeffrey's theory. Whether or not a terrorist group has a few or even a large number of members with personality disorders is irrelevant to the cause of terrorism.

There will always be enough normal individuals in a terrorist group to carry out various attacks even if all the psychologically troubled members were weeded out or never joined in the first place. It is not clear whether those terrorists who have abnormal personality characteristics would be any different in terms of their desires to join a terrorist group even if they were cured. Their commitment to a particular cause could very well attract them to a life of violence anyway.

This view is supported by Martha Crenshaw. The difficulty in gaining access to individual terrorists for clinical research purposes has been speculative. The studies that have been conducted point more toward normality than to psychological problems. "What limited data we have on individual terrorists suggest that the outstanding common characteristics has been normality," writes terrorism analyst Martha Crenshaw.[19]

A psychiatrist who examined four Red Army Faction members before their trial found that they showed no particular personality type and did not suffer from any psychosis or neurosis. Furthermore, terrorist groups tend to reject potential recruits who seem more interested in danger and adventure than in commitment to the cause.[20] As psychiatrist Post notes, terrorists have a tendency to submerge their own identities into the group, so that a kind of group mind emerges. The group cohesion that emerges is magnified by the external danger, which tends to reduce internal divisiveness in unity against the outside enemy.[21]

An individual terrorist may also use the group to avoid any personal sense of guilt or responsibility for various murderous activities. If the killings are the result of a collective group decision, then the terrorist feels no shame. Once the group identity is removed, though, the terrorist is faced with his/her own individuality and the reality of the crimes he committed. This may explain, in part, why some terrorists never leave a group and why some groups continue to exist even as the world around them goes through dramatic changes.

Similar to other biological explanations of crime, theories advanced by Jeffrey imply that terrorism is a product of the individual. Jeffrey's approach can be criticized on several grounds. Such an explanation suggests that the solution lies in treating individuals rather than overhauling the social order that perpetuates the social imbalances of power to generate crime.

The religious theory that says that there is moral justification for killing people, holding that God is on one's side, fails to account for terrorist incidents that do not have fundamental religious connotations.

Also, the psychological theory which asserts that terrorism is a result of personality disorders fails to refute the reality that the solution does not lie with treating individuals but rather with overhauling the social order that perpetuates the social imbalances of power to generate crime.

Not all terrorists are mad people, as previous theories seem to suggest. The evidence that has been gathered by the U.S. Federal Bureau of Investigation (FBI) suggest that most of the nineteen alleged terrorists who hijacked the planes that bombed New York and Washington were well-educated men, some from wealthy families.

The psychological theory has failed to point out that psychology is only helpful in understanding the group dynamics of terrorists. They live a life underground, dependent on each other for support and nurturing. The us-them dichotomy is very paramount in the thinking of terrorists.

The General Legal Responses to Terrorism

The offense of terrorism has been criminalized in the Penal Code Act of Uganda (1990) under section 28(1), which states that any person who engages in or who carries out acts of terrorism is guilty of an offense and is liable to imprisonment for life.

According to Timothy Schofield (1998), the terrorism law fails to adequately address the practical issues associated with this emerging threat. Understanding these traditional legal doctrines is, however, a prerequisite to developing a new law specifically designed to prosecute and punish acts of terrorism.[22]

Consistent with traditional law enforcement strategies, the focus of anti-terrorism activity is on apprehension and punishment. The terrorism law does not address itself to whether loss of life should accentuate the penalty, as in armed robbery, or whether the dependents should seek civil remedies for the loss of life of their breadwinner.

Ngobi (2000) points out that terrorism is committed meticulously and secretly, with very many innocent people dying, yet, under our current law, you can only detain the suspect for the same period as a chicken thief and still the burden of proof lies with the prosecution. He observes that terrorist law, and one may add human rights guarantees, are very lenient to terrorists and, therefore, need to be changed or revisited.[23]

Ewing and Gearty (1993) support Schofield in respect to legislation against terrorism. In 1998, Mrs. Thatcher said the following about her government's legislative response to terrorism:

> Yes, some of these measures do restrict freedom. But those who chose to live by the bomb and the gun, and those who support them, cannot in all circumstances be accorded exactly the same rights as everyone else. We do sometimes have to sacrifice a little of the freedoms we cherish in order to defend ourselves from those whose aim is to destroy that freedom altogether a decision we should not be afraid to take. In the battle against terrorism, we shall never give in. The only victory will be our victory: the victory of democracy and a free society.[24]

It is difficult to counter the emotional power of such arguments. The former prime minister was right to express concern about political violence in the United Kingdom. In response to her arguments, the Prevention of Terrorism Act of 1989 was enacted. It emerged as a response to a campaign of terrorism that the Irish Republican Army (IRA) has waged in Britain since 1972.[25]

The act provides for repressive measures against terrorists and their sympathizers. It also reveals that silence during interrogation may be used against a suspect on the ground that it indicates training in anti-interrogation techniques.[26]

Section 14 of the Prevention of Terrorism Act includes the discretion to arrest without a warrant, where a constable has reasonable grounds for suspecting an offense against any of the proscription, exclusion, or financial provisions in the legislation. It also shifts the burden of proof to the suspect.

Undoubtedly, the leaders of the United Kingdom were subjected to a barrage of criticism that they were curtailing civil freedoms. However, Benjamin Netanyahu supports the United Kingdom's approach when he said that the leaders must have the courage to do what is required even in the face of the most stinging criticism. "Courageous action is in itself the best answer to the inevitable slings that the small-minded heap upon the statesmen facing great odds."[27]

Statesmen should reject this criticism, responding, as has the Supreme Court of the United States, that "it is obvious and unarguable that no governmental interest is more compelling than the security of the nation—and this includes unlimited civil liberties.[28]

In their article "Museveni Wants Law on Terrorism" in *The New Vision* (September 11, 2000) Kamali and Kameo report that President Museveni of Uganda has revealed that the cabinet will soon table an antiterrorism bill to deal with insurgents waging rebellion against the state. All persons captured in armed action against the government will be severely punished to serve as an example to all enemies of democracy. But as noted above, such measures do not appear to work as designed by their proponents as witnessed by the Brogan case.[29] In that case, four British citizens were detained under the Prevention of Terrorism Act. They were detained for many days contrary to Article 5(3) of the European Convention. The European Court of Human Rights upheld the holding that their detention infringed their rights as provided in the convention.

The first reaction of the British government to the ruling was one of anger and criticism. Mrs. Thatcher declared in the House of Commons that "we shall consider the judgment carefully and in doing so we shall consider the human rights of victims and potential victims of terrorism as well as the human rights of those suspected of terrorist involvement." After a period of indecision, it was announced that Britain would not accept the judgment of the court, arguing that there was a public emergency threatening the life of the nation.

Similar to Thatcher's approach to repressive legislation against terrorism is the United States's statement contained in the *Patterns of Global Terrorism, United States Department of State*, 1997, which states that the United States is engaged in a long-term effort against international terrorism to protect the lives of its citizens and hold terrorists accountable. "We will use a full range of tools at our disposal, including diplomacy backed by the use of force when necessary, as well as law enforcement and economic measures."[30] As a result, two new presidential decision directives were issued, on combating terrorism and protecting critical infrastructures. They will be considered below.

It is well to remember that terrorists are not like ordinary criminals who can be tracked down and interrogated to break down and talk. They are trained to be very hard and they do not break down easily during interrogation. Security officials are breaking the constitution by detaining suspected terrorists for longer than forty-eight hours. But suffice it to say that this is good for society.

TERRORISM AND THE VIOLATION
OF FUNDAMENTAL HUMAN RIGHTS

Chapter IV of the 1995 Constitution of the Republic of Uganda provides for the protection and promotion of fundamental freedoms and other human rights. The same constitution provides that the rights and freedoms of the individual and groups enshrined in chapter IV shall be respected, upheld, and promoted by all organs and agencies of the state and by all persons, the terrorists notwithstanding.

The same constitution provides that no person shall be deprived of his/her life intentionally except in the execution of a sentence imposed by a court of law following or after a fair trial by a court of competent jurisdiction.[31] Thus, though the provisions of the constitution are very clear, terrorists have continued to violate the rights of the people without any hindrance.

Since 1997, over twenty-eight terrorist incidents have been registered in Kampala alone. These incidents have claimed the lives of innocent people and injured many more. They have brought untold suffering and have negated constitutional provisions relating to the protection and promotion of human rights. Not only have the rights of innocent people been violated but also those of suspected terrorists, who quite often have been found innocent.

Nevertheless, today there is a greater awareness of human rights globally and nationally, an inevitable consequence of democratization. The primary duty of law enforcement agencies is to respect and uphold the human rights granted by the constitution of Uganda. Resort to extralegal measures like torture of suspected terrorists have come under scrutiny by the courts and human rights bodies.

The Human Rights Watch report entitled "Breaking the Circle: Protecting Human Rights in the Northern War Zone" has documented scores of killings of unarmed civilians, dozens of rapes, and hundreds of beatings by the security forces over the last three years. The report warns that the acquiescence of the international community to human rights abuses in Uganda serves to undermine respect for human rights both here and worldwide.[32]

In their article entitled "Gazette Safe Houses," Alfred Wasike and Edith Kimuli report that President Yoweri Museveni of Uganda directed that all secret detention places in Uganda (also called safe houses) be gazetted.[33] This directive came as a result of complaints of arbitrary arrests and torture of suspected terrorists in illegal detention centers.

The above reports are a clear testimony of violation of human rights. Though those who engage in terrorism activities should not be handled with kid gloves, the innocent ones should not be denied their rights on the pretext of fighting terrorism. Investigations should be carried out and evidence obtained before arrests are made. Even the suspects deserve to be treated humanely, as the constitution of Uganda stipulates.

The Administrative Measures in Uganda

According to the U.S. Department of State Bulletin of November 1995, the face of terrorism has evolved with the development of technology, modern transportation, highly lethal weapons, and other technological advances. It has enhanced the capabilities of the contemporary terrorists. While the tools of the terrorists are considered more destructive than those available in the past, the ability to use these new destructive devices has also been increased.[34]

In Schofield's study (1998) an observation is made that the use of nonconventional weapons by terrorists will spread rapidly.[35] A nuclear device or chemical or biological weapon of mass destruction in the hands of a terrorist is well within the realm of possibility. Publications with instructions on how and where to obtain the necessary materials for the construction of a nuclear device are readily available in the print and electronic media.

Schofield further argues that specialized units fighting terrorists should be equipped to meet the challenges posed by terrorism. Has the government of Uganda equipped specialized units to combat terrorism thereby protecting the rights of its people? Frank Pearce in his *Global Crime Connections* (1993) asserts that governments are not equipped to deal with the rapidly changing situation, and that they show little or no interest in attempting to remedy their inadequacies. He contends current efforts to control are counterproductive, producing as many problems are they are designed to solve.[36] Likewise, Opiyo Oloya's argument article entitled "Uganda Ill Prepared to Help Terrorist Victims"[37] is consistent with Pearce's comments. He notes that Uganda needs to wake up in a hurry to face the reality of urban terrorism. He states that officials who should be fully prepared have responded in a knee-jerk fashion with no plan for evacuating victims and securing affected areas.[38]

The same criticisms are echoed in Mugunga's article "Slipper-Clad Police Used Matches in Bomb Aftermath." He reported that Museveni's Uganda government security apparatus simply does not have the capacity to combat terrorism.[39] This was evidenced during the grenade blast in Wandegeya's Bermuda Triangle in April 1998. The author explains that at Bermuda, seasoned personnel trampled all over the crime scene, totally oblivious of the fact that they were essentially destroying or tampering with the evidence in the process.

The author further adds that among the mobile police patrol officers, there was no sign of a bomb disposal expert. Instead, police personnel rounded up the still shaken citizens and subjected them to rigorous questioning. The more senior officers who usually crowd high-profile crime scenes engaged in their walkie-talkies as they reported to their superiors.[40]

The response time and operational coordination are yet another wanting area in the force. This was seen during the attack on Speke Hotel, right in the heart of Kampala and not too far from police CID headquarters and the central police station. It took close to twenty minutes for police to react to two 999 emergency calls made by a journalist immediately after the blast went off.

We concur with the authors of the article because it should not take long for the dispatch man in the signal room to communicate with mobile patrols for them to react rapidly. This does not call for additional resources but rather for better training and efficiency in operations.

However, the government should also equip specialized units to combat urban terrorism. Mugunga further reported that several of the policemen who responded to the Speke Hotel blast turned up in bathroom slippers.[41]

They did not have gloves and exposed themselves to danger when they proceeded to plaster their bare hands all over the floor in search of material evidence. Also, there wasn't any floodlight; instead, matches were struck to provide light. There was no video recording that would have provided a near permanent record.

It is imperative to point out that the police's capacity to contain semiconventional war is fair but when it comes to urban terrorism, very few of our so-called intelligence people even recognize the term. It is alien to them and there is no doubt that they would be at a loss when confronted with the complex technology at the disposal of the terrorists.

Partnership with Other Agencies

Crime affects everybody, not only the victims and the police. Preventing crime is not something that can be done by the police alone. The cooperation of the community is essential and the police must work in conjunction with other agencies at various levels. A partnership approach to crime reduction is therefore a key element of the work of police.[42]

We are convinced, however, that underscoring the police's role in fighting terrorists does not imply that the wider society has no role to play or that its role is of no significance.

Everybody shares the costs of preventing crime and dealing with offenders. The quantifiable costs of crime amount to billions a year, quite apart from the unquantifiable personal and social costs. The reduction of crime therefore offers a substantial financial dividend as well as other benefits to the community.

Nature of Terrorist Activities in Kampala

Uganda has finally shed its international reputation as a country of mass killings and gross human rights violations. With Idi Amin's reign of terror firmly consigned to the past, the country is now trying very hard to regain its image as the "Pearl of Africa." Since President Yoweri Museveni of Uganda came to power in 1986, there has been increasing political stability and economic development. Uganda is the first country in Africa to introduce universal primary education and to successfully reduce the spread of the AIDS epidemic.

However, the northern and recently the western parts of the country have been largely excluded from this success story. In these areas, a forgotten terrorism war is going on which has already claimed over 150,000 people. Rebels have continued to kill and abduct children. One vivid example is the 139 girls of St. Mary's College Aboke in Northern Uganda who were abducted by the Lord's Resistance Army, one of the deadliest guerrilla armies in the world, led by a religious fanatic, Joseph Kony. Several thousand other children have been burnt by terrorists in their homes and schools.

Rebel groups largely comprised of soldiers of vanquished armies have regrouped to wage war on the National Resistance Movement government. The most durable insurrection has persisted in northern Uganda and has taken on international dimensions, with rebels supported and sponsored by neighboring countries. Another full-scale insurrection led by the Uganda People's Army (UPA) was defeated in Teso in eastern Uganda. Other groups, namely the Allied Democratic Front and the Uganda Salvage Rescue Front, operate intermittently in areas around the Rwenzori Mountains in western Uganda and in low-level rebel activities in areas of Kampala City.[43]

With government forces maintaining pressure on them, these groups have, in their desperation, often resorted to terror tactics that have resulted in the torture of innocent civilians, the destruction of property, the detonation of bombs, robberies, abductions, and hostage taking.[44]

Since 1997, over twenty-eight urban terrorist incidents have been registered; twenty-two of these incidents have occurred in Kampala alone. The terrorist activities in Uganda have mainly been associated with the work of three rebel groups, namely, the Allied Democratic Front (ADF), the Uganda Salvage Rescue Front (USRF), and the Lords Resistance Army (LRA).[45] In the Nairobi and Dar-Es-Salaam bomb incident alone of July 1988 over 200 people were killed and over 500 were injured.[46] Still, the September 11, 2001 terrorist attacks in the United States of America left even more people dead, many injured, and much property destroyed.

The United States Department of State 1997 Report on *Patterns of Global Terrorism* indicates that 304 acts of international terrorism were registered in 1997 and this figure is eight times more than what was registered in 1996. According to the same report, 221 persons were reported dead and 613 wounded.

The idea of defeating terrorism continues to be spread by politicians and policymakers. The very first paragraph of the executive summary of the U.S. President's Commission on Aviation Security and Terrorism, which was established in the aftermath of the Pan Am 103 bombing, is indicative of the tendency to view terrorism as a finite problem. It reads, "National will and the moral courage to exercise it are the ultimate means of defeating terrorism.[47]

Similarly, President Museveni has condemned bomb blasts and other terrorist acts that have occurred in Uganda and elsewhere and described them as "barbaric acts which evil-minded terrorists have inflicted on innocent people."[48]

Although the National Resistance Movement (NRM) government that also began as a terrorist group and assumed state power in 1986, it has since made impressive gains in restoring and maintaining peace and tranquillity in the country. However, its efforts have been intermittently disrupted and, in some areas, severely curtailed.[49]

Over twenty-eight terrorist acts by way of throwing improvised explosive devices (IED) and grenades have occurred since 1997, in which, by December 1999, 52 and 197 people have been killed and injured, respectively.[50] Of all the cases that occurred, 89 percent were in the Kampala district, with concentration in the divisions of Katwe, Old Kampala, and Central Police Station.

Terrorists in Kampala are known to be coordinating their activities using modern communication equipment, including cellular phones. The central and busiest area of Kampala, policed by the central police station, has been affected most.

The statistics in table 12.1 indicate dates, place, nature of terrorist blasts, and people killed or injured from April 1998 to October 2000.

Intelligence reports revealed that the crude bombs were composed of FM-receiving units, nine-volt long-life batteries, wired wristwatches, high-

Table 12.1. Statistics of Bomb Blasts in Kampala between April 1998–October 2000

Date	Place of Incident	Nature of Blast	Persons Who Died	Persons Injured
4th April, 1998	Speke Hotel	I.E.D	1. Goikoi 2. Gasper Ndimusaba	3
4th April, 1998	Nile Grill Restaurant	I.E.D	1. Eunice Yunus Ssanya 2. Rebecca Gonza 3. Lukia Namagembwa	1
12th July, 1998	Slow Boat Bar and Restaurant	I.E.D	NIL	7
12th July, 1998	Isabella Pub, Makindye	I.E.D	12 (Not identified)	—
10th April, 1998	New Taxi Park	I.E.D	NIL	4
11th April, 1998	Old Taxi Park	I.E.D	1. Medi Kasujja 2. Francis Lutalo	11
1st May, 1998	Serena Pub Makindye	Grenade	NIL	4
6th May, 1998	Owino Market Police Post	Grenade	NIL	1
7th May, 1998	Nateete Market Grenade		1. Sunday	10
24th May, 1998	Kafumbe Mukasa Road	Grenade	1. Semakula Jamada 2. SPC Nakinja 3. Not Identified 4. Not Identified	3
30th May, 1998	Liberty Investment Nakulabye	Grenade	1. Margaret Kemigisha 2. Kisembo Rujumbi 3. Onenchan (Pharmacist)	13
14th Feb, 1999	Telex Bar	I.E.D	1. Boruk Gonfa 2. Silver Katusiime 3. Florence Sendagire 4. Lubwama Sulaiman 5. Margret Namusoke	
5th October, 2000	Kasubi Market	Grenade	1. Kezia Nabalogo	8
		Total	53	77

Source: Uganda Police Force and the Chieftaincy of Military Intelligence Reports.

explosive detonators, and locally made inductor coils. Technical experts found that the FM-receiving unit was usually set in the frequency used by the president's office.

The October 22, 1998, bomb at Najjanankumbi that killed the lone terrorist who was assembling it could have been triggered by the normal communication by president's office personnel. Quite often, the equipment and chemicals used in the manufacture of the bombs are acquired locally from some Kampala shops.

Terrorists have not attacked local people only. Foreign missions in Uganda have received bomb threats from anonymous callers. In September 1999, the U.S. embassy, the British High Commission, the Royal Danish embassy, and the European Union and its sister missions temporarily closed on several occasions for a few days due to such threats.

Concrete barriers erected at U.S. properties are still in place, while the police and the military personnel provided by the Uganda government are still guarding the American embassy in Kampala. Metal detectors have become a common feature in many public places in Kampala and many city residents have become more security conscious.

Kampala's Parliament Avenue and other roads where buildings housing American offices and their residences in Kololo and Nakasero Hills have been turned into one-way roads and barricades have been erected on them, making it practically impossible for motorists to go near them. As a result, terrorist attacks have since not occurred as anticipated, possibly because of the intensification of the security precautions on foreign mission premises.

THE LAW ON TERRORISM IN UGANDA

The government of Uganda, as noted earlier, is in the process of enacting a new law to curb terrorism. According to section 5 of the draft bill, all terrorism offenses are to be extraditable. Section 28 of the Penal Code Act is to be repealed. Section 6 will make terrorism offenses triable and bailable by High Court.

Sections 11 and 17 of the bill seek to widen the definition of a terrorist to include those who persuade or recruit people into terrorism, those who procure materials, those who finance, and those who carry out propaganda for terrorists. The burden of proof is to be shifted from the state to the suspected terrorist.

The new law will provide for the punishment of persons who plan, instigate, support, finance, or execute acts of terrorism.[51] It will also proscribe terrorist organizations and make provisions for the punishment of persons who are members of, or who profess in public to be members of, or who convene or attend meetings of, or who support or finance or facilitate the activities of terrorist organizations.[52]

It will provide for investigation of acts of terrorism and will facilitate obtaining information in respect of such acts that will include authorizing interception of correspondence and surveillance of persons suspected of planning or being involved in acts of terrorism.[53]

More specifically, the bill seeks to make terrorism an extraditable offense. The bill states that terrorism shall not be regarded, for the purpose of extradition, as a political offense or as an offense inspired by political motives. In addition to the above, the offenses under the Terrorism Act will be triable and bailable only by the High Court and on conviction will carry a mandatory death sentence.[54]

Next, the bill empowers police officers or other public officers to use reasonable force in the execution of their duties under the law and protects them from any civil or criminal prosecution.[55]

However, the bill has not addressed the following important areas: powers to deregister, revoke license, or deny registration for any organization, business, NGO, or individual, known to sponsor or support terrorism in any way, or who is connected with a terrorist organization; tightening gun control by civilians and tightening immigration laws.

The government of Uganda has failed to tighten gun control and immigration laws in the wake of terrorist threats. The continued existence in Uganda of heavily armed civilians is a grotesque distortion of the idea of civil freedom, and it should be brought to a speedy end. Similarly, this era of immigration free-for-all should be brought to an end. An important aspect of taking control of the immigration situation is stricter background checks of potential immigrants, coupled with the real possibility of deportation.

Protective Measures by the Uganda Police Force

Intelligence reports were received over a period of time that the threat of terrorism was imminent in Uganda. Consequently, in 1997, a committee consisting of relevant security organs with police as the lead agency drew up a plan, the National Plan to Combat Terrorism, in response to the anticipated threat.

The action plan would focus on four broad strategies: (1) accurate threat assessment, (2) protection of targets, (3) neutralization of terrorists, and (4) contingency planning.

Threat Assessment

Threat assessment can be defined to as the process of investigation by security organizations of hostile countries that pose a terrorist threat. Security organs will provide information about the members, how they are organized and armed, their capability and deployment, and what they are planning.

According to the same officials, a Joint Analysis Team (JAT) under the leadership of the Police Special Branch was formed in 1998 to collect and analyze all terrorism-related data as received from the various intelligence services. From this data, it has built a database from which all the task force operations were centered. It has also made periodic reports to higher authorities who needed to be informed of the progress of counterterrorism efforts.

Furthermore, counterterrorism desks were established within the Special Branch and Criminal Investigation Department organizations for the purposes of penetrating terrorist targets and for the coordination of investigations of all the terrorist incidents. These desks were to cooperate with those in other security services, namely, the Internal Security Organ, External Security Organ, and Chief of Military Intelligence. As a result, terrorist targets have been infiltrated and several arrests have been made. This has reduced terrorist attacks in Kampala.

Protection of Targets

This entails the application of security measures to protect vulnerable facilities and persons from terrorist attacks and includes a variety of measures, the details of which are considered below.

a) Installation of CCTV.
b) Hiring of specialized security firms to carry out guard duties.
c) Many security checks have been instituted by use of technical searching equipment and hired personnel.
d) Various seminars have been conducted in which various departmental security officers share ideas in respect to terrorist activities.
e) Accessibility to most of those installations has been limited to the legal entrances established.
f) Identification systems have been created and are being enforced.
g) Parking areas are closely supervised.
h) Arrangements are underway whereby plans for future construction of important premises and key installations must obtain security approval before they are approved.

In addition, about 120 incident commanders have been trained. Their duties include the recovery of materials for evidence and intelligence purposes after bomb blasts and other related incidents, sensitizing people on how to evacuate buildings in case of bomb-related incidents, responding to any bomb-related scenario like telephone bomb threat calls, dealing with suspected bomb items, sensitizing the public about bomb awareness, and taking charge of bomb sites.

Furthermore, the authorities have instituted a sensitization program that is aimed at educating the public about terrorism generally and what to do in case one sights a suspected item, what to do in case of a telephoned bomb threat, how to practice good housekeeping, and how to watch out for suspicious characters who might be terrorists. Much of this work is to be carried out by the incident managers, community liaison officers, and divisional/district police commanders.

Even the electronic media is increasingly playing a big role in this exercise. With the assistance of the proprietors of FM radio stations, Radio Uganda, and television stations, different messages have been designed for the listeners and viewers educating them about terrorism and bomb attacks. Thus, for example, the Nairobi bomb scene and other visual aids are frequently used to drive the message home.

In the case of security personnel, real explosive materials are used to make improvised explosive devices, and they are shown to them. In effect, this eases their work when carrying out searches. So far, the sensitization drive, which started in June 1998, has covered most of the likely targets throughout the country, with some good results.

As a result of the sensitization drive, a good number of people are becoming alert as far as abandoned objects such as polythene bags, suitcases, and motor vehicles. Indeed, about five calls are made daily to the information room regarding abandoned items, and there is a positive response from the public when cordoning off bomb scenes before and after such incidents.

As a security protective measure, the protection of VIPs especially in Kampala has been stepped up. All the VIPs who are entitled to protection are provided with plainclothes bodyguards and police uniformed guards, both during day and night periods. In addition, the training of protection officers has been stepped up. Much of this counterterrorism training is being provided by the U.S. Antiterrorism Assistance Program personnel. Thus, it is hoped, this will enable the Uganda Police Force and allied agencies to cope with the current wave of terrorist attacks.

The process of transforming the current task force into a professional permanent and autonomous antiterrorism unit under the Uganda police is well underway. The police now have a core group of fifty officers who undertook an advanced tactical firearms and rescue techniques training program in 1995 by West Marcia Firearms Experts, in Cairo, Egypt, in 1998, and the United States of America in 1999. In addition, 210 officers have benefited from the

American-sponsored Antiterrorism Assistance Program in the following courses: post-blast investigations, vital installations security, surveillance detection, aviation security, major case management, explosive incident countermeasures, crisis response team, terrorist crime scene investigations, and hostage negotiations.

Even though the capacity to handle forensic investigations in relation to terrorist attacks still leaves much to be desired, the Uganda police does have the capacity for bomb demolition and disposal. About 120 incident commanders and 68 police officers have been trained in improvised explosive disposal and explosive ordinance disposal, respectively. The police have sniffer dogs for detecting explosives, equipment for dismantling explosive devices, and equipment for investigating after bomb blasts. As a result, the police have become more efficient in detecting and investigating terrorist activities than ever before.

Accordingly, the Uganda police have taken a vigorous approach to promoting partnership. A number of structures to give partnership a more permanent footing have been put in place. Crime prevention panels that help to promote initiatives to prevent crime, neighborhood watch schemes, and formal police and consultation groups have been set up across the country.

However, police tend to emphasize a partnership approach during crisises but they pull away from it when there is calm. When terrorist activities were at their peak, many resources were channeled to the above programs. Later some programs were stopped because the government stopped funding them.

It would also appear that the police have neglected virgin areas of policing that include identification of problems and situations that are likely to result in the commission of crimes. It has failed to put measures in place to ensure reduction of opportunities for the commission of crimes through preventive measures.

Above all, the design, layout, and structural orientation of Kampala does not generally cover the needs of security. It is a security standard that demands that, before any construction, renovation, and modification of any structure is made, security should be consulted. However, this is not the case in Kampala. The result, not surprisingly, is that the police find it difficult to make Kampala safe. In situations of high threat security, the unplanned infrastructure will become a secondary danger.

It is particularly important for the police to involve the public in the campaign against terrorism because physical security measures alone cannot eliminate the threat. It is particularly important to let them know that security is a societal responsibility that can be achieved through training and education programs.

RECOMMENDATIONS

The constitution of Uganda provides that all power belongs to the people who shall exercise their sovereignty in accordance with the constitution.[56] Therefore, whoever desires political office should seek the consent of the people as provided in the constitution[57] but not through terrorism. Likewise, modernity in politics is about moving from exclusion to inclusion, from repression to incorporation. The threat of terrorism should therefore involve the condemnation of everyone. Uganda shall not develop if its political discourse is completely at odds with the realities of the security problem.

We need to go beyond simple explanations for terrorism. The idea that it is the consequence of simple religious fanaticism or some sort of mental depravity or a wicked subculture may not be wholly acceptable. Scientific methods demand that we look beyond such simple explanations and focus on history, namely, the shift of cultural influences that have defined the last two decades.

The long-term prevention of the threat of terrorism will require a methodical search for its underlying causes and a concerted effort to find longstanding solutions. It will require a rethinking of the foreign policies and actions of the developed nations toward the Third World and a focused attention to the well-being and freedom of all the peoples of the volatile regions of the world.

Domestically, there is a need to reassess the legal instruments necessary for combating homegrown terrorism. A legal framework to address the loopholes in the current law on terrorism in Uganda should be put in place.

The biggest constraint to fighting terrorist activities has been the absence of an enabling infrastructure. The government of Uganda should allocate greater resources to the police to make it more effective, thereby safeguarding the rights of all.

Enhancing strategic and tactical antiterrorism skills for police, law enforcement, and security officials should be considered while adhering to accepted human rights standards. Greater emphasis should be placed on the training and sensitization of all security officials to bring about attitudinal changes.

The Uganda Police Force should assess the protective measures in place to safeguard people against terrorist activities with the view to making them more effective.

The police should improve basic investigative capabilities to ensure the seizure and prosecution of terrorists.

The quality and development of a carefully monitored intelligence gathering system that does not impinge on the rights of the innocent should be developed.

Above all, the terrorist uses violence to erode the resistance of both public and leaders to his political demands. The resistance of a society to terrorist blackmail can be strengthened by counterterrorist education that clearly puts forth what the terrorist are trying to achieve, elucidates the immorality of their methods, and explains the necessity of resisting them. The government should prepare education programs and include them in the curriculum.

One may agree with Benjamin Nentanyahu, when he said, "Familiarity with terrorism in its complete rejection would create a citizenry which is capable of living with terror, not in the sense of accepting terror, but rather in the sense of understanding what is needed for society to survive with the least damage."[58]

CONCLUSION

It should be noted that terrorism is not a passing phenomenon. It will persist and terrorists will remain mobile, able to strike at targets anywhere at any time provided its causes are not dealt with.

While security precautions against terrorists can be taken by authorities of different countries, addressing the causes has to be the responsibility of the wider international community. There should be an international regime designed to punish terrorists and an international coalition for ameliorating the kind of prior injustices which give rise to terrorism.

Uganda should develop a comprehensive strategy to defend its people from terrorist attacks. This calls for better intelligence, effective law enforcement, increased domestic and international cooperation, and appropriate laws.

When considering protection of people's human rights against terrorist activities, we should not ask how—but rather, why not. This may be the most effective remedy against conventional considerations for those fighting terrorists. To contribute to this goal will be our task in the years to come.

The salient point to be underlined is that nothing justifies terrorism, that it is evil per se, that the various real or imagined reasons proferred by the terrorist to justify their actions are meaningless. Terrorism's underlying message is that every member of society is "guilty," that anyone can be a victim, and that therefore no one is safe.

The long-term prevention of the threat of terrorism will require a methodical search for its causes and a concerted effort to find longstanding solutions—thus, the need for closing ranks and fighting this evil from society.

NOTES

1. Benjamin, Netanyahu, *Fighting Terrorism: How Democracies Can Defeat Domestic and International Terrorists* (New York: Noonday Press, 1995), 3.

2. *Overview of Terrorism*, U.S. Department of State (November 1995), 30.

3. *Overview of Terrorism*, U.S. Department of State (November 1995), 30.

4. *Overview of Terrorism*, U.S. Department of State (November 1995), 30.

5. *Overview of Terrorism*, U.S. Department of State (November 1995), 31.

6. *Overview of Terrorism*, U.S. Department of State (November 1995), 31.

7. See paper presented to police officers by Bob Ngobi entitled "Terrorism and the Right to Life in Uganda. Are There Protective Measures?" at a human rights workshop in Mbale, February 2000.

8. Ngobi, "Terrorism and the Right to Life in Uganda."

9. Ngobi, "Terrorism and the Right to Life in Uganda."\

10. *Overview of Terrorism.*

11. *Overview of Terrorism.*

12. *Overview of Terrorism.*

13. D. Simon Jeffrey, *The Terrorist Trap* (Bloomington: Indiana University Press, 1994).

14. Jeffrey, *The Terrorist Trap*, 309.

15. Jeffrey, *The Terrorist Trap*, 309.

16. Jeffrey, *The Terrorist Trap*, 309.

17. Martha Crenshaw, *The Causes of Terrorism*, cited in Jeffrey, *The Terrorist Trap*, 308.

18. Jeffrey, *The Terrorist Trap*, 308.

19. Jeffrey, *The Terrorist Trap*, 308.

20. Jeffrey, *The Terrorist Trap*, 308.

21. Jeffrey, *The Terrorist Trap*, 308.

22. Timothy Schofield, *The Environment as an Ideological Weapon to Criminalize Environmental Terrorism* (Boston, Mass.: Boston College Environmental Review, 1998–1999), 7.

23. Ngobi, "Terrorism and the Right to Life."

24. K. D. Ewing and C. A Gearty. *Freedom under Thatcher: Civil Liberties in Modern Britain* (Oxford: Clarendon Press, 1993), 208.

25. Ewing and Gearty, *Freedom under Thatcher,* 231.

26. Ewing and Gearty, *Freedom under Thatcher,* 218.

27. Netanyahu, *Fighting Terrorism,* 307.

28. See *Haig vs. Agee*, 453 U.S. 280, 307 (1981).

29. Ewing and Gearty, *Freedom under Thatcher,* 224.

30. See *Patterns of Global Terrorism*, 11.

31. See chapter IV of the Uganda constitution, 1995, that provides for the protection and promotion of fundamental and other human rights and freedoms.

32. Milton Olupot, "Kakooza Raps Amnesty," *The New Vision* (March 20, 1997): 8.

33. Alfred Wasike and Edith Kimuli, "Gazette Safe Houses," *The New Vision* (November 4, 1998): 3.

34. U.S. Department of State Bulletin, November 1995, 7.

35. Timothy Schofield, *The Environment as an Ideological Weapon,* 7.

36. Frank Pearce et al, eds., *Global Crime Connections: Dynamics and Control* (Toronto: University of Toronto Press, 1993), 4.

37. Opiyo-Oloya, "Uganda Ill Prepared to Help Injured Victims," *The New Vision* (April 21, 1999): 21.

38. Jim Mugunga, "Slipper-clad Police Used Matches after Bomb Aftermath," *Sunday Monitor* (April 19, 1998), 21.

39. Mugunga, "Slipper-clad Police," 21.

40. Mugunga, "Slipper-clad Police," 21.

41. Mugunga, "Slipper-clad Police," 21.

42. *Reducing Crime in London,* 1992.

43. *Reducing Crime in London,* 1992.

44. *Reducing Crime in London,* 1992.

45. *Reducing Crime in London,* 1992.

46. *Overview of Terrorism,* U.S. Department of State.

47. Jeffrey, *The Terrorist Trap,* 9.

48. "Museveni Condemns Bombers," *The New Vision* (February 16, 1999): 1.

49. See the *Uganda Police Annual Policing Plan,* 1998.

50. See *Uganda Police Crime Report,* 1999.

51. The Suppression of Terrorism Act (1999): 9.

52. The Suppression of Terrorism Act (1999): 9.

53. The Suppression of Terrorism Act (1999): 9.

54. The Suppression of Terrorism Act (1999): 8–9.

55. The Suppression of Terrorism Act (1999): 24.

56. See Article 1(1) of the constitution of Uganda, 1995.

57. See Article 1(4) of the constitution of Uganda, 1995.

58. Netanyahu, *Fighting Terrorism,* 146.

BIBLIOGRAPHY

Amnesty International Report, 1997.

Basic Principles of the Independence of the Judiciary, Paragraph 1.

Brodie, Thomas G. 1976. *Bombs and Bombing: A Handbook for Detection, Disposal, and Investigation for Police and Firearms Departments.* Springfield: Charles Thomas.

Constitution of the Republic of Uganda, 1995.

Ewing, K. D., and C. A. Gearty. 1993. *Freedom under Thatcher: Civil Liberties in Modern Britain.* Oxford: Clarendon Press.

Forsyth, Frederick, 2001. *The Day of the Jackal.* Pleasantville, NY: ImPress.

Gibbons, Don. 1992. *Society, Crime, and Criminal Behavior.* 6th ed. New Jersey: Prentice Hall.

Graw, G. Joseph. 1981. *A Criminal and Civil Investigation Handbook.* New York: McGraw.

Jeffrey, D. Simon. 1994. *The Terrorist Trap.* Bloomington: Indiana University Press.

Mugunga, Jim. 1998. "Slipper-clad Police Used Matches in Bomb Aftermath." *The Sunday Monitor* (April).

"Museveni Condemns Bombers." *The New Vision* (February 16, 1999): 1.

Mutumba, Richard. 1997. "Rights Abuses Continue–Wambuzi." *The New Vision* (July 25).

Netanyahu, Benjamin. 1995. *Fighting Terrorism: How Democracies Can Defeat Domestic and International Terrorism.* New York: Noonday Press.

Ngobi, Bob. 2000. *Terrorism and the Right to Life. Are There Protective Measures?* Paper presented to a human rights workshop in Mbale, January.

Olupot, Milton. 1997. "Kakooza Raps Amnesty." *The New Vision* (March 20): 8.

Opiyo-Oloya. 1999. "Uganda Ill Prepared to Help Injured Terrorist Victims." *The New Vision* (April 21).

Overview of Terrorism. 1995. U.S. Department of State, November.

Patterns of Global Terrorism. 1997. Washington, D.C.: U.S. Department of State.

Pearce, Frank, et al., eds. 1993. *Global Crime Connections, Dynamics, and Control.* Toronto: University of Toronto Press.

Reducing Crime in London. 1992.

Schofield, Timothy. 1998–1999. *The Environmental as an Ideological Weapon to Criminalize Environmental Terrorism.* Boston, Mass.: Boston College Environmental Review.

The African Charter on Human and Peoples Rights.

The Penal Code Act, Chapter 106, Laws of Uganda, 1999.

The United Nations Convention against Torture and Other Cruel, Inhuman or Degrading Treatment.

The United States Bulletin, November 1995.

The Uganda Police Crime Report, 1999.

Uganda Police Annual Policing Plan, 1998.

Uganda Police Inspectorate Report 1997–1999.

Wasike, Alfred, and Edith Kimuli. 1998. "Gazette Safe Houses." *The New Vision* (November 4): 3.

13

Counterterrorism Domestic Security Developments and the Challenges of the Rule of Law in Australia

Jenny Hocking

> The countries that have done their best against terrorism are those that have kept their cool, retained a sense of proportion, questioned and addressed the causes, and adhered steadfastly to constitutionalism.[1]
>
> —Justice Michael Kirby, 2001

The contemporary national security threat of terrorism has proved to be a turning point in the nature and extent of internal security operations, spearheading a revival of domestic countersubversion activities at a time of intense criticism not only of their encroachment into domestic surveillance but even of their continued existence in the wake of the end of the Cold War. In the Australian instance, the renewed security mandate of counterterrorism was described in the early 1990s by a former head of Australia's most significant domestic security intelligence body, the Australian Security Intelligence Organisation (ASIO), as "security growing a new limb."[2] These developments, common to many Western nations, have not been without controversy. In particular, the suspension of aspects of the rule of law under counterterrorism provisions have led to concerns that forced confessions and the use of torture whilst under detention have caused miscarriages of justice.[3] The core principles which distinguish liberal democratic regimes from authoritarian ones, identified by Crelinsten as "the rule of law; openness and accountability of government; and the maintenance of a bond of trust and confidence between citizens and government that results from an electorate that is informed about public affairs," have increasingly been put under strain by the expansion of security operations according to a broad mandate of counterterrorism.[4]

COUNTERTERRORISM: THE FIRST WAVE

In the early development of a counterterrorist strategy in the mid-1970s, Australia drew heavily on the British model, despite their clear differences in the nature and extent of political violence. The British model, in turn, drew clearly on five main aspects of counterinsurgency theory and practice: the use of exceptional legislative measures; the maintenance of vast intelligence collections; the development of preemptive controls on political activity; military involvement in civil disturbances; and the development of a strategy of media management in times of crisis.[5] The exception to the wholesale adaptation of this model in Australia's counterterrorism strategy to date, however, has been its continued use of the existing criminal law against terrorist offenses. Unlike Britain, Australia's broadly counterinsurgency-based approach has retained this important element of what Crelinsten terms the "criminal justice model" and, until the events of September 11, 2001, has not adopted the particularly problematic use of "exceptional powers."[6]

Nevertheless, a slow but steady shift has occurred as the counterterrorism mandate has developed, taking the security structure away from a purely defensive—and hence marginalized—orientation and incorporating its key elements into the broader criminal justice process. Any remnant of the maintenance of a model of security operations as separate from policing in countering terrorism in Australia has been challenged in the wake of the September 11 attrocities in America. Just three weeks after these attacks, Attorney-General Daryl Williams announced dramatic proposals for the restructuring and expansion of the powers of Australia's major domestic intelligence collection organization, ASIO. In particular, these changes would comprehensively merge the once distinctive feature of the security function, preemptive intelligence collection and analysis, into the reactive intelligence gathering role of policing.

It remains unclear what dramatic change in the nature or level of terrorist threat in Australia exists to support such significant changes. Official reports have long remarked upon the relative tranquillity of Australian political life, that Australia has not shared the political extremism of terrorism so common elsewhere, nor is it likely to in the future.[7] Yet, despite Australia's admirable record as a relatively calm and nonviolent political order with a healthy declamatory civil society, spokespeople from government, media, and security organizations have consistently and perversely depicted a threat which is significant, expanding, and proximate. In a statement which posits this threat despite acknowledging its absence, the attorney-general suggested, "the profound shift in the international security environment has meant that Australia's profile as a terrorist target has risen and our interests abroad face a higher level of terrorist threat . . . there remains no known specific threat of terrorism in Australia."[8]

It is disturbing to see the ease with which established political and legal protections, central to any notion of the rule of law, were tossed about in the months following the September 11 attacks, threatening to undermine the very structures the "War on Terror" was ostensibly seeking to protect. Aspects such as trial by jury, innocent until proven guilty, and equality before the law have been dispensed with or at best heavily compromised in the conduct of a parallel "war" on domestic terrorism.

History abounds with examples of the ease with which a security crisis can slide into an authoritarianism in which acceptable political discourse and action are constrained, even formally proscribed. This can arise most overtly from the institutional changes to security structures discussed here, but also from the construction of an internal cohesion through the denial of popular legitimacy to expressions of dissent and through the creation of social and political divisions which allow a politicized notion of security threat to emerge. In the Australian context, this latter has been augmented by the controversial and inflammatory policy of mandatory detention of refugees and the demonization of this group as "illegals" and even as "terrorists." Talk-back radio abounds with comments which elide these groups, such as those of the high-rating "shock jock" Stan Zamanek: "I am continually pissed off with this nonsense about the bleeding hearts saying 'Let's open the detention centres and let everybody out.' Doesn't anybody remember September 11?"[9]

In such a heavily politicized atmosphere, a tremulous public may readily accede to demands for increased security measures, even those which so clearly diminish established legal and political protections. It was in just this climate that the restructuring of Australia's major intelligence collection body was announced.[10]

COUNTERTERRORISM: THE SECOND WAVE

Briefly, what has been proposed is, first, to grant ASIO powers of detention, even of those "not themselves suspected of terrorist activity" for up to forty-eight hours (renewable at least twice), for interrogation incommunicado and without access to legal representation. Furthermore, in what constitutes a sweeping removal of the right to remain silent, refusal to answer any questions put during detention (in the absence of legal representation) would carry a penalty of five years imprisonment. Second, the government announced the creation of a new category of offenses: "terrorism" and "preparing for or planning terrorist acts," drawing on the British *Terrorism Act 2000*. The Australian government issued by means of regulation a list of deemed "terrorist" organizations for which finances and property were to be seized. Finally, extensive and unprecedented powers for the attorney-general or any other delegated minister to proscribe, by declaration and without trial, political organizations which the minister considers a danger to security have also been announced.[11]

The merging of security intelligence capabilities and law enforcement mechanisms through the detention and interrogation powers proposed for ASIO would effectively fuse security operations with those of domestic policing. As such, these recent changes represent an end to traditional notions of internal security and the beginning of a broader domestic notion of "security policing," supporting Farson's observation that counterterrorism is "the zone where persons with coercive capacity must work alongside those with the information to prevent political acts of violence from occurring."[12]

Taken overall, these proposals would establish a new orthodoxy in ASIO's activities, moving it clearly into the arena of preemptive "security policing" and overturning aspects of both the rule of law and of long-established civil and political rights.[13] It would also mark the closure in ASIO's gradual shift toward a strategy of total, preemptive surveillance of an ever-present internal "enemy," an end to the political struggle to maintain a more focused, more democratic, and more accountable notion of national security.

AUSTRALIA'S DOMESTIC SECURITY HISTORY

When Ben Chifley, the Australian Labor Party (ALP) prime minister, reluctantly established ASIO in 1949, he did so under the undoubted political duress of intense Cold War security demands. Chifley intended that ASIO would confine its activities within the narrow bounds of defense-related, quasi-war activities rather than the pervasive security surveillance of domestic political activities. The reasons were both constitutional, as a federal authority ASIO could look only toward a genuinely defense-oriented matter, but also political. The ALP knew well the dangers to political engagement, to legal protections and to parliamentary process, that widespread politically based surveillance had already posed to the radical highly unionized constituency out of which had been born the world's first Labor Party.[14]

In an attempt to reconcile the view that peacetime security matters within a democratic polity ought to be a civil rather than a military concern with the strong military and intelligence pressure to create ASIO, Chifley appointed a judge, Justice Reed from the South Australian Supreme Court, as the first director-general of ASIO. In this way, ASIO again adopted the British model in maintaining a distinction, functionally and operationally, between security and general law enforcement, while at the same time linking these through the special branches of the state police forces. Farson has noted this British model as distinct from the American approach, which gives the FBI "a joint mandate to conduct criminal and national security investigations."[15]

The early incarnation of security in Australia had three unique features: it was based on this functional and philosophical distinction between policing and security activities; "national security" was seen as an arm of defense rather than of domestic concern; and finally it focused in its perception of threats to security on subversion as radicalism—most clearly on communism and communists. In the Australian instance, there were crucial political and legal imperatives to be met by effecting such a clear distinction between security and policing operations, and by the defense orientation of threat perception. Yet, over the Cold War–dominated decades which followed, ASIO's surveillance activities strayed into areas of civic political activities which would now appear faintly ludicrous were their protection not so central to the maintenance of a healthy and diverse public sphere.

This marked the beginning of ASIO's widespread approach to political surveillance which characterized this polarized era and lasted until a series of revelations of its excesses in the mid-1970s led to tighter controls. It has since been revealed that ASIO's own understanding of its key definitional term "subversive" was not only heavily politicized but based on what the subsequent Royal Commission into ASIO's operations over this time drily noted, was its "tendency to think of anyone they chose to call 'left-wing' as subversive."[16] ASIO had maintained files on church meetings for peace, on the New Housewives Association, the Fellowship of Australian Writers, antiwar campaigners, and on countless Labor Party politicians including the South Australian premier Don Dunstan, the future treasurer Jim Cairns and the future attorney-general (and minister responsible for ASIO) Lionel Murphy. There were no such files revealed on Liberal Party (conservative) politicians. Similarly, within the state police forces, Special Branches which had served effectively as ASIO's regional offices were, "Like the Maginot Line all defences against anticipated subversion, real or imagined, were built on one side."[17] Of greater significance and damage to those unwittingly placed under surveillance were ASIO links with key sections of the media which provided a means of publishing highly damaging and frequently spurious intelligence gossip about key political figures. This was revealed through Justice Hope's Royal Commission in 1977, and was the one aspect of ASIO's activities which Hope criticized roundly.[18] The use of media outlets in this way remains one of the most powerful avenues for the public destruction of individuals who have been improperly targeted and on whom private and personal, rather than security, intelligence material is collected. These well-documented transgressions highlight the dangers to democratic practice of an expansive and unaccountable notion of "national security."

Nevertheless, throughout these troubling times, ASIO did maintain a formal distinction between its surveillance activities and the law enforcement focus of state police forces. In part the containment of domestic intelligence operations around defensive notions of security threats reflected Australia's federal structure and its consequent jurisdictional jealousies, but it also reflected a broader recognition of the judicial and political concerns that these functions of law enforcement and surveillance remain separate. To do otherwise, to allow those who collect intelligence to also be those who initiate prosecutions, would be effectively to criminalize those on whom such intelligence is maintained (in secret, without review, with no knowledge of its source, its veracity or its purpose). This distinction between the functions of law enforcement and security surveillance has become increasingly blurred: first, due to the expansive shift in the national security discourse itself (from "subversion" to "terrorism" to "politically motivated violence") and second, from the development of surveillance technologies that have allowed for an immeasurable increase in not only the collection of intelligence but also its transmission to other bodies.

From "National Security" to "Security Policing"

The proposed changes in ASIO's intelligence-gathering powers to include coercive interrogation whilst under detention would take that surveillance into the previously contested arena of general law enforcement with attendant fundamental policy issues of the appropriateness of its collection and integration across a wide range of civil authorities. The intersection of traditional national security intelligence activities with those of law enforcement can be seen as an example of what Brodeur describes as "high policing" in which the police function is "reaching out for security threats."[19] In particular, it imposes a framework for intelligence collection structured around pre-emption, a military-based doctrine out of which has developed counterterrorist strategy and in which a key security imperative of the state is to anticipate threats. In this constructed state of permanent crisis, peacetime is seen only as a time before wartime, allowing ostensibly "exceptional" powers to become routine. In recognition of the security paradigm which underpins it, this shift in the philosophical approach to police intelligence is perhaps more properly described as "security policing."[20]

In this context it is important to recall that ASIO holds, as do most Western intelligence agencies, extensive powers of intrusion, surveillance, and data maintenance through what are termed its "special powers." These are set out in the legislation which governs ASIO's activities, and include the power to break and enter premises, remove records or documents or any other thing, intercept mail, listen to and record telephone conversations, intercept e-mails, monitor computer records, place individuals under personal surveillance, and place tracking devices on individuals and vehicles.[21]

These special powers turn around the key definitional term of "national security," which has seen several incarnations over the decades—revealing in itself the essentially contingent nature of "national security." An indication of the breadth with which ASIO has interpreted its "national security" mandate (the core definition on which the exercise of its "special powers" turns) can be gauged from the *Church of Scientology* cases in 1980 and 1983. The Church of Scientology sued the director-general of ASIO, arguing that ASIO had continued to characterize it as subversive, and therefore had continued to subject it and its members to surveillance and intelligence collection, even after ASIO had determined that the church was *not* in fact a security risk. This, the church argued, thereby constituted an improper use of ASIO's powers.

The *Church of Scientology* cases provided a rare opportunity to test the legal extent of ASIO's powers of intrusion, surveillance, and removal of personal records in the name of national security; in particular, to test ASIO's capacity to reach its own determination of the circumstances in which it could activate its "special powers." A majority of the justices found that ASIO was *not* bound to cease to obtain intelligence about an individual even if it had been established that the individual was not a security risk This ruling was breathtaking, giving ASIO virtually unlimited scope in determining the limits of its domestic surveillance operations. The majority of the justices appeared to accept the contention of ASIO's counsel that an individual's future activities may render presently innocuous behavior "relevant to security." This ruling therefore legitimated the collection of material, not only on individuals and groups who have been judged a potential security risk but also on those who have in fact been judged *not* a security risk. As the *Australian Law Journal* dryly noted, "on this analysis no one in Australia would be exempt from surveillance by ASIO."[22]

Not all High Court justices agreed with the unlimited potential this handed to Australia's largest domestic intelligence organization for unfettered surveillance. Foremost among the dissentients was Justice Lionel Murphy. As a one-time attorney-general in Gough Whitlam's Labor government of 1972–75 and a long-time critic of ASIO's unaccountable expansion into civil surveillance, Murphy had moved in 1973 to exercise close ministerial accountability over the traditionally quasi-autonomous national security decisions of ASIO.[23] In his minority judgment from the High Court bench a decade later, Justice Murphy reflected further on the need for greater legislative control and oversight of security organizations, in particular recognizing that the practice of political surveillance in the civic arena, and the public awareness of this practice, generates "a climate of apprehension and an inhibition of lawful political activity even at the highest levels of government. . . . Experience thus shows that for a free society to exist intelligence organizations must be subject to administrative supervision and amenable to legal process."[24]

Detention without Trial

Of the several changes to Australia's counterterrorism strategy announced in the weeks following September 11, the core proposal and that which has met with the greatest disquiet is that which grants ASIO powers of detention, specifically, to detain and question any individual for forty-eight hours (up to 144 hours by renewal) without charge, in the absence of legal representation or even notification to another party that detention is occurring.[25] Those being held would not be able to exercise their right to remain silent and would face five years' imprisonment for refusing to answer questions. These detention and interrogation powers would be exercised by warrant to be issued by a federal magistrate or a legal member of the Administrative Appeals Tribunal. The latter, being appointed for limited tenure, does not have traditional judicial independence and allows this procedure to be seen as little more than a rubber stamping of executive power. In this instance, the proclaimed safeguard ensured by the warranting provision, for an already draconian and contentious detention power, may appear illusory.

Particularly alarming is the suggestion that ASIO agents will be able "to question people *not themselves suspected of terrorist activity*, but who may have information that may be relevant to ASIO's investigations into *politically motivated violence*. The Australian attorney-general has spoken of his concern that police cannot under current law now detain and interrogate people in the absence of any suspicion of involvement in a criminal offense attaching to them. It is no doubt an indication of the extent to which the priorities of the state in self-protection have superceded those of its citizens in the rule of law that Williams, Australia's chief law officer, sees this not as one of the great protectors from the arbitrary use of executive power, a crucial part of ensuring justice, but as a "problem." A close reading of this statement indicates a reference to people being detained and questioned not about terrorism but about politically motivated violence: "We need to question people . . . who may have information that may be relevant to ASIO's investigations into *politically motivated violence*." Once again there has been an easy shift from the more extreme threat of "terrorism" into the less marginal and therefore more expansive field of "politically motivated violence."

The reach of these powers of detention is such that it would encompass all Australians, including those under no suspicion, even children. The attorney-general has been asked specifically whether the proposed power for individuals to be placed under detention, in the absence of any suspicion and with no legal representation nor any necessary notification, could include children. He responded, "It's possible. . . . There is no reason for making an exception in respect of any particular category of person."

The suspension of the right to remain silent and against self-incrimination during this period of detention has been designed as a coercive measure, such that a failure to answer questions put during detention (in the absence of legal representation) will result in five years' imprisonment. However, an even broader notion may be in play here. Williams spoke not of an offense of refusing to answer, but of an "offence in the process of failing to respond *appropriately*."[26]

The use of a coercive sanction of five years' imprisonment for failing to "respond appropriately" raises a further question about the status of the intelligence gathered through this process: in a situation of coercive interrogation where the threat of five years' imprisonment is used, what evidentiary value will attach to any intelligence gathered in this way? The power of detention in the absence of even a suspicion of wrongdoing, with the suspension of the right to remain silent and targeted at an entire populace, is solely an intelligence-gathering exercise in which nothing can remain private and "responding appropriately" becomes the sole means of release. Gossip and unsubstantiated reports on the actions and beliefs of others lead us into the authoritarian and now well-documented dangers of McCarthyism.

Finally, given that in Australia it is a crime to reveal the identity of an ASIO agent, what avenue for legal redress is there if someone is injured or harmed whilst under interrogation during detention? We need to consider that this establishes a situation in which ASIO officers may well be placed beyond the reach of the law, creating another vacuum in legal accountability for security operations.

Universalized Surveillance

With these proposed powers of detention, ASIO, for the first time in its history, will be able to move directly into law enforcement, and it will do so according to an all-encompassing concept of its target population. Indeed, the attorney-general has described these powers in exactly this light: "What we need to be able to do is to be able to get maximum information, maximum intelligence, in order to prevent any terrorist acts being committed." The chief of the Australian army, Major General Cosgrove, has similarly referred to the merging of the functions of the military, the police, and security services as an important element in universalizing their surveillance potential. "Whether it is guarding against or reacting to terrorism, law and order and the security forces must have the same and perhaps some additional information facilities which bring greater synthesis and synergy and analysis and discrimination for a more conventional battlefield. We must have the ability to make each constable or soldier a sort of 'Karnack the all-knowing.'"[27]

This desire to become an "all-knowing" surveillance society rests on an equally universalized notion of threat, one which shifts the justification for extreme measures away from the present and into the fear of an unknown future. In this intellectual fortress in which anything is possible, arguments for an expanded security sector are no longer based in present-day realities but in the unknown, and opposition on these terms becomes unarguable.

DEFINITIONAL ISSUES

The use of the term "terrorism" in itself compounds the problems of an uncertain counterterrorism mandate. The discourse of "terrorism" highlights the fear and the terror which all violence creates, yet constructs no precise criminal act. Through its carriage of an implicit yet overwhelming moral illegitimacy, the language itself neatly averts consideration of complex questions of causation. It is a powerful terminology and one which allows for the ready adoption of extreme measures that would otherwise be strongly resisted.

George Bush's description of the events of September 11, for example, as "terrorist acts against all freedom-loving people everywhere in the world" is an effective closure, allowing no possibility of further analysis. In particular the simplified depiction of "terrorists" versus "freedom-loving people" provides no means of understanding an element of causation in what is, of course, a far more complex reality. From this intellectual closure stems the crude denunciation of those who seek to understand causative factors in these attacks, as also condoning them.

The language of "terrorism" which is now so commonplace, is essentially unsatisfying, "a cliché in search of a meaning" in the words of a much earlier Christopher Hitchens, a debasement of language, destructive of understanding.[28] Not only is the key term "terrorism" ambiguous, it has proved impossible to universally define. In this sense the unstated assumptions of morality and of legitimacy which attach to the discourse of terrorism, its essentially ideological construction, tell us more about the speaking position of those using it than it does about the events purportedly being described. But it is precisely this linguistic and political imprecision surrounding the very notion of "the war on terror" that allows its unlimited expansion—like a multi-headed Hydra of which the alleged culprit Osama Bin Laden's is but one. That the language of "terrorism" functions closer to pathology than to politics can be seen in the description of the perpetrators of these recent attacks as having "an evil hatred of modernity." The crucial question of causation has nowhere been explicitly posed yet has again been implicitly answered in the language itself, as lying in the realm of the psychopathic, not the material. Yet it is precisely these questions that need to be confronted and examined, for without them no country can devise an appropriate response.

In the Australian context, the appropriate response must be located, first, in recognition of the remarkably low level of political violence and a consideration of the relationship between this relative lack of political extremism and a viable liberal democratic pluralism. From this must follow a clearly articulated attempt to balance security priorities with those of a healthy and dynamic multicultural polity. In this way Australia might avoid effecting the political marginalization and quasi-criminalization of political agitation that has occurred in countries adopting a counterinsurgency-based response to terrorism. For many years, despite the development of a powerful counterterrorism structure, the Australian response has not included the specification of "terrorist" offenses in criminal law. From the first wave of international terrorism in the 1970s, it was strongly argued to government: "The best safeguard against new terrors and apprehensions may lie in the rigorous enforcement of existing criminal law rather than in making new laws expressly about 'terrorism.'"[29] The report went on to note that the crux of the difficulty in introducing "terrorism" as a specified crime, lay in

> pondering what exactly is meant by "terrorism," now a popular, but amorphous, term. . . . A crime ordinarily is a particular act, done voluntarily and with intent to perform it . . . but terrorism is not defined by reference to specific deeds, but in general terms, the "use of violence"; and not with specific intent, but with an ulterior object, "for political ends," a most imprecise term. . . . This would appear to make criminal responsibility depend upon an ulterior intention or motive, an unusual ingredient of a criminal act.

Yet the new powers for the Australian security organization include specified offenses of terrorism in precisely these terms, resting, as do attempts to define terrorism in criminal acts elsewhere, on this essential element of ulterior intent. These offenses have been broadly defined, as including "threats of violent attacks intended to advance a political cause . . . which endanger Commonwealth interests."[30] Clearly, almost all political protests readily fall within this catch-all terminology. Indeed the new crimes of "terrorism" and of "preparing for or planning terrorist acts" draw on the British *Terrorism Act 2000*. These would be subject to a penalty of life imprisonment.

ECHOES OF THE COMMUNIST
PARTY DISSOLUTION ACT (1950)

The imprecision over the language of "terrorism" and its application lead to concerns that counterterrorist security measures will be broadly targeted in ways that are neither appropriate nor efficient, ways that may impinge upon legitimate political agitation and dissent. Historically, such concerns are not misplaced in the Australian experience. It is almost exactly fifty years since the final defeat of the Liberal prime minister Robert Menzies's several attempts to pass the *Communist Party Dissolution Act* (1950), which sought to outlaw political organizations by executive decree based on advice from the security service, at a time of presumed international and national crisis against the then scourge of communism.

The powers of proscription through declaration provided to the governor-general through this act extended far beyond the Communist Party of Australia through its provisions to similarly outlaw and criminalize membership of "affiliated organisations." The Act sought to outlaw political organizations by executive decree, without trial, and with a reversed onus of proof, it criminalized any continued support for proscribed organizations through its punitive sanctions, of five years imprisonment, for anyone who continued to in any way participate in the operation of "declared" affiliated organizations or to support any policy which was also supported by the Communist Party of Australia, even to "carry or display anything indicating that he is or was . . . in any way associated with an unlawful association," such as badges or flags. The breadth of this particular provision was such that it could include those who supported, for example, free and secular public education, support for the United Nations charter, or the peace movement. The Communist Party Dissolution Act was therefore the most profound challenge not only to established legal protections including the right to trial, to know your accuser, to freedoms of expression and political association, and indeed to the separation of powers but also to the nature of Australian constitutionalism itself.

The similarities between the proscription aspect of the current counterterrorist proposals with those of the Communist Party Dissolution Act bear further examination. The intense political and legal struggle to defeat this earlier authoritarian act reveals much of the core concerns about the current proposals, to limit acceptable political behavior and thereby to circumscribe effective democratic practice. Like the Communist Party Dissolution Act before it, these proposals similarly would allow for an executive banning of organizations, with no role for the courts in this process. The power of executive declaration is in itself a clear breach of the separation of powers which ought to ensure that such matters are judicial and not political decisions. In the introduction of a range of crimes of association with proscribed organizations, it also reverses the onus of proof in a number of sections. In these aspects the current proposal, as did the Communist Party Dissolution Act, does away with established protections before the law.

Following the passage of the Communist Party Dissolution Act by Parliament, its constitutionality was challenged before the High Court in a case led by the deputy leader of the Labor Party, Dr. H. V. Evatt. Evatt, first elected president of the United Nations General Assembly, a "libertarian warrior" in Justice Michael Kirby's description, believed passionately that this act was not only unconstitutional but that it was profoundly antidemocratic. In a 6:1 decision, Chief Justice Latham dissenting, the High Court ruled in Evatt's favor. It was a judgment which continues to protect all of us from the arbitrary abuse of executive power, "truly an 'epochal' decision, probably the most important ever rendered by the Court" which confirmed that the High Court would not allow its judicial functions to be usurped by Parliament.[31]

The intense political and legal struggle to defeat this earlier authoritarian act reveals much of what remains an ongoing desire on the part of security organizations, to limit acceptable political behavior and thereby to circumscribe effective democratic practice. Specifically, the Communist Party Dissolution Act allowed for an executive finding of guilt not found since the days of the Star Chamber, reversed the onus of proof, and removed even trial by jury in these matters. As Labor leader Ben Chifley argued in Parliament, the bill "strikes at the very heart of justice. It opens the door for the liar, the perjurer and the pimp to make charges and damn men's reputations and to do so in secret without having either to substantiate or prove any charges they might make."[32] The separation of powers, the established legal protections of trial by jury, the presumption of innocence, and, of course, judicial review itself are surely all there precisely because they protect citizens and our civil liberties from arbitrary executive power. In key respects, therefore, the Communist Party Dissolution Act did away with the "great principles of justice" as the former High Court justice Lionel Murphy called these established protections before the law. Such fundamental assaults on freedom of political association and natural justice in particular were, at that time, unprecedented in liberal democratic nations during peacetime, with the exception of the apartheid regime in South Africa, the provisions of whose Suppression of Communism Act (1950) it drew freely upon.[33]

The civil liberties concerns raised by such an exceptional legislative response to issues of national security were clear in the justices' questions during the course of the case. Justice Williams asked, "Does this mean that Parliament could say that the existence of John Smith, an ordinary citizen, is a menace to the security of Australia and require that he be shot at dawn?" Justice Kitto contended, also during argument, "You cannot have punishment that is preventive. You can't remove his tongue to stop him speaking against you. That is wide open to a totalitarian state."[34]

Despite this overwhelming failure at the High Court, Prime Minister Robert Menzies then determined to pursue the passage of this legislation through a referendum to amend the constitution itself. Again, Dr. H. V. Evatt maintained an equal determination to defeat it. That Evatt succeeded by the smallest of percentages, gradually effecting a shift in public opinion away from an initial 73 percent support for the proposal, has been described as "Evatt's greatest contribution to liberty in his own country," demanding as it undoubtedly did, "the sacrifice of personal ambition to the defence of basic constitutional rights."[35] For many would argue that Evatt's emphatic victory in every sphere of governance over the repressive security legislation of the Menzies government also ensured the Australian Labor Party's electoral defeat for years to come. If this is so, it was an outcome which Evatt anticipated and accepted in order to meet what he considered a more insistent need: "I regard the result as more important than half a dozen general elections. The consequences of a mistaken vote in an election verdict can be retrieved. But an error of judgement in this constitutional alteration would tend to destroy the whole democratic fabric of justice and liberty."[36]

LIMITING POLITICAL DISCOURSE

Today Australia faces such a threat to the "whole democratic fabric of justice and liberty," no less momentous despite Evatt's insistence on the unconstitutionality of the powers to proscribe political organizations, for these executive powers are now being sought again. The Security Legislation Amendment (Terrorism) Bill 2002 provides the means for the attorney-general (or delegate minister) to "outlaw terrorist organisations and organisations that threaten the integrity and security of Australia or another country,"[37] on the basis of his or her satisfaction that the decision is made upon reasonable grounds. The elevation of executive power in this way has strong echoes of the earlier attempts to pass the Communist Party Dissolution Bill 1950 in its banning of political organizations by executive decree, in aspects of its reversed onus of proof, and in its introduction of broadly defined criminal offenses. The bill, therefore, contains serious erosions of the principles of the rule of law and due process in a number of sections dealing with the proscription powers of the attorney-general and the creation of criminal offenses in relation to proscribed organization and terrorist offenses, in the name of combating terrorism.

The struggle over the state's perceived need for broader security power addresses these same issues of the need to protect our basic legal and political rights in the face of these revised priorities. Surveillance on this scale allows ultimately for the preemptive control of political conflict and dissent, which may or may not protect individual citizens but which certainly protects the state itself. It presupposes that democracy is infinitely divisible, that by suspending the rule of law for whole classes of people we do not equally remove it from society as a whole. Justice Dixon had noted precisely this tendency of the state to protect itself through an executive superseding of democratic institutional power in his powerful judgment in the Communist Party dissolution case:

> History, and not only ancient history, shows that in countries where democratic institutions have been unconstitutionally superseded, it has been done not seldom by those holding the executive power. Forms of government may need protection from dangers likely to arise from within the institutions to be protected. . . . [T]he power to legislate for the protection of an existing form of government ought not to be based on a conception . . . adequate only to assist those holding power to resist or suppress obstruction or opposition or attempts to displace them or the form of government they defend.[38]

The collapse of the World Trade Centers—brutal, unprecedented, and broadcast live—has, of course, propelled many countries toward reaction. The fear, insecurity, and uncertainty, captured on camera and replayed again and again to an ever-more alarmed public, rapidly became part of a seamless rush to action. In this, the inevitable call to arms and indeed individuals' demands for it, can be seen as a personal resolution, a means of regaining control of an otherwise uncontrollable and incomprehensible situation. Yet it is precisely these situations that call, not for precipitous action, but for reflection, not for vengeance or retribution, but for justice. They call, above all, in the midst of this chaos, for the retention of the rule of law which remains the fundamental protector of democratic practice.

The gradual, subtle shift of counterterrorism strategy toward a universalized surveillance has critical implications for the expression of political rights and the ability for citizens to engage openly in a dynamic and dissenting space crucial to democratic participatory politics. The Italian theorist Luigi Bonanate, for instance, argues that "a society acquainted with terrorism is a blocked one"; that "terrorism unmasks a democracy which is only formal."[39] If we consider that acts of extreme political violence, labeled terrorism, may reflect a systemic failure in participatory democratic practice, then the narrowing of acceptable political discourse and legitimate political activity may well be one of the precipitating factors of terrorist activity. If so, then what is needed as part of the struggle against terrorism are not further constraints on effective political participation but a more inclusive politics, not less democracy but more. Yet the current climate of crisis and uncertainty neither encourages such structural outcomes nor inspires such political reflection.

Just one month after the tragedy of September 11, Justice Michael Kirby of the High Court of Australia gave a powerful speech urging the protection of our legal and political rights, an adherence to the great principles of justice: "The countries that have done their best against terrorism are those that have kept their cool, retained a sense of proportion, questioned and addressed the causes, and adhered steadfastly to constitutionalism."[40] Our challenge now is to hold steadfastly to our civic traditions, to the rule of law, to equality before the law, and to defend the rights of suspects even in the face of such assaults. Ultimately, a healthy dynamism, a welcome diversity, and a broad political space within which domestic politics and its dissentients can thrive may be our greatest protection.

NOTES

1. Justice Michael Kirby, "Australian Law—After September 11, 2001," paper presented at the 32nd Australian Legal Convention, October 2001, at Canberra, Australia, 4.

2. In Jenny Hocking, "Charting Political Space: Surveillance and the Rule of Law," *Social Justice* 21, no. 4 (special international issue, Winter 1994): 67.

3. Dilip Das, "Impact of Antiterrorist Measures on Democratic Law Enforcement: The Italian Experience," *Terrorism* 13 (1990): 89–98; Peter Chalk, "The Response to

Terrorism as a Threat to Liberal Democracy," *Australian Journal of Politics and History* 44, no. 3 (1998): 373–88.

4. Ronald Crelinsten, "The Discourse and Practice of Counter-Terrorism in Liberal Democracies," *Australian Journal of Politics and History* 44, no. 3 (1998): 389–413.

5. Jenny Hocking, *Beyond Terrorism: The Development of the Australian Security State* (Sydney: Allen & Unwin, 1993), 21.

6. Crelinsten, "Discourse and Practice," 390.

7. Hocking, *Beyond Terrorism*, xii.

8. Daryl Williams, "Upgrading Australia's Counter-Terrorism Capabilities" *News Release* 18 December 2001, at http://www.law.gov.au/ministers/attorneygeneral/mediamn.html. (accessed 15 February 2002).

9. Stan Zamenek, quoted in *The Australian,* 16 February 2002.

10. Daryl Williams, "New Counter-Terrorist Measures" *News Release* 2 October 2001, at http://www.law.gov.au/ministers/attorney-general/mediamn.html (accessed 26 October 2001).

11. Security Legislation Amendment (Terrorism) Bill 2002.

12. Stuart Farson, "Security Intelligence versus Criminal Intelligence," *Policing and Society* 2 (1991): 65–87, 67.

13. Hocking, "Charting Political Space."

14. See, for example, the discussion in Ian Turner, *Sydney's Burning* (Melbourne: Heinemann Press, 1977); and Frank Cain, *The Origins of Political Surveillance in Australia* (Sydney: Angus & Robertson, 1983).

15. Farson, "Security Intelligence," 66.

16. Justice R. M. Hope *Royal Commission of Intelligence and Security Fourth Report,* Vol. 1 (Canberra: Australian Government Publishing Service, 1977), 128.

17. Justice White, *Special Branch Security Records Report* (Adelaide: Government Printing Service, 1977), 52.

18. Hope, *Royal Commission,* 128.

19. Jean-Paul Brodeur, "High Policing and Low Policing: Remarks about the Policing of Political Activities," *Social Problems* 30, 5 (June 1983): 507–20.

20. See Hocking, "Charting Political Space" for an earlier elaboration of this argument.

21. ASIO Act 1986.

22. *Australian Law Journal* 58, no. 2 (February 1984): 68.

23. Jenny Hocking, *Lionel Murphy: A Political Biography* (Melbourne: Cambridge University Press, 2000), 162–67.

24. Justice Lionel Murphy, *Church of Scientology Inc. v. Woodward* (1982) in Jean Ely and Ron Ely, *Lionel Murphy: The Rule of Law* (Sydney: Akron Press, 1986): 71–78.

25. Australian Security Intelligence Organization Amendment Act 2002.

26. Daryl Williams, *Lateline,* 27 November 2001 (my emphasis), at http://www.abc.net.au/lateline/s427336.htm (accessed 18 February 2002)

27. Peter La Franchi, "Army Chief Warns on Terrorism," *Australian Financial Review* (13 November 2001): 11.

28. Christopher Hitchens, "Wanton Acts of Usage–Terrorism: A Cliché in Search of a Meaning," *Harper's Magazine* (September 1986): 66–70.

29. Victor Windeyer, "Opinion on Certain Questions concerning the Position of Members of the Defence Force When Called Out to Aid the Civil Power" in Hope,

Protective Security Review Report (Canberra: Australian Government Printing Service, 1979), Appendix 9, 291.

30. Daryl Williams, "New Counter-Terrorist Measures" *News Release* 2 October 2001, at http://www.law.gov.au/ministers/attorney-general/mediamn.html (accessed 26 October 2001).

31. George Winterton, "The Significance of the *Communist Party* Case," *Melbourne University Law Review* 18 (June 1992): 630–58, 653.

32. In Jenny Hocking, "Robert Menzies' 'Fundamental Authoritarianism': The Communist Party Dissolution Referendum 1951," in *Arguing the Cold War*, ed. Paul Strangio and Peter Love (Melbourne: Vulgar Press, 2001).

33. Justice Michael Kirby, "H. V. Evatt, the Anti-Communist Referendum and Liberty in Australia' *Australian Bar Review* 7 (1991): 93–120.

34. Justices Williams and Kitto in G. Winterton, "The Significance of the *Communist Party* Case," 656–57.

35. Justice Michael Kirby, "H. V. Evatt: Libertarian Warrior" in *Seeing Red: The Communist Party Dissolution Act and Referendum 1951: Lessons for Constitutional Reform* (Sydney: Evatt Foundation, 1992), 1–22, 5.

36. Herbert Vere Evatt, in Allan Dalziell, *Evatt the Enigma* (Melbourne: Lansdowne Press, 1967), 2.

37. Daryl Williams, Attorney General, Second Reading Speech, *Security Legislation Amendment (Terrorism) Bill 2002* House of Representatives *Hansard* March 2002.

38. Justice Dixon, "Australian Communist Party v. Commonwealth," *Commonwealth Law Reports* 83 (1951): 187–88.

39. L. Bonanate, "Some Unanticipated Consequences of Terrorism," *Journal of Peace Research* 16, no. 3 (1979): 197–213.

40. Justice Michael Kirby, "Australian Law—After September 11," 4.

14

Safeguarding Human Rights of People in Counterterrorist Operations

S. Subramanian

All human rights are derived from the dignity and the worth inherent in the human person and their availability and enjoyment by the citizens are the hallmarks of a liberal democratic society. Violent groups use terrorism as a means to force their will and ideology on the society. Terrorists attempt to create an atmosphere where the "fear of death" is the dominant experience. To create the required impact terrorists indulge in brutal and inhuman acts affecting the dignity of the citizen. Counterterrorist measures initiated by the state often violate the human rights of citizens under the pretext of expediency and for reasons of state. Thus, the citizen gets victimized both by the terrorists as well as actions of the state. To ensure that this does not occur, the state should embark upon a massive human rights awareness campaign for the police and the security forces.

The preamble of the Universal Declaration of Human Rights (UDHR) proclaimed by the UNO on 10 December 1948, states:

- the recognition of the inherent dignity and of the equal and inalienable rights of all members of the human family is the foundation of freedom, justice and peace in the world;
- disregard and contempt for human rights have resulted in barbarous acts which have outraged the conscience of mankind; and
- it is essential, if man is not to be compelled to have recourse, as a last resort, to rebellion against tyranny and oppression, the human rights should be protected by the rule of law.

Since democracy is the government of the people, by the people, and for the people, UDHR in Articles 18 to 21 stresses freedom of speech, assembly, right to choose freely the representatives to govern the people. Dissonance is endemic in a democratic polity and people are expected to resolve their problems in a peaceful manner after extensive consultations and debate. However, terrorism seeks to impose its views on people, through mindless violence.

The Federal Bureau of Investigation (1999, 2) has defined terrorism as "the unlawful use of force or violence against persons or property to intimidate or coerce a government, the civilian population or any segment thereof, in furtherance of a political or social objective." Political movements adopt various violent means to make the governments and people accept their viewpoint and demands. Terrorism specializes in using the "fear of death" as the weapon to subdue dissent. In all recorded cases of highjacking, kidnappings, hostage taking, etc., this fear has been successfully used to extract compliance. Even powerful nations, which proclaimed "no negotiations with the terrorists," were forced in the past to deal with terrorists and negotiate with them to save innocent lives. To heighten their image of ruthlessness, terrorists indulge in wanton and unspeakable atrocities against civilian populations. This fear psychosis affects the quality of life in a democracy and prevents people from enjoying their basic rights to liberty, equality, and fraternity.

India has been experiencing terrorism of all varieties for over two decades including the Sikh militancy; the left-wing political extremism, the Communist Party of India-Marxist-Leninist (CP-ML), and Pakistan-sponsored Islamic fundamentalist movements. During the decade 1990–2000, in the state of Jammu and Kashmir alone, over 6,000 civilians and 2,200 security personnel have been killed. Terrorists have been targeting democratic nonviolent political parties too and have killed over 300 prominent political workers (Khare 2000, 14). In the southern state of Andhra Pradesh, where "People's War Group," a CP-ML outfit, is wreaking havoc, during the same period, 1,715 civilians and 344 security personnel have been killed and public property of considerable value has been destroyed (Interface 1999, 5).

Even while denouncing and undermining the established state, the terrorists, after committing crimes against humanity, have been taking full advantage of the constitutional guarantees and the protection of the "Rule of Law." Since they operate under the cloak of secrecy, it has become almost impossible for the security forces to gather evidence and prove the cases against terrorists in a court of law. The proof beyond reasonable doubt will seldom be available. Very few terrorists get punished by a court of law. This has led to widespread cynicism and lack of credibility for the democratic order and judicial system in the view of the common man. The frustration in dealing with an unknown enemy, who chooses his own time and place to strike, and the legal constraints and operational restrictions under which these forces act also lead security personnel to lose their faith in the efficacy of the concept of rule of law. Consequently, in field conditions, excesses that affect the dignity of the citizen often take place.

The common man is at the receiving end all the time and suffers. Terrorists attack him: those living in remote and inaccessible areas are forced to provide shelter and food to terrorists on the run; their womenfolk become the victims of terrorists' lust; and male breadwinners are killed and women and children are left destitute. On the other hand, the common man is subjected to intensive interrogation by the security forces to reveal the identity and movements of terrorists. Counterterrorist operations also place many irksome restrictions on the movement, freedom of speech, and other rights of the citizens in the affected areas. Terrorists use improvised explosive devices and land mines extensively to kill or maim security forces and the public remains a mute witnesses to this. Due to fear of reprisal, they seldom give any information to security forces. In a clever and diabolical manner, terrorists create an impression in the minds of security personnel that the people are also supporting them, whereas in fact it is the fear of death that keeps them away from the security personnel. Unable to identify friend from foe, security forces, in uncontrolled fury, target innocent people. When peoples' human rights are violated, the alienation against the established order gets exacerbated. Faced with a Hobson's choice of choosing between the two evils, people find it easier and more practical to covertly side with the terrorists and save themselves from reprisals.

The primary objective of counterterrorist operations is to protect the lives and properties of the people from terrorist attacks and restore order so that democratic institutions can function effectively. Order should be maintained in accordance with the law. It is possible to fight terrorism without violating the dignity and human rights of people. To maintain order, people's freedoms need not be trampled. Use of third degree, torture, forced disappearances, nonjudicial killings, etc. will make the security forces embrace the cult of terrorism and they will no longer remain a disciplined force. In a liberal democracy, means are more important than ends. Indiscriminate repression by security forces is incompatible with the liberal values and principles of liberty, equality, humanity, and justice.

The best antidote for terrorism is good governance. While displaying firmness in fighting the terrorists to protect the people, a liberal democracy should also uphold the rule of law. Under all circumstances, democratic institutions should be allowed to function in terrorist-affected areas. Many democracies are tempted to resort to draconian laws, martial law, and army rule to deal with terrorism and to restore order. This amounts to the remedy being worse than the disease. This very act strengthens the cause of terrorists and upholds their contention that the existing democratic system is ineffective in protecting people. Democratic governance is a basic human right and it should always be ensured.

Security personnel should remember that to fight an unseen enemy, superior armaments and tactical training alone would not produce the results. They need grassroots intelligence, which will come only from the people living in the affected area. If they are alienated due to the violation of their dignity and human rights, the people will not cooperate with them. Security forces should follow the golden principles of proportionality and operational necessity while using force. They should avoid unnecessary suffering to local population by carefully selecting the means of operations that would cause minimum damage to life and property.

Whatever the circumstances, a liberal democracy cannot survive disregarding the human rights of its people. Dissent is a democratic right. Only when violent and unacceptable means are adopted to express dissent, undermining public safety and morality, should the state step in. It should fight the criminality involved in terrorism, always keeping in mind that the terrorist is also a human being, though indulging in inhuman acts. Paradoxically, terrorism thrives only in a democratic environment! In a totalitarian or dictatorial setting, it will die in infancy.

Security personnel should remember that force and violence are passing phases in a society. The response should be ethical and lawful. They are there to serve the people in distress. Their actions should create confidence in the minds of the people. Respecting the dignity of the people at all times will automatically ensure that human rights are not violated. In the history of the world, nowhere has terrorism been defeated by force. Only conciliation through democratic and humane means has produced results.

It is the responsibility of the state and the leadership of the security forces to propagate among the security personnel an attitude that under no circumstances are the human rights of citizens to be violated. Stringent punitive action should be taken against the erring personnel. Systematic training should be imparted to the personnel in the minimum use of force and how to handle people in difficult situations without affecting their dignity. Human rights principles should become part of the regular curriculum of training for security personnel.

"Liberty and Democracy become unholy when their hands are dyed with the blood of the innocents" (Mohandas K. Gandhi).

REFERENCES

Federal Bureau of Investigation. 1999. *Terrorism in the United States: 1997.* Washington, D.C. U.S. Government Printing Office.

Khare, Harish. 2000. "Kashmir: Where Do We Go from Here?" *Hindu* (April 2): 14.

"Interface. Feature by the Government of Andhra Pradesh." 1999. *Hindu* (December 19): 5.

15

A Future for the ETA?

Irwin M. Cohen and Raymond R. Corrado

On December 28, 2001, the European Union released a list of groups and organizations that it considered to be terrorist in nature. This international list included the Basque separatist group ETA (Euskadi Ta Askatasuna—Basque Homeland and Liberty), which operates primarily in Spain.[1] Motivated, in part, as a response to the terrorist attacks on September 11, 2001, in New York and Washington, the subsequent "war on terrorism," and the desire to appear united against the threat of terrorism, the unanimous adoption of this list by the European Union is not simply symbolic. By being defined as a terrorist organization by the European Union, ETA is subject to various serious consequences, and not just within Spain's jurisdiction. Specifically, this policy requires the fifteen member-states to freeze the assets within their jurisdiction of any terrorist group on the list, and to jail any person within their borders whose name appears on any of the group's membership lists. In addition to having much of its international legitimacy and stature undermined by being defined as a terrorist organization by this conglomerate of states, ETA has also become the last, albeit most active, nationalistic antistate terrorist group waging a sustained campaign in Western Europe.

ETA's political goal is independence for the two to three million Basques from what it perceives to be the historically repressive Spanish national government controlled by the majority Castilian ethnic group. However, while the ETA once enjoyed a significant amount of support from the citizens of *Euskadi*, the Basque country, since the end of its self-declared fourteen-month cease-fire in 1999, it has seen its public and political support wane dramatically. In this chapter, we will provide a plausible explanation for this decline in support for the ETA. It will be maintained that this change in public support did not occur primarily because of the disenchantment among

Basques with ETA's tactics of kidnapping and/or murdering politicians, military and police officers, members of the judiciary, journalists, professors, and a growing number of innocent civilians. In effect, it is not the public's growing desire to seek a peaceful solution to the question of Basque independence, but rather the changing structure of Basque society resulting from industrialization and globalization, the institutionalization of liberal democratic values, the political devolution or federalization of Spain since the death of General Franco, an increased recognition of the economic, social, political, and cultural costs to the Basque region of ETA terrorism, the substantial gains made by nonviolent Basque nationalist political parties to protect and defend the Basque culture and language, and the concessions made by the national government to most of ETA's demands. In fact, it may be argued that with the exception of amending the 1978 constitution of Spain to allow for a Basque referendum on independence, granting complete independence to the Basque country, completely removing all Guardia Civil from the Basque country, and the release of all ETA terrorists from prison, all of ETA's demands have been met. Albeit, while these outstanding demands represent some of the core political goals of ETA, the systematic concessions made by several Spanish governments have been important in explaining the decline of Basque public support for ETA.

There are parallels between the history of the Basque region and ETA, and Northern Ireland and the Irish Republican Army (IRA). However, a more complete parallel case that provides a better understanding of ETA and the Basque region can be found in the history of ethnic nationalist terrorism in the province of Quebec in Canada. In the Basque country, Northern Ireland, and Quebec, there are substantial segments of the population who support independence movements. Yet, in repeated elections, independence propositions have been opposed by a majority of the respective electorates. Similarly, ethnic nationalistic terrorist organizations have emerged, including ETA, the IRA, and the FLQ (Front pour la Libération du Québec). All these groups used violence against the symbols of the state and its agents, as well as "innocent citizens." Except for the FLQ, the IRA and ETA have successfully resisted any military attempts to defeat them.[2]

However, unlike the IRA, and much like the French separatists in Quebec, ETA does not enjoy any significant support outside their region. Moreover, among Basques, the sense of victimization and discrimination by the national government, which is instrumental for sustaining any public support for a terrorist campaign, is diminishing. This lack of support for ETA reflects the evolving economic configuration among the various regions of Spain. The Basque region is among the most economically stable regions in Spain, the per capita income is higher than in the rest of Spain, and this wealth is spread equitably between ethnic Basques and non-Basques.[3] While language ethnically distinguishes the Basque from the rest of Spain, religion does not. Most critically, 52 percent of people living in the Basque region define themselves as both Spanish and Basque, with only 29 percent identifying themselves as Basque only.[4] Politically, the Basque region has more autonomous power than any other region in Spain. This is evident in the Basque regional parliament having direct local control over the school system, tax collection, welfare, health services, police, agriculture, and fishing.[5] Given this economic-political profile, there are several fundamental reasons for the dramatic reduction in support for ETA and its tactics of terrorism. As mentioned above, many of the historical issues that gave rise to ETA have been redressed. Of critical importance is the trend of the Basque region continuing to be governed by the recently reelected moderate Basque Nationalist Party (PNV). Nonetheless, despite these unfavorable trends against ETA, after forty years of terrorism, there is a significant portion of the Basque population that supports even greater autonomy and even independence from Spain. Yet, what has changed dramatically is the diminishing number of people who remain committed to terrorism in order to achieve these goals and those willing to support terrorism.[6] Given the complex political context, it is necessary to distinguish, on the one hand, between the political conflict between the Basque regional government and politics and the federal government and national politics situated in Madrid, and, on the other hand, the violent conflict between ETA and the Spanish government.

THE ORIGINS OF BASQUE NATIONALISM AND ETA

While almost certainly Europe's oldest surviving ethnic group,[7] the traditional Basque territories encompass the four provinces of northeastern Spain and the three immediate cross-border provinces in France.[8] The contemporary period of violence to preserve the integrity of the Basque regions of Spain dates back to the Carlist wars in the early nineteenth century. At that time, the traditionally oriented Basques joined the conservative monarchy in fighting the forces of political liberalism, an ideology that was seen as a threat to the deep-seated rural Basque culture linking the farm, village, towns, extended family, and the Roman Catholic Church. The next threat occurred in the late nineteenth century when the industrialization of the Basque regions initiated a fundamental transformation toward urban development. Major industries evolved rapidly in the cities of Bilbao and San Sebastian. Equally critical was the influx of "immigrants" from the poorer, less industrial regions of Spain, who were drawn to the Basque country by the availability of jobs. Bringing with them their Spanish language and regional cultures, their concentration in Basque cities made these so-called immigrants even more visible and distinctive.[9] Finally, it was from their ranks that unions and socialism emerged and came to be viewed by the conservative and tradition-bound Basque elite as another threat to the survival of their culture and people.[10] Contemporary Basque nationalism can be traced, therefore, to the "foreign" political and economic trends emanating from the Madrid-based Castilian elite who were seen as deliberately facilitating the demise of the Basque people. For many Basques, this threat could only be met by creating a Basque nation that would preserve the centuries-old regional rights of the Basques symbolized in the ancient *furores*, or written codes, defining a citizens' rights and the relationship between regional and central authorities.[11] In effect, these *furores*, which were lost during the Spanish unification of 1876, recognized the economic, political, and cultural distinctiveness of the Basque homeland.[12]

During the final half of the twentieth century, other critical events further set the stage for the eventual founding of ETA. First, the Second Spanish Republic was established in 1931. By siding with the Carlists, the Basque provinces, despite the popular antipathy toward the politically dominant socialists of the Republican regime, were recognized briefly as an autonomous region. However, the Spanish Civil War (1936–1939), which pitted the democratically elected Republican government against General Francisco Franco's military rebellion, ended with the demise of the short-lived Republic and the onset of the Franco dictatorship in 1939.[13] As before, the Basque sided with the losing side in the conflict. With the rise of his regime, General Franco was able to implement his concept of Spanish nationalism, which focused on the sanctity of a united and centralized Spain. To achieve this goal, Franco's regime imposed severe measures against any expression of Basque cultural and political identity. As historian Jose Maria Garmendia argues, Francoism made the Basques' perceived occupation of the Basque country real and effective.[14]

The regional nationalisms of the Basque and Catalan areas were ruthlessly suppressed. For a short period, immediately following World War II, there was hope among the anti-Franco forces that the victorious allies would force the fascist regime from power. However, the Cold War that quickly ensued took precedence, and, in exchange for the use of military bases in Spain, the United States accepted the legitimacy of the Spanish dictatorship.[15] Bolstered by his newfound international support, Franco systematically strove to abolish the cultural basis of Basque nationalism by forbidding the use of the Basque language either publicly or privately. Franco's regime reacted brutally to any expressions of Basque nationalism. The Madrid-directed Civil Guard were given a free hand to ruthlessly violate basic civil rights in the systematic campaign to maintain a centralized and unified Spain. Basque political leaders were either imprisoned or forced into exile, usually immediately across the border in the French Basque region.

During this period, the Basque Roman Catholic Church, as it had been throughout history, remained a focal point for the preservation of the Basque culture; it subtly facilitated the use of the Basque language and literature. The rapid decline of the Basque language, *Euskera*, to the point where only 25 percent of Basques could speak it, became the central cultural symbol and rallying point for all Basque Nationalists.[16] Mountain climbing, hiking clubs, and other subterfuges also were utilized to perpetuate the Basque culture, and, eventually were used by the ETA leadership to meet, plan, and recruit.[17]

The initial concept of ETA arose among a small group of university students in Bilbao. Nationalistic and ideological antistate terrorist organizations often emerge from universities because of the nature of such institutions. Students meet routinely in classes and lectures, as well as in informal groups to discuss an array of topics. Invariably, controversial political and cultural issues attract a certain number of the more radically oriented idealists among students who typically take courses in history, political science, humanities, and philosophy. While not restricted to these types of students, nonetheless, it is not uncommon for more radical students to coalesce around these subjects. Knowledge of the history of Basque nationalism made such students aware that the traditional organizations, including the long-standing conservative Basque Nationalist Party, had failed to overcome the powerful political, police, military, and economic forces perceived to be allied against Basque nationalism. Disillusionment with nonviolent approaches, therefore, set the stage for ETA. While these student activists initially entertained the notion of working through the youth wing of the PNV, in 1959, they instead chose a revolutionary approach.

ETA was created by several university students on July 31, 1959.[18] This date was purposefully selected for its symbolic value as it celebrates and honors the patron saint of the Basque country, St. Ignatius of Loyola.[19] This nationalistic link to the past is extremely important in order to comprehend the purpose, values, and contemporary goals of ETA. ETA's nationalistic idealism is linked to the nineteenth-century Basque nationalist movement of Sabino de Arana who forged an ideology based not only on the Basque culture and language but also on the centrality of the Roman Catholic Church. Arana believed that it was necessary to protect the Basque territory from the loss of its culture and language and the influx of immigrant workers from other regions in Spain.[20] In order to achieve this, Arana argued that the Basque region had to become independent from Spain. To forward this agenda, Arana formed the Basque Nationalist Party (PNV).

In the face of the Franco dictatorship, ETA leaders debated both the ideological basis of their organization and the appropriate strategy to obtain the goal of an independent Basque state for nearly a decade.[21] While moving through different phases, ETA eventually defined itself as a Marxist-Leninist movement committed to the principles of Basque independence and social-ism through the use of violence.[22] Similar debates were occurring among radical university students simultaneously in many Western countries. Civil rights, anticolonial, and anti-Vietnam War movements arose in the United States, Northern Ireland, France, Germany, and Italy. In all those countries, revolutionary terrorist organizations eventually emerged as the choice for small groups, principally university students, who sought to combat the forces of aggression not only in dictatorships such as Spain but also in the liberal democracies of Western Europe and North America. Yet, for ETA, the IRA in Northern Ireland, and the FLQ in Canada, the choices concerning ide-ology and strategy were confounded by an ethnic nationalist component. In contrast, within Western Germany's Red Army Faction, Italy's Red Brigade, Japan's Red Army, and the United States's Weathermen, the ideological de-bates focused on the appropriate organizational strategies to be derived from their mixture of anarchist and neo-Marxist ideological goals. While these goals, paradoxically, were far more elusive to define than the ethnic nation-alist goal of an independent nation-state, the latter goal became intertwined for many ETA leaders with the socialist goal of a more equitable distribution of wealth or living standards for the working-class of the major Basque cities.

By the late 1960s, the Basque areas had experienced another major indus-trial expansion and had become the wealthiest region of Spain. As a result, more non-Basque immigrants were drawn to this region's cities only to be concentrated in the more deprived working-class sections.[23] These immi-grants could be potential allies of Basque nationalism since they suffered sig-nificantly from the Madrid-directed capitalist elite's economic and social policies. For example, during the recessions endured by Spain in the 1960s, these workers suffered the highest unemployment rates. Even during more expansionary periods, their wages and benefits were kept low to make Spain more competitive than other manufacturing countries. The low wages and lack of social benefits, such as adequate housing and medical care, were ex-acerbated by Madrid's policy of redistributing the manufacturing-based wealth of the Basque economy to the less productive, but more loyal, re-gions of Spain. If approached properly through mass-based organizations, such as unions and eventually worker-based political parties, these "immi-grant workers" could have been converted to the obvious advantage of an independent Basque nation.

Still, under the repressive police and paramilitary apparatus of the Franco regime, the risks of choosing a broad movement strategy were opposed by certain factions among the ETA leaders who argued instead for a more nar-rowly defined ethnic- and nationalist-based strategy. ETA preferred to rely on recruiting from those individuals who were committed above all to the goal of preserving the Basque culture through the establishment of an independent nation-state. The method that ETA adopted was the "spiral of action-repression-action," or the selective use of violence against the most oppressive symbols of Spanish occupation, such as the police, the Civil Guard, and the military.[24] This terrorist tactic is based on the notion of gaining widespread public support by being the victims of harsh government repression in response to a terrorist attack.[25] Given the brutal experience of many Basques with Franco's police and military tactics since 1934, ETA leaders expected that their terrorist acts would result in indiscriminate violent countermeasures by government forces against the general population, in the form of human and civil rights abuses. In turn, this state violence would generate greater support for ETA "guerrilla" or terrorist violence against the Spanish oppressors. In theory, the spiral of violence would increase to the point where a majority of Basques would support a civil war and, therefore, a level of violence that would force the Spanish public and political leadership to give up on what would be a too costly occupation of the Basque colony. This strategy was not entirely farfetched, given the numerous successes of guerrilla movements, such as in Vietnam and in Algeria against the French and in Kenya against the British. Given that the Basque region was developing an advanced industrial economy, and, therefore, was fundamentally dissimilar to these historical examples, this ideology and strategy debate concerning tactics and policy, in one form or another, continued throughout ETA's early existence, and is still being debated today.

The *lucha armada* (armed struggle) and *guerra revolucierara* (revolutionary war) began in 1968 when the police killed a respected ETA leader during a shootout.[26] In response, ETA assassinated a notorious police chief, Meliton Manzanas, outside his home. As predicted, the Franco government's response was immediate and indiscriminately furious with the imprisonment, torture, and exile of thousands of Basques in the militarily besieged region.[27] During this government crackdown, sixteen ETA leaders were arrested and tried in Burgos in 1970, with six ETA members receiving death sentences.[28] These severe dispositions resulted in massive demonstrations, backed by various distinct segments of the population in the Basque region, for the condemned men. In addition, ETA also kidnapped Eugene Beihl, the West German honorary consul in San Sebastian, and demanded lenient treatment for the convicted defendants in exchange for Beihl's release.[29] With demonstrations throughout Spain demanding that these death sentences be rescinded, the threat of increased street violence, and growing international pressure from the governments of Sweden, Norway, Denmark, West Germany, France, Belgium, the Vatican, and Australia, for Franco to commute the death sentences, Franco backed down.[30]

However, even with this "victory," ETA, as a viable nationalistic entity that could challenge the power and authority of the state, barely survived this period of government repression. Their survival was partially due to the charismatic leader, Eustatus Mendizabel, who was able to maintain the cause's public legitimacy and political allies, and an unexpected influx of new recruits from disillusioned members of the youth wing of the PNV. This occurred because while the PNV supported the long-term political goal of ETA, namely, the complete independence of the Basque country from Spain, it does not support the use of violence to achieve this goal. However, because of the lack of progress on Basque independence, and the increased repression of the Franco regime, there was a segment of the Basque population that had grown impatient with the PNV's political approach. As such, with the influx of new recruits and the harsh policies of the Franco regime, ETA was revitalized. This set the stage for its most spectacular act, the assassination of Luis Carrero Blanco, the Spanish premier and designated successor to Franco.[31] This single audacious act was symbolically critical because it kept alive the strategic utility of violence in the face of the overwhelming failure of ETA to foment a general uprising of the Basque people against the oppressive Franco regime.

Even with the successful assassination of Blanco, the inability of ETA to either progress substantially toward independence or create a mass uprising against the central government in Madrid raised a crucial policy debate within ETA and led to internal dissension. The main issue was that if the predicted uprising did not occur under the existing "ideal" circumstances of massive repression, perhaps a broader political strategy, including cooperation with other Basque nationalist organizations, might be more helpful in gaining popular support. This caused a split in ETA into two groups, ETA-*Zarra*, or old ETA, and ETA-*Berri*, or young ETA.[32] Following further internal disputes, ETA-*Berri* divided into two subgroups, ETA-5 and ETA-6. Two factions quickly emerged within ETA-5. One faction challenged the dominant militant faction's strategy of unnecessarily risky terrorist acts that not only brought about virulent repressive government reactions, but also alienated many supporters within the Basque and non-Basque communities. Again, the challenging faction resurrected the strategy of working with broad-based organizations, not only in the Basque regions, but also in Spain and Western Europe to achieve independence. This faction saw labor and human rights organizations as critical to the cause of Basque nationalism. The two factions split formally in 1974 following a bomb attack on a Madrid café. The emerging groups became known as the ETA-*militar*, who favored violent actions, and the ETA-*politico-militar*, who favored building a political base, but also employed the tactic of kidnapping people for large ransoms.[33] These two groups symbolized the evolving strategy debate that intensified with the death of Franco in 1975 and the unexpected quick initiation of a transition to a liberal democratic multipolitical party system, which continues today.

ETA IN THE POST-FRANCO ERA

With the death of General Franco in 1975, Spain began the process of transforming its political ideology from fascism to democracy. In 1977, Spain held its first democratic elections. In the Basque provinces, the PNV, which demanded autonomy from Spain, won a clear majority, including ten senate seats, thus, ensuring the protection of the Basque culture and language.[34] By 1978, Spain had a democratic constitution that entrenched civil and political liberties and began the process of devolution of powers to the regional governments.[35] And, while the devolution of power was not enough to garner support for the constitution from the majority of the electorate in the Basque country,[36] or to appease the PNV, which was the only major democratic party to call for the abstention in the constitutional referendum, ETA found that it had lost much of its international support and sympathy. As Corrado argues, ETA was no longer viewed internationally or domestically as a group of freedom fighters opposing a fascist regime, but as a terrorist group in violent conflict with a fledging democratic state.[37]

As such, the immediate issue for the leadership of ETA was whether to continue using terrorism to achieve the goal of Basque independence or to ratify the new proposed constitution that provided the politically autonomous Basque and Catalan regional parliaments with considerable power over taxation, as well as economic and cultural domains. The pro-negotiation groups and ETA factions were pitted against the anti-negotiation ETA factions over the next twelve years. By the early 1980s, many from the former group had negotiated an amnesty agreement with the Spanish government regarding its imprisoned and exiled members. In return, most of ETA-*politico-militar* essentially disbanded its members, with former supporters typically joining various Basque socialist parties and coalitions after 1977.[38]

Even within the hard-line faction of ETA, the negotiation issue remained unresolved. Following the ratification of the new constitution, the political context evolved rapidly in Spain. Despite ETA's attempts to provoke the reactionary factions of the Spanish military police and civil guard through several assassinations of their members, liberal pluralistic democratic institutions and processes seemed to take hold quickly throughout Spain. Most importantly and symbolically, an attempted military coup d'etat to ensure the integrity of all Spain through a military regime was stymied by the quick opposition of King Juan Carlos, and the wide rejection of such a regime by most of the Spanish people. Most critically, key segments of the military and police heeded the king's call for loyalty to the constitution.[39]

The key Spanish Socialist Party, led by Prime Minister Felipe González, dominated the post-Franco era. González governed for fourteen successive years and was defeated only in the spring of 1996. González projected the image of supporting the gradual evolution of a more federal relationship with the Basque and Catalan regions. In fact, his government was able to remain in power only by fomenting a coalition with Catalan nationalist political parties. During this period, Spain became a full-fledged member of the European Union, which brought not only a vast new protected market for Spanish, especially Basque, products but also crucial major economic development grants for the poorer developed Spanish regions. Supposedly, this would lessen another long-standing Basque grievance, namely, the unfair redistribution of Basque wealth to these economically poorer regions. Spain's economy, while not anywhere near the advanced levels of the European Union's most powerful economies, such as Germany, nonetheless had been drawn along by an enormous momentum which included: the uninhibited flow of Spanish laborers throughout the stronger EU economies; the standardization of business, labor, and human rights codes; and the enormous influx of capital as well as tourists and retirees who became dominant fixtures in Spain's coastal resort communities. In effect, despite the current stagnant growth and high unemployment characteristics of the first half of the 1990s, Spain had become fundamentally and irrevocably integrated into the European Union after nearly a half-century of isolation during the Franco regime. This structural transformation was an overwhelming contextual fact that posed in many ways one of the ultimate challenges to ETA's existence and historical role.

One might have expected ETA to simply fade away in this context as it was increasingly being regarded by many within the Basque country, and throughout Spain, as an obsolete response to a political system that no longer existed. Spain was proving to be a robust young democracy, and through the process of devolution, the Basque country had been granted autonomy and a regional parliament had been established. The Basque region was governed by the PNV in coalition with the Socialists, who shared, among other things, a common platform against ETA terrorism.[40] Nonetheless, during this time, ETA hard-liners increased their rate of murder.[41] Realizing that its decision to abstain from regional and national elections may have been a mistake, ETA-PM formed a coalition political party to participate in the next round of elections. This lead ETA-M to also sponsor a coalition, HB (Herri Batasuna—Popular Unity), to contest the coming elections.[42] Breaking away from the PNV in 1978, HB was formed as a more militant group in support of ETA and the use of violence that attracted young Basque voters.[43]

While the exact link between ETA and the HB, or Popular Unity political party,[44] remains unclear, many scholars contend that the relationship between ETA and HB parallels the links between Sein Fein and the IRA in Northern Ireland. Presumably, HB and Sein Fein are the legitimate or legal political expressions of their illegal military or terrorist organizations. The assumption has been that, while the leadership of the two types of organizations are separate, they nonetheless coordinate their policies to a certain degree. Historically, HB has refused to oppose terrorism in all circumstances, yet it has condemned specific ETA acts, such as the 1994 bombing of a store in a working-class area of Barcelona that killed twenty-one people. This admitted ETA mistake (its warning to evacuate the area was not effective) resulted in a substantial drop in electoral support for the HB both within the Basque province and in its drive to garner support in other regions of Spain. In fact, this reduction in political support even reached the European Union where HB had previously won an unprecedented seat to the European Parliament in Strasbourg. The subsequent loss of this seat occurred partly as a result of the Barcelona bombing. In addition to losing this seat, HB lost two of its thirteen seats in the Basque Parliament.[45] Still, after the 1994 election results, HB remained the third-largest political force in the Basque country with 16.3 percent of the total vote. Consequently, HB has raised the general issue again of the utility of terrorism as a necessary element in the strategy to gain an independent Basque nation-state.

In addition to the Barcelona bombing, other contemporary ETA actions have produced similar public condemnation. For instance, in September of 1993, 50,000 people marched in the city of San Sebastian to demand the release of Julio Iglesias Zamora from ETA captivity. Perhaps the action that has caused the most damage to ETA's public image was the murder of a small-town councilman, Miguel Angel Blanco, in 1997. After his kidnapping, ETA issued an impossible demand for Blanco's release. The terrorists insisted on the transfer of 500 ETA prisoners from all over Spain to the Basque country within forty-eight hours. Once this deadline passed without government compliance, ETA executed Blanco by shooting him in the back of the head.[46] The public's response to this terrorist act was immediate and overwhelming. While it is estimated that over one million people marched in anti-ETA protests throughout Spain, in the Basque country, protest turned to violence where many of the offices of HB were attacked.[47]

Prior to these events, Spain's Congress of Deputies elected Jose Maria Aznar prime minister in May 1996 after forming a majority coalition with several regional political parties. Given this political arrangement, it was unlikely that Aznar would attempt to reverse the regional decentralized trends of the previous four González governments. As well, during the election campaign, Aznar bitterly rejected Socialist Party contentions that his Popular Party (PP) would revive the repressive social and political policies of the fascist Franco regime, even though the PP initially was a product of this right-wing movement. Aznar convinced a near majority of younger Spanish voters that he and his party were centrists and, therefore, rejected all ideological extremes. Instead, he promised an honest and noncorrupt government that favored lower taxes and economic growth. This strategy focused voter frustration and anger with a 22 percent unemployment rate, slow economic growth, government-business financial scandals, and, most important, the accusation that former premier González was associated with the secret government Antiterrorist Liberation Group (GAL).[48] GAL death squads had been implicated in the killings of twenty-seven ETA members between 1983–1987. Over the past ten years, several key senior police and government officials have been tried and convicted for their direct and indirect participation with this state terrorist death squad.[49] Given the popular furor against GAL and its illegal counterterrorist tactics, Aznar's government has continued to resist resorting to a similar strategy in his attempt to defeat ETA.

Perhaps sensing that Spain would never concede to ETA's ultimate demand for Basque independence, the Basque's increasing intolerance of ETA tactics and subsequent waning support, and the influence of the Good Friday peace agreement in Northern Ireland, ETA entered into a self-declared cease-fire with Madrid on September 16, 1998.[50] At the time, many within Spain believed that the purpose of ETA's cease-fire was not a demonstration of their commitment to renounce the use of violence to achieve their goals, but a tactic to reduce government counterterrorist activities, enable ETA to regroup and resupply themselves, and advance its political agenda in the upcoming Basque parliamentary elections. These beliefs were further supported by the clear progress that ETA's political arm made during that election. The Euskal Herritarrok (EH) became part of the ruling coalition government in the Basques' regional assembly and saw its share of the vote to the European Parliament increase by nearly a fifth.[51] Political support for ETA increased from 15.5 percent to 19.5 percent. With their increase in popular support and their cease-fire in place, ETA made several demands of Prime Minister Aznar's People's Party. ETA demanded that the government accept a Basque right to self-determination, and wanted the national government to be bound by the results of a Basque referendum on independence. In addition, ETA wanted a firm schedule for the withdrawal of all Spanish police from the Basque country and the release of all ETA terrorists who were being held in Spanish jails.[52] Aznar's government quickly rejected these demands and, similar to the Good Friday Peace Accords, countered that before any negotiations could occur on any of ETA's demands, ETA had to unconditionally disavow the use of violence and turn in all their weapons. Even with this hard line, Aznar did make some conciliatory gestures. He agreed to move ETA prisoners closer to their homes and to give ETA exiles the opportunity to return to Spain. Still, Aznar would not consider the issue of independence, nor accept the ETA's argument that they needed to retain their weapons in order to protect themselves from government agents.

In late 1999, after fourteen months of a cease-fire that only produced one meeting between ETA and Aznar's government, ETA declared that it was resuming its violent campaign for independence. ETA claimed that no progress had been made on this central issue and that Aznar's government was using the cease-fire for its own political capital. Since the resumption of violence, ETA has murdered thirty-five people and injured many more. With their return to violence, ETA, and its political party EH, suffered a clear setback to its popular support. For instance, at the beginning of the 1998 cease-fire, support for the EH was at 18 percent. However, in the elections that occurred six months after the ETA returned to violence, support had plummeted to 10 percent, and its seats in the Basque Parliament fell from fourteen to seven.[53] For the first time, Basque voters clearly said no to violence and terrorism.

THE FUTURE OF ETA

At the end of 2001, ETA remained a viable organization with the clear capability of being murderously effective in targeting high-profile politicians and police officials. ETA's durability is impressive given its reduction in public support, the increasing effective government counterterrorism policies, and because it has essentially lost its strategic logistical sanctuary in neighboring France.[54] Various Spanish governments have put considerable pressure on France to stop ETA from operating in its adjacent Basque provinces and other areas. Since 1978, various measures by French authorities have made it more difficult and dangerous for ETA to plan, operate, and maintain safe houses in France.[55]

Recent estimates of ETA's core membership suggest that it has declined considerably since the early 1990s. In all likelihood, ETA has many more members in Spanish and French jails, an estimated 500, including most of its leaders, than it has commandos capable of carrying out terrorist attacks.[56] Moreover, unlike the IRA, for example, ETA does not have an American or European lobby to raise funds or provide fresh recruits.[57] This poses a serious problem for ETA because the new generation of potential ETA recruits has not experienced the crude totalitarian tactics of the Franco regime. Instead, they have lived in Basque provinces that have been governed for over twenty years by moderate Basque nationalist politicians who openly espouse the key cultural symbols of the Basque culture. As one indicator of this decrease in cultural discrimination, the Basque language, *Euskera*, is spreading. Many schools in the Basque country teach only in *Euskera*.[58] As such, it is growing increasingly difficult to attract new members because life in the Basque country is not too bad, when compared to the rest of Spain, and Basques face little discrimination from either the central or regional governments. The relative low standard of living and/or high levels of discrimination are typically essential for an antistate terrorist group remaining viable and being able to replenish their supply of young people willing to engage in violence.

There are several other key issues that have contributed to the general decrease in public support for ETA. Clearly, ETA's abandonment of the 1998 cease-fire, and its continued tactic of indiscriminately killing innocent people, has transformed their once solid base of support into widespread hostility. Where thousands of people once took to the street in protest and solidarity when an ETA member was killed or imprisoned, tens of thousands now protest each new ETA terrorist attack. Not only are peace movements gaining support and momentum, but Basque political parties that have traditionally supported ETA and/or the use of violence, such as EH, have seen their popularity and political influence decrease. As mentioned above, in the last election EH lost about 8 percent of their popular support and several seats in the Basque parliament.

It is becoming more difficult for Basques to tolerate or support violence in a functional democracy. More so because many of ETA's demands have been realized. Spain's 1978 constitution gave exceptionally strong support and protection for minority rights, and the Basque government has autonomous control over everything from education and health care to the police force.[59] The Basque country, like the other sixteen regions, or *comunidades autonomas*, is autonomous with real political power. As mentioned above, the Basque country collects its own taxes, staffs its own police forces, and continues to be governed by a Basque nationalist government. And, while many in the Basque country support the principle of greater autonomy, and even eventual independence, fewer people are willing to support the use of violence to achieve this ultimate goal.

Moreover, Spain's economy has been transformed over the past twenty-five years. Since it joined the European Union in 1986, Spain's economy has privatized and opened to the world. Real GDP growth has been at or near 4 percent for the past four years and unemployment has dropped from 24 percent to less than 14 percent.[60] Moreover, ETA terrorism has a genuine economic cost. Tourism is significantly down in the Basque country.[61] Furthermore, it is estimated that damage to private and public property by ETA and their supporters costs tens of millions of dollars every year.[62] In addition, over the years, ETA has extorted vast sums of money from large and small businesses under the guise of a "revolutionary tax" to finance their terrorist activities.[63] Not only have the extortion, kidnappings, and murder of businessmen placed a significant drain on Spain's economy, they have damaged the ability of the Basque country to attract foreign investment.[64] As political scientist Gurutz Jauregui points out, ETA's great contradiction is that it is attempting to apply a Third-World revolutionary strategy to a highly industrialized country.[65]

It can be argued that most Basques are primarily concerned with family, jobs, and the future. Continued ETA terrorism puts these basic values at risk.

Nonetheless, ETA is likely to continue as long as it solely represents the pure concept of Basque nationalism. Throughout its organizational history, the half-dozen attempts to compromise its use of violence to gain an independent Basque homeland have ultimately failed. Several militant groups have emerged from the original ETA determined to use the tactics of terrorism in an attempt to gain their absolute vision of Basque nationalism. However, it seems extremely unlikely that any Spanish government would ever negotiate the dismemberment of Spain, even though there is a general acceptance that regional parliaments do not threaten the national integrity. In effect, unless the Aznar coalition government reverses this trend, ETA will no longer be able to invoke the once obvious historically oppressive symbol of Spanish colonialism with the same degree of effectiveness that it has for most of its existence.

NOTES

1. "EU Puts Basque, Mideast Groups on Terrorist List," *Reuters* 2001, at <http://dailynews.yahoo.com/htx/nm/20011228/wl/attack_eu_list_dc_1.html> (accessed 28 December 2001).

2. "But Basque Aren't Irish," *Economist* 340, no. 7975 (1996): 42.

3. "But Basque Aren't Irish," *Economist* 340, no. 7975 (1996): 42.

4. "But Basque Aren't Irish," *Economist* 340, no. 7975 (1996): 42.

5. Janice Valls-Russell, "Terror and Politics in Spain," *New Leader* 78, no. 7 (1995): 8.

6. Pablo Sanchez, "Two Basque Police Officers Shot Dead, ETA Blamed," *Reuters*, 2001, at <http://dailynews.yahoo.com/h/nm/20011123/wl/spain_shooting_dc_2.html> (accessed 23 November 2001).

7. Al Goodman, "Attack by Basque Separatists Fail as Support Dims for Terrorists," *Christian Science Monitor* 87, no. 106 (1995): 6.

8. Paddy Woodworth, "Why Do They Kill?" *World Policy Journal* 18, no. 1 (2001): 3.

9. Robert P. Clark, *The Basque Insurgents: ETA, 1952–1980* (Madison: University of Wisconsin Press, 1984), 16.

10. Robert P. Clark, *The Basque Insurgents*, 16.

11. Raymond R. Corrado, "Basque Nationalist Terror: ETA," in *Encyclopedia of World Terrorism*, ed. Martha Crenshaw and John Pimlott (Armonk, N.Y.: Sharpe Reference, 1997), 572.

12. Gurutz Jauregui, "National Identity and Political Violence in the Basque Country," *European Journal of Political Research* 14 (1986): 592, 588.

13. Jonathan R. White, *Terrorism: An Introduction* (Belmont, Calif.: Wadsworth Thomson Learning, 2002), 189.

14. Paddy Woodworth, "Why Do They Kill?" 5.

15. John Sullivan, "Forty Years of ETA," *History Today* 49, no. 4 (1999): 34.

16. Paddy Woodworth, "Why Do They Kill?" 4.

17. Peter Waldmann, "Ethnic and Sociorevolutionary Terrorism: A Comparison of Structures," *International Social Movement Research* 4 (1992), 241.

18. Gurutz Jauregui, "National Identity and Political Violence in the Basque Country," 592.

19. Raymond R. Corrado, "Basque Nationalist Terror," 572.

20. Gurutz Jauregui, "National Identity and Political Violence in the Basque Country," 588.

21. Raymond R. Corrado, "Basque Nationalist Terror," 572.

22. Paddy Woodworth, "Why Do They Kill?," 5.

23. Paddy Woodworth, "Why Do They Kill?," 5.

24. Paddy Woodworth, "Why Do They Kill?," 6.

25. This tactic has been successfully used by many terrorist organizations. Currently, Hamas and Islamic Jihad have used a similar approach of engaging in a minor to moderate terrorist attacks and using the subsequent Israeli retaliation as a way of garnering increased international and domestic support for their aims and objectives.

26. Raymond R. Corrado, "Basque Nationalist Terror," 573.

27. Mark Kurlansky, *The Basque History of the World* (New York: Walker & Company, 1999), 243.

28. Raymond R. Corrado, "Basque Nationalist Terror," 573.

29. Cyrus Ernesto Zirakzahed, *A Rebellious People: Basques, Protests, and Politics* (Reno: University of Nevada Press (1991), 184.

30. Mark Kurlansky, *The Basque History of the World*, 244.

31. Raymond R. Corrado, "Basque Nationalist Terror," 573.

32. Clifford E. Simonsen and Jeremy R. Soindlove, *Terrorism Today: The Past, The Players, The Future* (Upper Saddle River, N.J.: Prentice Hall, 2000), 98.

33. John Sullivan, *ETA and Basque Nationalism: The Fight for Euskadi 1890–1986* (London: Routledge, 1988), 186.

34. Mark Kurlansky, *The Basque History of the World*, 271.

35. Paddy Woodworth, "Why Do They Kill?," 6.

36. 11.3 percent of Basques voted no to the constitution, while more than 40 percent of Basque voters abstained from the election and others cast blank ballots.

37. Raymond R. Corrado, "Basque Nationalist Terror," 573.

38. Robert P. Clark, *Negotiating with ETA: Obstacles to Peace in the Basque Country, 1975–1988* (Reno: University of Nevada Press, 1990), 79.

39. Paddy Woodworth, "Why Do They Kill?," 6.

40. Paddy Woodworth, "Why Do They Kill?," 6.

41. In 1980, ETA claimed ninety-one victims, as compared to sixteen victims in 1975.

42. John Sullivan, "Forty Years of ETA," 35.

43. Mark Kurlansky, *The Basque History of the World*, 276.

44. In 1998, Herri Batasuna changed its name to Euskal Herritarrok (EH) and became the official political arm of ETA.

45. "Where Is the Basque Gerry Adams?" *Economist* 333, no. 7887 (October 1994): 57.

46. Fred Coleman and Thomas Omestad, "Millions Say 'Basta' to Terror," *U.S. News & World Report* 123, no. 4 (July 1997): 42.

47. "A Murder Too Far," *Economist* 344, no. 8026 (July 1997): 46.

48. Mark Kurlansky, *The Basque History of the World*, 289–91.

49. Paddy Woodworth, *Dirty War, Clean Hands: ETA, the GAL, and Spanish Democracy* (Cork, Ireland: Cork University Press, 2001), 434–40.

50. Mark Kurlansky, *The Basque History of the World,* 301.

51. "More Talks?" *Economist* 351, no. 8124 (June 1999): 54.

52. "A Period of Calm and Turbulence," *Economist* 353, no. 8144 (November 1999): 55.

53. "Aznar Hurt, ETA Clobbered," *Economist* 359, no. 8222 (May 2001): 46.

54. For most of ETA's existence, key leadership and operational structures remained in France just beyond the legal jurisdiction of Spain's police and military.

55. Mark Kurlansky, *The Basque History of the World,* 285.

56. Paddy Woodworth, "Why Do They Kill," 8; Mark Kurlansky, *The Basque History of the World,* 298.

57. "The Murderous Minority," *Economist* 357, no. 8198 (November 2000): 11.

58. "The Murderous Minority," *Economist* 357, no. 8198 (November 2000): 11.

59. Paddy Woodworth, "Why Do They Kill?," 3, 8.

60. "Spain: A Country of Many Faces," *Economist* 357, no. 8198 (November 2000): 4.

61. "Robust Basques and Regional Catalans," *Economist* 357, no. 8198 (November 2000): 12.

62. Paddy Woodworth, "Why Do They Kill?," 2.

63. Benjamin Jones, "Basques Fight Back," *Europe* 332 (January 1994): 43.

64. Mark Kurlansky, *The Basque History of the World,* 302–303.

65. Gurutz Jauregui, "National Identity and Political Violence in the Basque Country," 596–97.

REFERENCES

"A Murder Too Far." 1997. *Economist* 344, no. 8026 (July): 46–48.

"A Period of Calm and Turbulence." 1999. *Economist* 353, no. 8144 (November): 55.

"Aznar Hurt, ETA Clobbered." 2001. *Economist* 259, no. 8222 (May): 46–48.

"But Basque Aren't Irish." 1996. *Economist* 340, no 7975 (July): 42.

Clark, Robert P. 1984. *The Basque Insurgents: ETA, 1952–1980.* Madison: University of Wisconsin Press.

———. 1990. *Negotiating with ETA: Obstacles to Peace in the Basque Country, 1975–1988.* Reno: University of Nevada Press.

Coleman, Fred, and Thomas Omestad. 1997. "Millions Say 'Basta' to Terror." *U.S. News & World Report* 123, no. 4 (July): 42.

Corrado, Raymond R. 1992. "Basque National Separatists Terror: ETA." In *Encyclopedia of World Terrorism,* edited by Martha Crenshaw and John Pimlott, 572–76. Armonk, N.Y.: Sharpe Reference.

"EU Puts Basque, Mideast Groups on Terrorist List." 2001. *Reuters.*

Goodman, Al. 1995. "Attack by Basque Separatists Fail as Support Dims for Terrorists." *Christian Science Monitor* 87, no. 106: 6; at http://dailynews.yahoo.com/htx/nm/20011228/wl/attacl_eu_list_dc_1.html (accessed 28 December 2001).

Jauregui, Gurutz. 1986. "National Identity and Political Violence in the Basque Country." *European Journal of Political Research* 14: 587–605.

Jones, Benjamin. 1994. "Basques Fight Back." *Europe* 332 (January): 42–44.

Kurlansky, Mark. 1999. *The Basque History of the World*. New York: Walker.

"More Talks?" 1999. *Economist* 351, no. 8124 (June): 54.

"Robust Basques and Regional Catalans." 2000. *Economist* 357, no. 8198 (November): 12–13.

Sanchez, Pablo. 2001. "Two Basque Police Offenders Shot Dead, ETA Blamed." *Reuters* at http://dailynews.yahoo.com/h/nm/20011123/wl/spain_shooting_dc_2.html (accessed 23 December 2001).

Simonsen, Clifford E., and Jeremy R. Soindlove. 2000. *Terrorism Today: The Past, the Players, the Future*. Upper Saddle River, N.J.: Prentice Hall.

"Spain: A Country of Many Faces." 2000. *Economist* 357, no. 8198 (November): 3–4.

Sullivan, John. 1988. *ETA and Basque Nationalism: The Fight for Euskadi 1890–1986*. London: Routledge.

———. 1999. "Forty Years of ETA." *History Today* 49, no. 4: 34–36.

"The Murderous Minority." 2000. *Economist* 357, no. 8198 (November): 11–13.

Valls-Russell, Janice. 1995. "Terror and Politics in Spain." *New Leader* 78, no. 7 (9 November): 7–9.

Waldmann, Peter. 1992. "Ethnic and Sociorevolutionary Terrorism: A Comparison of Structures." *International Social Movement Research* 4: 237–57.

"Where Is the Basque Gerry Adams?" 1994. *Economist* 333, no. 7887 (October): 57.

White, Jonathan R. 2002. *Terrorism: An Introduction*. Belmont, Calif.: Wadsworth Thompson Learning.

Woodworth, Paddy. 2001. *Dirty War, Clean Hands: ETA, the GAL, and Spanish Democracy*. Cork, Ireland: Cork University Press.

———. 2001. "Why Do They Kill?" *World Policy Journal* 18, no. 1: 1–12.

Zirakzahed, Cyrus Ernesto. 1991. *A Rebellious People: Basques, Protests, and Politics*. Reno: University of Nevada Press.

IV

CONCLUDING REFLECTIONS

16

Addressing the Needs of Victims

Noël Brennan

Hello. I am delighted to be here today on behalf of the U.S. Department of Justice and to be among my esteemed colleagues from the United States and from around the world. I would like to thank Dr. Dilip Das and Alex Schmid for inviting me to participate in this meeting and for their effort in organizing and bringing together this distinguished panel. I appreciate this invitation to share what we at the Department of Justice have learned about terrorism, mass violence, and its victims. The subject of the needs of victims of terrorism is very much in the developmental stages and we have much to learn from one another.

Before I begin, I would like to tell you about the Department's Office for Victims of Crime (OVC). OVC's mission is to enhance our nation's capacity to assist crime victims by providing leadership to change attitudes, policies, and practices to promote justice and healing for all victims of crime, whether federal, state, or local. OVC accomplishes this in many ways. OVC administers program grants, trains professionals, supports direct services, develops and sponsors demonstration projects, promotes public education and awareness, and publishes information for national distribution. Within the Justice Department, OVC serves as an advocate on behalf of victims in policy development. But what is most unique about OVC is how it puts to work for victims the dollars of criminal offenders. Let me explain. The Crime Victims Fund, administered by the OVC, is derived not from tax dollars, but from the fines, assessments, and penalties paid by federal criminal offenders. Nearly 90 percent of this money collected each year goes to the states in the United States to help fund victims' programs to provide lifeline services to help victims heal. This translates into help for over 4,000 local victim services agencies, including domestic violence shelters, children's advocacy centers, and rape treatment programs. In addition, these funds are used to reimburse victims for expenses resulting from the crime, including medical and mental health counseling costs, lost wages, and funeral expenses. Since 1986, OVC has distributed more than $3 billion to individual states to support victim services and none of this came from taxpayer dollars! That provides a snapshot of what OVC does.

As you know, a goal of terrorism is to send a shocking message to the public and to a government to encourage political change. Terrorism causes extreme psychological effects on its victims. Terrorism is usually directed at noncombatants. Terrorism is intended to create an extremely fearful state of mind—not just in victims but in the wider audience.

Through our experience with the victims of the Pan Am Flight 103 bombing, the Oklahoma City bombing, and the embassy bombings in Kenya and Tanzania, the Department of Justice has learned that the emotional and psychological crisis created by terrorism affects many people, especially children, and lingers long after the last piece of rubble has been cleared and the defendants have been sentenced. Healing of the emotional and psychological damage is usually extremely costly, both financially and in terms of human suffering and the loss of human potential. Yet, despite our experiences in these bombings, we know that federal, state, and local planners often fail to plan ahead to address the mental health and other needs of victims of terrorism.

Lessons learned have taught us that effective crisis response should be immediate, clinically sound, community based, at a level that is psychologically and emotionally appropriate, and include long-term services. As with every other aspect of a response to terrorism, plans and interagency agreements need to be put into place at the local, state, and federal levels before the terrorism occurs. These plans need to be closely linked to planning efforts by first responders.

Experiences in Oklahoma City and other terrorism cases demonstrated that our federal response plan for a terrorism mass-casualty incident did not include an integrated, mental health plan for such disasters. This oversight created the following serious ambiguities:

- Who is in charge of mental health/victims services?
- What assistance and monies are available for these services?
- What are the protocols for allocation of these funds?
- How are responses and services coordinated among agencies?
- What are the roles and responsibilities of participating agencies at all levels? How are they distinct from one another?

In the United States, the federal government is responsible for working on issues at a national level while the states, territories, and the District of Columbia are responsible for working on issues at the state level. This system results in two sets of laws, policies, and procedures—one federal and one state. At this point, we will keep matters relatively simple by ignoring the city and county issues.

It is critical that states also develop a disaster mental health plan and enhance their capacity to provide an immediate and ongoing response to terrorism and mass-casualty crimes. This is important because it is at the community level that the ongoing care of disaster mental health victims must be provided and maintained for a period of years after a terrorism event.

From the literature on traumatic stress and victims, we know that victims of intentional disasters have higher rates of psychological distress than do those who have experienced natural disasters. Traumatic stress associated with terrorism can range from relatively mild, short-term symptoms to full-blown post-traumatic stress disorder (PTSD). The effects can be extensive and can persist over long periods of time. While PTSD is a primary diagnosis, other disorders, including depression, acute anxiety, substance abuse, and various psychoses, may also occur. In addition, a variety of other symptoms, such as physical ailments, personality changes, and harm-seeking behavior, may result. Onset of symptoms may be delayed for days, weeks, or even months.

Victims of terrorism experience some unique issues related to the criminality of the event. The following factors increase the level of traumatic stress for terrorism victims:

- the realization that a devastating act and the resulting death and damage was an intentional act by other human beings;
- the extent of the physical and emotional damage to victims;
- the sense of loss of control, safety, and questioning what it all means;
- the length of time it takes to rescue the injured, recover and release bodies, and identify victims;
- the extent and intrusiveness of news coverage, especially repetition of disturbing visual images; and
- involvement in the criminal justice system, which can be lengthy and convoluted.

Unlike natural disasters, the effects of terrorism extend beyond direct victims to those who identify with the victims, such as coworkers and school-aged children. Beyond emergency medical treatment and physical safety, the immediate needs of victims and surviving family members after an act of terrorism include information, the ability to communicate with family members, privacy, protection from the media, and crisis counseling.

Like natural disasters and other types of crime, significant secondary trauma may be experienced by those who work with victims in the aftermath, including rescue workers, investigators, other first responders, mental health providers, and criminal justice professionals. The effects on responders can be significant, particularly since both agencies and the public tend to see responders as "heroes." Given this label, the responders may not feel free to acknowledge how negatively they have been impacted by their involvement in the aftermath of the terrorist act.

As we continue to learn, we are able to improve services to victims. Victims who waited years for services, and victim advocates who were moved into action because of the lack of rights and services have helped make changes. Now we have laws that establish victim rights, services, and compensation. In 1988, when the Pan Am 103 bombing occurred, the U.S. government did not respond to the victim families effectively. But we learned from the Oklahoma City bombing and the Khobar Towers and embassy bombings. Working with victim families and advocates in response to these incidents taught us lessons we now use to shape our response to terrorism and mass violence.

PAN AM 103

The bombing of Pan Am 103 took the lives of 270 victims from twenty-one countries. The average age of the victims was twenty-seven years old. There were 189 American victims with family members residing in forty-six states. The Office for Victims of Crime is providing support to the family members of the victims in preparation for the upcoming trial which will occur nearly twelve years after the incident. The international nature of the crime and the trial presented huge obstacles for family assistance which OVC has been challenged to overcome.

We have established an international toll-free information telephone line in our office for victim families in Washington, D.C., that is accessible from sixteen countries where victim families are located. We are working closely with the Crown Prosecution Team, the Scottish Court Service, and the Scottish Police; they provide regular updates for the information line. In addition, we have created a secure website for victim families to give them updated and comprehensive information about the case and the trial. Receiving 59,000 hits within its first three months of operation, the website provides updated information on the case, an "electronic scrapbook" of archival information on the bombing and the victims, information about victim services, and a discussion forum for the families to communicate with one another.

We also have funded three Family Liaison Officers who will coordinate victim services throughout the trial. Services to the victims' families will include providing assistance in locating lodging, arranging local transportation, counseling, and legal explanation about Scottish law and procedure to families. We are working with the Scottish officials to arrange closed-circuit viewing at four secure remote sites for the victims' families. We will provide funding for two victim family members to attend the trial in the Netherlands or to go to one of the remote court sites for one week. Through this assistance, we are attempting to provide much needed services for the victims' families.

OKLAHOMA CITY BOMBING

The Oklahoma City bombing was a wide-scale act of domestic terrorism and the blast killed 167 men, women, and children and injured 853 others. Extensive property damage occurred to the Murrah Federal Building and to the surrounding area. The American people were shocked and horrified that their safety and security could be threatened like it had within minutes.

In the immediate aftermath of the Oklahoma City bombing, we learned that we must have a number of safeguards in place. I will share eleven of them:

- A coordinated death notification system involving teams of professionals who have received specific training in death notification.
- Adequate numbers of mental health and victim services professionals, who are well trained in disaster mental health and crisis response.
- A central place, with security, for victims and families to go for information, crisis intervention.
- Critical incident stress management services and incident review for rescue workers and other first responders, including a secure place to go for crisis debriefing and updated information.
- A mechanism for screening and coordinating volunteer counselors and other support persons. In Oklahoma City, more than 2,000 volunteer counselors arrived on the scene following the bombing.
- Coordination of victim assistance/mental health services with the disaster response.
- Close coordination and a process for transitioning services and assistance to victims from one agency to another.
- Creation of an accurate list of victims with contact information.
- A plan for managing stress and mental health needs of staff working with victims.
- Identification of and development of a plan for accessing funds for emergency services.
- Assistance for families with the media. Selection of spokespersons to address mental health issues and needs of victims and family members.

Based on what we have learned from these incidents, we believe that planning for an effective response to victims and surviving family members must include emergency crisis counseling and intervention, including death notification and, eventually, long-term mental health services for some individuals.

Responding to victims of terrorism requires the development of relationships and protocols to address coordination between first responders, including law enforcement, victim services, and mental health professionals. Without preexisting relationships and plans, communities will have difficulty addressing these important issues.

EMBASSY BOMBING IN EAST AFRICA

On August 7, 1998, two bombs were detonated simultaneously at the United States' embassies in Kenya and Tanzania. It was determined that these bombings constituted an "act of terrorism" against the United States. As a result of the bombings, hundreds of individuals, including twelve American citizens and scores of employees of the United States government, were injured in the blasts.

Immediately following the bombing, OVC provided funds to the State Department and the U.S. Attorney's Office for the Southern District of New York, which is the jurisdiction where the trial will be held, to help. Because statutory use of funding is limited to United States citizens, the Department of Justice was constrained in what it could do.

The State Department was authorized to:

- provide financial assistance to the victims for unreimbursed or covered medical and mental health counseling expenses, lost wages and loss of support, and burial costs;
- cover emergency travel costs required to obtain services;
- host meetings with the victims and government officials to provide information about the status of the investigation and government assistance available to the victims; and
- secure a victim assistance specialist to serve as a liaison between the victims and the State and Justice Departments.

With funding from OVC, the U.S. Attorney's Office was authorized to support an additional victim-witness assistance specialist position to provide the rights and services mandated by federal statutes and delineated in the *Attorney General Guidelines for Victim and Witness Assistance.*

The specialist was responsible for identifying all victims of the bombing, providing information regarding the status of the investigation and prosecution, and providing reasonable protection from harassment to the victims, as necessary.

Assistance provided by OVC included:

- providing guidance to State Department employees regarding allowable costs for payment with Federal Victims of Crime Act funds;
- interceding with State Crime Victim Compensation Programs on behalf of the victims and providing supplemental funding to the crime compensation program to cover benefits paid to victims;
- assisting State Department employees in the coordination of the family briefings; and
- responding to specific victim inquiries regarding services and assistance needed.

OVC has proposed the following support for victims during the upcoming trial:

- creating a separate waiting area during court proceedings;
- intervening on behalf of the victims and witnesses with their employers and creditors;
- assisting with logistical information, including transportation, parking, child care, translator services, and other prosecution-related services;
- preparing victim impact statements regarding the social, psychological, and medical impact of the crime on any individual against whom the offense was committed;
- advocating for the victims' interest at the time of sentencing which may include addressing restitution issues;
- establishing a secure website on the Internet for victims;
- establishing an international toll-free information telephone line for victims' families;
- linking to the State Department embassy cable network; and
- supporting Crisis Counseling and Mental Health Treatment Services during the trial.

As you can see by the services that we are proposing to assist the embassy bombing victims during the trial, that we have learned a number of lessons.

CLOSING

In closing, let me add that we at the Department of Justice continue to work with survivors and families of victims of the incidents we discussed today. We developed a working group to deal with the needs of victims of terrorism. We funded a number of projects to develop model agreements and protocols to respond to victims in the event of an international terrorist incident. Other current efforts include developing a curriculum on providing psychological assistance to victims of mass casualty and terrorism and developing models for coordinated crisis response plans for states and local communities.

Thank you for the opportunity to learn from you and to share the lessons we have learned in the United States. To learn more about the Justice Department's Office for Victims of Crime, please check our website on the Internet.

Thank you.

NOTES

The speech was presented at the "Terrorist Victimization: Prevention, Control, and Recovery," an ancillary meeting of the Tenth U.N. Congress on the Prevention of Crime and the Treatment of Offenders, 12 April 2000, at Vienna, Austria.

17

Impact of Antiterrorism Measures on Democratic Law Enforcement: The Italian Experience

Dilip K. Das

It is, no doubt, a great credit to the Italian police that they were successful in their battle against terrorism. However, this battle should also teach them a few valuable lessons. The police in Italy must remember that in the beginning they had not enough intelligence on the nature of terrorism that devastated the country for many years. Such a glaring lack of intelligence seems to suggest an absence of rapport with society at large. After the terrorists were defeated with increased legal powers and other means of physical might, the police lost the support of the press, which had stood by them during the bad days. Moreover, the discouraging response to a police recruitment drive also indicates that the police were losing popularity. Sensitivity to public feelings based on the strict observance of democratic norms of law enforcement must always remain the cornerstone of any police strategy.

INTRODUCTION

The methods and procedures used by Italian institutions responsible for antiterrorist measures, which during the last fifteen years seem to have successfully controlled the major groups that indulged in daring and reckless acts of violence, are examined here. The police in Italy have also been accused of violence. And, it has been said that many measures used by the police and other agencies responsible for containing terrorism were devoid of the norms of democratic law enforcement. Although this is a rather vague expression, the qualities that should characterize the enforcement mechanism in a democratic community are given below. This account is based on the statements of two eminent American jurists and a noted English scholar.

The following is an account of a few police measures for handling Italian terrorists between 1979 and 1982, as reported in two British periodicals, namely, *The Economist* and the *New Statesman*. Referring to "special powers" for handling terrorists, *The Economist* commented,

> Italy's governments over the past 10 years have long refused to bring in special powers to defend themselves against a much more widespread terrorist challenge. But on December 17, Mr. Francesco Cossiga's weak minority government startled civil libertarians by issuing a series of antiterrorist decrees which seem dangerously close to the thin line between legitimate self defense and repression.[1]

New powers given to the agencies of law included "mandatory life imprisonment" for killing judges, police officers, lawyers, and other connected with the prosecution of terrorists. For inflicting injuries, terrorists were to face twice the usual term of imprisonment. Bail provisions against terrorist suspects were also made extremely stringent. According to the new laws, the police could question such detainees for up to two days before formally charging them or allowing them legal assistance.

For nearly a year, the urban guerrillas of Italy's Red Brigade have growled in frustration as the police have cracked their whips. Far-left gunmen have been rounded up or killed in shootouts with the police, and the number of terrorist attacks has fallen sharply, from some 2,400 in 1979 to little more than 1,000 last year.[2]

Referring to the reports that "police repeatedly tortured suspected left-wing terrorists," the *New Statesman* reported "accounts of systematic beatings and various forms of torture." The same source reported that prisoners under trial were kept in detention for excessively long periods for the purpose of police interrogation.

In another report it is said charges that the police have roughed up suspects are not new in Italy but according to one of the Verona defense lawyers, reports of systematic torture "are unprecedented. . . . Italian police seem to have sometimes been in too much of a hurry to worry about legal niceties."[3]

Thus, there were increased police powers of detention for interrogation, more "shootouts with the police," terrorist suspects "roughed up" and "repeatedly tortured" by the agents of law enforcement, "accounts of systematic beatings" and so on.[4]

Such allegations have prompted me to examine some of the measures that the police in Italy used to combat terrorism. I hope this examination will provide the police and other institutions of justice in Italy—as well as other countries—an opportunity to reflect on their methods of operation.

Definitions of Terms

In this context the phrase *democratic law enforcement* means moral sensitivity in regard to the impact of a particular method of police operation.

That kind of moral quality is represented by the sentiments contained in the following statement used by Chief Justice Earl Warren: "The methods we employ in the enforcement of our criminal law have aptly been called the measures by which the quality of our civilization may be judged."[5]

Briefly, democratic law enforcement as used here calls for police methods and procedures that demonstrate the culture and refinement of times. These must not betray indifference to the tolerance and tough-minded fairness, which distinguish a society as civilized. In other words, the police must avoid "cruel and unusual" methods of operation in order to conform to the civilized norms or legality.

Antiterrorist Measures and Democratic Law

Second, included within the concept of democratic law enforcement are the restraints that government agencies must exercise in order not to present incorrect codes of behavior to the public. The need for governmental restraint is explained by Justice Brandeis: "In a government of laws, the existence of the government will be imperiled if it fails to observe the law scrupulously. Our government is the potent, the omnipresent teacher. For good or ill, it teaches the whole people by its example."[6]

Third, democratic law enforcement is the balance between official restraints and individual freedom that calls for wisdom and humanity in the performance of enforcement tasks. The following statement provides an insight to the need for avoidance of disorder and protection of liberty: "Any nation which so orders its affairs as to achieve a maximum of freedom from public disorder may fairly claim a prize among the highest achievements of the human race."[7]

In brief, democratic law enforcement implies concern for the impact of police measures on moral values, which contribute to the quality of life. It calls for sensitivity on the part of the agents of law enforcement to the examples they set by their actions. They must not indulge in incorrect, deceptive, or repressive behavior to gain momentary advantages. True, the efficiency of law enforcement in a democratic society is the guarantee of security for enjoying the fruits of liberty.

ITALIAN TERRORISM AND AGENCIES OF LAW ENFORCEMENT

The birth of terrorism in Italy can be traced to the bomb incident in Milan on December 12, 1969, when twelve people were killed and eighty injured. However, the first manifestations of terrorism were regarded as casual events perpetrated by isolated anarchists and not as the deeds of an armed opposition that would challenge the authority of the state itself. This inability on the part of the Italian intelligence community to assess the real danger of the new threat gave the terrorists enough time to organize themselves by re-cruiting young militants, laborers, and members of the lower middle classes who suffered most from economic disparity, political insecurity of Italian de-mocracy, and cultural antagonism. The terrorist organizations of the Right and the Left (Red Brigade, Front Line, etc.) could recruit more than 10,000 followers taking advantage of the serious political instability of the 1970s that prevented Italy from launching immediate and efficient countermeasures against terrorism.

One characteristic of ideological terrorism is the difficulty the state has in meeting its claims and finding a common ground for negotiation. Normally, the ideological posture is utopian in keeping with its neo-Marxist founda-tions. Pisano explains the rapid expansion of the terrorist impact on Italy as follows:

> In the Italian experience, domestic terrorism is substantially the product of frus-trated social, economic, or political aspirations, whose degeneration into vio-lence has been and is made possible individuals, parties, "collective," "commit-tee," "clubs" and sundry other aggregations which, in consonance with revolutionary doctrines, advocate revolutionary solutions or, more subtly, insti-gate subversion, political violence and terrorism.[8]

The terrorists were organized rather efficiently. They had a pyramidal structure, their militants formed the nuclei, which operated at citizen levels in groups known as "brigades," and their national organs were called "columns." In addition to those involved in these organizational structures, there were many others who were known as "flankers." They were not di-rectly involved in terrorist operations, but they gave important logistic sup-port, including information. Among various people who joined the terrorist organizations, mention may be made of many intellectuals, for example. Pro-fessor Toni Negri, a political scientist from the University of Padua; Professor Aldo Semerari of criminal anthropology at Rome University; and others such as Paolo Signorelli, a teacher of history and philosophy; and Claudio Mutti, who taught literature. It is said that "The intellectuals of the far-right will be joining a cloisterful of jailed intellectuals who are alleged to have been re-sponsible for the far-left terrorism of the past few years, headed by Professor Antonio Negri. With teachers like these, Italy's young can hardly be blamed for flocking to the cause of terrorism."[9]

Thus, Italian terrorism became a unique phenomenon for the Western world insofar as a high number of people of different ideological persua-sions joined the ranks of the terrorists.

Within ten years of the Milan catastrophe, there emerged in Italy two ma-jor trends in the growth of terrorism: the leftist factions and rightist groups who were neo-Fascists and neo-Nazi. Among the leftist groups, the most im-portant were the Red Brigades (BR), Front Line (PL), and Workers Autonomy

(AUTOP). Notable BR actions included abduction of the president of the Christian Democratic Party and former prime minister Aldo Moro in 1978. So far as the Front Line was concerned, their most spectacular action was a raid at the Industrial Management School of Turin where five instructors and an equal number of students were victims of mass leg shooting.

According to Pisano, AUTOP "preached unlawfulness, subversion and violence."[10] He adds, "the Armed Revolutionary Nuclei (NAR) and Revolutionary Action (AR) were small rightist groups who were 'imitative of leftist targeting pattern.'"[11] However, the Italian terrorists were also supported by many foreign countries, including Russia and Czechoslovakia, for "dynamic commitment to anti-Western internationalism."[12]

The number of incidents and acts of crime involving terrorists in the sixteen years between 1968 and 1984, can be seen from the statistics given in table 17.1.

Italy is a country with many agencies of law enforcement. There are various classes of the police, namely, the Carabinieri, the State Police, the Treasury Police, and the Municipal Police. Established in 1814, the Carabinieri have been serving the country both as a police force and an army. Its strength is about 100,000 personnel. Some three decades after the Carabinieri came into being, in 1834 to be precise, the State Police were created for the administration of public security. In 1943 they were brought under the control of the Ministry of Defense, although they were directed by the Ministry of Interior insofar as their security duties were concerned. This force was made a purely civil police force of about 90,000 persons by Act 121 of 1981. These two forces—the Carabinieri and the State Police—have been in

Table 17.1. Terrorist Incidents and Crime

Year	Incidents	Murders	Injuries	Abductions
1969	352	17	135	—
1970	317	8	56	1
1971	484	4	21	—
1972	494	5	13	2
1973	365	41	73	4
1974	515	30	159	4
1974	640	14	23	5
1976	1202	12	24	1
1977	1988	20	49	1
1978	2243	36	135	1
1979	2135	31	174	—
1980	1107	132	314	1
1981	737	27	82	5
1982	548	26	86	1
1983	412	4	17	2
1984 (part)	157	5	3	—

the forefront of Italy's law enforcement efforts against the terrorists. However, the success of the Italian government's strategy against terrorism is dependent on many factors that need to be critically examined to determine whether democratic law enforcement has been kept in mind during the operation of the strategy.

THE MAJOR STEPS AGAINST TERRORISM

Coordinated intelligence onslaughts, police arrests of terrorists, destruction of their hideouts, trial and long sentences, and the repentance in terrorist ranks, as well as exposure and discord created by confessions were some of the cornerstones of the police action that would evolve over the years.

State-Sponsored Coordinated Intelligence Service

In 1974 the first antiterrorist office, entitled Ispettorato Generale per la Lotta al Terrorism, was created, under the control of the Ministry of Interior for the exclusive purpose of an intelligence operation against terrorists. Here the State Police and the Carabinieri were gathered under one banner for coordinated intelligence and overt activities. As the combined action started to advance, more tightening of centralized operations, characteristic of the new intelligence setup, took place. In 1977, the Intelligence Security Service (SID) was divided into two sections: namely, the Military Security Intelligence Service (SISMI) for international and military intelligence and the Democratic Security Intelligence Service (SISDE) for domestic security matters. Regarding combined police powers and resources it was said: "Parliament will have less say in the government's decision to shake up the security forces to improve co-operation between three main branches, the regular police, the carabinieri and the finance guards."[13]

The strengthening of police measures in an unprecedented manner was noted in other areas too. All of northern Italy's antiterrorist operations were placed under the command of a Carabinieri general allegedly "responsible to nobody" but whose powers were comparable to "those wielded by a Spanish military governor under Franco."[14] It was felt that "Italy's government ha[d] overreacted against a diversionary attack by a retreating army."[15] The special intervention group (Gruppo di Intervento Speciale) was a "state secret," whose training consisted of "electronic eavesdropping, use and disarming of explosive devices, interrogation and surveillance, martial arts, and special weapons."[16]

Higher Budget Allocations for Police Training

According to Colonel Ferrari (personal communication, 1987), during the years of advancing terrorist menace, police training in handling arms became more effective and fighting-oriented to achieve an edge not only over the terrorists but also over armed criminals in general. All officers and most noncommissioned officers of the Carabinieri were required to attend special courses to improve shooting skills. Greater financial support received from the government helped in replacing older models of police weapons with more sophisticated ones. Ferrari mentioned that the police emphasized the following aspects in the fight against terrorism:

1. Increased time and resources for training.
2. Improving commitment of the police personnel.
3. Strengthening investigative techniques.
4. Greater attention to the improvement of various aspects of the organization, particularly SWAT teams and intelligence units.

All police officers and other observers point out that Italian police training in arms and weapons did not change substantially, but because of higher budget allocations, they could spend more on weapons and provide more effective training for handling them.

Wider Powers for Judiciary and Police

However, terrorism has had a tremendous impact on the courts and laws for combating those crimes with terrorist association. Many magistrates were assassinated by terrorists, and such killings conveyed the impression that "the battles of society against terrorism are fought, in the end, by solemn middle-aged men in black robes droning on about obscure points of law."[17] Even the start of the trial of the Red Brigade defendants involved in the murder of Moro, the former prime minister, was delayed for two years. The obstacles faced by courts and magistrates can be seen from the following description: "In their attempt to abort the trial, the Red Brigades murdered a Genoa magistrate. . . . The start of the trial was delayed for two years. But once it got under way it was a model of due process, despite occasional walk out and outbursts by the defendants."[18]

The Moro trial took the jury 100 hours, and the presiding judge, fourteen jurors, and the lawyers had to sit for three months despite many threats to their lives, highlighted by the murder of a police officer who took part in the investigation of Red Brigrades.[19]

Nevertheless, such experiences as these led to the developments of much wider powers for the judiciary and the police in regard to search, seizure, wiretapping, interrogations, and other methods, making some critics wonder whether "free societies, if they want to stay free, have to fight terrorism" with "precise counter-terrorist measures" or lashing out "in generalized fury" against suspected revolutionaries.[20]

The following lists some of the new laws passed to fight terrorism:

By 1974, laws governing police interrogation were made more severe. Prior to that time, police interrogation without referring the matter to a public prosecutor was illegal. This trend was given its fullest expression in Section 225 of the Code of Criminal Procedure in 1978 following the Moro incident, which made police interrogation without informing the prosecutor and without the presence of a lawyer much less difficult.

Section 152 of May 1975 gave police wide powers to search for weapons. Commonly known as the Reale Law (named after the justice minister of the time), this law covered police searches of persons, cars, and other belongings. It also forbade the wearing of masks, turbans, and other devices for camouflage. Section 533 of 1977 has made stop-and-frisk laws more severe.

Law Moro, Section 191 of 1978, following Moro's death, gave the police powers (apart from the wide powers of interrogation mentioned above) to search buildings or entire blocks of buildings.

Section 625 of 1979 legalized preventive detention for a period of up to twelve years. This section also referred to Repentance Law, which would later on become a powerful but controversial measure.

In fact, the laws against terrorism made immediate arrests, summary trials, and refusal of bail easier in regard to persons found in possession of illegal weapons. Police restrictions concerning custody of suspects, searches, and identification of people were reduced. Laws for trying police agents for committing acts of violence against terrorists were made less stringent. They were given powers to confiscate immovable property used as terrorist operations. All landlords renting apartments or rooms were required to give the names of tenants to the local police. Collaborators with police investigations were given special reductions in their sentences, even if they committed very serious crimes and their cooperation could have been secured by extralegal means.

ANALYSIS OF THE NEW MEASURES

After the Reale Law, complaints were heard that the police became "dangerously gun-happy," and statistics were quoted to show that after the promulgation of the law "some 150 fatal shootings of civilians" took place within the next ten years.[21] On March 9, 1985, plainclothes officers shot and killed an unarmed man on a crowded street in Trieste, and the person involved was a teacher of mathematics and a member of the Workers' Autonomy. It appeared that the police were not cautious and, as a matter of fact, the head of the local antiterrorist squad was replaced following this event. It was at this time that the Italian press started a campaign against police powers, although the cooperation of the press and other media was extended to the police, judiciary, and prison authorities during the height of antiterrorist operations. *The Economist* commented on the cooperation of the media, "Many newspapers have also been practicing a form of self-censorship, refusing to give undue prominence to terrorism or to publish the terrorist "communiqués." The state television network, the Rai, last week refused to show a videotaped interrogation . . . although the terrorists had demanded a showing."[22]

The Italian media also received praise for recognizing that "terrorism thrives on victories-by-display," and refusing to publish terrorist "communiqués" without creating confusion regarding the media's responsibility for maintaining "the fine line between keeping the public informed and giving terrorists free advertising space."[23] The latest round of antipolice publicity could be regarded as genuine fear that the Italian police were able, by the wave of terrorism, to exercise powers that softened democracy.

However, police commanders interviewed (Ferrari, personal communication, 1987) maintained that, although to a certain extent the atmosphere of danger might have caused a limited growth in the use of weapons and also mistakes in their use, the newly acquired powers did not make the police trigger-happy. Section 53, which was enlarged to give the police more powers, seemed to have never been used in its modified form. According to them, police behavior did not undergo any change for the worse as a result of Section 625 of 1979, which established a form of preventive detention and arrest, *"fermo di pubblica sicurezza,"* permitting the police to detain anyone for forty-eight hours on suspicion if there is reasonable ground to believe that he or she was preparing to commit a terrorist act. The police were quick to point out that the new section was consistent with Article 13 of the Italian constitution.

Nevertheless, these powers were considered as too dangerous to leave in police hands. It was maintained as follows by some:

> But it is the new police powers that are drawing most of the fire. The police can now arrest and question and terrorist suspects for up to two days before they have to be charged or are entitled to call their lawyers in. A magistrate can extend the questioning period by two more days. The police have frequently complained that defense lawyers' blocking tactics make effective grilling of suspects impossible.[24]

It was feared that "powers could be abused." The police authorization to search terrorist hideouts including nearby buildings, taping of telephones used by suspected terrorists without authorization by a magistrate, proof of identity to the police by anyone paying more than $25,000 to a new bank account, and so on, received mixed acceptance.

In the struggle against terrorism, two laws, Section 625 of 1979 (Legge Cossiga) and Section 304 of 1982 (Legge Sui Pentiti), which were very useful "from operational and pragmatic standpoint" have caused considerable controversy. These laws award a substantial reduction in penalty if a terrorist collaborates with the police and the judicial authority. Antonio Savasta, General Dozier's chief jailer and a multiple murderer, took advantage of this so-called repentance law to gain freedom. According to the other legal provision, if a terrorist defendant disassociates from his group, he can secure a smaller reduction in sentence. Regarding these laws, Ferracuti observes,

> The tactical success of these laws is undeniable. . . . "Repented" or "Disassociated" terrorists are estimated to number at least 40 percent of the official 2000 terrorists currently serving time or waiting trial in Italian prisons. . . . Police operatives and administrators favor the extension of the laws. Arguments pro and against range from moral to legal, and philosophical considerations.[25]

Ferracuti adds, "Disassociation may be the acknowledgment of defeat, the reality analysis of the impossibility of carrying out the grandiose revolutionary project." He argues that it is an expression of political realism and not moral internal change." Again, he explains that "collaboration may be a cold calculation of possible benefits, and essentially, betrayal." However, "its morality is indefensible" although it is "technically important."[26] Thus, he finds these laws essentially unethical:

> The prospect of reduced sentence makes the voluntariness questionable because of the obvious psychological pressure involved in the process. . . . Repentance has previously been given legal status in the Italian legal system only in the analysis of the convict to be granted conditional release, an Italian equivalent of parole. However, what is being implied is that the subject has changed (Rawedimento) from a criminal to a non-criminal value system.[27]

CONCLUSION

It appears that "political terrorism in Italy can be considered defeated" although "both hard core terrorists and conservative elements of the state machinery . . . may actively fight attempts at pacification." And "repentance and disassociation" have provided only "a tactical tool, and not a final solution."[28] The future danger and the present success should not lull the police to the fact that antiterrorist measures could do them a disservice if the attitudes and practices of the late 1970s and the early 1980s are not constantly reviewed and analyzed by the Italian police.

Italian society has been deeply divided in its reaction to the powers given to the agents of justice in their fight against terrorism. It appears that even the highly successful repentance laws are opposed by more than 30 percent of Italians.[29] But the police need to carry the people with them. It must be realized that terrorism flourished because the perception of serious social discrimination was widely shared in Italian society. In a survey conducted by *L'Espresso*, it was revealed that 21 percent of the country's youths believed that the Red Brigades were fighting for a better society. On the other hand, police operations, roadblocks, street raids, and wide visibility of the armed forces seem to have had some effect on the people. This phenomenon assumed such serious proportions that the police had difficulty in recruitment.

It is, therefore, essential that police measures should be informed by the sociopolitical realities of Italy: namely, "a tradition of political violence," the "anti-Fascist" heritage, and the "dubious legitimacy" of Italy's political system dominated by the Christian Democrats but marked by "clientalism" and "laborious compromises" while the communists are without a voice in the governing of the country despite their numerical strength, and "the anarchic transformation of the society in the 1950s and 1960s from [a] semi-rural to [an] industrial stage."[30]

Already, the government seems to have felt the need to liberalize some of the laws. Now, Sections 31–34 of 1987, for example, require the presence of an attorney and approval of a public prosecutor before interrogation, and more restrictions on police powers of search have been envisaged.

NOTES

This chapter was previously published in *Terrorism* 13 (1990): 89–98. Reprinted with permission.

1. "Terrorism," *The Economist* (December 22, 1979): 31–32.
2. "Terrorism," *The Economist* (January 10, 1980): 14–16.
3. John Phillips, "Beating Terrorists," *New Statesman* (February 19, 1982): 40–41.
4. "Even Terrorists Can Admit Failure," The *Economist* (March 13, 1982): 46.
5. *Coppedge v. United States*, 82 U.S. 438 (1962).
6. *Olmstead v. United States*, 277 U.S. 438 (1928).
7. T. A. Critchley, *The Conquest of Violence* (New York: Schocken, 1970).
8. Vittorfranco S. Pisano, "Terrorism in Italy: From Dozier's Rescue to Hunt's Assassination," *The Police Chief* (1984): 138.
9. "Terrorism," *The Economist* (September 6, 1980): 41.
10. Pisano, "Terrorism in Italy," 139.
11. Pisano, "Terrorism in Italy," 139–41.
12. Pisano, "Terrorism in Italy," 139–41.
13. "Terrorism," *The Economist* (December 22, 1979): 31.
14. "Terrorism," *The Economist* (December 22, 1979): 31.
15. "Terrorism," *The Economist* (December 22, 1979): 31.
16. M. Daniel Rosen, "At War with the Red Brigades," *The Police Magazine* 5 (1982): 42–48.
17. "Terrorism," (1978): 45.
18. "Terrorism," (1978): 45.
19. "Terrorism," (1978): 45.
20. "Terrorism," (1980): 16.

21. "Terrorism," *The Economist* (1985): 41.

22. "Terrorism," *The Economist* (August 8, 1981): 44.

23. "Terrorism," *The Economist* (January 10, 1981): 44.

24. "Terrorism," (1979): 31.

25. Franco Ferracuti, "Ideology and Repentance: Terrorism in Italy." Paper presented at the Conference on the Psychology of Terrorism, Washington, D.C., March 16–18, 1987, pp. 9, 10–16.

26. Ferracuti, "Ideology and Repentance."

27. Ferracuti, "Ideology and Repentance."

28. Ferracuti, "Ideology and Repentance."

29. Demoskoea, quoted in Franco Ferracuti, "Ideology and Repentance: Terrorism in Italy." Paper presented at the Conference on the Psychology of Terrorism, Washington, D.C., March 16–18, 1987.

30. Martha Cranshaw, "An Organizational Approach to the Analysis of Political Terrorism," *Terrorism* 8 (Fall 1985): 490.

Index

About the Contributors

Dr. Mamdooh Abdelhameed Abdelmattlep is currently the head of the Police Research Section and security expert at the Research and Studies Center of the Sharijah Police in the United Arab Emirates. He is also the advocate at the Supreme Appeal Court for the State Council as well as a legal adviser. Dr. Abedelhameed has degrees in criminal sciences, management and organization and its application on the police, a master's of science in police sciences, and a Ph.D. in police sciences. He has served various law enforcement roles throughout Egypt and Qatar.

Noël Brennan, Principal Deputy Assistant Attorney General, United States Department of Justice, Office of Justice Programs.

Dr. Irwin M. Cohen is a postdoctorate fellow at the School of Criminology at Simon Fraser University. Irwin's areas of interest focus on young offenders, juvenile justice, political crime, mental health, and Aboriginal victimization. He has coauthored several manuscripts on torture, terrorism, juvenile justice, young offenders, restorative justice, and mentally disordered offenders. Irwin has also acted as the project director and a coprincipal investigator on several research projects focusing on serious and violent young offenders, and Aboriginal victimization. Irwin is a member of the Institute of Mental Health, Law, and Policy at Simon Fraser University.

Dr. Raymond R. Corrado is a full professor in the School of Criminology and the Department of Psychology at Simon Fraser University. He also is a visiting fellow at Clare Hall College and the Institute of Criminology, University of Cambridge, and a founding member of the Mental Health, Law, and

Policy Institute at Simon Fraser University. Dr. Corrado has coauthored three edited books, *Issues in Juvenile Justice, Evaluation and Criminal Justice Policy,* and *Juvenile Justice in Canada,* as well as having published various articles and book chapters on juvenile justice, young offenders, terrorism, mental health, and victimization. Currently, Dr. Corrado is completing a variety of projects involving comparative juvenile justice, state terrorism, mentally disordered offenders, and Aboriginal victimization.

Dilip K. Das, Ph.D., is a professor at State University of New York, Plattsburgh. He has written extensively on comparative and international policing. He is founder/president of the International Police Executive Symposium which, among other activities, brings together police practicioners and researchers every year to deliberate on important topics in the world of policing. The proceedings are published as books. He is also the founder and Editor-in-chief of *Police Practice and Research: An International Journal,* a quarterly devoted to strengthening globalization of policing and collaboration between police practice and research. A human rights and policing consultant to the United Nations, Das is currently working on the World Police Encyclopedia, which will contain essays on police of every country. He works closely in all these endeavors with his wife Dr. Ana Mijovic-Das, professor Peter Kratcoski, and Lucille Kratcoski.

Kelly R. Damphousse is an associate professor in the Department of Sociology at the University of Oklahoma and director of the Center for Crime and Justice Studies. His research interests include domestic terrorism, drugs and crime, and homicide. He is codirector of the American Terrorism Study and is currently assisting in the creation of a national terrorism database, composed of individuals indicted by the U.S. government for acts of terrorism. He also directs the Oklahoma County and Tulsa County Arrestee Drug Abuse Monitoring (ADAM) program sites. His work has been published in *Criminology, Deviant Behavior, Crime and Delinquency, Homicide Studies,* and in several book chapters.

Dr. Jenny Hocking is head of the National Key Centre for Australian Studies at Monash University in Melbourne, Australia. Dr. Hocking's biography of the late High Court justice and former attorney-general Lionel Murphy, *Lionel Murphy: A Political Biography,* was published by Cambridge University Press in 1997; a paperback edition with new epilogue and a forward by Justice Michael Kirby was published in 2000. She is also the author of *Beyond Terrorism: The Development of the Australian Security State* (Sydney: Allen & Unwin, 1993). In 1999, Dr. Hocking was awarded an Australian Research Council QEII Research Fellowship for which she is currently working on a biography of the late Australian author Frank Hardy. Jenny Hocking has published widely internationally and within Australia on Australian politics and security issues, is a frequent media commentator, and has been academic adviser on several films and multimedia productions, including documentaries on the Office of Governor-General (*A Mirror to the People*) and on the High Court of Australia (*The Highest Court*), both screened on ABC-TV. In 2002, Dr. Hocking was awarded a Harold White Fellowship with the National Library of Australia.

Dr. Ely Karmon holds a B.A. in English and French culture from the Hebrew University, a License in International Relations from the Institut d'Etudes Politiques, and a License in Bantu languages from the Ecole de Langues Orientales in Paris. He took both his M.A. and Ph.D. at the Department of Political Science at Haifa University. He served as adviser of the Anti-Semitism Monitoring Forum of the Israeli Government Secretariat and is adviser to the Israeli minister of defense. Dr. Karmon is senior research scholar at the Interdisciplinary Center in Herzliya. He also lectured at the Department of Political Science at Haifa University (1992–2000) on the subjects of international terrorism and European extremist parties and organizations. His fields of research include international terrorism, political violence, and extremism, the strategic influence of terrorism and subversion in the Middle East. Dr. Karmon has written extensively on international terrorism and has participated in numerous international conferences. His forthcoming book is *Coalitions between Terrorist Organizations (1968–1990): European Revolutionaries and Palestinian Nationalists–Painful Partnership. And What about the Islamists?* by Kluwer Law International (Den Hague, London and Boston, 2002).

Peter C. Kratcoski, Ph.D., is emeritus professor of justice studies at Kent State University and adjunct professor of justice studies at Kent State University's regional campuses. He has also served as Chairman of the Department of Criminal Justice Studies at Kent State. In addition, he has acted as a consultant for approximately 100 criminal justice, juvenile justice, and social service agencies. He has authored four books, written numerous articles for professional journals, and presented many papers at both national and international professional conferences. He previously served as editor of *The Journal of Crime and Justice*, and is currently North American editor of *Police Practice and Research*. He is the official recorder for the International Police Executive Symposium, and has written a number of articles and book chapters based on the topics that were the focuses of IPES meetings.

George Millard is the police chief of the Sao Paulo State Police, professor of Civil Police Academy in the state of Sao Paulo, former director of narcotics in the Department of Sao Paulo, and has been the assistant director, Internal

Affairs and Head of the Tax Fraud Division. He has an LLB and MBA from Mackenzie University (Sao Paulo) and a postgraduate diploma in sociology (Sao Paulo). He is a visiting professor, College of Law, in the University of Florida. Mr. Millard is an adviser to the Board of International Association of Asian Crimes Investigators, senior researcher in the Center of Financial Crimes Studies in the University of Florida, and lecturer in Cambridge Symposium on Economic Crime (England).

Dr. Ashraf Mohsen is currently serving as the political counselor of the Egyptian embassy in Madrid. On the 18th of September 2001, he was nominated by the Secretary General of the United Nations to serve as the counterterrorism expert in the Security Council Resolution 1363 regarding sanctions against the Taliban. Prior to assuming his post as the Egyptian consul in San Francisco, Dr. Mohsen was the director of the Counterterrorism Unit in the Egyptian Ministry of Foreign Affairs from 1998 until 2001. From 1994 until 1998, Dr. Mohsen was the first secretary of the Egyptian embassy in Tel Aviv-Political Affairs, where he followed the peace process. He also served in the Egyptian embassy in London during the Gulf War, after joining the Egyptian diplomatic service in 1985. Dr. Mohsen has worked extensively on the development of extremist Islamic groups and has published several articles on that issue. From 1998 to 2000, he participated in various counterterrorism meetings as an individual expert as well as representing the Egyptian government. He also participated in the drafting of several regional and international counterterrorism conventions, including the UN convention on Suppression of Terrorism Financing and the African Counterterrorism Convention. Dr. Mohsen received his Ph.D. and MA from the School of Oriental and African Studies, University of London, after graduating from the American University in Cairo.

Gerhard O. W. Mueller received his baccalaureate degree from the Castle of Ploen College, Germany. He obtained his J.D. from the School of Law at the University of Chicago and earned an LL.M. degree from Columbia University. He served as chief of the United Nations Crime Prevention and Criminal Justice branch from 1974 until 1982. In this position, he directed the policies of the United Nations and assisted member states throughout the world in their struggles against terrorism. He is chairman of the Board of the International Scientific and Professional Advisory Council of the United Nations Program in Crime Prevention and Criminal Justice. Dr. Mueller is also the editor and author of several hundred books and articles. He is a professor at the Rutgers University School of Criminal Justice.

Steven Kasiima Munanura is a graduate of Makerere University, Political Science and Sociology (1990). He mastered at Makerere in the Department of Philosophy in the field of Human Rights. He has served as office in charge of Mbale and Capchorwa Police Stations in the Uganda Police Force from 1993 to 1996. He has also served as a superintendent of police in charge of police inspections and quality assurance from 1996 to 2000. He is currently the district police commander of Masaka district in Uganda. His research is in the field of human rights promotion and protection, gender, children, and refugee issues. He has researched and published the following: "Political Change and Problem of Violence: The 1979 Kiziba Massacres in Bushenyl District" and "Terrorism and Its Challenges to Human Rights Protection in Uganda: A Case Study of Kampala." He is currently carrying out research entitled "The Use of Maximum Force in Policing: A Case Study of Uganda Police Force."

Alex P. Schmid (b. 1943) is a historian by training but later worked in the fields of sociology, political science, and human rights. He held the Synthesis Chair on Conflict Resolution at Erasmus University in Rotterdam. He taught international relations at the Department of Political Sciences of Leiden University and was an Einstein Fellow at the Center for International Affairs, Harvard University. Alex Schmid was research coordinator of the Interdisciplinary Research Programme on Causes of Human Rights Violations (PIOOM) at Leiden University and one of the founding members of FEWER, the London-based Forum on Warning and Early Response. He served on the executive board of the International Scientific and Professional Advisory Council of the United Nations Crime Prevention and Criminal Justice Programme (ISPAC) and the steering committee of Conflict Early Warning Systems of UNESCO's International Social Science Council. Professor Schmid was academic director of the International Student Symposium on Negotiation and Conflict Resolution, an international summer school organized by the Institute for International Mediation and Conflict Resolution (Washington, D.C.) with Erasmus University, Rotterdam. Dr. Schmid has authored and edited more than 100 publications, including more than fifteen books, among them the award-winning *Political Terrorism*. His latest three edited publications are *The Rule of Law in the Global Village: Issues of Sovereignty and Universality* (Milan: ISPAC, 2001), *Countering Terrorism through International Cooperation* (Milan: ISPAC, 2001), and *Immigration Policy: A Search for Balance in Europe* (Driebergen: Synthesis, 2001). Since 1999, Dr. Schmid has been officer-in-charge of the United Nations' Terrorism Prevention Branch in Vienna. He coorganized the ancillary meeting "Terrorist Victimization: Prevention, Control, and Recovery," in April 2000, on which this volume is based.

Amy Sellers, Department of Justice Sciences, University of Alabama at Birmingham, is a research associate for the American Terrorism Study. In 2000, she received an M.S. in Justice Sciences from the University of Alabama. Her previous publications include a chapter titled "Terrorism and the American System of Criminal Justice," in *Handbook on Criminal Justice Administration* and "The Prosecution and Punishment of International Terrorists in Federal Courts: 1980–1998," (with Brent L. Smith, Kelly R. Damphousse, and Freedom Jackson) in *Criminology & Public Policy 1(3)*.

Dr. Andrew Silke is a forensic psychologist formerly based at the University of Leicester and now working for the Home Office. He is an associate fellow of the British Psychological Society and has been actively researching political violence in Northern Ireland and elsewhere since 1993. He is the editor of *Terrorists, Victims, and Society: Psychological Perspectives and Terrorism and Its Consequences* (Wiley, forthcoming). He has written extensively on a wide range of issues relating to terrorism and political violence and has spoken on the subject at numerous national and international conferences.

Brent L. Smith received his Ph.D. from Purdue University in 1979. He then served two years in the U.S. Army as an instructor in the Department of Military Police Operations and the Counterterrorism course at the U.S. Army's Military Police School. He then moved to the University of Alabama at Birmingham in 1981. Dr. Smith's research has focused primarily upon social movements and government response. Terrorism, and how the polity responds, has been of continuing interest throughout his career. Dr. Smith's publications on terrorism have appeared in *Justice Quarterly, Terrorism: An International Journal, Studies in Conflict and Terrorism*, and most recently in a series of articles appearing in *Criminology*. He is the author of *Terrorism in America: Pipe Bombs and Pipe Dreams* (SUNY Press, 1994). Following the Oklahoma City bombing, Dr. Smith testified before the U.S. House of Representatives Judiciary Subcommittee on Crime at the hearings on the Oklahoma City bombing (May 1995) and again at the congressional hearings on Violent Antigovernment Groups in America (November 1995). In 1996, he was an invited discussant at special hearings on the status of research and terrorism convened by the National Research Council's Committee on Law and Justice. In addition to serving as professor and chair of the Department of Justice Sciences at UAB, Dr. Smith is the project director and principal investigator for the American Terrorism Study, a research project originally funded by the National Institute of Justice and currently funded by the Oklahoma City National Memorial Institute for the Prevention of Terrorism.

Dr. S. Subramanian is a leading crusader of human rights in India. Dr. S. Subramanian served with distinction in the Indian Police Services (1958–1992) and held prestigious appointments of director-general of Central Reserve Police Force and the National Security Guards. He was founder and director of the elite Special Protection Group and director of the National Police Academy. He also served as the minister in the Indian embassy in Bonn, Germany. He held senior appointments in the intelligence bureau, Central Bureau of Investigation, and Andhra Pradesh Police.

Ayako Uchiyama is currently a deputy director of the Department of Crime Prevention and Juvenile Delinquency of the National Research Institute of Police Science at the National Police Agency. She has also been engaged in research work there since 1968 after she finished her BA in education at Tokyo University. The main fields of her research include causes of delinquency, female delinquency, lifestyle of organized crime members, various damages of victims of crime, and child abuse. Between 1976 and 2000, she has presented many papers, sixteen of which were in English and over 100 in her native tongue.

Arvind Verma has served in the Indian Police Service occupying many senior administrative posts. He is a consultant to the Bureau of Police Research and Development, Government of India, and is engaged in a number of projects related to criminal justice in India. His doctoral work was concerned with the development of new tools of analyses using fuzzy logic, topology, and other "qualitative" mathematical techniques. His research interests are in policing, comparative criminal justice systems, policy issues, research methods, mathematical modeling, fuzzy logic, and geographical information systems. He works at the Department of Criminal Justice, Indiana University at Bloomington, and is the managing editor of *Police Practice and Research: An International Journal.*